WOMEN
ON FOOD

for all of us

Library of Congress Control Number: 2018958809

ISBN: 978-1-4197-3635-3
eISBN: 978-1-68335-681-3

Printed and bound in China

10 9 8 7 6 5 4 3 2 1

Abrams books are available at special discounts when purchased
in quantity for premiums and promotions as well as fundraising
or educational use. Special editions can also be created to
specification. For details, contact specialsales@abramsbooks.com
or the address below.

Abrams Press® is a registered trademark of Harry N. Abrams, Inc.

ABRAMS The Art of Books
195 Broadway, New York, NY 10007
abramsbooks.com

WOMEN
ON FOOD

Charlotte Druckman

+ 115 Writers,
Chefs, Critics,
Television Stars,
and Eaters

Abrams Press, New York

INTRODUCTION

So many roads and so much opinion
So much shit to give in, give in to
So many rules and so much opinion
So much bullshit but we won't give in

—Le Tigre, "Hot Topic"

Dear (Potential) Reader,

This is where I'm supposed to tell you what you're getting into.

What you're getting into is an anthology about women in—and on—food. That means women who work in or around food in some capacity, and what they think about that ... and what they think about what you expect them to think about that.

Because when you think about women in the food world, you probably have some ideas about who or what you're going to find. Women have a long history in the kitchen and of writing about such matters. But how much freedom have we had in that? And how much freedom have we had in how it's been parsed and packaged?

"What does it say about us that a woman who speaks the truth of her experience should be dismissed for telling more than the world feels comfortable with hearing?" Joyce Maynard asked in September 2018, in her essay for the *New York Times Book Review*. You could apply this to any experience and, beyond that, to any woman who does more with her medium, or in her profession, than the world feels comfortable with.

Women are capable of, and have been doing more in—and on—food than we have been given credit for or seemingly been allowed or encouraged to share. And the ways in which we have been allowed or encouraged to share whatever has been codified as acceptable have been limited.

What if we could speak the truth, and what if we could speak it completely, as ourselves? What if we could be analytical, furious, funny, serious, sad, harsh, silly, challenging, old-fashioned, avant-garde, creative, macho, pensive, unforgiving, unforgivable, opinionated, neutral, just plain weird, or all of the above? What if we could revisit some of the accepted tropes—take another, different look? What if we could talk about what it's like, really, to work in the food industry or food media, to get a meal on the table, or feed a community? And what if we could write about that without having to match the format of or adhere to a particular genre or style? Whose stories would we tell? How would we choose to tell them?

These are the questions I asked myself and the upwards of one hundred women I recruited to contribute to this book. Together, we've answered them in all kinds of ways.

I told you this was an anthology. You probably have ideas about that, too. I did. I tend to think of anthologies as academic or boring, as pages and pages of essays. Sometimes that's exactly what you want to read and, the good news is, you have lots of options. But anthologies can be more than that, and they can offer readers a more varied experience. Maybe you're in the mood for an essay, or maybe you'd just like a quick laugh, or maybe you want something a little more intimate and conversational. Maybe you're in search of a history lesson or a catharsis. Maybe you just want to hear from some people you haven't heard from before.

This anthology has a healthy portion of original essays, all commissioned exclusively for this project. Most are prose, but as you will see, there are a few visual surprises thrown in. The contributors are all people I personally love to read—their talent is unequivocal; their perspectives are unique and vital.

It's risky, you might be thinking, to create a from-scratch anthology. Usually, the essays have already been published elsewhere and deemed the most exemplary of their genre before they're selected for what will then be sold as a "best of" compendium. I've always worried that, not unlike institutionalized awards, these collections encourage conformity on the part of writers. I wanted to create a situation where there was no pressure to conform; where the work had been "chosen" before it was written.

Similarly, there is no prioritization of topics in this anthology. It frees things up structurally, allowing pieces to be placed together that might relate to each other in subtler ways. The result is an interweaving of multiple threads throughout the book and, what I was most excited by, an organic emergence of themes: motherhood, domesticity, and, in its many forms, the work of cooking come up a lot. Race, class, and cultural assimilation do, too. No one will be shocked to learn that sexism and feminism are everywhere in these pages. So is power, which is at the root of everything.

Serious. That's what you're thinking now. *This all sounds rather serious. What happened to the "quick laugh" option*? Some of it is sobering. But a lot of it isn't—scout's honor! In addition to the essays, there are interviews with some of the people (in food) I most admire—from different walks of culinary life and at different stages in their careers. Those conversations have been edited for your reading pleasure and ease. And to keep you entertained—and on your toes—there are unexpected outtakes and outbursts, and a powder keg of truth from a powerhouse of a chorus that tells it like it is, and how it should be.

I kind of like to think of it as a variety show, in book form, with me as your emcee.

So let me do a quick costume change, and I'll be right back with my pal Sadie Stein and some very important revelations about one of the most famous food writers ever.

LEXICON

Are there any words or phrases *you really wish* people would stop using to describe WOMEN CHEFS (or really, women, period)?

JAMIE FELDMAR

Women.

ESTHER TSENG

"Best female chef" as a participation trophy.

THERESE NELSON

Women chefs. I appreciate the power of female energy, but it's used far too often as an aside and not a qualifier. In 2018, I heard a well-known chef suggest that there aren't more women in this work because it's too hard and I think the suggestion that women lack the fortitude for this industry is still too closely embedded in the way we use the term.

ALISON ROMAN

I wish they'd stop qualifying us as women. We are chefs, writers, cookbook authors. It's 2019—we can drop the *woman/female* as a preface, I promise.

EMIKO DAVIES

Um, *female* chef. It implies that chefs are normally or should be men (like *female* doctor, ugh). Can she just be called a chef?

ANDREA NGUYEN

I'm not a chef. I'm a professional home cook. Some of my close friends are chefs.

LIGAYA MISHAN

Nothing specific, but I hope that as writers we will always stop and think,

Would I use this word or describe this aspect of a person if they were of a different gender (or orientation), and if not, should that make me pause and think twice here?

MONIQUE TRUONG

Beautiful, attractive, young, former model.

ALEX VAN BUREN

Gorgeous. Sexy.

REBEKAH DENN

Tiny, trim.

JASMINE LUKUKU

I do not want to hear ANYTHING about a woman's weight when I'm reading a profile about her work as a chef. It's such a common trope in the female chef profile. It always makes me roll my eyes.

KRISTINA GILL

Obviously, anything that focuses on appearance, or makes a woman seem an unlikely candidate to get as far as she did.

AUBRIE PICK

I read a profile on Elizabeth Warren the other day that started by describing a cardigan she was wearing, and then used that cardigan as a metaphor for how she operates as a person and a politician. And I nearly threw the magazine across the room. So many profiles of women start with a physical description meant to tell the reader something about the personality of the woman being profiled. And usually in terms that you just don't see in profiles of men.

MAGGIE HOFFMAN

Bitchy. Emotional. Sensitive.

CATHY BARROW

Sassy.

TAMAR ADLER

Perky.

JULIA SHERMAN

Feisty!

JULEE ROSSO

"The Girls"—as we were always referred to collectively, and it sounded condescending every time.

NICOLE TAYLOR

Chick. I hate that word. Is it a chicken? It sounds so cheap. It sounds like an animal. Does it really mean *chic* like fashion?

CHANDRA RAM

Pioneer. Matriarchal. Ball-busters.

REBECCA FLINT MARX

Nurturing. Ugh.

Strong. Because that implies that the default for women is 'weak.'

Badass. It's like *interesting*: so bland as to be almost meaningless. It's a token word that only conveys pandering, along with the (food) media's (somewhat condescending)

efforts to make up for lost time/ recognition/opportunity/respect where women—chefs and otherwise—are concerned.

HOLLY DOLCE

Any modification to the word *boss*: boss babe, girl boss, badass boss bitch. It makes me even crazier when women describe themselves this way. You don't see dudes being like, *Hey! I'm a Boy Boss.*

WENDY MACNAUGHTON

Badass. There's a built in bias in that word. It's often a synonym for "woman who does something you don't expect a woman to do." I use it all the time and I'm trying to knock it out of my vocabulary.

What about words or phrases used to describe male chefs (or men, at all) that you'd like to ban?

THERESE NELSON

I wish terms like *tough, badass, hardcore* were meant to describe strength. What they really do is assign a kind of toxic masculinity to men in ways that perpetuate it in insane ways. I think strength is a virtue that men and women need, but there is a way in which we talk about male strength that diminishes women while also marginalizing men, as though all they can be are these one-dimensional caricatures as opposed to fully formed people. The whole narrative is bad for everyone.

JASMINE LUKUKU

Can we stop with the *rogue/bad boy* nonsense? There are other virtues like creativity, curiosity, and kindness that are much more intriguing.

REGINA SCHRAMBLING

Kill *celebrity chef.*

MONIQUE TRUONG

Traveler, in search of, rebel, obsessed, hard-drinking.

ESTHER TSENG

Pioneer. Saying they "discovered" anything. *Bad boy. Falstaffian* (whereas women chefs would be considered *fat*).

REBECCA FLINT MARX

Genius. Badass. Towering. King. God. Pirate. Lion. Lion is the worst.

NICOLE TAYLOR

Bro. I use the word but I hate it because it means everything I hate when we say Bro Culture. Nothing positive about the word *bro*. Maybe the men need to come up with an alternate way to describe Bro Culture because it's all negative.

SIERRA TISHGART

Visionary!

Daring!

Innovative!

NAOMI TOMKY

Rock star, genius, self-taught when what they really mean is "didn't go to culinary school."

Sadie Stein

Sadie Stein could write about anything—spreadsheets, watching paint dry, golf—and I would want to read it; she brings an unexpected perspective and unforced wit to every sharply observed situation she finds herself in and every story she drafts.

I had an idea in mind for her essay when we met at Café Loup, a Greenwich Village haunt that we're both fond of. But as we sat there gossiping with our glasses of wine (and Sadie spreading a more-than-passable country pate on some sliced baguette), something rather remarkable happened.

For a long time, I'd been harboring a secret—a lack of love for a food writer held up as the ultimate, shining example of her profession by most who engage in it or are interested in its subject. I saw my inability to appreciate her work the way others did, so zealously, as a shortcoming. But it just didn't speak to me. I thought maybe one day I'd have the courage to put this in writing.

And then, just as I was about to tell Sadie about her potential topic, she blurted a confession of her own—the same one, in fact, that I had been too cowardly to blurt myself. In that moment, the universe reminded me that kindred spirits do exist, and made it perfectly clear that Sadie had to write the following essay, which, no doubt, will leave you as much in awe of her—and rightly so—as almost everyone else we know is of this literary paragon—or was; the following might change their minds, or elicit a few more confessions.

Serve It Forth

When I turned eleven years old, my grandfather made his annual visit to New York from Monterey. He always timed his visits to overlap with my birthday. Per usual, he'd brought as many massive, decrepit suitcases as the budget airline would allow. (Each visit lasted a month.) From these he produced packages of ancient rope licorice, tarnished pieces of silver, various knives and weapons he'd picked up at tag sales, and dozens of books. That one could find these things in New York was irrelevant; being able to transport them at no additional cost seemed to him a remarkable feat that had the further benefit of, in some way, cheating the system.

For this particular birthday, my grandfather threw a heavy, seventies-issue paperback book onto my bed, *How to Cook a Wolf*. He said, "Read that. You'll need it. She's quite a gal."

At twenty, in London on a junior year abroad and suffering from a bad case of flu, I was sent a care package by a British family friend who lived nearby, a bon vivant and gourmet. It contained a pack of Solpadeine, a plastic container of homemade chicken stock, and a raw egg, which I was instructed to beat into the broth for extra nourishment. Oh, and a copy of *The Gastronomical Me*. "The best food writer going," he'd written on the flyleaf.

When I graduated college, my boyfriend's father, knowing I liked to cook and read, presented me with a generous gift: a vellum-wrapped first edition of *Consider the Oyster*.

On a date to a then-new West Village hotspot with serious culinary bona fides, a nice young man with an interest in food gave me "one of my favorite books"—*Serve It Forth*.

I still own them all. I own most of her other books, too. It seems for the better part of my life, men have been pushing M. F. K. Fisher on me. I've never had the heart to tell them I don't much care for the writer John Updike called "poet of the appetites" and of whom W. H. Auden wrote, "I do not know of anyone in the United States who writes better prose."

Thanks to that prose, Mary Frances Kennedy Fisher's is a well-documented life. Born in Michigan in 1908, she was raised from early childhood in California—a defining motif in much of her work. A long stint in France with her first husband proved formative, as detailed in *The Gastronomical Me*; she would return there all her life.

Upon coming home to California during the Depression, Mary Frances began to read about culinary history at the library. The short essays on gastronomy and philosophy that arose—she'd originally read them to guests before dinner—caught the attention of a friend of a friend in publishing and ultimately became her first book, *Serve It Forth*. It was well-received. While plenty of mostly male writers wrote about food and travel, and plenty of mostly female ones wrote about nutrition and home cooking, what she called "humanistic-gastronomic writing" was hers alone. She had, in effect, created a new genre.

Was it a genre especially suited to the male palate? From the beginning, men liked Fisher's books; at a time when women were routinely overlooked or condescended to by male critics, her work was universally celebrated.

The next chapter of Fisher's life only enhanced her legend—her affair with Dillwyn Parrish, whom she would later marry, at the Swiss artist's colony where they briefly lived with her first husband and which culminated in Parrish's suffering and ultimate suicide. In the midst of this, her 1940s output was remarkable by any standard. (*Consider the Oyster*, published in 1941, is thought by many her finest work.) And yet, from a professional standpoint, it was only the beginning: She would go on to write the wartime manual *How to Cook a Wolf* and gain wide readership through magazines like *Vogue, Town & Country*, and the burgeoning *Gourmet*. Her translation of Jean Anthelme Brillat-Savarin's *The Physiology of Taste*, the founding bible of French gastronomy, was accounted a revelation that brought the classic to a new generation of sybarites.

A crony of James Beard and Craig Claiborne and a mentor to countless rebels waking to the pleasures of the table, Fisher spent much of her life in picturesque locales, having what looked, superficially, like equally picturesque adventures. But her life was hard by any standard: filled with death, caregiving, money troubles, and the stigmas and difficulties of being a single mother. Her death, at eighty-three, at the fabled "Last House" in Glen Ellen, California, came after a long battle with Parkinson's. And through it all, her work, more than twenty books in total.

In 2014, the late food writer Josh Ozersky issued what can only be called a screed against the cult of Mary Frances. He ranted, "I personally find her work to be dull, monotonous, and eventually stupefying, like the endless chatter of some lady you sit next to on a bus . . . Fisherism is, not to put too fine a point on it, a straight-up form of cultural hegemony." Ozersky hated everything about Fisher. He painted her as a vapid snob whose legacy of self-indulgent, unapologetically bourgeois navel-gazing was the original sin of food writing as we know it. The piece—as intended—provoked a minor uproar. Five years later, it already reads as profoundly dated, almost quaint; food writing has changed a lot since both their times and much of the essay presents as barely veiled misogyny.

But then, so too does the uncritical adulation he was responding to. Ozersky wasn't wrong: Fisher was able to inspire a sort of slavish, thoughtless genuflection that today reads (to me) almost as a soft dismissal. In her *New York Times* obit, the author praised Fisher's "ebullient embrace of the slow, sensual pleasures of the table" which, in turn "was matched by her cool acceptance of sudden violence and evil." As usual in discussions of Fisher, the *Times* was quick to comment on her looks, describing her as "a beauty and an enchantress." Even Ozersky gets in the inevitable mention of her physical charms: "Being outrageous [*sic*] good-looking didn't hurt, either—she was, on top of being rich and smart, so gorgeous that Man Ray once photographed her for his own pleasure. Fisher had it all, and she knew it."

While Fisher was unquestionably an attractive woman, I wish they'd knock this off; what they mean, one supposes, is that she had an active love life, some of it with married men, and bore a child out of wedlock—and apparently no one can accept that anyone but a stunning vixen was capable of such a feat. I always find myself wondering: Why do they mention it at all? Perhaps because, if her subject was the table, it was not, exactly, the domestic one. She was very much a woman and not, particularly, a wife.

My own complaints about Fisher were never Ozersky's; in fact, I remember feeling somewhat irritated that he'd forced me into defending her so rabidly. But, on the other hand . . . what were my complaints? I have never enjoyed being told what I ought to like. At times, I have even felt a perverse and juvenile pleasure in rejecting what was, to others, sacrosanct—an impulse that should rightly be binned with the CD collection.

For the purposes of this piece, I was determined to reconsider my long-embedded resistance to Fisher's spell. If I could not be wholly dispassionate, then at least I would be well informed. I reread her entire oeuvre, her letters, and her posthumous work; I looked at every interview I could find and at what film remains—most of it dating from late in her life, when Fisher was already very ill.

Her fans were just as right as Ozersky. Fisher is indeed a wonderful stylist, crystalline and—overused word—elegant. She writes with enviable economy and lack of sentimentality. There are sentences in her work—particularly her memoir—that really *can* rival anything of the period for grace and pith. Take this, from *How to Cook a Wolf*:

> Another thing that makes daily, hourly thought about wherewithals endurable is to be able to share it with someone else. That does not mean, and I say it emphatically, sharing the fuss and bother and fretting. It means being companionable with another human who understands, perhaps without any talking at all, what problems of basic nourishment confront you. Once such a relationship is established, your black thoughts vanish, and how to make a pot of stew last three more meals seems less a nightmare than a form of sensual entertainment.

Fisher was a fearless pioneer who made unconventional choices and forced readers to take food writing seriously as an art form. She was unencumbered by the dicta of midcentury morality. She was unapologetic and smart. She encouraged the women of America to think beyond the limitations of their palates and circumstances, and in the process credited them with intelligence and taste—or at least the capacity to develop these. She was a pro: She wrote to earn her living, and throughout her life was remarkably prolific and disciplined, never allowing the artist's ego to outstrip the professionalism of the working writer. She was tough: She wrote some of her most iconic work while her second husband was being consumed by a painful disease, and after he took his own life.

What's more, her writing on France should qualify as some of the most evocative travelogues produced in the twentieth century, and it's unarguable that for anyone who wants to study the essay, food writing, or the lost craft of the letter, Fisher's body of work is essential.

Still, I don't love it. Or, rather, I don't enjoy it. As Cyra McFadden once observed, "Food is what she wrote about, although to leave it at that is reductionist in the extreme. What she really wrote about was the passion, the importance of living boldly instead of cautiously; oh, what scorn she had for timid eaters, timid lovers, people who took timid stands, or none at all, on matters of principle."

The scorn, I feel. That's not what I'm looking for when I read about food, or anything else. When I read about food, I want to be made hungry—coarse but true; I know this consigns me to the philistines.

Certainly, her descriptions are nothing if not vivid. "The first thing I remember tasting and wanting to taste again is the grayish-pink fuzz my grandmother skimmed from a spitting kettle of strawberry jam," she wrote in *The Gastronomical Me*. Who can forget that—or her first boarding-school oyster, viscerally tied to experiences of erotic awakening and horror? Or the tangerine peels she left to dry on her Strasbourg window ledge as a new bride? Or, for that matter, "The smell of good bread baking, like the sound of lightly flowing water . . . indescribable in its evocation of innocence and delight."

Very lovely. Very elliptical. But I've never been so much as tempted to cook one of the recipes in her many books. (Okay, once I made the nasturtium leaf sandwiches, which failed to electrify my grandfather's gin-rummy group as they had her mother's tea parties.) Some of this is, of course, a matter of changing times and tastes; it's not as though A. J. Liebling sends one leaping off to the kitchen in search of sweetbreads. (That Elizabeth David does is a testament to her particular genius.)

To be sure, despite the vast range in which she cooked, the kitchen was not Fisher's favorite subject, an omission addressed by Joan Reardon's excellent *Among the Pots and Pans*. There's a curious fade-to-black when it comes to the stirring and grating. As Amanda Hesser wrote in her introduction to *The Art of Eating*, "For me, her life as a cook will always feel like a missing piece." I would go further; for all the eating, I miss her life as an eater. She was not *greedy*. Although she alludes to rapture, she's never rapturous about the recipes she presents. Her restraint in this regard seems both obscurely secretive and deliberately modest. "The following has always pleased me," she says of a rabbit casserole; of a ration-friendly "War Cake," "I'm not ashamed of having loved it . . . merely a little puzzled, and thankful that I am no longer eight." "Edible and consistently interesting," she calls one lamb stew.

Even if she's describing a blue trout stumbled upon in the Alps, there's no sense the reader could replicate even a part of the experience; it's beyond us, because we are not M. F. K. Fisher and were not in the Alps with a lover and a crazy waitress, and, while that's all very well in writing, it's a different matter altogether when you are reading in order to imagine an experience, a dinner of your own. I am not inspired to imagination by her descriptions; neither am I sated.

The funny thing is, when anyone reminisces about eating with Fisher, they make her meals sound appealing and appetizing: the chicken legs her grand-nephew Luke Barr recounts in the introduction to *Provence, 1970*, or Reardon's description of guest menus the Parrishes offered up before his death: "They typically served a first course of chilled green beans and tomatoes or other seasonal vegetables, followed by an entrée of rare steak or curried lamb with Indian rice. A compote or fresh or preserved fruits usually concluded the meal. When they dined alone, Mary Frances prepared a cheese souffle with a light salad, or broiled lamb chops garnished with herb butter, or scrambled eggs and toast." Ruth Reichl, in *Comfort Me with Apples*, remembers a picnic of chicken sandwiches. Yet these are not the preparations one imagines from her books. To enter into the meals, as she describes them, one has to have been there. And here, perhaps, I should confess another prejudice. When I read a magazine interview in which someone talks about the four historical figures they'd most like to invite to dinner, I always wonder: *What makes you think they'd accept? That Virginia Woolf would just love to hear your thoughts on politics, that Dorothy Parker would consider you a wit? Would you actually want to cook for Madame de Staël—or Christ?* For whatever reason, I tend to assume most fixtures of the literary canon, for example, might be hard work. That, even if we spoke a common language, they might not have much to say to me. M. F. K. Fisher gives me this feeling in spades.

A *Gourmet* tribute, literally quoting the great woman's letters, is enough to give a hostess chills: "Nothing seemed to annoy Fisher like fussiness. 'Miss E. cannot eat a dozen things . . . because of a recurrent pain in the gall bladder, or she cannot chew them w/ her double clickers or she is prejudiced against them for unknown but probably racial reasons.'" And, if fussiness was reprehensible, nonfussiness was even more irksome: "They will eat anything that is set before them," she writes of two dinner guests. "They chomp right through, making appreciative noises on schedule." I'd be petrified.

And for me, relaxation is key to enjoyment. To my mind, truly evocative food writing—the sort that whets the appetite—is an act of generosity. It's second only to, maybe, erotica in its need to connect in both a universal and particular manner with the reader. And in the same way, that is far more difficult than it might seem. To me, Fisher is not a generous writer. Not in her cool, critical descriptions of family; not in her barely veiled contempt for the average American palate as she found it; not in her blatant self-absorption and frequent bouts of self-pity, as when she complains of having grown up a repressed minority—an Episcopalian in a largely Quaker town. I can appreciate that it's these same qualities that made her so fearless in life and so lucid in prose, not to mention gave her the confidence a memoirist requires. But that doesn't mean I want to hang out with her—even if she does come off much the best of the jerks parade—led by the snide Richard Olney—that is *Provence, 1970.*

Not every food writer needs to be a cozy confidante (although favorites of mine like Diana Kennedy, Florence White, and Edna Lewis effortlessly *are*). Elizabeth David can be plenty acerbic, Jane Grigson doesn't hold your hand, and Gabrielle Hamilton and Nigel Slater don't encourage you to think of them as best friends. I love reading their books. I once made a frantic three-hour trip to the Bronx Meat Market overwhelmed by the need to prepare Tamasin Day-Lewis's "gluey" oxtails with grapes; Julia Reed's description of a BLT once sent me to the bodega at 2 A.M. And the fact that we have all made at least half the recipes from Laurie Colwin's *Home Cooking* essays *after not a single one worked* is a testament to both her charm and her enthusiasm. Do you need to like a writer in order to like her work? No—unless she's exclusively writing about herself—an irony, given M.F.K.'s professed disdain for the personal essay—in which case you need to at least get along.

Because, at the end of the day, this was Fisher's subject. Not food, not eating, and certainly not cooking. Fisher was a pioneer, and if she spawned a thousand imitators, she certainly also cleared the way for female food writers to be cozy *and* rigorous, adventurous *and* domestic—serious writers and serious eaters who could not merely talk about appetites but express them. M. F. K. Fisher never felt that she had that luxury. Instead, she was her own muse. She was self-sufficient—a quality that one can admire without wanting to hold it close, or have it as a dinner companion. And I'm quite sure that she wouldn't care a whit that I thought so.

A Conversation with Betty Fussell

Although Betty Fussell has authored a dozen books on subjects like corn, steak, and American regional cuisine, it would be inaccurate—and inadequate—to call her a food writer. What would be accurate—and still, probably inadequate—would be to say she has pushed the boundaries of what food writing could be, especially—but not only—for women. I think of her as an anthropologist and of food as her probing tool.

She is fascinated by the underpinnings of the human condition—by where we come from and who we are, not so much in the existential sense, but in the here and now of the physical world. You see it in the viscerality of her prose; every page of her 1999 memoir, *My Kitchen Wars,* is ripe with it:

> We were discovering what the French had known forever, that food was like literature and art, and that sex was above all like food. But the subtext was always sex. We wanted to have our cake and eat it, too, but we didn't want Betty Crocker cake mix anymore. We wanted dacquoise and génoise and baba au rhum at the end of a Rabelaisian banquet flowing with still wines and sparkling conversation. Every new food opened up new sexual analogues. To explore the interstices of escargots with the aid of fork and clamp, each shell in its place on the hot metal round, each dark tongue hidden deep within the whorls and only with difficulty teased out and eased into the pool of garlic-laden butter—what could be sexier than that?

I don't know. Certainly not most of this country's so-called food writing, definitely not the writing expected of women on any subject. She is ninety-two now, and her voracious appetite for knowledge and experience hasn't diminished. From her retirement home in Montecito, she made pronouncements like "There is no human nature; human nature is gone" and shared her opinions on gender, food media, genetics, kale, and more.

You think forty's old. Are you kidding me?

I think, from the perspective of pop culture, there's no middle. It's like either you're young or you're not, right?

Either you're young or you're old.

Or, it's just, as long as you're young that's what matters, and the rest is nobody cares. Because everyone's so obsessed with youth and youth culture.

But the youth culture has been with me from the beginning of my birth in 1927 because of movies. Okay. This is a whole century in which women thought that over twenty-five was old, and therefore didn't exist, because it didn't exist on the screen.

Yeah. And it hasn't changed that much. It really hasn't.

This is part of the last century.

I have questions for you. My first is about your childhood. In *My Kitchen Wars*, you talk about your religious upbringing a lot, and these really deep-rooted feelings of guilt, but then also how you rebelled against it. Do you think that set you on the course for rebellion, or do you think that it's just who you are, and you would have, in any situation, ended up pushing against what was put in front of you?

Yeah, yeah. For me, the puritanism of my culture comes directly from the Scottish Puritans. Since my genetics is Scots and we are an ornery lot, they're inseparable—nature and nurture—on this, because the nature is

Scots are ornery people. How would I know what I would be otherwise, because I'm not?

Well, okay, to take that idea of rebellion forward, for you, there's a connection between food and rebellion that runs through your work.

Of course, because if I'm a rebellious, ornery kind of a kid, it's going to show up in everything.

But do you think at some point you became conscious of it and really started working with it deliberately?

Absolutely.

When did that happen for you?

College, when I discovered for the first time that the Bible wasn't history. Literally. I majored in philosophy because there was nobody in my childhood that didn't believe that the Bible and history were synonymous.

There's something in this idea of the kitchen war—that the kitchen could become a battleground. For most women it wasn't so much a battle; you became docile and you just did what you were supposed to do. You know?

You don't know that because you don't have enough evidence of it. I've watched tons and tons of movies. I have now watched all the movies, I think, that are available from the thirties, forties, fifties, and sixties—and the seventies. You see the shifts in pop culture. You see middle-class women discovering the (servantless) kitchen where they can compete with each other to excel. You see them adopting these stereotypes of each other because that's what they see in the media as role models. There's no impetus to rebel from that until they discover the kitchen is their only domain. It's very easy.

The kitchen doesn't become a battleground until either the man or the woman says, "I don't like what's happening here. I don't like this scene." The woman can say it over and over again, and the man can be deaf to it, or the woman can see that her only mode of survival is to say nothing. In movies of the fifties, you get this terrible batch of women in aprons who do nothing but cry. They either cry, or they cry in the kitchen, or they hide in the kitchen, or they hide someplace in the bedroom and cry. They are so wimpy, you can't believe it.

CD

If you want to talk about the kitchen as a battleground, I have been seeing that in food writing because for so long it was where women got sent. It was like, "Well, this is the thing you can write about. You do that." And then it became a source of entertainment, and it became a business; restaurants became big business. Now you see more male editors of food magazines. You also see men getting to write the juicier stories a lot of times—

BETTY

This was always true. This is not new. What's new is that there are fewer magazines and newspapers. The online world, it is not about readers; it's about viewers. Your main audience is much more eclectic. Good god. This seems to me a huge, huge, huge revolution, but it's not tidy the way you want it to be. Women didn't even exist on the women's page except within the tight little—they were sequestered to [food], just the way they were sequestered to the kitchen, but change was that food became fashionable, so guys got into it. Okay, that's a good thing!

CD

When you first started writing about food, it seemed like you chose it because it was a safe and nonthreatening place. Just because you had your husband, Paul Fussell, who was this writer, and there was so much tension between the two of you regarding your doing anything that would be threatening to him. I think your work, the books that you've written, the articles you've written, really fight against that. I wonder how much of that was conscious, but also if you've gotten any pushback from editors along the way when you wanted to do that kind of writing about food that really wasn't the kind of writing expected of women.

BETTY

Yeah. The main pushback was I couldn't get published. Because I wasn't doing recipes.

CD

That's exactly my point and my question. How did you push through that? How did you manage still to be able to do it? And did it become easier at any point?

BETTY

Yes. But let's see. I began writing food articles in 1960 for *Travel & Leisure*, because we were traveling so much. And that's when I had to appear first as B. H. Fussell, because you couldn't get published as a woman any more than M.F.K. [Fisher] could. Publishing belonged to men in every sense, but everything did.

CD

When did it become easier for you? Or did it never become easier for you?

BETTY

The first and only break I got was when the *New York Times* food page–women's page, became the Lifestyle section, but it had a woman editor [Charlotte Curtis]. Oh god. Wonderful woman and rare, but she was very much under the thumbs of all the male editors on the *Times*. But it was when Craig

Claiborne stopped being the main food editor, and then there was room for Mimi Sheraton and Ruth Reichl, etc. But only when it enlarged to Lifestyle, because they found, *Oh, there are people interested in that who aren't just stupid little women.*

CD

What about in terms of books and getting book deals. Did you find that challenging?

BETTY

Challenging? I found it impossible. If you wanted to publish a book without recipes, you were crazy. You had to fight everybody, including—if you were lucky enough to get one—an agent. Everybody. Because that was the definition of a cookbook. But a lot has been written on this. The implication of cooking and food was simply how-to, because that is mechanical, and that's simple, and it's what the tradition of the food industry is—all of those things working together naturally. Anything that is not that was scary to everybody.

CD

They didn't know where to put it, right?

BETTY

Yeah, because bookstores didn't know.

CD

I always say that people have a really hard time with anything that is cross-genred.

BETTY

You betcha. They will always have trouble with this, even with the magic of multimedia, because the book industry is not set up that way. We are having a total revolution of the book industry, but they've been like lemmings going over the cliff instead of saying, "Hey, we could seize this and use it." No, they don't.

CD

When did cooking shift from being a chore for you and a way to keep up appearances or even compete with your neighbors? When did it become something that you did for pleasure's sake? When did you realize that you liked it?

BETTY

I liked it from the beginning because I had never done it. It's like Julia [Child] in that sense, and Julia represented the tip of the iceberg of women who had never cooked. The reason I had never cooked was the opposite of Julia's: mine was poverty; hers was wealth. It doesn't matter if this is still an entirely new world that is intriguing and wonderful and exciting. What I have always loved about food is that it is transitory. It is immediate. You get results, good or bad. You're not at it for ten years before you discover it's junk that you made.

CD

Well, there's also the idea that some people really like the repetition of it and other people (like me), don't really like to make the same thing twice. I always want to be trying something different and challenging myself. A lot of it's driven by curiosity.

BETTY

Right. I agree.

CD

That seems like another aspect of it, which is that it's the doing but it's the doing something you haven't done and that being the thing that drives it.

BETTY

That's the pleasure. I've always said there are two kinds of cooks. I'm your kind of cook. The other kind of cook is somebody who is a Julia. Julia wants to perfect it. She has always had that engineering thing. It is a process, which you can perfect, and that appeals to guys much more. That appeals to bakers as it does to surgeons. Who are the best bakers? Surgeons. Or vice versa. They're aligned. It's precision. It's measuring. It's quantitative in effect. Whereas improvised cooking is whimsical, organic, all the things you don't get rewarded for in a machine society.

BETTY

I wanted to talk to you about the idea of sex and food, and, to go back to this idea of pleasure, of things like lust and hunger. This was definitely not part of cookbooks and of women cooking. If it was, we weren't supposed to talk about it, obviously.

BETTY

Except for Julia, who meant something different by "Bon appétit." That was not the introduction to the *Joy of Cooking*. Notice that "joy of cooking," it is joyless by contemporary sense.

CD

Yes. I was wondering when you started to really tap into that as a writer. It's one of the things that I love the most about *My Kitchen Wars*. It shouldn't have been such a rare thing in the late nineties, when it came out, to read about that connection between sex and food and have someone be so honest and embracing of it. But, I realized it was. You write about when you tapped into it in the kitchen, but when did you start making that connection in your writing?

BETTY

It was always there in my writing. My food writing from the beginning was about sensations, because food is such an easy and automatic avenue to that. That's another of the pleasures of improvised cooking, because your focus has to be on what's in your hands, what's on the board. How does it feel? "Whoo! Very hot pan!" "Oh, watch it, that. It's curling, it's spinning. It's alive!" This is the real thing. It is alive.

CD

Maybe you always knew, but it was different from what other women who were writing about food were doing; it definitely was not on the page. If you read anything in the women's pages, or you picked up a cookbook, you would not get that sense. You would not feel the sensuality of it. You sort of see it in Julia, but it's more like she's having a gay old time than—

BETTY

Right. She's having a gay old time in the process. There are two people, the English writer Elizabeth David, and very much of course M. F. K. Fisher. And this is the French tradition, anyway; anybody who is at all familiar with French literature of any kind. There are all these models, and I'm a book person, so it was very easy to pick up from Elizabeth David that, *Ooh, something wonderful is going on here,* because it combines history and interest in culture and the wider, deeper prospect of the world around you and your relation to it as a little tiny person with a body.

CD

One of the things that I was also really struck by, writers don't often talk about how hard the process of writing is—I mean, that idea of really working on it so that you become good at it—and that's something that you've written about. How do you think your writing has changed?

BETTY

That's easy because the first part comes from being married to a guy who was born a writer. I was not born a writer. I had always written. I had written from the beginning, stuff in school, which I loved to do, but I loved to improvise. For which I would often be punished.

CD

Why can't improvising be another version of being born a writer? What does that mean?

BETTY

Okay, this would have to do with reporting. When I went to work for the [New York] *Times*, they employed me. I mean, I wasn't an employee; I was just a freelancer for them. They were interested in my content. As one, I forget which, male editor said, "Well, you're a lousy reporter, but a good writer." I had to learn what form to put my improvisations in, as I did in graduate school. I had to learn the forms of what is an essay, at which I'm lousy. I'm a terrible expository writer, and I really hate exposition.

CD

What dictates or motivates your choice of subject matter? Did you find that it changed at all? I still love that story that you wrote for Darra Goldstein's magazine *Cured*, about the fermented corn drink, tejuíno. I was wondering where those ideas come from for you.

BETTY

That's standard cliché, this one, because tejuíno would be a popular drink, which Mexicans in the United States, some, have never heard of. In Mexico it is totally everybody's drink—that's peculiar, and, of course, because it's related to corn. Why are we interested in corn? Because this is communal history. In food, we are always talking about other people, other creatures. We're talking not just about ourselves. The curse of writing.

CD

The curse of writing.

BETTY

The curse of blogs. The curse of Facebook. Truly. People have become extremely isolated and narcissistic. Boring. Boring. Boring. Food is this perfect window into other people, which is automatic. Major difference. The food is not a subject. It is a vision, a way of life as is art a way of life, whether it's writing or anything. It's a way of perception. It's a way of proceeding.

It's a way of relating to the universe that you find yourself in, little pieces of dust that we are.

CD

Yes. This is a question that's just a little bit silly, but it's fun.

BETTY

Nothing's silly.

CD

I love how you write these descriptions of eras and gender roles, but you use food as the marker. Things like: "These were the smiling Eisenhower years in which Ike ran the country and Mamie turned the lamb chops with the same nauseous cheer." If you had to assign foods to different decades, which would you choose for each decade? What do you think were some of the definitive dishes of the thirties, the forties? I'm seeing the lamb chops, but then obviously, we had all these different changes, thanks to Julia Child, and the end of the Cold War.

BETTY

Well, if I try . . . this is just a kind of a wildly free association.

CD

Yes. That's good.

BETTY

Yeah, okay. That means it's always gonna be personal. The thirties would be, for me, a can of Del Monte Peaches, actually. The forties would be white oleo (margarine) that you have to mix with the yellow coloring in the package to make pretend butter.

CD

I love it.

BETTY

The fifties would be—what was the casserole we all made out of cans, again, because we were learning to cook before Julia? We weren't really learning to cook; we were desperate. The fifties would be macaroni and cheese casserole. Something that was easy. You didn't have to know anything. The sixties, okay. Julia is in the works . . . let me skip to the seventies, because the seventies will be a soufflé, a chocolate soufflé. The eighties could be a beef Wellington, but it could also be a salmon en croute. The nineties, what we were eating in the nineties? Let's say prime rib with béarnaise. That's nineties. And the double aughts, that'll be a quinoa salad.

BETTY

Quinoa.

CD

Now, what is it, teens, our current decade?

BETTY

Yeah.

CD

Okay. Oh god. Kale. Kale. Kale.

BETTY

Kale, everywhere kale, yeah.

CD

Can we please leave kale to the thirties? Send it back to the farm movement, which it never was a part of. I'm missing the sixties. For me, but it's not characteristic, because we were mostly living abroad in the sixties—it meant French baguette and real butter. Does it work?

BETTY

Yeah. It works. Okay. Originally, of the sixties, you wrote, "the ideologues of the feminist movement seemed to me as narrow or dogmatic as the Calvinists of my youth." It's fifty-plus years later, and we're in the midst of the #MeToo movement. Having seen all the different waves of feminism and types of feminists, how do you look at what's happening now?

CD

I argue all the time with my feminist younger friends, let's say my daughter's age—those in their forties, fifties, and sixties. The extremity of the ideology, which is what it is now, it will produce its own horrific backlash, which is already happening. Practically, I think it's a bad move. Ideologically, I think it's a bad move because you are ruining people's lives for something that is a very indeterminate and insoluble problem of gender division. Boys are not girls, and girls are not boys.

BETTY

Do you see any other way out of it or through, or do you think that this is something that is part of the human condition?

CD

Everything is part of the human condition. Right now, we have a cultural moment of extreme conflict, which we have not always had, great America. It is riled naturally by the people who are at the head of the country that we have elected or allowed to be elected. It is rife in the Congress. It is rife in all people who are in positions of power because they have had a free ride postwar, the beginning of the time when America grew up and became a political global power. We've had half a century and more of being, "Thump, thump, thump. The greatest power on earth. Yeah!" You pay for that kind of hubris, boys and girls. It's just a matter of time, and meantime, people you love will be harmed and hurt and killed. And other people will not, in unjust fashions. Yeah. So nothing is easy here, kids. Don't create categories and pretend there's an easy way, when it's not a problem that needs solving. It's ourselves, all of us.

BETTY

Kind of related to that, but maybe not. How do you think food writing can be a feminist act?

CD

I don't think it should be. That's easy. Food breaks through the stupid categories we put on things. I hate the word *feminism*.

Can you talk a little bit about the documentary project, on Eves? It sounds so cool.

BETTY

Yeah, because the media food world, I mean, the television food world, for obvious reasons, has been the domain of guys—for the usual power reasons, and guy chefs and wonderful writers like Anthony Bourdain who [was] both. Okay. But it is a male point of view. The part that I want to capitalize is that there is a Female Point of View that is distinct from the male point of view formalized in our industrial structure. It doesn't get aired. I've been working about four years on this because Eve is a natural subject for me. There have been wonderful books on Adam and Eve, and who the hell was Eve. I've decided that my definition of the difference between Adam and Eve and the garden is that the guy obeys rules. God is the rule maker. So the guy says, "Well, here we are. Yes, God, we're doing this, and we're doing that, just like you said." Eve said, "Well, why shouldn't I? Why?" She asks why. She's the daring one. The garden of Eden is dead because there is no change. If there is no change, there is no life. God has said, "No, there will be no life here." When he said, "You shall not become mortal because I want you as potential—not as real," Eve made us real because she dared.

CD

You were saying it's been hard to get the project picked up, why?

BETTY

That's easy. Because I'm not in the loop. I'm dead. Nobody's heard of me in the current TV world. I'm not a household name. I'm not Julia Child. It'd be hard enough to get the right show for Julia now, actually.

CD

I think about that a lot. I think if Julia were here now, what she'd be doing.

BETTY

Yeah, and it's a good question, because it would answer a lot about what media is up to, and what it wants to be up to, and what it could be up to.

CD

This is not the most interesting question, but still something I'm curious about, which is what you cook these days, and also, do you look at new cookbooks, or do you not care that much at all?

BETTY

I never look at cookbooks anymore, and I regret it because I'm missing a lot of wonderful books. I cook every day. The only meal I have in the old-folks' home is breakfast 'cause that is easy. That is my social hour. The rest of the day, I'm on my own. If I can't cook—I discovered this here—I get to feel desperate the same way if I'm not writing. Something's missing. What is it? You can call it an addiction or an obsession. I don't. I call it my way of life has altered radically by being in an old-folks' home, and I want to participate in my food. I don't do that by going to the dining room and sitting there to be served. Which is what most people here want. I don't want that.

CD

But is there an option for people to cook if they want to?

BETTY

Oh, you can. There is. We each have these little closet kitchens.

CD

That sounds so depressing. A closet kitchen.

BETTY

No, it's not. You always make do with what you have.

CD

That's true. I'm thinking back to your splendid kitchen you described, the Lilac Lane kitchen in Princeton, then I think about the closet, and you know?

BETTY

I don't miss that at all.

CD

You don't?

BETTY

It was another lifetime. It was another moment. This is the moment now. What saves me is that the greenmarket on Saturday mornings, the downtown farmers market, is sensational, naturally; it would be, in Santa Barbara. All year long, I have flowers, fresh seafood, fresh wonderful pasture-fed meats, produce, produce, produce. You follow the seasons. Oh, yeah, California has seasons. Yes, yes. The stone fruit is in now, so it's peaches, and apricots, and nectarines. Then you get that and you have it with raw cream from the market from the most gorgeous cows you ever saw.

CD

Wow.

BETTY

It's all there. All you have to do is get into the van and go. Usually I'm the only person in the van. Sometimes, there are two.

CD

My last question is a bit of an annoying one, but I ask it anyway. Do you have any regrets, professionally?

BETTY

My only regret, truly, is that I haven't finished the current work in progress, which I wanted to have finished in 2018 because I like the sound of 2018. This one won't be finished until 2019.

CD

Is this the memoir, the second installation of the memoir? I cannot wait to read it.

BETTY

Yeah. This is the *How to Cook a Coyote.*

WRITE THIS, NOT THAT!

Is there a STORY—or a GENRE OF STORY, or a SUBJECT MATTER—*you wanted to write* and were told you couldn't—or were made to feel as though you couldn't ... and you're pretty sure it's because you're a woman?

KATHLEEN SQUIRES

Luckily, I don't think this has ever happened to me.

MONIQUE TRUONG

I'm going to modify your question: *"pretty sure it's because you're a woman of color?"* I had been living in Helsinki for three months, courtesy of a writing fellowship, and I pitched a travel article about a particular area of Finland—a comprehensive, well-researched pitch complete with restaurants, hotels, and culinary highlights of the region—to food magazines and major US newspapers, all of whom I had written for previously. No takers. Why? They, most likely, couldn't fathom the connection that I had or could make with this region of the world. Women of color are rarely afforded "expertise" or "connection" beyond the locale modifiers that appear in our bio. Our "world" is seen by these editors as small. How can we be a travel writer when our world is limited and proscribed by others in this way?

KRISTINA GILL

I'm a black woman, and I identify in that order. I think in my case this matters far more than the single aspect of being a woman. There are other factors besides race/ethnicity you could add to being a woman that would also change opportunity in different ways that don't apply to men. So although you may have some women who felt they couldn't, or were made to feel they couldn't because they were a woman, I've felt that black was the more limiting factor from the perspective of the person who was denying me the opportunity.

CATHY ERWAY

A lot of the subjects I propose are deemed unfit not because I'm a woman, but because they're about Asian food topics that are thought to be too esoteric or "niche." I'm not sure if these would be taken more seriously if I were a man proposing the exact same things and have no way of telling that. But it's an interesting thought experiment.

NAOMI TOMKY

I tend to do a lot of "Day in the Life" type pieces and have often felt that my access was limited by male chefs who felt like it would be annoying to have my lady-energy in the kitchen. I have no hard proof, but an inkling.

JAMIE FELDMAR

Oh man (ha, no pun intended, but maybe pun intended), yes. There was (and very much still is) a certain style of feature story, often a profile, that involves a writer "tagging along" with a chef (usually male) on various acts of culinary derring-do and/or discovery (i.e., hunting, fishing, searching for some legume previously believed to have been extinct in a remote jungle; usually accompanied with a surplus of drinking and swearing) often in "exotic" locations. As a young writer, not gonna lie, I loved reading a lot of these kind of pieces—how could you not? They are intentionally evocative and aspirational and appeal to those who think of themselves as adventurous and inquisitive—and wanted to write them. I pitched these stories, often working in conjunction with the PR teams who actually dreamed them up and dealt with the logistics (a nasty little not-so-secret, but neither here nor there, I suppose), and was never, ever assigned them. There would be times where, six or nine months later, I would see a version of a story with a chef in a location I had pitched, written by a man. Was it because I was too junior a reporter? Female? A terrible pitcher? A bad writer? I'll never really know, but I can't shake the feeling that gender played a role.

JORDANA ROTHMAN

I've only recently been thought of for those ride-along, Hunter S. Thompson kind of assignments— you know, the ones that begin in media res in an alley in Tokyo with so-and-so megachef cocked on Hibiki, singing "Show Me the Way to Go Home." No one wanted that from a female writer for most of my career, and I'm not sure anyone wants that from women now either (frankly I'm just not sure anyone wants that at all, which, actually, may be progress).

SIERRA TISHGART

An exposé on a prominent male restaurant group's history of mistreating their female employees (verbal abuse, not physical) because the subjects weren't "bad enough."

REBECCA FLINT MARX

I've been lucky in this regard: I can honestly say I've never encountered this problem.

REBEKAH DENN

An investigation on fraud in food labeling.

CATHY BARROW

I've wanted to write about women and whole animal butchery, but selling the story has been a struggle. It's been covered, now, in the form of profiles, but I can't get traction with a larger trend story.

When I tried to write stories about the intersection of food and business, I couldn't sell the pitch (which felt strange as I arrived in the world of food writing from some years as a small business owner). I had an early "in" with the founders of a fast-casual restaurant group with about six hours of interviews as background to a pitch. I had an exclusive line on expansion into new markets as well as a deal with Whole Foods in NYC maybe six months before it happened. At the time, I was writing regularly for both the *New York Times* and *Washington Post* Food sections whose editors suggested it was a stronger business story. I pitched to *NYT*

Business and the rejection email actually said something along the lines of "maybe you should just stay in the pantry."

ALI ROSEN

Working in food television, I have constantly hit a wall regarding the type of content I can be "allowed" to host. I once had a call with a major cable network about a potential show and they openly admitted that they haven't hired a female host for any program in years because their "audience doesn't like them."

Women in food TV are expected to fill certain archetypes and a lot of the more interesting cultural or in-depth content is naturally assumed to fall to men. And as you get older as a woman it is even worse. Think of all the food travel shows: You can name a lot with men who are forty or older, but can you name one with a woman in that age range? Women in that age range have to be hosts or cooks and not much else in-between.

TAMAR ADLER

I don't know if this is a good answer, but I feel like some of what I write is scorned because I'm a woman. I've not been forbidden from writing anything. But I think the reception of some things has been skewed.

This is well-covered territory, but if a man had written the following, it would not have caused even a ripple: "Though I cringe to admit it, I not only own, but love, a hand-forged egg spoon. Before my husband and I were given it as a wedding present, we used little campfire pie irons, which you can buy at any hardware store, and they worked just as well." It even has the words "hardware store" in it. But the response was cruel, aggressive, offended. The actual word choice and idea is really pretty neutral, but because of some idea about women or women who've worked at Chez Panisse, or something, I got crucified for it (Twitter crucified, that is.) I don't know exactly what the issue is. I'm not that smart. I only know that it has to do with gender.

JULIA TURSHEN

I've had plenty of stuff rejected, but I don't necessarily think it's because I'm a woman.

KRISTY MUCCI

I've pitched so many stories, to men and women . . . that I've been told are great ideas, but I don't get the go-ahead. I think in some cases, it's because I'm a woman, but in others, because I'm not in with the right crowd of women.

REGINA SCHRAMBLING

Never happened that I can recall.

Do you think there are certain genres of food writing—or even a particular type of voice or writing style, or point of view—that are consistently assigned to or associated with women, or, more specifically, women of color?

RUBY TANDOH

I feel that as women we are expected to put a huge amount of ourselves into our work, threading our personal story into the narrative, making our traumas public. I've been vocal about having had an eating disorder, because I felt that disclosure was important when I was writing pro-food, anti-wellness books and essays. But that story now has taken on a life of its own: Editors want that level of intimacy and self-disclosure in everything I write, whether or not it's relevant. It's women's lot to be defined by their subjectivity, it seems, whereas male writers have more freedom to approach food from the perspective of some kind of detached external observer (think critics, "experts," reporters, and high-end chefs). Whether or not it's possible or even desirable to look at food from an "objective" point of view is another issue entirely, but it's frustrating that food writing is so often divided along these lines.

DEB PERELMAN

Home cooking. Cooking for families. Cooking with kids. Lunchboxes. Grocery budgeting. How to clean your kitchen better. Guilt about food. Guilt about not cooking. Diets.

Everyone is fine with women cooking so long as it's an extension of their natural domesticity.

JASMINE MOY

Has any "How to get a quick and easy meal on your table" story ever been pitched or written by a man? Or is it left solely to the working or stay-at-home moms?

NAOMI TOMKY

I definitely think there's a bias toward women having to cover anything "homestyle" or home cooking—which is of course multiplied by the "immigrant" narrative.

LIGAYA MISHAN

I think that personal narratives are often seen as the province of women food writers—approaching food through the lens of one's own family tradition or history. This is particularly true for women of color, who may be expected to act as ambassadors/advocates for the foods of their childhood, and then may not be given a chance to write beyond that.

JULIA TURSHEN

This is a huge generalization, but I do believe women are asked more often than men for recipes, for home cooking stories, for food that makes people feel taken care of. Men, more often than women, are associated with food that impresses. People of color, especially women of color, are often asked to write about race—white people rarely are.

JAMIE FELDMAR

Yep. In a grossly oversimplified nutshell, I basically feel like food writing that's about home cooking and/or ingredients and/or some type of "traditional" cuisine and might involve recipe testing is women's work; writing about chefs, restaurant trends, and or/food culture goes to men. Obviously, there are exceptions to this (see: Julia Moskin, Kim Severson, Jane Black, et al.), but interestingly, I think it often leans toward women writing about chefs/restaurants/etc., and not often the other way around (i.e., I rarely see men write about home cooking, unless it is BBQ, or they are David Tanis).

EMIKO DAVIES

In general—and this is very broad—I do feel there is a sort of sexism about what is "female food" and what is "male food." For example: cakes and sweet things versus meat, vegan versus barbecue, chocolate versus alcoholic drinks. I wouldn't mind writing more about things like offal, but I think that's seen very much as "boy's food," at least here in Italy—I don't know many women who enjoy eating tripe even though it's a classic Florentine dish and at the lampredotto (abomasum tripe) van, it's always a group of men lined up or sitting there with their glass of wine and offal sandwich (and there's me with my daughters!).

EMILY FARRIS

I don't know many professional male recipe developers, that's for damn sure. There are chefs, and they do write recipes, but as far as recipe development behind the scenes, that feels like it's been women's work for a while.

While there are exceptions, food writing, in general, has been dominated by white women. That's finally starting to change and hopefully that will make us all better consumers—and people.

ESTHER TSENG

The genre of recipe stories where there's a buildup by way of a personal essay to a certain food, often cultural, and a recipe follows. I feel these are always assigned to women—whether because these are pitched more often by women or not, I'm not sure.

REGINA SCHRAMBLING

Recipe-writing is the quiet room. Women are always segregated cuz they can't come out dick-swinging.

ANDREA NGUYEN

Recipe- or technique-driven pieces often have female bylines. There have been many Asian American folks working in test kitchens! We can and do write other things.

White women have cornered the market on really trendy stuff like cupcake books, inspiralizing, or books with *skinny* or *bitch* in the title. Can you imagine a black woman (or black man) being "allowed" to publish a book called *Soul Food Is My Bitch* or *Skinny Bitch* anything?

Black men and women are almost exclusively restricted to soul food and/or Southern food (which somehow when someone black is involved are one and the same) as if these are the only topics we could possibly have expertise in. Works by Bryant Terry, Stephen Satterfield, Chef Todd Richards, and even my cookbook about Rome show that there is a market for black authors in food who are not kept in that box, regardless of how the publishers choose to market the books. Even better, look at how James Beard Award winners Toni Tipton-Martin, Adrian Miller, and Michael Twitty's books were received. There was mass appeal. I think this points to the fact that when there is no diversity on your team—making decisions about who writes for you/ whose books you publish—you only worry about one demographic and you short-change yourself literally and figuratively.

TAMAR ADLER

I think that the woman as credible critic is a slim category. It might be changing? I can't comment really on women of color versus white women, but to say that if it's hard for a white woman to seem like a credible food critic, I imagine it's orders of magnitude harder for women of color, who fight credibility fights in every area of life. (NB: Since I answered this, Tejal Rao has been named the *New York Times*' California restaurant critic, so it's definitely changing . . .)

There's also an implicit double bind in womanhood and the life of the restaurant critic; that is, to seem credible, smart, and in control, women have, at least for a while, had to be thin—or I've read studies in which women who have larger bodies are seen as out of control and less credible and reliable than women with smaller bodies. And to be honest, I have wondered occasionally whether my own attachment to being a slim woman has affected my career. I don't eat that many pasta tasting menus—I mean, I eat some—but in the balance between my self-concept as a fit, taken-seriously woman and a serious food writer (who might need to surrender said self-concept), the first wins. I have a definite tendency to test certain recipes less because I don't want to eat ten pasta dishes or pies in a day. And I'm sure there are other times I miss out on an idea or a lightbulb because I'm thinking—I've already eaten at three restaurants this week. I have a feeling that this is different for men, who I think feel more free to sacrifice their bodies to their field and don't expect to be socially shunned for it.

REBECCA FLINT MARX

Profiles of lifestyle bloggers with a cookbook to flog; anything having to do with dieting/wellness (unless it's some guy eating nothing but Halo Top or Soylent for a week for *GQ*).

KRISTEN MIGLORE

I can't back this up or even share anecdotal experience, but my hunch is that service-driven pieces are more often handed out to women, while more writerly, voicier columns and features go to men—see *Eater*'s roundup of writers on [deceased Pulitzer Prize–winning food critic] Jonathan Gold (seven women to fifteen men, and they're pretty conscientious about such things).

CHRISTINE MUHLKE

Baking. Recipes. Entertaining stories. Trend roundups. Memoirs.

HANNA RASKIN

I suppose women are more likely to write about cookies, baby food, and hot male chefs.

CATHY BARROW

As most of my writing has been about preserving and about pies, I've stayed in my female lane, that's certain.

CHANDRA RAM

Certainly the food pages/women's pages of newspapers and anything having to do with entertaining, holiday cookies, and Easter bunny cakes. I remember reading Sally

Quinn's entertaining book, and she wrote about a pasta dish called Johnny Marzetti, calling it "a man's dish"! That's what I think newspaper food sections were designed to emulate.

But along those lines, the fact that desserts are what women write about, and pastry/patisserie are what men do, says a lot: women should bake the cookies, while men should create artistic desserts that earn them respect. Ugh. And it's worse for women of color, because I don't think readers want to hear from them unless it's a precious story about your grandmother cooking in a mud hut or trailer or something that says (my least favorite word) "ethnic," but can be put under amber for people who want to feel they had something "authentic" (another word I hate in food).

NICOLE TAYLOR

Baking. I feel like women are always in the baking category: pies, cakes … any kind of dessert. Even some of my favorite bloggers—*Smitten Kitchen*, etc.—the recipes I love the most from them are for baking.

I grew up around black women who baked all the time. Like big luscious layer cakes that weren't simple. Pies from scratch using lard. But the funny thing is, you don't see that many black, particularly Southern, women, writing about the big cakes and pies and intricate pastry stuff. I would love to write more about Southern cakes and pies—those of the black church ladies, black

PTA moms that learned from their grandma or aunt.

ALI ROSEN

The current think pieces we see on the lack of coverage of women in the food space have all been led by women.

Do you think there are certain genres of food writing, or even a particular type of voice, writing style, or point of view, that are consistently assigned to or associated with men?

VIRGINIA WILLIS

To answer your question I will ask you to consider a few questions: How many food sections in the past fifty years have been run and staffed by women? How many women currently work in magazine test kitchens? Now, think how many men are featured as the voice of that particular test kitchen? How many women work at food magazines and food websites and how many of them are run or headed by a man? I am not certain as I have not actually conducted a study, but it appears to me that the bulk of the work is done by women and men are disproportionally represented in positions of leadership.

KRISTY MUCCI

As far as I can tell, men have their pick. It feels like there's a bro club and the guys all hook each other up and help each other out, and they all get to do what they want.

It also feels like there's a girls club that does the same thing for its members. It's just at a smaller scale.

GINA HAMADEY

Anything vaguely food science-y.

JASMINE MOY

Anything to do with fire or mammals with their faces still attached.

NICOLE TAYLOR

Barbecue. I love barbecue. I grew up seeing men barbecue, but I also saw women preparing the meat and prepping the sides. Those are the most important parts—prepping the meat, seasoning and massaging the meat, getting it ready. A good piece of meat is important, but I feel like the sides are the most important. It's always women that you'll find whipping them up.

If I had to think right now . . . I can't think of three women writing about barbecue.

HANNA RASKIN

Other than barbecue?

As far as voice, I've been told that one of the reasons I'm not universally beloved is because I write like a man. (And my paper's studies show I'm most popular with educated white men aged sixty-eight to eighty-two, so maybe I do.)

TAMAR ADLER

I just feel like if men are doing basic, tender cooking—making a fire, cooking in it, or making soup, stuff like that, it's considered a return to the elemental, some kind of grand leap of concept, or coming back around from super conceptual to the real and homey. And when women do it, it doesn't deserve comment, or worse, is viewed as precious.

ANDREA NGUYEN

The bro tone created by and for men is there for them. But increasingly, that's become sexually neutral in publications like *Bon Appétit*, which drove that bus at the beginning. In food television and videography (YouTube) there's still a certain exaggerated, over-the-top voice used to draw attention to *extreeeeeme* food topics.

CATHY ERWAY

I actually once wrote a cooking beat for a now-defunct mens' lifestyle website. It was a lot of fun, but I was writing from the presumption that cooking was a novelty for this audience. In reality, home cooking is a novelty for a lot of young people (and older people!) regardless of sex these days. I think food writing for male publications often has an exaggerated bro-ness to its tone that can be exhausting, so it was refreshing that the editor wanted me to write this beat instead.

REBECCA FLINT MARX

Oh yes: the dick-swinging male chef profile. All of the time. If you're a dude, you get to follow David Chang to Tokyo. Or Francis Mallmann to his latest bonfire. Or Daniel Boulud to wherever he feels like drinking. But it's not just profiles of chefs; it's really profiles of any Serious Man, e.g., Harold McGee, Nathan Myhrvold.

As far as voice, I've noticed that a lot of guys tend to use second-person narration, as in: "You watch the sun set, smoke in your nostrils and blood and fat under your fingernails, and think, this, finally, is what it means to be a man."

JULIA TURSHEN

Profiles of "geniuses"!

ALI ROSEN

Oh absolutely. Most of the chef profiles and restaurant reviews are done by men. That is slowly changing (and thank goodness) but I still think they are predominantly male-oriented despite there being a larger prevalence of female food writers.

JULIA BAINBRIDGE

No, but I haven't been reading through this lens. In other words, I haven't made it my business to think deeply about the gender of the authors of stories I read.

KRISTINA GILL

Plain old American white men (and women) seem to have free rein for any genre, even genres to which they have no particular ties—a story/book on Mexico? No problem! Take a long trip and come back and write it.

ALEX VAN BUREN

Spirits coverage! I'd love to see more women, nonwhite, non-straight spirits writers.

MAGGIE HOFFMAN

The drinks space, especially when it comes to cocktails, is still very male-dominated. Dudes assume that women have inferior palates and less experience. In the wine world, men who have been to Germany once act like true experts, while I'd be encouraged to play "beginner" even though I, too, have been there once. It's all quite outdated—women drink whiskey. Women know wine. Women can shake drinks all night—and taste them. And women can behave appropriately around alcohol— maybe that's the stereotype that needs knocking down first. Women can taste booze and not turn into shrieking idiot party girls.

EMILY FARRIS

Restaurant reviewing! Not even food is free from the male gaze.

ALISON ROMAN

Travel, with regard to food writing especially, is nearly always given to men. RESTAURANT REVIEWS. Can every newspaper start fresh? MEAT. Why does meat = men? I, for one, love meat. I cook it and eat it and really love it. In fact, I have a bit to say about it. But honestly what gets me going the most is the "expert" hat. "Ask a Chef" or "Ask an Expert" almost always means "Ask a Man." I've seen men who haven't worked in restaurants or magazines in years get gigs where an "expert" is required and it's . . . LOL, it's because they are a man.

DEB PERELMAN

Buffalo wings. Football food. Restaurant culture. Single malt. Extremely detailed articles about coffee beans and technique. "You're doing this wrong in the kitchen." (This = whatever the topic is; doesn't matter if the writer is actually an expert, only bravado is required.)

JORDANA ROTHMAN

If you are granting wishes, mine is to never have to read another story about a bro discovering noodles.

CHRISTINE MUHLKE

Boozy chef profiles. Street-food guides to Asian metropolises. Fishing and hunting tales.

AUBRIE PICK

There's a certain type of embedded reportage-style food photography that I only really see male photographers getting assigned. Two weeks with an indigenous tribe hunting and pit-cooking wild pigs? Fishing remote schools of fish in deadly waters? Harvesting wild thyme with Bedouins in the mountains of Jordan? Almost always shot by a white guy. Which isn't to say that there aren't talented, hardworking female photographers who would be awesome at taking on those kinds of assignments, and I'm sure there are some that are getting them, but it's often the exception, not the rule.

CHANDRA RAM

I hate that men seem to own restaurant reviews and food travel shows. The former, because reviews are service journalism for the (huh, male) readers newspaper advertisers care about, and they tend to want to get advice on how to spend their money from a man. And they appreciate and respect negative criticism from a man, where as a negative comment from a woman is perceived to be bitchy.

Similarly, any sort of food/travel seems to belong to the likes of Tony Bourdain, Andrew Zimmern, and David Chang. Why can't a woman travel around and discover new cultures? Wouldn't the women in communities those men visit have so much more to say to a woman traveling the world to share their stories?

ESTHER TSENG

I feel like TV shows where different cultures are explored are always assigned to men—especially when there are copious amounts or varieties of food being consumed, because I feel there's this unspoken rule that people are uncomfortable watching females eat a lot, or they're not used to watching females on TV who aren't caretaking or showing a recipe.

YASMIN KHAN

I'm so over watching middle-aged, middle-class white men dominate food and travel media. In the broadcast world, women are predominantly depicted staying home on the ranch to cook for our families and then it's the men who go off and adventure and eat some crazy shit in a foreign street market. I'm over it. We need more female-led food travel shows. Women approach other cultures, travel, and people in a different way than men. We ask different questions, we seek different experiences. Executives need to wake up and hire more women to produce, direct, and present food and travel shows. I'm hungry for it!

Tejal Rao

Tejal Rao's stories remind me of the Dutch artist Johannes Vermeer's paintings. You're probably familiar with his most famous, *Girl with a Pearl Earring* (c. 1665), and how the details of the subject's costume are rendered—the way her Turkish turban drapes, or her jacket creases, and that pearl glistens; they give the impression of precision and imprint the image on our brains. When Tejal writes a profile, she does something similar. In just two sentences, she takes us behind the griddle of a food cart, or into a room, and we can visualize it as if someone gave us VR goggles: "She rolls up the sleeves of her oversize orange sweater to pull whole tilapia from a garlicky marinade, which she will pan-fry and serve with the browned plantains, a salad of raw onions, tomatoes, and herbs and a homemade hot sauce. She warms groundnut soup on the electric stove until the windows fog up and the whole room is swaddled with the scent of peanut butter and chilies." That's from an article she wrote about British food writer Ruby Tandoh. I see it painted, in Vermeer form: Woman Standing at a Stove.

Or, look at how she described a dish back in 2013 when she was the restaurant critic for New York City's *Village Voice*: "a squelch of root vegetables and pickled lichen in a murky chicken broth, and a bright egg yolk shone through it like the sun behind clouds." The words turn into a still life as you read. A few paragraphs down, she makes a masterpiece of a hot dog. "The long, curved weenie comes in a soft, pockmarked Swedish flatbread known as tunnbröd, with a billow of smooth, hot mashed potatoes, brown mustard, fried onions, and a bushel of fresh, feathery dill." Most writers only dream of being able to depict things so poetically. For Tejal, it seems as natural and regular as stirring brown sugar into a bowl of oatmeal or rinsing a glass.

These days, she's using her descriptive powers to review the California dining scene for the *New York Times*. In the following essay, she brings her poetry to one of the humblest, most perfect things in the world: jam.

The Fruit Saver

Have you ever supremed an orange? You don't just push your fingers in and peel it. Instead, you cut the ends off (look, already, you've wasted some fruit). Then you sit the orange flat and use a knife to strip away what's left of the rind, curving the blade along from top to bottom, working your way around. Cut and turn. Cut and turn. The idea is to produce clean orange segments with no peel, or pith, or membrane, but this is hard to do without wasting a lot of fruit (and impossible to do without wasting a little). June Taylor's citrus preparation deviates completely from this technique. It wastes nothing. Standing in her kitchen in Berkeley, she cuts segments away from the whole orange, still attached to the rind, cutting around each piece so that nothing is left when she's finished but an empty sheath of white membrane, like a deflated, juicy balloon. "Marmalades are like that," she said. "You have to know what you want your end marmalade to be like, and then you work backwards."

For the last thirty years, Taylor has sought out and preserved some of the most wide-ranging, delicious fruit in California, zigzagging across the state to meet surly farmers in Home Depot parking lots, tracking down rare citrus through word of mouth, testing gnarled branches in people's backyards by climbing into them, and striking deals with the trees' owners. She has rushed to pick up figs in the summer so she could preserve them at just the right moment, and recently drove to Napa for some "absolutely drop-dead gorgeous" plums.

"I used to climb this one Rangpur lime tree for about fifty to sixty pounds of fruit a year, but now they just FedEx it to me," she said, with some relief—Taylor is sixty-eight years old, and the work of running a jam business is more physically demanding and less glamorous than it might seem through the soft filters of Instagram. In December, she waits in agony for clementines, Meyers, navels and blood oranges, following the crush of Japanese citrus—yuzu and sudachi. All winter, her head is in candy making, syrups, and marmalades, and when she finally looks up in April, or May, it's time to put up rhubarb.

Every summer, Taylor drives her van sixty miles north from Berkeley, toward a cluster of Red Cloud apricots in Winters, California, watered by the reservoir of Lake Berryessa. And as she walks with the farmer Hector Melendez-Lopez, she worries that this year might be the last for her and the Red Cloud. The last time she pries out the stones and roughly chops the flesh and simmers it with lemon and orange juice and sugar and extols its sweet, quiet glories in the way of a jam maker, with hundreds of small glass jars. It might be. "I got 180 pounds this year," Taylor said, which sounded like a lot of fruit. "But from those same trees, I used to get 500, 600 pounds."

The Red Cloud apricot gets its name from the brilliant splotch that marks it. Its smooth orange flesh coats the mouth like softened butter. Full and round and sweet, its meat is charged with a floral perfume. In texture, it's not grainy, or stringy. And because the Red Cloud is more than just a sugar bomb, because it has a bop of acidity, it is a fruit beloved by cooks. It is also, quite possibly, going extinct. Taylor, America's most revered jam maker, a master of the form and a godmother to a movement, preserves the apricots each year and she suspects that this variety might grow in one old and increasingly unproductive orchard in northern California, the one belonging to Melendez-Lopez—and nowhere else.

Though Alice Waters mentioned the fruit in her book, *Chez Panisse Fruit*, work on the subject is rare. If the Red Cloud disappears, there are other fruits, sure. Other apricots. The Patterson apricot represented nearly half of the American apricot crop back when there was a bigger market for the canned stone fruit. "It went from the height of the apricot crop to no one really knowing it," said Taylor sadly. "It has good structure and very good acid and a beautiful apricot flavor. So I'm doing my little stabbing bit in the world of jams to bring it back." Lately, as her Red Cloud source dwindles, Taylor has been using Pattersons more and more.

For decades, Taylor has devoted herself to seeking out organic, often esoteric, endangered varietals, quietly building an appreciation for the diversity of their flavors and textures, in some cases recovering them from near disappearance, simply by working with them. This work is not twee. Taylor stands and cooks and boils and jars Patterson and Royal Blenheim apricots. Santa Rosa plums and July Flame peaches. Josephine raspberries, Nagami kumquats, Page mandarins, and Sudachi lemons. (Meyer lemons, too, but frankly, she's over them.) Tayberries, in small supply and therefore in competition among younger, trendier jam makers, have been familiar to Taylor for a decade.

The particularities of these names might seem excessive, but Taylor uses them with intention. "If I use a fruit's name, the customer uses the fruit's name and the farmer might grow more of the fruit. And this is the way small farmers get supported," she said, standing on a stool, stirring a pot of juice and sugar. "If you don't have a name, you don't exist."

*   *   *

June Taylor's name is on every jar she sells, on every box of candied peels and fruit pastilles. "What we do is the most detailed hand labor—eight hours of standing and cutting oranges and lemons into tiny triangles. And we work with the most gorgeous fruit. But people don't always see that." What do people see? They see what they want: A woman in Berkeley—once the epicenter of a food movement, now a shorthand for its preciousness and privileges—in a flowy cardigan and dangly earrings, selling expensive jam.

But Taylor is a tenacious guardian to the constellation of California fruit. "I do what I want," she said. "It doesn't come from a place of confidence, it comes from a fierce place. The little working-class person who wants to show everyone who we are. It's this voice in me, always, and it's saying, I'll show you."

*　*　*

Taylor was born in a blitzed, rubbled London just after World War II, into a working-class family from Scotland and England. When the city was bombed out, families like hers were pushed up north into the council estates where she grew up, near the fields and the forests of Hadley Woods. She is exuberant now, but she was a painfully shy kid. The kind who walked around with her head down, picking up abandoned bird's nests and mouse skeletons and glinting rocks and beautifully shaped leaves, then arranging them all into museums of feather and bone in her bedroom, miniature exhibitions of the natural world. She was the kind of kid who was more at home in nature than under a roof.

Right by her home there were mansions—proper mansions—and rich families with butlers who answered the doors. When she and her brother were feeling exactly the right ratio of bored to bold, they'd go knocking on doors, to see if anyone would pay them to wash the already gleaming cars in the driveways. Taylor's family didn't have a car. In their driveway, they grew potatoes. Her mother sewed their clothes. And in a greenhouse, built by Taylor's uncle, a carpenter, the family grew tomatoes. It was Taylor's job to water them after school.

Taylor's mother worked in shops and in telecommunications. Trained by the army, she handled the phone lines on an American military base in Devon. "She came from the underbelly of the working class, the underbelly of Glasgow, and she was always the life of the party," said Taylor. She hated to cook, like Taylor's grandmother, who opened cans of potatoes when her granddaughter came round. "Have you ever had canned potatoes? Oh my god. I remember looking down from the tenements in Glasgow. I remember how dark it was. I remember the smell." But Taylor's mother did make jam. It wasn't precious, just a chore. But it's precious now: Taylor saved a single jar of her mother's blackcurrant jam and it sits, unopened, on the shelves in her Berkeley kitchen, right next to her own. "It's never going to be opened," said Taylor.

Taylor's father—and this is a story Taylor hates to tell—worked for the same company his entire life. Though he got a scholarship to a fancy school where all the boys wore capes and buckled shoes, his family couldn't afford the books. So instead, he was sent to the labor exchange, took the first job he got, and stuck with it until he was asked to leave at fifty-nine. In as a tea boy, out as an export manager.

"My father always told me I was a worker bee, too," Taylor said. In school she took years of home economics, French cooking and sewing, preserving and mending. "People think you learn everything from your mum and your granny, no way," she said. "I thought, *I'm not learning to type, I'm not being anyone's secretary!*" In university, Taylor studied sociology and occupational choice: How do you end up doing what you do? How much is determined for you? And how do all the small, seemingly innocuous decisions you make pile up to shift the course of your life? The research and field work were exciting, taking her all across the country to interview people for hours at a time, to ask any questions she wanted about the twists and turns of their lives. But the bulk of the work was academic and dry, and the answers seemed rigged. "All these old, white professors, still debating objectivity versus subjectivity," said Taylor, rolling her eyes, gesturing obscenely with her sticky wooden spoon. She wanted out.

Taylor worked at a supermarket and a newspaper, until she could buy one of those plane tickets where you hop on and off as much as you like, as long as you keep flying in the same direction. She traveled on her own through the United States with a list of phone numbers she could call—friends of friends of friends. Taylor went to New York, to Florida, to Nevada. "I wanted to go to Albuquerque because I couldn't pronounce it," she said. "I wanted to go to Las Vegas, because I'd dated a croupier." One of her last stops was in San Francisco, where she landed without a coat. It was freezing. She called the numbers in her journal and got lucky when someone picked up and told her to come on over.

* * *

The nature writer Robert Macfarlane has written at length about the relationship between language and landscape. About what's lost when the diversity and specificity of words dissolves and what's gained when it is preserved. An example: Once you learn that the word *ammil* refers to the drippy-shaped ice that forms on frozen branches when a thaw is interrupted by a freeze, you see the ice differently. You see it broken down into its moments; you see it changing throughout its life (it has a life!). In short: You become more likely to recognize its particulars. And if you see and taste a Santa Rosa plum, which Taylor describes simply as "ballsy, as in, it's got balls," well, maybe your fruit glossary expands, too, and your understanding of the plum and its variations deepens.

There's no sign outside Taylor's kitchen in Berkeley. "I never put the business sign out because I couldn't decide what I wanted it to say," she said. But Taylor calls her kitchen the Still Room, after the secondary kitchens dedicated to processing plants in old manor houses, typically run by the woman of the house or her house-keeper, who had to stay out of the way of the main cook. These rooms used to have a still at their center, for distilling the essence of flowers and herbs. It's been a long time since these kinds of spaces were in popular use—by the time the journalist and cookbook author Isabella Beeton wrote about the still room, for Victorian house-wives of the nineteenth century, the concept was already outdated.

In *Mrs. Beeton's Book of Household Management*, a book obsessed with class and domestic hierarchy in a distinctly British way, the still-room maid's duties were outlined as menial, and include dusting the housekeeper's room and lighting her fireplace. If the still-room maid worked very hard, Mrs. Beeton suggested, she might be lucky enough to get promoted out of the annex and move up into the main house. It was not an esteemed department. But Taylor chose the name with care. "The still room was the woman's place," she said. "I'm recognizing the work of women typically done in lowly classes. There's nothing shameful about it, but it's never been given true recognition for its beauty, this work women have done for centuries."

In the still room, pickles, confectionary, preserves, syrups, and infusions were all made to mix up home remedies and to stock the pantry. Its tools were all of a jam maker's best friends: large pots, glass jars, beatup sieves, spoons, fine muslin, apple corers, cherry pitters, vegetable peelers, and paring knives—the same kind of tools Taylor and her small team of two cooks reach for most days.

Taylor started jamming when her son was born, thirty years ago. She wanted to feed him only the best food. "I looked at him and thought, *Oh, you're perfect. I'm not giving you commercial fruit!*" So she began preserving fruit for her baby from the Berkeley farmers market. She still does minimal preserving with minimal cook-ing. Because of that, her jams are high in acidity. And the lower sugar content means they have fairly short shelf lives once the jars are unsealed. Rather than using second-tier fruit, the kind damaged or unfit for eating, she chases down the best she can and makes every cut into it count, trapping its vibrancy. That is her concern: "to keep the flavors vital," as she puts it.

Taylor's other work includes flavored syrups, made with layers of herbal or fruit infusions. "The syrup is the elemental piece of confection, it is liquid and sugar and it is amazing," she said. A few years ago, she decided to stop wasting any of the fruit, candying peel and turning juice into fruit cheese, or pastilles, thick and bouncy, cut with a knife. "A new process opens you up to new ways of enjoying fruit," she said. "It shows people, this is something you can eat; it's not something you reject. I've been thinking about that so much over the years. We take a citrus fruit and throw away the peel, and barely eat the inside, and have no relationship to the leaves of the tree, or the bitterness of the fruit, why not?" Jams, and all the confections related to fruit, are just new ways of enjoying it.

She often describes fruits she approves of as "ballsy"—like the Santa Rosa plum—and those she finds boring as "wimpy," and she pumps her middle fingers in the air to express anger. Her clogs, likely coated in a thin layer of sugar syrup, stick to the floor so she can be heard constantly sticking and unsticking, peeling herself away as she moves around. "I love this, but I can't do it for a lot longer," said Taylor, who isn't sure what will happen when she's ready to stop working. She worries that if she sells the business, it won't run the way she likes. Besides, no one's ever approached her about buying it. "I've dedicated half my life to this craft," she said. "All I know is I don't want it to die."

Taylor pulls her long-handled wooden spoon back and forth along the bottom of the pot, feeling for the change in the drag, a resistance, an indication that more water has evaporated and the pastille is ready to pour. "I'm always trying to tell people, I don't make jam, I *preserve*," she said. Jam making is vague. Taylor likes specificity. Besides, *preserving* points directly to the heart of her work, to the names she's kept in circulation and the process she's mastered—to the mosh of pectin gelation and sugar, which draws out moisture, so that microbes have nowhere to bloom and a plum can be suspended in time, in glass, indefinitely.

A Conversation with Pim Techamuanvivit

Some of you may not be old enough to remember Chez Pim, but if you've read or kept a blog, you should know it's in part because of hers. Launched in the early days of blogging, it was one of the first to get major attention, and to function, even if unintentionally, as a source of information for readers in search of recommendations for what to read or to see, where to eat, or what to cook. Its success led its creator, Pim Techamuanvivit to give it a focus: food. After her pioneering turn in the blogosphere, she broke into artisanal jam making well before "small-batch" anything became a lifestyle phenomenon. Based in the Bay Area, the tech industry's hub and the source of figs good enough to be placed, unadorned, on a plate and served to deep-pocketed diners, she seemed primed for both pursuits.

But, in 2014, when she opened San Francisco's first upscale Thai restaurant, there was a real concern as to whether or not that city could wrap its head around the concept—how could this woman be a chef? And what would a non-fusion restaurant that refused to serve Western favorites like pad thai and presented food based on traditional Thai recipes in a less casual setting look like? No pad thai, really?! (Really.) Unsurprising to anyone who knows the Bangkok native, she could very much become a chef-restaurateur, and a damned good one. What Kin Khao, her first venue looks like, is a Michelin-starred success.

Since she opened in 2014, multiple projects have followed: In 2018, she took over Nahm, a fine dining establishment in her hometown that arrived in 2011 and had previously been run by Dave Thompson, an Australian. It had ranked on the World's 50 Best Restaurants list for the previous five years and received a Michelin star. (For the record, those accolades have carried over.) She collaborated on a food hall in San Francisco International Airport that was unveiled in 2019, and, a few months later, introduced her adopted city on the West Coast to Nari, a restaurant that pays homage to the women who taught her how to cook, some of whom you'll hear about below. There's lots to respect about Pim: her prescience, her perseverance, her willingness to take risks, her commitment and ability to perfect whatever project or profession she pursues, her frank acknowledgment of her privileged upbringing, her massaman curry, her jam . . .

Can you talk a little bit about your childhood in Bangkok and specifically what role food played in it?

PIM

My grandmother was a great cook. My eldest aunt, who sort of supervised the kitchen when I was growing up, is an amazing, amazing cook. So I grew up with really good food around me all the time and I just took it for granted. I was interested in eating good food. I was not really that interested in cooking it, because it was available everywhere. I was kind of, *Ehhh, cooking is sort of not really my thing. We have cooks . . .*

CD

You weren't that interested in cooking, but I know your aunts taught you and I think you were maybe . . . were you out of college or in your twenties?

PIM

I was already shipped off from Thailand. I was in the US and going to graduate school and realizing that I can't get anything the way I want. As I spent more time in the US, I came to a realization that if I wanted to eat the food I grew up with, I had to learn how to do it, because no one else was going to cook it the way I wanted for me.

Actually, this was the turning point: When I would go home, I would smuggle back all these ingredients that I could use to cook simple things. I was still on my parents' payroll. And my mom would take me shopping, so I would come back to school with a suitcase full of new clothes. But also I would smuggle in jars of chili jam, and one year it broke in my bag.

CD

Oh no, in the new clothes?

PIM

There was no taking out chili jam. It got on everything and anything. So I was like, *Oh, I have nothing to wear.* It sounds so terrible and vain. But I was like, *Next year I am learning how to do this. This is not a long-term strategy. I can't have it breaking in my bag every year.* Yeah, so the next year, I went home again and asked my aunt to teach me how to make my grandmother's chili jam. And that was because it was one of those things—even in Thailand—people don't make themselves; they buy it from the store. But at our house we always make it and it's always kind of a big production. When my aunt made a giant batch, she would have help cutting garlic and shallots and everything. And for the next day or two I would drive around to relatives' houses dropping off jars of chili jam. That was what we would do. And then I went from there, because I grew up around a lot of these old dishes that we would eat at our house and may not be that common outside, and I just wanted to learn how to make them all because I'm always hungry.

CD

Did you enjoy doing it?

PIM

Oh, I loved it. I like to try to figure things out, giving myself a puzzle to solve. I know what the end product is going to be and I'm going to figure out how to make it. And I'm lucky. I was also around people who knew how to cook, like our family cook who just died two years ago and was also trained by my grandmother. She would make everything from scratch. I was used to that and I learned how to do all the dishes I loved to eat growing up to feed myself.

CD

You and your siblings all studied in the US. You went to grad school here. Was that your choice or something that your parents wanted?

PIM

It's a difficult thing to explain without sounding elitist, but there's a certain class of people in Thailand. It's like if you're born into a certain class in the UK, you send your kids to boarding school when they're five or whatever. This is what was expected of us. You spend some years abroad studying whatever you want to study—it doesn't really matter—and then you come home and get married and have kids and work or not work, it doesn't matter.

CD

You decided to say in California while the rest of your family stayed in Thailand and I wonder if, when you were younger, you imagined you'd end up living elsewhere, not in Thailand, and how the separation was for you.

PIM

When I was growing up, I spent a lot of time with my grandfather, my mother's father, who was kind of my backer. He was always like, *You can do anything you want.* When I was in school, I would get into all kinds of trouble because I wasn't a very nice student. And my mother would be called in to see the principal and then occasionally she would complain to my grandfather, and my grandfather would say things like, *You have a kid who's doing well at school, quite well in fact, but has a problem and she's not trying very hard. But she's still doing fine at school, right? Would you rather have a stupid kid that's really, really trying hard and still failing? What would you prefer?*

He was the reason that I could do what I wanted and, basically, had a pretty free childhood where I could study what I wanted. And then he passed away when I was just starting high school . . . and living with mom all year was a little bit difficult.

CD

You seem somehow always ahead in terms of your professional choices. So you were in tech pretty early—

PIM

I just sort of kept going to school because I thought that's my excuse to stay away from home, to still live my life before I have to go back to Thailand and follow rules and all of that. I was doing a PhD in San Diego and when I was getting close to finishing and realizing that everybody ended up with jobs in some strange town, I met someone and came up to Netscape [in Palo Alto] to do a summer gig. It was so much fun and it was just the beginning of Silicon Valley and everything was so exciting. And what was supposed to be just a summer gig turned into, *Oh, do you want a real job?* So I sort of fell into it.

CD

You can come up with a reason for each thing just happening, but, okay, you were one of the early bloggers—not even food bloggers but early bloggers. What about that?

PIM

Blogging, I also kind of fell into it. I knew some people early on doing it and I knew Meg Hourihan, who was one of the founders of Blogger. We had mutual friends and my friends were blogging and I was like, *This is kind of cool.* Today it would be more like, *I see you said something funny on Twitter,* but back then there was no other forum for it. I didn't want to report on the big things that were going on in my life. I wanted friends to know about this book I'm reading or this funny thing I overheard someone say in a café. So it became a way to document my life for friends and family that were far away. And it was a little self-indulgent and naval-gazing and all of that; it was about pretty random things—they were called web logs for a reason in the early days, because people wrote about whatever, anything. It was kind of your diary out there in the world. I shifted the focus to food when I started getting more attention. It became, *Ah, I can't write about anything personal anymore.*

I went back and edited out all of the not-so-ready-for-publication stuff. It was different when the web was a small place. It wasn't out there like it is today. So yeah, it became *I'm just going to write about restaurants and food.*

If someone asked me to teach them how to be a successful blogger, I don't really have anything to say, because it was a time and a place . . .

CD

But it really took off and you can't say that for everyone else's.

PIM

True, but at the same time, if I'd started my blog ten years after I did and I had the same voice and told the same stories, I wouldn't have been as big a deal either, right? It's just I wrote early on and then when blogs became a thing, people started writing about it, and there just weren't that many people and I was an interesting story.

CD

And when did you decide to leave Silicon Valley and make food your full-time career?

PIM

That was 2005 to 2006. I was approached to write books and there were television people talking to me and there was all this interest around food. It was about the time when I'd spent seven or eight years in Silicon Valley and was realizing that this was not the career path I wanted. I could afford to take a couple of years' break to think about what I wanted to do with my life and figure out what path I wanted to follow. So I just took a break.

CD

Okay, now here's another example, which is when you started making jam. It was really early on in what would become the new artisanal movement. It ended up being so representative of an entire small-batch moment. I know it "just happened," but Pim, there's something in it. There are too many coincidences for this "just fell into it" claim. I think you might have some special sixth sense.

PIM

Oh, maybe. I don't know, but the jam thing was just because I was around such amazing products in the Bay Area. And I was curious, and I was also a little bit bored. Because it was when I was in a relationship with [Chef] David [Kinch]. A lot of my effort was in maintaining that relationship, right? I didn't really realize it at the time. I was focused on making the relationship work and being there, around someone with a really, really difficult schedule. And for me, going back to work full-time was not an option because my sixth sense probably knew that wasn't going to work if I wanted to stay in that relationship. I consulted a little bit, and I was bored. There wasn't much to do. I started looking around for something interesting that I could do and where I could be in control of my time. With consulting, I could decide when I could take on a project, how much I was going to work, and what I was going to do, and I was lucky because those consulting gigs basically supported my jam-making obsession. There was no profit in making those jams, I could tell you, for real.

CD

You stopped blogging around 2011. And I know they're unrelated, but you stopped selling the jam, too. I wonder why you ended each of those things when you did.

PIM

I can only do something if it really, really interests me. I blogged for years without any kind of advertising. It was just something that I found interesting, that I wanted to do, and then blogging became a little bit more commercial. I made money blogging. It was great. I wasn't that interested in growing it.

People kept asking me, "Oh, could we write for Chez Pim? Do you want to turn it into some blog where you have multiple writers?" And I was like, *It's called Chez Pim*. I didn't really stop blogging; I stopped blogging regularly. I was still doing things. I just did it on my own schedule.

CD

And what about the jam? Was that more because you realized you were opening Kin Khao?

PIM

Yeah. Pretty much. I only really sold jam for a couple, maybe three seasons. Not that many years.

CD

I think I just fixated on it because I love your jam. What made you decide that you were going to open your own restaurant and be a chef, and what were the biggest challenges and obstacles in doing that?

PIM

The Thai restaurant was something I had thought about for a long time. Like, *Maybe I should open a Thai restaurant; maybe I could just do something very small and cook the dishes I want to eat that you can't find in other Thai restaurants*. One thing that got me seriously thinking about it was how successful the jam was, actually. I mean, I think my jam is great. But if you look around, there are amazing jam makers out there in the world, right? I'm a better Thai cook than I am a jam maker. I think I have more to contribute, more to add to that. It's like I don't really have anything new to say about jam. But Thai food is different. And I thought, *If people really love the jam so much, then this Thai restaurant thing isn't such a crazy idea.*

CD

Did you feel the psychological challenges of just proving to people—and even to yourself—that it was a thing that you could do?

PIM

Nobody really thought I could do it, I don't think.

CD

But you thought you could do it. Did you question yourself?

PIM

I totally questioned myself. That's one of the main reasons why Kin Khao is the way it is and where it is because I really had no idea this was going to work. I knew my food was good, but I had never worked in a restaurant before, let alone actually run one. I never have even been a server. I was kind of tangentially seeing what went on at Manresa [Kinch's restaurant], but I never worked there, either. So, I didn't know I could do it. That's why it took me a long time to find a space and to find something that I felt comfortable enough to do. San Francisco is really expensive and it's a very expensive place to run a business. When I started looking, I was like, *Wait a minute, you need $2.5 million to open a small restaurant in the city?!* And I thought, *I can probably raise $2.5 million, but can I really, with a straight face, tell people that they can give me money and I will return it to them?* I wasn't sure.

This space at this [Parc 55] hotel became available, and we figured out a way I could do it so that I did not need to find $2.5 million to start a restaurant. I did it mostly on my own, with my best friend in Bangkok. And we just opened it. Because I did it in a way where I really didn't need to have twenty or twenty-five investors with $100,000 each, I could do things that are comfortable—cook food I wanted to cook. There was no pressure to do things to make as much money as possible.

That's really interesting because I think that the model in the last few years has been crowdsourced investment—

PIM

For me, crowdsourcing a restaurant—if you look at a lot of projects, you have to offer a lot more than what people give you, right? You offer discounts. You offer special dinners. And I think at the end of the day, you end up with more commitments than what you gain. I was willing to gamble and see if this was going to work and I did it with a small enough pot of money that I could afford, instead of having lots of investors who were wondering when they were going to get their $2.5 million back, which was gonna be really hard.

We went through the early months saying, "This is the menu we're going to make. There's no tom yum. There are no dishes people recognize, because I don't want to cook those dishes. I want to make these." And we could do it because there was no one looking over the numbers every week going, *But when are we ever going to get the return on our money?* We went in half and half together.

CD

What did it mean to you, personally, but also within the context of San Francisco dining, to open a Thai restaurant in the Bay Area and at a higher price point?

PIM

I wanted to do everything from scratch, and I wanted to use the same ingredients that I want to eat. If I go to the Saturday farmers market at the Ferry Building to shop for myself, when I'm going to shop for a restaurant, I will also shop there. I had that goal in mind; I thought that there was room for a restaurant that's different. The one thing I said jokingly about Kin Khao, and it's really true: I kept waiting for someone to open up a Thai restaurant I wanted to eat at. And nobody did.

CD

So you just did it.

PIM

I did. And I knew that if we're going to really go for something that is different, we might not have the easiest time of it. When we first opened Kin Khao, people came to the door and they were like, *You're a Thai restaurant right? Great, so you have sushi?*

CD

That's hilarious and awful.

PIM

There were people who would just ghost us. They'd sit down and we'd drop the menu. The server would chat a bit about what we'd do, and the next thing we'd know, we'd look at the table and there are these menus and water, and no people, because they didn't recognize anything and left. But I stuck with it, because I knew that there would be enough. You know how I say I fell into things? I think I'm so lucky that I somehow caught on to things early on and became known—had a lot of followers on social media and whatever. When I started making jam, I didn't have to wait for someone to write about it.

CD

You had a built-in audience.

PIM

Absolutely. I saw that if I tried to do something, I could get enough attention thanks to my good luck—people would at least come and give it a try. But I needed to be able to back it up. You can get people to come once because they're curious about this restaurant that Pim opened, but if they didn't like it, they wouldn't come back.

The most valuable thing I did before I opened Kin Khao was to sit down with a writing pad and write down things I didn't know how to do. It really helped. Then I knew I needed to find someone to help me set up the front-of-house, and maybe I needed a professional chef to run my kitchen, because even though I knew how to cook all of these dishes, I did not know how to cook for two hundred people a night.

CD

It seems like you really love it—that you just threw yourself into it and that you also get a huge amount of gratification and joy out of it.

PIM

It's so much fun. It's really scary because, even though with other things I'd done, I'd put myself out there and I was used to the ugliness that came with attention—like people wanting me to get my nose done because the picture in my blog was not pretty—at the same time, Kin Khao was much more personal, even more so than my blog; it needed to be, for a successful business.

CD

Did you feel like you got any flak or pushback for being a woman or just for presenting Thai food in a more elevated way?

PIM

Yeah, and we get it today. People are used to dealing with Thai restaurants in a certain way. They still complain that we're not adaptable, that we're not willing to make something spicier or less spicy for them. One thing that I tell all of my staff and my kitchen, in front and in back, is that you really can't please everybody. There are going to be some people who come in and they want pad thai and no amount of anything we make is going to make them happy because they want pad thai and they want it spicy.

CD

Do you feel like now that you've proven the restaurant and yourself, you've gotten the respect that you should? Do you think you've gotten the same amount of respect that established male chefs in the Bay Area have or that white chefs doing Thai food have?

PIM

Yes, to a certain degree. When I first opened Kin Khao, I resolutely did not call myself a chef because I have a certain respect for the profession. I know it takes a certain type of work, running a professional kitchen, to be called a chef, and this is all my food, but Michael [Gaines] was my chef because he ran the kitchen.

And then when Mike left to open his own restaurant, people asked, "Your chef left. Is the food going to change?" And I was like, *Why would it change? It's going to be my food Michael Gaines used to cook. I am as much a chef of Kin Khao as anybody is the chef of their restaurant. I'm not running the kitchen schedule and I'm not ordering food, but this is my restaurant. This is my concept. These are my recipes. This is my food. Nothing goes on the menu without it being me . . .* I'm just not what people think of as a traditional chef.

CD

And you have the Michelin star, and what that means, especially for business can't be underestimated.

PIM

It helps and it hurts a little bit. It's not what you think of as a Michelin-starred restaurant and I was really, really surprised—very happy and very flattered, and just elated for my staff, but I didn't expect it. The first year that we got the Michelin star, I remember thinking, *Maybe I need to find tablecloths. Maybe I need to change the service, and maybe I need to do things that make me worthy of it . . .* Trying to cook and thinking about satisfying critics or lists or stars, to me it's like being in an abusive relationship. You keep thinking, *If I do this one other thing, he's going to love me more.* Or, *If I dress like this, he's going to love me more.* And no, it doesn't work. I don't know why I got a Michelin star. I think it's because our food is really good. I don't want to change anything; I'm just going to stick with what I do and what I know, and I'm not going to try to please anyone, because it's futile.

CD

This is actually a coincidental question; I'm not suggesting that one is related to the other, but I wanted to ask about dating a chef. The tendency is to assume that your food career took off because you were dating a male chef.

PIM

Yeah, that's definitely what people say. I mean, when somebody wrote that I leeched my Michelin star off of David Kinch or something—

CD

It simultaneously legitimizes your work but it also undervalues your own ability to do it, because the assumption is: How could you have possibly done that yourself?

PIM

Right and people wrote about how, with the help of my boyfriend, the chef David Kinch, I opened the restaurant and I was like, *No, with the help of my best friend I grew up with in Bangkok, I opened a Thai restaurant.*

CD

And it seems like you've actually achieved more in the food world—as an entrepreneur, and as a restaurateur, and as a chef—after you broke up with him. I'm wondering if there are ways in which he helped you find your way, but also ways in which he hindered you or the relationship hindered you.

PIM

I think it was definitely the thing where you are in a relationship, and you put a lot of energy into keeping that relationship and being the caretaker of the relationship. And I think a lot of women get into that situation. The way I saw that, I was the one who was spending more energy taking care of myself, and taking care of the relationship, and it's

not something that comes from a position of weakness. It's from a position of strength—I could take care of myself; I didn't really need a lot of emotional support; I'm strong . . .

Despite people thinking that I did the blog and I do a lot of these things for attention, it wasn't really. I was happy for him to be the star and the focus. But also what people don't remember was that, when I started going out with David Kinch, he wasn't David Kinch, the three-Michelin-star chef of today. He had this little restaurant in Los Gatos that, if they did thirty covers a night, it was a busy night. He was thinking about closing the restaurant when I started going out with him.

CD

You were diagnosed with breast cancer not that long after you had opened Kin Khao. How did you manage to get through battling that illness and keeping the restaurant going? How did you find the strength emotionally?

PIM

I got through it with a lot of help from friends and family and people who work for me. Because before that, I felt like I was Atlas holding up the heavens at Kin Khao; if I wasn't there every day something was gonna fall around everyone's ears and it was all gonna come crashing down. All of a sudden, I just had to step away and everybody at Kin Khao just totally stepped up. All of a sudden, there's a schedule for who's going to take Pim to the hospital and pick her up and cook for her, and it was amazing. I had so many friends step in, because we all live away from our families these days. My community took care of me.

CD

You also have to be okay with accepting help, which is another thing. People are so proud or they have a hard time even saying they need help in the first place.

That's definitely the one thing I tell friends when they find themselves in a place where they really need to accept help. You really need to understand that it's as generous to accept help as it is to offer it, because it's really hard for people to wrap their mind around that. You're being really generous in letting your friends step in. You also have to be there to help them in return.

CD

I wanted to ask you about Nahm and about how that came about.

PIM

I met Christina (Chris) Ong, the owner of the Como Group a couple of years ago, through a mutual friend. Around the middle of 2017, she mentioned that David Thompson was going to leave to open a bunch of new restaurants, with another group. She said, "We own a hotel in Bangkok and we own the restaurant and we would like to keep it going. Would you be interested in taking over?" She kept going to restaurants in Bangkok and didn't feel like there was anyone who had the touch and understanding of food that she felt I had, and she really wanted me to think about going to Bangkok. And I said, "I'm really very, very touched and very flattered that you asked me, but Bangkok? I don't live in Bangkok. My mother lives there."

I'd always done things that I started myself. It was a very different prospect for me to look at stepping in to take over a restaurant that someone had built and been so closely identified with. That was another thing that made me take a long time before I agreed.

CD

What made you decide to do it?

PIM

I went to Bangkok in January [2018] and I spent some time in the kitchen and the markets, and I started thinking about actually cooking with these ingredients. I also talked to Jan [Suraja Ruangnukulkit], who, at the time, was the first sous chef in the kitchen. We went out to eat, we cooked, we spent time in the kitchen, and it became possible in my head: I could figure out how we could do it, how we could set the menu and change it often enough, and how I could remotely be on top of something with my name and my face on the door. I knew I had this woman who's an amazing chef and she's a great manager. And we have very similar palates. I felt like I could work with her and have her run the kitchen in the way that I want to run it when I'm not there. I could see the path.

CD

At any point, were you scared? Once you got there and you saw it and you thought, *Yes, I want to do it*, was there any fear in it?

PIM

There's always fear in everything, I guess. A new dish you put on the menu, you ask, "What are people going to think?" I'm not unfriendly with fear. I get it. But I also look at it and say, "Well, the worst thing that could happen is I fail." And I'm okay with that. It's a possibility.

CD

What's it like to be back in Bangkok and cooking, and to be that close to your family again?

PIM

It's definitely different. I left Thailand when I was so young. I was not quite twenty. I've never lived in the city as a fully grown woman before. Frankly, a lot of my family, I don't know if they know what to make of my cooking for a living because it's like, *Oh right, didn't you go to school and do other things, and you're running restaurants?!*

What does your family think of your food though? I'm especially curious about your aunt, who taught you.

PIM

Neither one of my aunts is cooking anymore. One passed away and the other one has Alzheimer's, so it's really sad.

CD

Did either of them ever get to have it while they were still here and present?

PIM

I went to visit my aunt Chawiwan when she was still a little bit present. I showed her pictures of food at Kin Khao and she said, "You know how to cook? You know how to make this?" And I said, "Yes, I do. You taught me." And then I showed her a picture of the chili jam clams, which has my grandmother's chili jam, and she said, "Oh yeah, *nam prik pao* [chili jam]. You can't buy that stuff, it's not very good what people sell." And I said, "I know, I make it." And she asked me, "You know how to make that? That's very good. Is it like ours?" I said, "Yes, it's ours. You taught me." It was really touching. She saw all these things and she was amazed that I could cook, but she didn't remember that she taught me.

CD

I sense that in Thailand, women cooking professionally is not a big deal, but I wonder if it's a big deal in a restaurant like Nahm?

PIM

There are a lot of women. Meghan [Clark, chef de cuisine at Nari] made this observation that in the beginning, only the girls were in the kitchen. When I talked to them, they started gathering around and listening and really paid attention. And Meghan was like, *I think we should fire all the boys. Because they don't care.* They didn't care. They were just kind of skulking in their corner, doing their stuff.

Then it changed. One day, this guy at the curry station came over to join the girls. He was really paying attention. And I was like, *Oh hey, we've got one boy today.* That's a win. And then the circle started growing, and now . . . I could be working with just one person on one station, and all of a sudden I look up and it's like everybody gathering all around listening. I think that's really great.

CD

What are your future business plans?

PIM

Well, I just want to keep cooking. I want to keep being inspired by food and enjoying it, to enjoy cooking it and eating it. I'll take business opportunities that make sense to me. I don't aspire to have a Kin Khao or Nahm in every major city of the world or anything. I think when you are a businesswoman, you have to entertain growth and expansion possibilities, and it's about providing for people who work for you, creating a good business so that you have this ecosystem of everyone making a great living and making great food together.

CD

I'm so happy for you, Pim. But I still miss my old friend, jam.

PIM

Yes, I know. My old friend, jam. It's really not bad.

Soleil Ho

Before I'd read anything Soleil Ho had written (unless tweets count), I'd heard her voice on the podcast she cohosts with Zahir Janmohamed. I haven't gotten into podcasts the way most people have. *Racist Sandwich* is one of a handful I subscribe and actually listen to, regularly. In the words of its creators, it offers a fundamental but seldom heard perspective, "that food and the ways we consume, create, and interpret it can be political," and it does so with humor and humanity and with a much more comprehensive purview of who and what "food" as an industry or cultural phenomenon encompasses. They expose racism in fields where you might never have thought to look for it and dissect issues of class and economic inequality. Had it not been for Episode 50, "Detroiters are Fighters," I might not have been introduced to Devita Davison and the work she does, and I never would have interviewed her for this book (see page 144), which would have been everyone's loss—mine most of all.

Once I realized (late to the game) that she writes, too, I began tracking Soleil's byline. There were literary essays and restaurant reviews for various feminist magazines and a chapbook titled *Hungry Ghosts*. In December 2018, she was named the new restaurant critic for the *San Francisco Chronicle,* where we can now read her weekly. She has a way of calling out irresponsible acts of cultural appropriation or teasing apart racial stereotypes that is never holier than thou and often leaves you enlightened, and laughing. When she told me she wanted to write about video games, for the first time possibly ever, I got excited about that topic, because I knew she'd make me care about it, learn, and enjoy the process. And she did.

Ms. Pac-Man's Revenge!

When I first picked up *Harvest Moon 64*, a farm simulator game that came out on the Nintendo 64 in the late nineties, I had two objectives: to marry a cute girl and eat a piece of cake. The first task would, I quickly found out, involve days of wooing, small talk, and daily gift optimization, but the second would be quite easy. After selling a few turnips, I could afford a slice of sweet, pixelated perfection—with vanilla frosting and bright red strawberry slices sandwiched between two layers of white cake and a whole berry on top. Potentially, though, you could go the entire length of the game without buying a piece of cake. Instead, you could opt to replenish your stamina (much-needed for a full day of chopping wood, watering crops, and milking cows) with cheaper berries foraged in the mountains or raw fish pulled straight from the water. But where's the fun in that? For the first time, I'd found a game that simulated the pleasure of eating something delicious for its own sake.

It was 1999 and it's not like food was a new element in gaming: it had been a staple—literally, as in, a necessity—of many earlier releases. To replenish your health in side-scrolling arcade fighters like *Streets of Rage* and *Double Dragon*, all you needed to do was kick a trash can and eat the hot dogs and roasted chickens that popped out. In *Castlevania*, players can restore health by hitting walls to potentially unearth plated roasts—spoken of among fans as "wall meat."

It can be an enemy, too: one of the most iconic food games is a longstanding arcade regular called *Burger Time*, where the player is a chef attempting to make a giant burger while avoiding attacks from malevolent sausages and eggs. In *Super Mario RPG*, a gorgeous, multi-tiered wedding cake (strangely named "Bundt") turns sentient and goes on a rampage, attacking Mario and his friends.

Food might also make an appearance as a reward, like the iconic Black Forest cake in *Portal*. In these games, marketed for an audience that was probably not of the gourmet persuasion, food is less feature, more window dressing: None of them dwells on how the food actually tastes.

Why has food, which is arguably an essential part of our day-to-day lives, been so marginal in so many games? It could be due to ingrained assumptions about their intended audiences: If these products were meant to appeal to men, why waste effort on rendering food when one could focus on more masculine motifs, like monsters and spacecraft? And yet, one of the earliest examples of game developers' thinking outside of the box and bringing food to the forefront is one of the earliest games: Pac-Man. In an interview with Eurogamer, the game's developer, Toru Iwatani, admits that his inspiration for the overall design had culinary origins. The fruits that Pac-Man eats up are easy to spot, but the design for the protagonist himself is, notoriously, related to food, too: "I was trying to come up with something to appeal to women and couples. When I imagined what women enjoy, the image of them eating cakes and desserts came to mind, so I used 'eating' as a keyword. When I did research with this keyword I came across the image of a pizza with a slice taken out of it and had that eureka moment. So I based the Pac-Man character design on that shape." In a burgeoning scene where games were mainly about shooting asteroids and aliens, *Pac-Man* stood apart for having gameplay that only asked the participant to eat.

In a 1982 article in *Electronic Games* magazine, critic Joyce Worley wrote, "No discussion of women as electronic gamers would be complete without a deep bow in the direction of Midway's incomparable *Pac-Man*. The game's record-shattering success derives from its overwhelming popularity among female gamers." Before *Pac-Man* came chomping through his maze and arcades repositioned themselves as family-oriented establishments, Worley claimed, women were rarely sighted playing on the game machines. In his book, *Atari Age: The Emergence of Video Games in America*, Michael Z. Newman writes,

> [I]n North America, *Pac-Man* appealed widely to children and women in addition to male players, and to both more casual and more serious visitors to arcades. Its financial impact was staggering: it earned one billion dollars in revenue in its first fifteen months in the United States, and the home console version was predicted in the pages of *Time* to be a bigger money-maker than *Star Wars*, a widely recycled factoid.

Iwatani's gambit was so successful that the company subsequently produced *Ms. Pac-Man*, which came with its own rom-com-esque storyline, as an explicit thank-you nod to their female fans.

Since *Pac-Man*, we've seen food emerge as a staple in what are known as "casual games." These would be the intuitive and noncommittal variety that tend to be more popular among women and comprise the bulk of food-centered games, including *Candy Crush Saga, Overcooked, Farmville, Cookie Clicker,* and *Cooking Mama.*

When I was a teenager, in the early days of browser-based Flash games, I became obsessed with a very simple cooking game, which asked only that I drag pieces of raw beef onto a photo of a grill, where it would start to sear with a satisfying hiss. The game, *Yakiniku,* by indie developer Yoshinao Mori, matches your pace, supplying more and more plates of raw beef as each batch finishes. It appealed to me with its simplicity: in the midst of chemistry homework, interpersonal drama, and hormonal nonsense, focusing on the act of searing virtual beef and dipping it in BBQ sauce was an amazing way to allay anxiety. I could imagine I was dining solo at some old-school Japanese restaurant, free to zero in on the frivolous question of how well-cooked I'd prefer my beef to be. In casual games like this one, where there are virtually no stakes or storyline beyond what the player is willing to fill in on their own, such a simple set-up works quite well.

Though food has long been a staple of casual games, and a few production-heavy console games have featured food-themed minigames as well—like the sushi-eating contest in *Pokémon Stadium* and the Iron Chef–style competitions in *Suikoden 2*—it's been rare to see food and cooking at the center of the action. But recently, those games that fall into the "hardcore" category have begun to embrace it as a motif worth exploiting. *Final Fantasy XV* (*FFXV*), a high-budget Japanese role-playing package released for the PS4 in 2016, quickly garnered attention for its involved cooking minigame. Players can concoct dishes for their fighting party to eat to replenish their health, but these are not the generic roast chickens of the *Streets of Rage* days. If they choose to dig into the one-hundred-plus recipes listed, they can make photorealistic dishes reminiscent of Hainanese chicken and rice, nasi lemak, xiaolongbao, truffled risotto, and cassoulet. If they don't care to go to the trouble, they can just stick with toast and Cup Noodles (who probably paid big money for product placement in the game). One of the sidequests even asks players to journey in search of the perfect extra ingredient to make their instant Cup Noodles really sing.

In an interview with *Eater* at the end of 2016, *FFXV* director Hajime Tabata cited "meshitero," a dramatic portmanteau of "food" and "terrorism" that roughly translates to "food imagery that strikes indiscriminately." The development team was so serious about the realism of the food, they went camping (much of the game takes place as a road trip) and took photos of the food they were able to create outdoors. Part of their quality control was, of course, taste testing: If a dish didn't taste good to the team, they wouldn't put it into the game. "Recipes were just one element of the camping scenes, but the catalyst for our obsession was the high quality of the food graphics that the camp team was able to create in the pre-production phase," Tabata said. "We have to create truly delicious-looking food scenes similar to those that appear in movies and anime." Any fan of Studio Ghibli films like *Spirited Away* or *Howl's Moving Castle*, in which the glistening of dumplings and crackliness of fried eggs is rendered in careful detail, could see the relation.

The Legend of Zelda: Breath of the Wild, released the following year on the Nintendo Switch, also features a robust cooking element capable of producing charmingly cartoonish renditions of curries, stews, and rice balls for characters to eat. Though there are distinct recipes, players are invited to experiment and combine ingredients haphazardly to see what happens. The improvisational spirit of cooking is all there—an aspect that's bolstered by the fact that players must hunt and gather the components, from whole fish to wild mushrooms to moose meat, on their own. And *Stardew Valley*, an immensely popular fantasy farming simulator similar to *Harvest Moon*, includes seventy-one recipes for dishes the player can make and gift to NPCs (non-player characters).

The culinary improvisation introduced in *Breath of the Wild* and in later versions of *Harvest Moon* got a little bit closer to the truth of what real-life cooking is like. Rather than asking players to follow predetermined formulas, the games invite them to reason out what ingredients would go with each other. Like any real life chef, the player is lead to ask, "What can I make with what I have on hand?" The recipes in *Breath of the Wild* are shared with the player verbally by non-player characters, so sometimes they'll make suggestions like, "You could also throw a couple of berries in there," or "Use whatever meat you've got."

It's a lot like what Tom Colicchio and Samin Nosrat have done through their cookbooks, *Think Like a Chef* and *Salt Fat Acid Heat*, respectively. Rather than being filled with standardized recipes, with measurements and processes clearly outlined, these books focus on the psychological aspect of cooking. They show the reader how to use foundational ideas and flavors to build dishes on their own. I remember reading Colicchio's "Trilogy" chapter as a high-schooler and being awed by the idea that, by flexing a reliable three-ingredient combination like ramps, morels, and asparagus, you could create a huge variety of dishes. His approach asks the reader to look at the ingredients they have and build ideas from them, like a chef would with the spread of produce she picks up at the farmers market. The set of skills Colicchio and Nosrat try to build with their writing seems especially good for novices who might be overwhelmed by all of the terminology and techniques assumed by conventional recipe books. While it's rare to see their philosophies echoed in mass market recipe collections online and in print, it's even stranger to see major video games subtly prompting players to think this way through in-game mechanics.

With these newer, more involved iterations of virtual eating and cooking came more cross-platform coverage of the games: both food publications like *Eater* and gaming outlets like *Kill Screen* and *Inverse* began to play host to conversations about the culinary aesthetics of new releases. The fact that these food and game publications, whose mastheads and readership respectively skew heavily female and male, had enough shared material to construct a Venn diagram is significant because of how cloistered-off the games publishing world has been for the majority of its existence. Criticized in recent years for catering to an audience of mainly white straight men at the expense of the diverse gaming public, the adjacent publishing sector has faced major growing pains. On the one hand, movements like Gamergate, a precursor to the modern, online alt-right movement, have frequently moved to silence critiques by white women, queer people, and people of color in order to preserve control over their patch of land. And on the other, outlets like *Waypoint*, *VICE*'s gaming vertical, have worked to diversify their stable of writers and add an element of critical consciousness to their published work.

At the very least, the increased presence of food in games has prompted a shift in participation and coverage among many mainstream gaming media outlets: now, readers swap recipes in article comment sections, news verticals report on food brand partnerships with game studios, and writers often post listicles describing the "best" digitally rendered dishes of various games. On the surface, at least, the mainstream gaming media has become more receptive to including "feminine" content, though it remains to be seen if that will translate to more inclusivity of non-men in that world at large. If *Pac-Man* is any indicator of how things may go, then perhaps there is a chance that positive change may occur.

Outside of the mainstream gaming media, there's another pattern of fusion happening: a few gamers, mainly women and queer men, have started food blogs that focus exclusively on the dishes that appear in games. You might find recipes that turn the 1Up mushrooms from *Super Mario* into cake pops or real-life adaptations of fantasy game health potions into fruit smoothies. Part of the puzzle is figuring out how to make dishes that provide very little information to go on: It's not like the games' recipes involve much more than a list of ingredients for the player to gather. For example, a Google search for "cinnamon butterscotch pie," a food item used in the game *Undertale*, unearths multiple attempts by bloggers—and random kids on social media—trying their hand at the imaginary confection and bonding over their successes (or failures). For a blogger like Everett, the man behind the *Stardew Valley* Recipes page, the process of puzzling out how to make something like the Strange Bun is a game in itself. The Strange Bun, crafted in-game out of a periwinkle, flour, and Void Mayonnaise, a black sauce made from a witch-cursed egg, has no real-world equivalent. For those following at home, he eventually settled on preparing a yeasted, savory pastry with a filling made from canned snails—no Void Mayonnaise required.

As I browsed through the recipes on popular video game food blogs, I could hear my chef voice nagging, saying things like, *They should have used real butter,* or *Why did they use pre-made whipped cream?* The photos are often a bit janky and dim, with results naturally looking like emulations of pixelated images more than real food. But that was me missing the point: These sites are far from the precious food blogs that I've gotten used to, where, if a post isn't sponsored by General Mills or Blue Apron, everything is perfect and bespoke, with the food a natural complement to the writer's diary-like prose. Even the cooking videos that I've found, which often require more production effort than written blogs, are pretty awful. *Eurogamer,* a popular games journalism site, produced a video in 2016 where one member of their team re-created a recipe for "hagfish quenelles" from *Dishonored 2*. Armed with a list of ingredients specified in-game and a slim knowledge of what quenelles even are, the host ends up making a dish that, at best, looks like it fell out of a Soviet Army MRE: a beige, lumpy mess. (Ironically, the version posted by *Nerds' Kitchen,* a

Polish blog, looks way better.) The popularity of these blogs and videos, especially among gamers, might not only be due to their subject matter but also to the fact that they validate the experiences of their audience and meet them where they're at.

In addition, there's a fascinating new type of instructional food videos, mainly by men, that caters specifically to people who play video and PC games. With titles like, "Top 10 Gamer Foods," "The Perfect Gamer Food," and "Brain Food for Gamers," sometimes the videos are just lists of snack foods, like chips and candy, that the host enjoys, and sometimes they feature actual, if rudimentary, recipes. In "8 Simple Microwave Recipes for Gamers," the hosts demonstrate how to use pantry items to prepare quick, single-serve meals like a biscuit made with Spaghetti-Os and a mug quiche. In a curious marriage of YouTube genres, they conduct their cooking lessons through the frame of a Let's Play video, "playing" the lesson with controllers and commentary as if it itself is a game.

The idea of there being a distinguishable sort of "gamer food" or "food for gamers" speaks to the cultural hold this hobby has on people who take it seriously as an identity. It's not like there are similar videos about "snacks for knitters" or "podcaster recipes." The closest comparison might be to the subset of people within the tech world who make up the core consumers of Soylent, the Ensure-like meal replacement smoothie that purports to do away with the inconvenience and messiness of food and enable an uninterrupted work life. For them, food is something marginal—like the garbage-can roast chicken picked up to replenish hit points—to consume while pursuing more important tasks.

However extreme my doom and gloom visions of sad couch dinners in cups may seem, this trend runs up against what may be a very real problem for gamers: A recent Canadian study found that, in a small sample of adolescents who played games, subjects ate more calories while playing, despite not performing any physical movements beyond handling a controller. Interestingly, an article on the study posted by *Lifehacker* generated comments that spoke to the contrary: Commenters said that playing games often made them forget about eating entirely. One wrote, "It's the case of 'I'll eat when I get this far' turns into 'Oh my god it's 1 A.M. and I haven't eaten since lunch.'" Regardless of whether an individual eats more or less, it seems apparent that gaming does effect diet in some way. Videos about gamer food are speaking to this idea, whether they're simply reminding gamers to eat anything at all or giving them the tools to consume more nutritious options.

While the boom in game-related food content is interesting in its own right, one has to wonder if the approach the more popular blogs and videos take is informed by gender, especially when it comes to their amateurishness. On some level, the looseness of the creators with regard to their culinary skill levels and the food they make could be an affect that is informed by the patriarchal notion that men just aren't naturally meant to cook or take care of themselves, so the assumption of skill and expertise common to female-led food media would be inappropriate for a mostly male audience of gamers. It would, in a word, make them "inaccessible." The emphasis here tends to be on the novelty of imitating video game content in real life, as a sort of extension of the live-action role playing (LARP) tradition, or on optimizing caloric intake without disrupting one's play session to pause and make an involved meal. Blogs like *Lvl.1 Chef*, which revel in the work it takes to perfectly execute game food, are a much rarer breed.

In a sense, this contrast runs parallel to the gender imbalance in the audiences for casual versus hardcore games. Though the Entertainment Software Association, a US trade association for the game industry, puts the gender ratio of female to male players at roughly forty to sixty (sans any data about players who identify as nonbinary), in 2016, game analytics company Quantic Foundry found that the kinds of games played varied heavily according to gender. In a survey of 270,000 players, they found that, across twenty-three genres, proportional female participation varied from 2 to 70 percent, with matching and farm/family simulator games sharing the lead and sports, racing, and shooter games sitting at the very bottom of the chart. Nonbinary respondents, who made up 1.1 percent of the pool, favored farm/family simulators and exploration games. *Harvest Moon*, the game that fed me my first slice of pixelated cake, would certainly be at the very top for the former category.

The mainstream games that I referred to earlier, including *FFXV* and *Breath of the Wild*, fall in the middle of the chart. It's safe to say that the majority of games that meaningfully incorporate food in their designs and narratives are the ones that appeal most to female-identifying players. It's clear, given the results of the survey, that within the umbrella of "gamer" or "people who play games," there's a great deal of varying experiences and personalities, with quite a bit of diversion along gender lines. This can speak to the difference in the tenor of gaming and food videos, with some appealing to the Soylent crowd and others to enthusiastic home cooks.

Rather than being anything subversive or educational, could the inclusion of food in games play a part in the gender segregation in the gaming industry? Food itself could potentially become a signifier for less "serious" games that won't be as hyped up or lauded by the gaming media. There is also the dark possibility that it may be a way for developers to superficially pander to female consumers without having to, say, include well-written, gender diverse characters into their narratives or reckon with hiring and firing practices that punish women and nonbinary employees for being outspoken about gender issues in the industry. The tying of "female" with "casual gamer" has deleterious effects on women in the games industry, as noted by a *Kotaku* investigation into sexist hiring practices at Riot Games, the developer behind the hardcore game, *League of Legends*: "[T]alented women have fallen through Riot's hiring processes because they weren't considered 'core gamers,' which one source described as 'an excuse.' Two sources familiar with Riot's hiring practices say the company checks interviewees' *League of Legends* stats prior to bringing them on campus for interviews."

This kind of surface-level appeal without impact, the kind that I think we're quite used to within capitalism, might be all that we get. After all, as much as we've talked up the freshness of Ms. Pac-Man as an early female game protagonist, her narrative was all about her romance with Pac-Man: We don't even know her name.

And yet, despite the potential for the kind of gender-based consumer segregation that might pop up as the market for more casual games grows, perhaps including nice pixelated food benefits everyone. Maybe it's a good thing that gamer kids can see their favorite characters whipping up millefeuilles and paellas and be motivated to try it on their own. There might be some division among the gaming community regarding genre preferences and the binaristic gender stereotypes, but it's not like a game media reader can cordon off the sections of gaming publications that take food seriously as an element of game aesthetics. And a game like *Dishonored 2*, with its inclusion of a detailed recipe that intrigued its fans enough to get them to make it, really does walk the walk when it comes to representation, with a quietly diverse cast of characters who inhabit a wide range of roles. Finally, as food becomes an even greater and deeper part of game design, as we've seen in the releases of major developers like Square Enix and Nintendo, it has observable reverberations in fan culture, piquing interest in creative home cooking among a group of people who are often not catered to by mainstream food media. Sachka Sandra Duval, the lead narrative designer of *Dishonored 2*, told me via email that the game's hagfish quenelle recipe "was a reference to the famous dish that you find in most restaurants in Lyon, where [Arkane Studios] is located." Inspiring American gamers to make an authentic Lyonnaise dish that greats like Julia Child and Paul Bocuse would have recognized and savored feels like a coup in itself. We might not all be diving headfirst into making it, but I'm sure many of us have since wondered, "How do those taste?"

A future where even hardcore gamers might be able to rattle off recipes for laksa or bread pudding doesn't seem too far off, though we'll have to hold out for more developers like Arkane and fewer like Riot. Perhaps one day Tom Colicchio and Samin Nosrat's improvisational and, frankly, playful approach to cooking will permeate even further, inspiring more young cooks who grew up gaming, just like me. And maybe we will see people of all genders learning—and loving—to cook both digital and analog food. (Pro tip: Cake tastes even better when you make it IRL.)

COOK THIS, NOT THAT!

What is a type of FOOD *you wanted to cook* and were told you couldn't—or were made to feel as though you couldn't . . . and you're pretty sure it's because you're a woman?

CHRISTINA TOSI

Anything on the grill . . . GRRRR.

AMY BRANDWEIN

I think my fellow line cooks at my first restaurant were really questioning whether I could handle a grill for two-hundred-plus guests a night, and butcher pigs, rabbits, squab and fish, but when they saw me do it, it was settled. Also, a woman working the pasta station was sort of unheard of in an Italian restaurant in America—or at least in DC.

DIANNA DAOHEUNG

When first starting, I wanted to learn everything. Butchering in particular was not as friendly to women. So that was the one area I felt people would make you feel like you couldn't do it.

KIM ALTER

I once applied at a sushi restaurant. When I asked to speak to the chef to schedule a stage, I was told no woman should be allowed to work in a sushi restaurant. I automatically assumed it was a cultural thing and tried not to take too much offense, but he proceeded to tell me that a woman's hands run hotter than a man's and the fish should not be handled by a woman. I never went back to that restaurant. I also always look for women in sushi bars and have since only once seen one.

ANA SORTUN

Carving a turkey? Maybe . . . but I could have if I really wanted to.

BONNIE MORALES

I've been told that women are good at cooking nourishing food but that I could never succeed in a "real" kitchen. By that, they meant three-star Michelin kitchens, implying that precision cooking is best left to men.

CAROLINE FIDANZA

I was never explicitly told I couldn't cook anything because I was a woman, but I continue to feel that men tend to be reluctant to go into business with a woman as an equal business partner.

JOANNE CHANG

I honestly can't think of anything.

MASHAMA BAILEY

I don't believe in the question. Women are the center of all food. It starts in the home and everyone learns how to cook from those humble beginnings.

JENI BRITTON BAUER

Ice cream in 1996.

Do you think there are certain kinds of food—or styles of restaurant or culinary events—that are consistently associated with women, or, more specifically, women of color?

ANN CASHION

I think women are often associated with what I call "context" cooking . . . preparing food that has an origin story or resonates in some family, cultural, or traditional way.

ANITA LO

Women for the most part are expected to, and praised for, cooking "homey" and nurturing food. This is changing but hasn't gone away by any means. And women of color are expected to cook cuisines reflective of their race, which may or may not make any sense culturally.

JEN AGG

LOL, see [New York Times restaurant critic] Pete Wells's King review, which I believe perfectly encapsulates the way women are treated in the restaurant business, not as innovators, but as caregivers. It's revolting. Here, see! "What Ms. de Boer and Ms. Shadbolt offer is not a wild vision of new ways to cook but a solid vision of how to eat. They put pleasure at the table above gymnastics on the plate. For reasons I don't want to understand, I associate this trait with other female chefs around town, including Rita Sodi, Missy Robbins, Gabrielle Hamilton, Sara Jenkins, Angie Mar and April Bloomfield, another River Café alumna."

MASHAMA BAILEY

I think comfort food is considered food that women cook and I think that when people think of women of color cooking they only think of soul food.

TIFFANI FAISON

I think women are shoved into a narrative about caretaking that manifests in certain types of restaurants. There is a cultural expectation that the food women produce is meant to fuel, to support, and to show love and caring, not meant as a platform for intelligence, talent, and skill. I find that this manifests in the form of baking, comfort food, and more rustic cooking. Even in the baking and pastry world, women often aren't thought of as great technicians or exacting in their craft; it's just seen as yummy yum yums.

JENI BRITTON BAUER

Brownies, granola. Farmers markets.

NAOMI POMEROY

It's always the pastry, man . . . It's just like, I can't count the number of times I've told people that I was a chef . . . and they said: "Oh, I LOVE dessert!"

CHRISTINA TOSI

Pastry chefs—and it drives me crazy! I only ever worked for male pastry chefs, and there are plenty of amazing women throughout the industry beyond the beloved pastry kitchen.

UMBER AHMAD

Pastry and dessert are associated with women. Much to my dismay, when one speaks of pastry, the most prominent image that people describe is that of grandma's kitchen table, covered with a checked tablecloth, on which a platter of cupcakes covered in pastel buttercream sits. It's viewed by many as nostalgic. In fact, it's a form of misogyny. That sounds extreme, but it isn't. We, as women—as creators, as inventors, as businesspeople—are reduced to a stereotype without any room for deviance. In fact, we are nothing like grandmothers in kitchens. We are creative forces daring to present the last taste you walk away with, the crowning achievement to a meal, the focal point of celebrations. We take the simplest of ingredients and transform them into gravity-defying, visually stunning, forever memorable moments in one's life. When a man does what a woman does in pastry, he is considered a genius and a trailblazer. Why, then, are women not viewed through that same lens?

ERIN MCKENNA

Bakeries! And now since it's trendy, a gluten-free and vegan bakery would be even more spot-on. And tah-dah, I fit the stereotype.

CAROLINE FIDANZA

Baked goods. Cafés. Food in bowls. Healthy food. Salad.

EVA KARAGIORGAS

Grain bowls or colorful things in bowls—why are "healthy-ish" bowls always a female thing? I mean, they are yummy and I'm a mini health nut so more power to these bowls, but it's so trendy. I hate trendy. And I hate that this food trend is super female.

MICHELLE HERNANDEZ

While there may be an association like this in the States, from a global perspective, the majority of the chefs in the professional food industry are male. Few women head top kitchens or sections of the professional kitchen in the world to even make an association with a particular style possible yet.

Do you think there are certain kinds of food—or styles of restaurant or culinary events—that are consistently associated with men?

CAROLINA FIDANZA

Anything with bacon on it.

NAOMI POMEROY

Meat, BBQ, smoke, burgers, grilling, Steak. Man stuff—hahahaha.

ANN CASHION

I think men are often associated with molecular gastronomy, which mercifully, seems to be on the wane. Also, classic American pit barbecue is a male preserve for sure.

RACHEL BOSSETT

Barbecue still feels like a man's world. Roasting big ol' pieces of meat over an open fire is so primitive and is still more heavily dominated by men and masculinity than even many professional kitchens.

MASHAMA BAILEY

Whole animal cooking! I guess because it's more rustic.

GILLIAN SARA SHAW

When coming up in kitchens, early on in my career, 90 percent of the other (i.e., not pastry) departments were men . . . HOWEVER, I did work at a lovely place in Provincetown, Massachusetts, where the kitchen was mostly women.

EVA KARAGIORGAS

Pizza—all over the world pizza is always very masculine or made by men. Where are the lady pizzaiolos?!

MARISSA LIPPERT

Sushi?!? Is that a random answer?

SARA LEVEEN

Sushi! Like anything with such an established history and culture, it has its feet firmly planted in tradition and evolution is slow. I've read explanations for the lack of female sushi chefs that include menstruation (a woman's palate changes with her cycle which affects the precision) and the coincidence of the end of samurai and the birth of sushi (warriors and knives!). My baby sister just completed a two-year culinary program at Johnson and Wales and was invited back after her externship to the sushi bar at Makoto in Miami for a full-time position. I don't want to pressure her into this very difficult field, but I'm encouraging her to really stick with it because it's so rare and she'll be so badass.

JENI BRITTON BAUER

Korean. Meat. French.

CHARMAINE MCFARLANE

Mastery competitions in which the top placement and titleholders are usually men (e.g., Certified Master Chef, Certified Master Pastry Chef, Meilleur Ouvrier de France [MOF], etc.). Butchery, grilling, wood-fired cookery, and professional baking are cooking styles associated with men. I'm drawing a distinction here between professional and home baking because a woman's place has historically been relegated to sitting next to the hearth cooking and baking for her family. However, the village baker has historically been male. Once cooking becomes paid work outside of the home, it becomes men's work and if anyone doesn't believe me, name five professional male bakers and five professional female bakers.

BONNIE MORALES

Absolutely. Just look at the top restaurants in the World's 50 Best list and you'll have your answer.

A Conversation with Diana Henry

Diana Henry got kicked out of her consciousness-raising group at Oxford University for bad attendance. She would also very much like to try her hand at fiction. If you've read any of her twelve cookbooks, especially her first, *Crazy Water, Pickled Lemons* (2002) and her eleventh, *How to Eat a Peach* (2018), you no doubt hope she scratches that literary itch. Take a look, say, at this passage about Provence from the former:

> Of all the smells in the world—wild strawberries, bacon sarnies, the sweet bready scent of a baby's head—this is my favorite.
>
> A mixture of savory, lavender, wild thyme and rosemary, the aroma could not be described as "sweet." This is the garrigue, a sun-baked scrubland of poor soil, harsh light and olive trees. The smell is pungent—pine needles, pepper, camphor and citrus. I like it best in the morning because it's softer, promising hot weather and herb-marinated chops for lunch. By mid-day when every footfall releases its smell and your head is pulsing in time with the cicadas, you'll be almost drunk with it and half asleep.

I worry that she might not get to the novel-writing stage of her career because she claims to have a list of future concepts for cookbooks that will keep her writing those until the age of seventy-two—and at the rate she gets ideas, that list is likely to grow.

All these things I learned while staying at her house in London, which, to me, felt more like going home than visiting my parents at the apartment I grew up in. Diana, one of the UK's most preeminent cookery columnists and authors, lives with her sons, Ted and Gillies, who are, unsurprisingly, both what you'd call "good kids" and, more important, exceptional people. In the evening, I was greeted with the best cooking smells—familiar ones from my own childhood—as Diana would prepare supper for the boys, radio on, news streaming out into the kitchen and dining area. It's where this interview was conducted, on a comfy L-shaped sofa across from the dinner table.

CD

This is a question that I ask most people from the start, and you get a sense of it in *How to Eat a Peach* and in some of your other work, but can you talk about how your childhood and what or how you grew up eating informed your ideas about food and your cooking?

DIANA

Oh. Massively. I mean, huge. That's what makes you as a cook, I think. I started cooking when I was, honestly, about six. Because it was just something that went on all the time. My mom did it. In Northern Ireland, there's a big emphasis on baking. If you talk about people being good cooks there, you talk about them being good bakers. There's a lot of prestige in a very old-fashioned way—but nobody thought it was sexist, actually—attached to whether you can make cakes, wheaten breads, good pastry, all of those kinds of things. There's a great pride taken in that.

My mom, in one way she was very kind of a feminist. She wanted to do stuff. She didn't think she should be shackled by her sex and not be able to do what my dad did. But she did not ever denigrate the kind of stuff that you did in the kitchen. One of my earliest memories is sitting in our galley kitchen, on the countertop, while she brought warm wheaten bread out of the oven. And then slicing me off a piece—I like the heel, the end bit—and putting butter on that, and putting raspberry jam that was from my uncle's mother-in-law, Aunt Sissy.

So there were a lot of ways that food was attached to homeness, good smells, good times—and also, a sense of wonder. I have used the word *magical* in connection to food over a long time. For me, some bits of it were an area of enchantment in the way that fairy tales were.

There was also a thing where it was attached to what I read a lot. Something like *Little House on the Prairie*—all the Ingalls

Wilder books. I looked for it quite often. In *Anne of Green Gables*, there's the thing where they make stuff together. And *The Arabian Nights*, even though there's nothing specific about cooking, there were ingredients in it. And then *Miss Happiness and Miss Flower*, that Rumer Godden book—a lot of that stuff moved around and got mixed up in my head.

CD

Did your mom have cookbooks?

DIANA

Yes. And I was into those at a stupidly young age. She collected the Cordon Bleu series. And I don't like to think of it as a kind of fantasy, but it was another. It's about going places. So there were pictures of farm places in those, but also, of a life that I didn't live. This was in the late sixties. I just thought, *I want to do this and I want to go to these places where these kinds of things happen.*

CD

It was like reading for you, in a sense—I mean, that same way when you read a book and you enter a world and you want to be immersed in it.

DIANA

I completely think that's true. I think they weren't just cookbooks. I think they were about other worlds—other worlds and how to make things. So those two things were very central.

CD

Then later, you studied English at Oxford. And I noticed from following you on social media, you're a great reader. You post a lot about books that you're reading that are not cookbooks.

DIANA

Oh yeah.

CD

I would love to know which genres of literature have influenced your writing and who you really most love to read.

DIANA

Oh my god. I read a lot of American literature. And Irish. I don't think there's any fiction writer whom I read that's influenced me as a writer in any way that I'm aware of at all. But I do really love Jane Smiley. I went on a massive Alison Lurie phase. I've read everything that she's ever written. I think Richard Ford is phenomenal—anybody who can really talk about human relationships in a way that I would need three or four lives to get to grips with, I'm amazed by. And I love Richard Yates.

CD

You started out with your English degree, and then you ended up in television production at the BBC. Right?

DIANA

Yeah. I went to journalism school after Oxford. And there's a BBC traineeship, which is very kind of prestigious. They took twelve people on every year. I went through that. But yeah. I really wanted to work in television. Because you're making something from nothing at all. Books are a lot easier than television, 'cause television, you are making it with a big team. And you're making something that's 3D, and it's moving and living. You have all of the different elements. I got much more visual when I worked in television as well.

CD

While you were doing all of that television production, were you always cooking?

DIANA

Yes.

CD

And then you have Ted, right? And you felt like *I can't keep doing television*?

DIANA

I was doing exactly the kind of thing I wanted to do. When he was eight months I went back to work for Channel Four to do—it was a lovely series: it was about the social history of gardening in the UK in the twentieth century. But I was with this elderly woman, and she was just living out of London, and she was talking to me about the garden that her husband and she put together just after the war, and all I could think about was getting back home to Ted. I thought, *I don't care about these stories anymore. And if I don't care about these stories, I'm not gonna be able to do this well.* And also, I just wanted to get back home; I was upset about being away from him. And I went in on a Monday morning and I resigned. And I knew that was going to be the end of my television career.

CD

But you never regretted it.

DIANA

No. All I regretted was the six months that I spent going back because it was six months when he was with a nanny. And it totally broke my heart. I think he would've been okay, but I wouldn't have been okay, because there was just not a connection. And I didn't want to be home all the time. That was driving me mental. It was that difficult thing of, *What do I do that's kind of part-time and doesn't take me away from him?* And people had always said, "You should write about food," 'cause it was my complete obsession and joy and all the rest of it. And I'd been to cooking school for a year. (I left television for a year to go to Leiths School of Food and Wine just as a treat for myself.)

I left that [TV] job on Monday. On a Friday, someone had heard I was available—a publisher, who wanted someone to ghostwrite a book for Antonio Carluccio, his first vegetable book, and she got in touch with me and she asked me if I would do that. And I just thought, *Oh my god, I've just left television and now somebody's paying me to write about Italian vegetables and spend Thursday morning every week with Antonio!?* And it was very easy for me to ghostwrite because I'd done scripts and everything. I was good at doing someone else's voice. So I did that. And I did loads of reading. And I wrote that whole book. That was kind of great. The transition wasn't difficult.

CD

Did you ever think, *Am I selling myself short?* You know, that thought of: *Oh my gosh, I've had all this training in television and now I'm just gonna sit down and write about food?*

DIANA

Yes. I never had an aim to be a food writer. I had gone into television because I wanted to make documentaries that would change things. But the truth is, I wasn't really making documentaries that changed things anyway. I did feel that food writing wasn't a very important thing.

CD

That sort of nobler pursuit idea—

DIANA

Yeah. And I still don't really think food writing is a noble pursuit.

I really wanted people to cook and I wanted them to love it. 'Cause it had been such a joy for me my whole life, as much a joy as books. If there are two things I want people to do in life, it's read and cook.

CD

How did you find your voice as writer, and how did you find your voice as a cook? Did those things happen simultaneously because of the nature of cookbook writing, or were those separate processes?

DIANA

No, I think it was just all the same thing. I wrote *Crazy Water, Pickled Lemons* and that book had been in my head, but I never thought I'd write it. In fact, it was about what role food had played in my imagination when I was growing up, because I'd grown up in Northern Ireland.

You had to do so much with your head, because you were stuck in the countryside. When I then started to write, it was about the places that you went, through thinking about food and through thinking about ingredients, as much as anything else. It was what I had always been doing. It was a thing that you did in the kitchen, practically, but it was a thing that took you somewhere in your head at the same time.

In me, there is a longing for fulfillment, for going places. I think, in my books—except the ones which are very, very practical—that is part of it.

CD

You're prolific. You write at a tremendous pace, and you maintain it. In addition to the cookbooks, you've got the weekly *Telegraph* column, you do additional stories for other outlets regularly. You have a monthly column for Waitrose, the British supermarket chain, and some of the pieces you do are longer features—a travel piece or profile. Then you do radio. How do you manage that pace and that output?

DIANA

I do really long hours. I get quite annoyed when I have to go to sleep. I don't mean in a kind of, *Oh, I've got so much to do, I can't go to sleep.* It's like, *But I'd like to do such and such. I don't wanna go to sleep because it's just such a waste of time!*

People also sometimes suggest, rather meanly, that it's a displacement activity; I can't live with my bad feelings, so I'm busy working instead. I know there are people like that. I honestly love what I do. I'm very motivated by curiosity—curiosity and creativity. I love stopping as well, though. When I've got these periods when I can stop, it's like going to a big lake and drinking. I wish people wouldn't tell me, "Don't work." People have been telling me that for years.

CD

I wanna be like, *Listen folks, this is where my self worth comes from. Don't tell me not to do it.*

DIANA

It's my pleasure as well, and also I don't think they tell men this. I think they tell women this.

CD

They do not tell men this.

DIANA

Do you think anyone told Bach he should just give up and go to bed? Or whether he should just take a day off? Nobody said that to people like that.

CD

No one ever said that.

DIANA

No. People ran around them and they facilitated it. I hear all the time from friends about [how] they have fathers who are academics or something. It's kinda, *Shh, Daddy's working.* Nobody fucking says that in here, "Mummy's working." I'm in the middle of all the chaos, trying to orchestrate all the other things that need to happen.

CD

But this is something that I wanted to ask you: you're a single mother of two kids. A lot of what's happening with your work is you also need to support them. You love what you do, but this is also an issue of economic sustainability; this isn't, *I just love my job and I don't really care if I don't get paid.*

DIANA

No. If the kids were finished at school and college, there would be things I would cut out. But all I would do would be to fill them with work that I prefer.

CD

As a single parent, how do you balance the work, which is, in a way, also part of raising your family—

DIANA

I think it's an advantage and a disadvantage that what I do is—cooking is domestic, so my work can be done in the home. I don't think I am very good at balancing it all, I think they blur completely, but I think that's also because recipe testing can become supper. Although, it doesn't always, because my kids are picky, so then I end up cooking something else and getting quite resentful about that. I lose it.

CD

There's something else I've been thinking about which is, we have this idea of #wellness now. It's infiltrated the food world; it's certain ingredients, but also feeding yourself—that all of this is self-care. The one thing we never equate with self-care is the cooking itself. For me, it's a way of staying sane, and it brings me a lot of joy and a lot of calm. I know you've thought about it a lot, too. You've dealt with depression and you've written about how cooking has also centered you.

DIANA

I did try to write about this recently. I just put a thing out. It was the day after Brett Kavanaugh had been sworn in [to the United States Supreme Court]. I woke up the next morning and I just felt like . . . depressed, total shit, but not in a sad way. It was like, *Shit, is this coming? Is this gonna be a little episode?* And the usual things didn't work. Listening to music didn't work. Just having my sourdough and pot of coffee and blah blah, it didn't work. And the cooking did. For me, anyway, there's something about—well, the same with reading and writing—but just standing at the cooker; it's going back to a core self that has been there for years. Whatever else is happening all around you, there is that thing, which is essentially you. Then some things about it are quite rhythmic; some things are repetitive. In some way, it's the smells that help, the smell of a frying onion. There's just a kind of immutability and a continuity with cooking, which is lovely. It's a constant.

I had a breakdown in my late twenties, and I was in psychiatric hospital for quite a long time. I really, really was looking forward to getting back to cooking again. One of the things that got me through the last month I was in there, I thought about food all the time. I thought about dishes I wanted to make, then I thought about menus, then I thought about menus for a restaurant that I wasn't gonna have. I'd make out these menus. Late into the night, every night, they had two choices at every course, and I could imagine: Would they really choose the three things that would work perfectly, or would they take the wrong ones from each choice?

Then when I got home it was a bit scary, 'cause I couldn't do anything very complicated, 'cause I just felt drained. I didn't have as much energy. The first thing I did was just this marinated chicken and rice and a kind of yogurt on the side. You know when you say you don't forget how to ride a bicycle? It was a bit like that. It was like gradually getting back on the bicycle again, and I got my balance, and the bicycle started to move. Then it was like, *Oh, I've got this thing back again.* It was like going back to myself.

CD

Yeah. It also reminds of me of something I heard you say, that hope is what saves you; that hope is the most important thing to you. I feel like in some small way, being in that hospital and having those menus—that is something where you're already, without realizing it, imaging having a life after you leave.

DIANA

Oh god, yes.

CD

To me, that is a very practical, small hope, because you're just saying, "I will get out of here and I can make these menus."

DIANA

I think it was a big hope. What I don't understand is why food is so central to me. I don't know. I've wondered and wondered. Except that I suppose at home, that's the thing that was connected to good things. That's the only thing I can think of.

CD

This is a question that's gonna sound loaded, and you're maybe going to disagree with me, but fine. I think that British food writing is better than American food writing. Can you talk about what you think distinguishes British food writing from American food writing? Then maybe you can tell me which one you like better.

DIANA

I think I can tell you what distinguishes American food writing from British food writing. I think, especially when I started to write, here, a personal voice wasn't really encouraged. I think that Nigel Slater was the only person . . . and he wasn't really telling you an awful lot about himself. It was sensual and stuff like that, but you didn't know much about Nigel Slater's life.

CD

True.

DIANA

When I looked at American stuff, I thought it was very sensual. I thought some of it was funny as well—Calvin Trillin. And I totally adored Molly O'Neill's writing. I don't cook her recipes very much, but I think her writing is really wonderful because it was that thing that she writes about the aubergines—first cooking aubergines when they're listening to Nixon [resign]. I mean, Jesus fucking Christ, how did you do that? You want the aubergine. You smell the aubergine. It's in her life. I never cook an aubergine without thinking about that piece. And the aubergine, because she said it was this taste beyond what they knew, and that reflected the political situation at the time. Would that I could ever write like that. I don't know anyone here who can write about a food, a personal thing and a political situation all at the same time in one piece. That is extraordinary.

I just think the American voice—like we assume the American way of life, although not so much now—is freer. It's because you think individualism is important in a way. People can write the way they want. Here, when I did *Crazy Water, Pickled Lemons*, a couple of reviewers hated it. One of them said, "Oh, she's so full of 'I, I, I.' Who cares about what she thinks?" Well, what the fuck else do you care about?

CD
As we're talking, I'm realizing what it is for me that I like so much about British food writing: I think it has more to do with the collapse between the headnote and the recipe. Even though it's changed, I think of that style of writing a recipe where the recipe itself could be narrative; that is not American. American was really about that era of home ec and science and formulas.

DIANA
Yeah, that is more British. But I think only certain people got away with that here.

CD
But if I think back to the older British writers, even someone like a Jane Grigson or an Agnes Jekyll—there's not so much a distinction between a headnote and a recipe, and I love this idea that it's not categorical, that one can bleed into the other, and that the way you describe the process of cooking sounds like the way, now, that we write a headnote.

DIANA
I would really like to have that freedom in everything I do. I would like to be able to write more like that.

CD
That to me is British. That is not American.

DIANA
No, I concede that that's true. Well, when I said that I love American writing more, that's also 'cause I discovered it later. But the person who formed me as a writer was Jane Grigson, because I remember before her, I'd only had very instructive stuff that my mom had, and then I discovered Jane Grigson and it was like, *Oh my god, there's poetry in this, there's history, there are little sentiments about her life.* It wasn't really memoirish, but you were able to build up a picture of her and her life. There was really a connection. It was like having a chat. It was so layered, and there was a different approach to different things as well. There might be one essay in the *Fruit Book* which is very lyrical, and then you go into one which is really much more practical.

CD
Do you think there's any kind of relationship between gender and food writing in Britain? In terms of how people write or who's allowed to write what?

DIANA
God.

CD
I do feel like most of the great British food writers have been—

DIANA
Women.

CD
Women. When I think about whose shoulders food writing rests on, it's pretty much women.

DIANA

Yeah, well, we were in the home kitchen. But it changed when the celeb chef came along, so there were chefs doing it. They were nearly all male.

I got kind of pissed off because, here, I thought food writing was the kind of thing that "little women" did. I mean, there was the food writers' guild, which is our professional organization here and it was largely women, and then when cooking got to be a bit cooler, loads of men started to join. I just thought, *Oh, fuck off.* Because ten years ago, you just thought we were prancing around in pinnies.

CD

Also, I always felt like they gave us so little. There were so few areas where men were like, *fine, you can have that.*

DIANA

I know. Cooking was ours.

CD

You know what? We did a really great thing with it. We really created a genre that didn't exist. We found voices for ourselves where we didn't have them before, and now they've come in and they're like, *Hey, guess what? We can do this, too.*

DIANA

And we can do it better. And we can do it with more muscularity. We go all over the world and we can taste things you would never taste. Dangerous.

CD

I sometimes want to be like, *If you really are interested in the swashbuckling food lifestyle, you could also ask women to do that.* We can do that. We know how to do that, too.

DIANA

That's true, actually. I wonder why we haven't got a female Anthony Bourdain. Also, I think the whole chef thing, they may talk about food being more of a thing and look at restaurants being more of a thing, introducing ingredients, but I think they've done us, largely, a disservice in terms of what we cook at home.

CD

I was about to say, they've ruined home cooking. The other thing about it that kills me is that while we're being told that we have to make everything idiot-simple, as soon as it's a chef story, they can have us smoking things in hay.

DIANA

Yeah, I know. I like chefs because I think they're a bit crazy, and they're addicted to things, and they live large. I like that about them. I'm in awe of the techniques they manage to master.

CD

Yeah. Okay, we talk about cookbooks all the time. We love them. I wanted to know which are your trusted ones you go back to again and again?

DIANA

Alice Water's *Chez Panisse Menu Cookbook.* When I discovered that—oh my god, that was a day! I bought that on the same day as I bought Claudia Roden's [*The*] *New Book of Middle Eastern Food.* It was money that my granny sent me for my birthday and I was at journalism school in London and it was really raining and I went around the corner from my flat.

I took them back to the flat; I was in this basement flat, and I read them lying on the sofa, and then I realized suddenly it was dark. I could barely see the pages anymore. Those two books and *Jane Grigson's Fruit Book,* those are the books that made me a food writer I think.

CD

My last question for you: Is there something you wish people asked you more about your work? Or something that people don't realize about you or about your work that you would like to address?

DIANA

I know the recipe is important. That's mainly what I peddle, in fact. But I don't like to be thought of as just a recipe writer, because I think the recipes are just the little, small things that you pass on, but there's a massive thing all around it. I don't think I'm usually asked about that at all really.

To do something, if I now was at the position I was in when Ted was born, I probably wouldn't become a food writer. I hate that it's become a thing to do with fashion. Most of the people who tell me they want to be food writers, they want to be food writers because they think it's cool. I went into something that was deeply uncool. I got teased at university for it because I wasn't even liberated. People would keep telling me that I needed my consciousness raised. I shared a house with someone who said, "You know that you are enchained by this?" What, I'm enchained by my cooking? It really gives me the greatest pleasure in life apart from reading.

CD

I actually feel quite free when I'm cooking.

DIANA

So do I. I know! And it's so central to me. How dare you tell me that this thing that's at my very core is something I should be ashamed of? Fuck off!

Tienlon Ho

Even when I was burned-out on the, bro-therly, buccaneer energy of *Lucky Peach*, with its worship of the 1989 cult action film *Road House* and all things Anthony Bourdain, and its dizzyingly pulsating mash-up of graphics, I would always stop to read anything Tienlon Ho had written for that moment-defining magazine (same deal for Rachel Khong; if her byline was up there in the table of contents, I was going in). Tienlon went to the Central Asia steppes to retrace the "steps" of a caterpillar believed to possess magical healing powers because of a fungus that infected it. Closer to home (that would be San Francisco), she tracked down the last species of abalone that was until recently still legal to fish for (recreationally) in the United States and dive for off the Mendocino County coast. In the post–*Lucky Peach* era, I've followed Tienlon to *California Sunday*, where I found her name on what I think is the best story to have been published about chef René Redzepi (and he's been the subject of many). When the cookbook she's coauthoring with Chef Brandon Jew on the food and people of San Francisco's Chinatown comes out in 2020, you can be sure I'll have a copy.

She got more personal here, in what she sees as "a story mostly about me and my dad," which it is, although it's also about cultural heritage and how it holds up (or doesn't) as time marches on. But, Tienlon added, "My mom's family traditions and stories, like the one about my grandmother, an imam, and some homemade pork sausages, deserve their own pages." Now I'm desperate to know more about these sausages and waiting for those pages to be written.

The Months of Magical Eating

One night over dinner, when I was six months pregnant, I yawned.

My husband, a Connecticut-born son of an artist and a school secretary, smiled and stroked my hand sweetly in sympathy.

My father, a Guangdong-raised son in a long line of Chinese doctors, furrowed his brow, leaned in to give me a good look, and, dismissing my explanations of long hours at my desk and the obvious gestation, said what he has for nearly every affliction (from allergy to zit) that I've ever suffered: "You're not eating right."

What would be right, to start, were *yàn wō* (燕窝). Birds' nests. Half-moons of hardened saliva spat onto the walls of seaside caves by tiny swiftlets in Southeast Asia.

Dad also prescribed more soups, more ginger, more steaming and less frying, more actual meals and less snacking, and, of course, more rest. But while it seemed clear to me that I just needed to get to the other side by delivering this new person safely into the world, he seemed to think things could be better, now. So I couldn't refuse when he offered to take over all the cooking while he was in town.

The next morning, Dad took the bus to Stockton Street and returned, arms loaded with the remedy. There were stacks of birds' nests in a fancy box, and also pig parts, a chicken with black skin and bones, long white radishes and longer burdock, goji, longan, red dates, black vinegar, and packets of fungi, flower buds, and withered rhizomes.

He soaked the birds' nests overnight until they melted into white clouds that smelled like the ocean, then tweezed out the bits of down woven in. Then he dropped the softened nests with some rock sugar and water into a *dùn zhōng* (炖盅), a stoneware double-boiler, and heated them gently until everything was a wispy, jelly broth.

I ate it and somehow felt immediately less weary. It was the same with everything else he cooked.

I should have been used to it by now. Growing up with a father such as mine, whose roots reach deep in the very traditional Cantonese and Hakka cultures (the kind who keep records going back thirteen generations in the family shrine), a yawn might as well be a hacking cough. Mundanities like that, from the timbre of your pulse to the color of your tongue and the stench of your gas, are all clues into your current state of health. For most discomforts, there is always an antidote.

To sons of doctors of Chinese medicine, love is not a kind touch. It's a hot bowl of bird spittle.

I was raised by two scientists in Ohio, a place where medicine works hard and fast and comes in caplets, which means I tend to look at Chinese medicine like I do Instagram and Oprah (anything with hordes of devotees)—with at least as much skepticism as interest.

Chinese medicine as a system of diet, acupuncture, and the interplay of physical and mental health was written down some 2,200 years ago, and before and since, has been interpreted by trained specialists and well-meaning parents alike. Of all the ways to heal in Chinese medicine, food comes first.

This might seem especially prescient given the current obsession in the United States with functional mushrooms and bone broth, but the earliest doctors weren't thinking about food as wellness. They were thinking about not starving. Throughout Chinese medicine's development, famines in the Middle Kingdom wiped out millions at a time—more regularly than war or epidemics. And so, Chinese doctors wrote foraging, farming, and cooking guides. They wrote about how to render roughage more digestible, offal more delicious, and how to make every bite count. In old China, a footed soup pot, not a sword or a pen, represented power on banners and in songs. Wielded right, a soup pot prevented catastrophe.

Good health requires good food. In Chinese medicine, disease is disharmony, the result of vital energies in the organs blocked or for too long left out of whack. You don't just eat for flavor or nutrients. What you eat can counter your constitution (the product of your genes), your bad choices, and all the demands of living.

The Chinese medicine traditions that passed to me did not come as they typically would through the women in my husband's family (they have German roots), but through the filter of my father's vivid though distant memories. His begin in the mountains west of the Pearl River Delta and land in America, where he became a scientist developing vaccines and materials for space among other things that made his early years without plumbing and electricity feel worlds away.

My dad learned to read as sons of families rooted in tradition did, reciting the *Compendium of Materia Medica* (本草纲目), a massive tome of plants and prescriptions that is still the most comprehensive resource on Chinese medicinal foods since the first edition arrived five hundred years ago. When someone in his house fell ill, he picked bitter herbs and tender hearts of bamboo that grew on the hillsides to steep into soothing broths.

When my sisters and I were growing up in suburban Ohio, there were no neighborhood practitioners or medicine shops. Except for what shot up in our garden and the wild chives and dandelions, the plants that grew around our house weren't edible. Even imports were limited. The numbing Sichuan peppercorn (a pain reliever and gut cleanser) couldn't legally enter the United States until 2005.

At the two Asian markets in town, my parents usually skipped the dry goods aisle, which, for a long time, I took to mean that whatever boxes of twiggy herbs, flowers, roots, and seeds that made it over didn't do much. But actually, it was the opposite. My parents wanted to save them for vital moments. My dad would wonder how people ate curry leaves and chilies, big-ticket meds in all the books, with such abandon.

Naturally, my sisters and I developed a sense of how things we ate made us feel. I went so far as to turn down pizza most of the time, because the spices would make me *shàng huǒ*, or excessively heated. (Explaining this to friends was only slightly less embarrassing than the alternative—a rash across my face.) When you believe what you eat has the effect of feeding or draining the organs, speeding vital energies along or blocking them, even oregano on a pan pizza tastes like medicine.

Within our own house, there were culture clashes, too. My mom did not grow up as my dad did. Her customs are northern, from a family that lived on the same lands for eight hundred years, mixed with some Hui, a Muslim people with their own blend of remedies. My mother's grandfather and uncles were surgeons with modern Chinese and Western training. She was born in a state-of-the-art hospital in Chengdu, where my grandmother accepted painkillers in the Western way and stayed to rest for thirty days afterward in the Chinese way.

When it was her turn, my mom followed tradition by resting a month at home after giving birth, but she was an island in America's Midwest. She managed mostly on her own, first while my dad finished his dissertation and then when I arrived, while they juggled my two sisters. My mom says she subsisted on one particular high-energy recovery dish—a braise of pigs' feet and peanuts, which were both easy to find in America's corn belt and to leave unattended on the stove. That was about it for her and the Chinese way.

"Anyway, we didn't need those things," my mother says now. "We were young and healthy. We had central heating."

She doesn't say so, but I suspect there were other reasons for not holding so tightly to the past. Everyone knew, for instance, that ginseng grew wild not far from us in the wooded ravines and hollows of West Virginia. My uncle went foraging for them, until locals started welcoming people like him with "chink" and "gook," waving guns, and making it clear that those wandering *their* woods should go home. This was not long after Vincent Chin went out for pre-wedding beers one night in Detroit and was beaten to death by two men who got probation and a three thousand dollar fine. Connections to things far away made you less American.

At some point between empty nest and retirement, there was a reawakening. Visits to see me in New York, Chicago, and San Francisco included time for my dad to shop for quality herbs and consult with specialists about annoyances that had aged into aches.

He discovered he hadn't forgotten his childhood recitations. He remembered the three herbs for a stomachache, and the four for insomnia. He started bringing us jars of *liáng chá* (涼茶), a bitter drink involving flowering shrubs, to treat our colds. He remembered how to ferment rice wine and how to use it to make healing tinctures. He remembered that a broth made of that wine and *wū gǔ jī* (烏骨雞), chicken with black skin and bones, helps bring in a new mother's breastmilk. It was a recipe his own father had cooked for his mother eighty years ago.

And then suddenly, as it goes, I was pregnant.

*   *   *

In every medical tradition, there are countless books on pregnancy and birth, but that doesn't make it any less baffling when it is happening to you. When you grow a baby, it turns out, you are also growing yourself. You build new neural pathways in the brain. Your heart adjusts to pump a couple liters more blood. Your breasts transform into functioning glands. Organs move. The uterus stretches from the size of a pear to the size of a watermelon, and so on.

In Chinese medicine terms, all that change throws the yin and yang, your body's cool and warm qualities, into disarray. How well a mother manages to rebalance her energies with food, rest, and avoiding stress determines how well she ultimately recovers after the baby arrives. To add to the pressure, her ability to find equilibrium also determines the quality of the qi, or life force, she transfers to her baby.

Over the centuries, these principles have been put into practice through rules developed from trial and error mixed with a good dose of folk wisdom.

Anthropologists say traditions persist so long as they serve some purpose, real or perceived, for the next generation. I found the practical reasons behind rules surrounding pregnancy and childbirth are obscured by easier to remember superstitions. You avoid lamb chops, not because they are too yang and so make you *shàng huǒ*, but because your mother-in-law warned sheep can suffer seizures and eating them puts your baby at risk for epilepsy. Or you skip crab season not because of the threat of shellfish-borne illnesses, but because your neighbor said if you eat foods with many legs, your baby could grow an extra arm or act like they did (*sānzhī shǒu*, or extra hand, is slang for "pickpocket"). You buy sesame oil, not just because it's nutritious, but also because someone once said it makes the fetus slippery so that when the time comes, it can slide right out.

Other rules offer the benefit of offering unassailable defenses against the demands of people who aren't pregnant. For instance, avoiding strenuous work is justified in some Chinese medicine books by the existence of the *tāi shén*, your baby's feisty but touchy spirit that jumps around the house.

A calendar of its movements is documented in the *Zhulin Temple's Secret Remedies for Women* (竹林寺女科秘传), one of the world's earliest clinical books on obstetrics and gynecology. The baby sprite wanders into different precarious places according to the longitude of the sun and the phases of the moon, a schedule that must have confused billions of expectant parents over the centuries by now.

One day the spirit stands at the door, which has come to mean avoiding slamming doors or repairing them. The next day, it sits on the stove, which means no cooking. It moves around everywhere in the household from the stone mortar (no grinding soybeans!), to the henhouse (no cleaning the coop!), and the bed (no!). The tradition is so ingrained, that many households throughout Southern China and Southeast Asia still avoid loud noises, remodeling projects, knives, and sex during pregnancy even though few believe in the *tāi shén*.

Once baby-spirit and baby-body are united at birth, the rules train a spotlight on caring for the mother. After delivery, the Chinese medicine books describe her as a drained vessel too far on the yin side, susceptible to certain evils like "cold" and "wind" that, unremedied, will plague her for the rest of her life.

In Chinese tradition, the cure is a regimen of food, self-care, and these days, plenty of anachronisms. Birth marks the start of the rite of passage called *zuò yuèzi*, or sitting out the moon. Depending on your family, a moon can mean anywhere from thirty to one hundred days of dedicated time to recover from the previous nine months. There are massages, gentle exercises, and binding your abdomen with muslin. Family and friends are to provide foods for "tonifying and nurturing the mother's five key organs"—"not just to celebrate the child," prescribes the *Formulas Worth a Thousand Gold Pieces* (備急千金要方), a book of remedies that still followed fourteen hundred years later pops up on blogs and message boards for new moms. This generally means easy to digest seaweed or chicken broth in the first days after birth, graduating to more substantial, iron-rich dishes of offal for replenishing nutrients, and calorie-dense stews of pumpkin or peanuts and pigs' feet to boost lactation and energy in later weeks, with variations depending on individual needs, season, and region.

A dedicated time to rest makes sense to everyone. It sounds obvious even. The part of *zuò yuèzi* that most people outside the culture can't fathom is the deprivation. In English-speaking parts of Asia, *zuò yuèzi* is translated ominously as "confinement." And standard practice is to endure the following without exception: You cannot eat raw, cold, acidic, or spicy food. You cannot drink cold water. You can't have sex, use air conditioning, or take a bath or shower. You might be allowed to choose between grooming with a fine-toothed comb or a wipe-down with boiled water steeped with Chinese herbs. In some cases, you can't even brush your teeth, climb stairs, cry, read, or look at digital screens. You definitely can't leave the house.

These restrictions can drive even the most dutiful women in Asia crazy, too. On the message boards of Ci123's, China's largest parenting community with 150 million members, new moms commiserate over hiding their mobile phones under mattresses, secretly cracking windows, and sneaking showers while their minders are on grocery runs.

Usually, the worst consequences of strict *zuò yuèzi* are boredom and body odor. But a few years ago, during a massive heatwave in Shanghai, one new mother died bundled up in blankets, reportedly unable (or unwilling) to turn on the air conditioning, determined as she was to "obey the advice of her elders."

The grandmothers in charge draw on their own experiences from a now bygone age. They had no hairdryers, dependably sterile water, or Amazon Prime. Staying warm was work in itself. Ask a Chinese grandmother what caused her arthritis, and if she doesn't share a story about carrying a newborn on her back as she helped with the spring harvest, she's likely to blame herself for not wearing socks during her confinement.

Fortunately, I—as a daughter of a son of Chinese medical doctors who lives in San Francisco—had the benefit of leeway. First, not having to worry about grinding rice powder to make a paste to repair my paper windows left me energy to turn up our heater. And, conveniently, my husband knew nothing about these customs while my parents didn't even remember most of them.

To us, it made sense to ignore most of the rules and look at the principles behind them. Maybe because the farther away you are from your roots, the easier it is to see that what mattered before depended on circumstance. And because, as it is for all immigrants and their children, adapting the old ways is the family tradition until eventually the new becomes old again.

*   *   *

Chinese mothers who sit out the month have had the option of hiring a *yuè sǎo*, a confinement doula, to move in and cook for and guide them in the first months, since at least as far back as the time of Confucius and his disciples, who documented the practice two thousand years ago in the *Book of Rites* (礼记). In the month before the baby arrived, it states, a woman got a break—a room of her own and a "well-dressed maid" to tend to her and to her husband's questions. Until recently, though, such outsourcing was always done at home, under the watchful eye of relations.

Now in China and throughout Asia, generations that once lived together in one compound are thousands of miles apart. The journey home to see parents or in-laws is a yearly event.

You get situations like a mother telling a reporter, "My family is very busy working so they don't have enough time to care for me," as she sits alone in an immaculate Taipei confinement hotel. Parents are having children later, which means grandparents are older than they used to be and aren't able to travel or do all the heavy lifting required. Half of all new mothers in Taiwan now stay in a postpartum facility.

Confinement hotels are a hybrid of clinic and retreat with amenities like breast-feeding pillows, candlemaking workshops, and full-body decontamination showers/dryers for anyone entering a confinement room. The most popular birth hotels in the major cities from Singapore to Shanghai advertise science-based services. They are staffed by a battery of twenty-four-hour nurses that take the principles of Chinese medicine to counterintuitive places like limiting mothers from holding their babies to avoid rattling their soft bones and joints. Licensed dieticians count calories and nutritional content when creating menus from the array of dishes that balance yin and yang, stimulate breast-related meridians for lactation, and clear away heat. The dishes that have been part of the postpartum tradition for hundreds of years are made with free-range chickens and organic produce. There are still pots of red date and goji tea instead of water and plenty of pigs' feet. But now, there is dietician-approved cake, too.

During confinement in these "scientific" facilities, mothers are pampered in a fragile Victorian lady of leisure sort of way, spending much of the month alone save for scheduled visits from nurses and the newborns, who get the same treatment enclosed in the nursery, away from germs.

Isolation has its uses. It protected mothers and babies from serious infection when birth was for many, the medical texts note, "like awaiting death." But these days seclusion shields them from their families even while modern science tells us that too much time spent alone weakens the immune system and breeds postpartum depression and anxiety.

Back in my father's village, after a baby was born, toward the end of confinement, hordes of family and neighbors arrived to share a meal capped with eggs dyed red and sweet rice wine. They glimpsed the mother and baby, staying long enough to pass along *hóngbāo*, gifts of cash, to celebrate their shared burden of raising a child, before taking the party to the streets. But even this tradition, like everything else about *zuò yuèzi*, is being outsourced. You can have vacuum-sealed red eggs mailed to family and friends so that you never have to actually see them but they still know to send cash. A practice meant to soften the challenges of confinement by bringing everyone together at the end is now just a money grab. Having time for actual connection is an outdated notion.

To those outside the culture and, increasingly, even to those within it, the greatest anachronism is the idea of a grown woman on lockdown at home, subject again to her parents dictating what she can't do or eat because of her weakened state. It all sounds downright anti-feminist. In the West, we talk about getting back to business weeks after birth. We praise women the less they seem to be moms. We try not to talk about being tired or feeling unsteady about motherhood. Unlike the Chinese, here, we like to say we eat certain foods to be healthy and strong, not because our bodies are too weak to digest it.

It's true, *zuò yuèzi* probably wasn't born of empowerment. In its very earliest incarnation, its practices took a form common across all early civilizations that was motivated by fears of blood and menstruation and the mysteries of new life. There are still vestiges of that oppression. In the Shanghai dialect, a woman sits the month in a room called the *xuèfáng*, the blood room. And the best way to repair the supposed ills of not following the rules during *zuò yuèzi* is to have another baby. In other words, Confucius's well-dressed maid answers the door to help out but also to keep any bad luck from getting out.

But beneath those fears has always been the real need to draw clear lines to make time for a woman to heal and to transform into a parent. Just like failing to eat a diet that balances your energies or aggravating the *tāi shén*, all the bad things that can happen while simultaneously cradling your week-old infant and taking conference calls, are really just another way of saying, allotting time for rest does not make us weak but makes us strong again.

In Chinese, another name for the period of confinement is the gateway. It marks the crossing from one phase of life to another. In the past, and still today among some Chinese families, a woman was not really "in" until the birth of a child. So the gateway also stood at the juncture when a mother-in-law began the rituals of caring for her new daughter and teaching her the family ways. A new mother didn't always have to just take it. She was allowed and expected to be confused, uncertain, and emotional without bringing shame to anyone involved. Bonds were forged with the help of intense emoting and mutual sleep-deprivation.

Beyond recovery, beyond transitioning from woman to mother, the underlying motive of confinement has also been to connect generations through shared food, memory, and struggle. It was a time for growing a family.

* * *

When I was six months pregnant, I hadn't yet made much time to focus on baby-related things, because where should I begin?

It was around then that my dad suggested we brew an inky tonic of ginger and black vinegar to cure pigs' feet and eggs. It would take a few hours to prepare and another two months to finish. The black vinegar and ginger were heating elements: they would balance out all the yin. In the caustic brine, the cartilaginous feet and eggs would melt into a slurry of digestible calcium, minerals, and protein to be eaten beginning three days after the baby was born.

It took us a while to find the preferred ginger—not too young or old, not long stalks but round knobs. Then it took time to find the right large pot that could withstand months of holding acid. Dad special-ordered pounds of just hind feet, which have more bones and cartilage than the fore, to be halved along the bone, just so. Then there was the sourcing of a black vinegar brewed from sweet, glutinous rice.

It could be a lot more complicated, Dad said. There is a tradition of vinegar production in China's northeast, for instance, where parents harvest rice to make wine that they ferment at the bottom of a cold lake from the day their daughter is born until she marries. Then the precious vinegar is used for her confinement meals.

When we had finally assembled all the necessary ingredients and equipment, we sat down late one night at my kitchen table, scraping the skin off a few pounds of knobby ginger with spoons, in between blanching and plucking the bristles off the heap of pigs' feet.

We had to use the edges of spoons for the ginger, because peelers would bruise it and cause it to release too much of its juice too quickly. Also, Dad said, we could save the scrapings to dry and sprinkle in my first bath, the rhizome's skins being warming and naturally antibacterial.

In between the work and rinsing our hands to soften the burn of the ginger juice, we talked. He told me about his mother, my Nai Nai, and how she gave birth to her first child, alone on the dirt floor of the mud-brick house where he would grow up. How, when her daughter arrived, she was so utterly alone that she realized she had no way to cut the umbilical cord and so considered biting through it, but instead reached for the sharpest thing she had on hand—a shard of a bowl she rinsed with boiling water. With sheer will, she gave a new person to this world.

My dad left the black concoction on the stove in the big pot with instructions to bring it to a boil every ten days over the next few months until the baby arrived. I did so faithfully. As is often the case with tradition, the potential guilt kept me going even as it filled every room with an acrid cloud. (The vapor purifies the air, I reminded my poor husband.)

So the soup is where I began processing what was happening and considering life after the baby arrived. That may or may not have been my father's plan. But it was a side effect of Chinese medicine for our ancestors.

A dish meant to heal does so in many ways. A black slurry of pickled pigs' feet and eggs can't serve its purpose if that purpose and its origins aren't known. What is lost when there are no moments together sipping tea, breaking down ginger and pork until your hands are raw, and remembering how it had all been done before? What happens to all that is said in between?

There is magic in rules. After all, rules fill the void. They promise a semblance of certainty during a time when there is actually very little. But it's in the context where the magic lies.

These days, rules tend to exist stripped of their magic. While the Chinese are looking for comfort in "science-based" ones, Americans seem to be seeking the opposite. We look for remedies that can be taken as needed (as is convenient). We like the idea of ancient (Chinese and otherwise) wisdom, but we want the abridged version. We down Moon Juice to "expand [the] body's capacity to handle mental, physical and emotional stress." We pay ten times more to have the roots and fungi from the Chinese medical texts sealed up in pretty packaging, because the purpose of wellness is that it must confer a sense of virtue, and virtue must be hard won—if not through sacrifice, then with money. Across cultures, the approach looks different but the result is the same.

Confinement tells us that we are healthiest when we are not alone. But when it is reduced to a battery of rules, an emotionless regimen that can be bottled or outsourced, it becomes alienating and impersonal, just another form of wellness. Its bleak message is that inevitable moments in life are inconvenient. It makes us feel like we have to suffer to do the right thing. It makes us believe we are inadequate when we deviate. Wellness at its worst forces each of us to conform to the unrealistic expectations of everyone around us—our mother-in-law, our husband, or the stranger at the grocery store—and never to our own needs. In good times, rules help us (and the people who teach them to us) feel virtuous and in control. But in bad, they saddle us with guilt.

Here is what happened to me:

Thirteen weeks after I yawned and a week after the black elixir was finally ready, I went into labor. And at its height, my pulse racing, cervix fully dilated, I suddenly saw my Nai Nai.

I saw her, the woman I knew only as tiny and weathered, young and strong again. She squatted alone on a dirt floor waiting, like I was, for her firstborn, feeling all the same worry and uncertainty but so much more of it. And I burst into tears at that memory of something I would never experience—never need to experience—and at seeing the faces of my husband and people who cared about me nearby, helping me, and this new emerging being. Many times throughout my many hours of labor, like a vivid movie or an apparition, I saw my grandmother doing this miraculous thing, and in my own way, I was able to do the same.

In our first months back home, we all ate well. There was ginger-braised liver, pork kidney and congee, many chicken soups, and more. In a stupor, my husband made endless grocery runs. My sister braised pork ribs with white radish, ginger, and star anise. My mom gently braised her version of pigs' feet with carefully peeled peanuts, and brewed teas of red dates and goji, and sweet porridges of black rice and longan. She brought me the sour broth from the pickled eggs and pigs' feet to sip. It was grainy and thick like the sum of its parts had been compressed into each spoonful. My dad arrived and cooked us pork kidneys, pork rib, and seaweed soup, and took many more trips to Stockton Street. He made the chicken soup with rice wine that he remembered.

I remember what I ate, mostly because I wrote it down. But I don't need jogging to remember the morning my sister brought ice cream sandwiches. Or the afternoon my mom stood by my bed and held my hand, while I cried and she yelled, "Yes, tell me! Let it all out!" I remember waking up one morning to the sight of my husband cradling our daughter and realizing so much more deeply what it meant when he lost his mother to cancer seventeen years before. I remember the day after eating my mom's pigs' feet and peanut soup, how my milk came in suddenly like geysers. And I remember a few weeks after everyone had to leave, that my cousin came to visit and decided I looked too green. She started regular deliveries of pork, lotus, and cuttlefish soup, which she carried across town on the bus in a gigantic pot.

I remember being nourished by my family.

*　*　*

When you are so fragile and too tired to think beyond the fact that something so precious can be lost, turning to magic feels entirely reasonable. You do whatever you've been told. You might give up sushi, soft cheeses, wine, and caffeine. You might stop with the prosciutto. Eat more greens. You might eat the nests of tiny seabirds. Sometimes, feeling better is only a matter of having more protein in your diet. But sometimes, especially when you are about to be a parent, you just need that sense of being cared for again.

I didn't leave the house much for a couple months, not because I was following tradition, but because I was wrecked. The sun was too bright and the traffic too loud. It took me a couple weeks for my first real shower, not because I was trying to bolster my yang, but because of complications of my recovery. I was still too weak to lift my arms then to wash my hair, so I never washed my hair with ginger. It took me time—more than a few moons—to want to be unconfined. But that was just me.

If you are lucky, you might have this epiphany sooner than I did: That there is no right or wrong way to care for yourself while pregnant, to birth a child, or to become a mother. There is only your way, forged by the memories of your own childhood and shaped by your experiences since. At some point, you find yourself taking in all that advice and all those rules no longer with fear and guilt, but with interest and skepticism, and that is when you realize you have crossed the gateway, intact and improved.

One day, when things felt not back to normal but settled into a new normal, I was finally standing steady and strong on two feet. I held my new baby in my arms and opened the refrigerator to cook something for all of us, and there in the back was a jar of black eggs and pigs' feet glistening like onyx. With everyone in my family cooking and everything else, I never got around to eating them.

I still have that jar in my refrigerator, and whenever I see it, I feel immensely grateful. It is a jar filled with a family's strength, a nascent wisdom, and the memories of ages that allowed me to bear the weight of this new life barely started. I could never eat it.

THE TRUTH ABOUT MY MOTHER

What a lovely image we seem to have in our heads, that all the women who would become food writers or professional cooks grew up learning at their own mothers' knees, in the kitchen, our chubby little-girl hands pulling at their apron strings, our eyes following their every move as they made supper. We watched them baste chickens, and helped them mix batters (then licked the bowl), and cherished the moments together.

But how many mothers do you know like that? And how many grown daughters do you know who cook now, for whatever reason, because they had mothers like that?

REBEKAH DENN

1. The truth about my mom is she loves to cook because her own mother was obsessed with cleanliness and never let her in the kitchen as a kid.

2. Also, the truth about my mother is that she always appropriately credits recipes. She left me three phone messages once when I was mistakenly giving people the recipe for "her" famous Senate Brownies, which turned out to be from a community cookbook.

3. The truth about my mom is that one night, after my parents divorced and my older siblings left home, the fish she got for dinner smelled off, and she took us out for ice cream instead. Just ice cream. The best dinner of my teenaged life.

JASMINE MOY

She was a single mother, raising two small children, without any sort of child or financial support and that shit is HARD. It means we ate a lot of fast food, and for as much as people demonize McDonald's or anything non-organic or not home-cooked, if fast food wasn't as prevalent as it is (and was), I literally don't know if and how she would have fed us every night. We were also on food stamps for a period and literally the *last* thing a person in that situation needs is someone telling them what they can and can't use those food stamps on. That said, my mom, when she had the time and money, loved to cook. There were a few Midwestern staples that we ate a lot (think turkey tetrazzini, chicken and dumplings, meatloaf) and her Christmas cookie repertoire is the stuff of legend. She'd make forty different kinds and give platters of them to friends (and coworkers and the firemen down the street) in lieu of gifts.

KRISTY MUCCI

She can't cook, and I grew up wishing the food at home tasted better. She also let me start cooking—using the oven and stove and real knives—at age six.

CHRISTINA TOSI

She cooks and bakes to care, to nurture. She will shamelessly use margarine, nuts that have been in her pantry for five-plus years, the bottom of four different types of flour bags. She's a busy woman, but her love language is service, and growing up in the Midwest where most didn't have access or funds, service meant bringing someone a meal, or a sheet cake or a stack of cookies.

She let me buy any box of cereal at the grocery growing up but refused to let me throw a single box away until it was empty. LOTS of stale cereal memories, but that MILK at the end . . . ☺

WENDY MACNAUGHTON

She tried. She really did. My mom is a fantastic home cook, and when I was little she did her very best to impart that wisdom to me. I paid attention through the chocolate sauce lesson, then moved on to other interests like drawing and talking on the phone. I think it broke her heart a bit that I survived two decades living off protein bars and frozen veggie burgers. When I finally learned to cook it wasn't on purpose. I'd agreed to illustrate Samin Nosrat's *Salt Fat Acid Heat*, and in order to understand what I was looking at, why things do what they did, why they taste like they taste—and then communicate that through drawings—I had to learn how to do it myself. When I told my mom that I finally enjoyed making a meal, she was thrilled. It gave us another point of conversation and connection. Even more than that, I think she was relieved. She values food not only for sustenance, but also as a way to gather loved ones together, show care, and keep family traditions alive. And now I do, too.

ALISON CAYNE

Sometimes I make it sound like she only fed me Frosted Flakes and Lean Cuisine, but she made a killer spaghetti, cottage cheese crispy pancake, and her love of curry powder and canned fish definitely positively influenced my palate.

LIGAYA MISHAN

My mom was a child in the Philippines during the Second World War, which may explain her fondness for foods that last: powdered milk; canned peaches; Spam, which she crisped in a pan and added to Kraft mac 'n' cheese, along with frozen peas; and Tang, mixed with freshly squeezed calamansi from our back yard.

JENI BRITTON BAUER

She oversalts everything and makes everything with too much butter and cream.

NAOMI TOMKY

She has an unresolved vendetta against salt and fat . . . both in her cooking and her daughter.

NING (AMELIE) KANG

My mom is the only person in my family who doesn't know how to cook. Growing up she had two signature dishes (also the only two dishes she knows how to make for that matter), Congee with Thousand Year Egg and Instant Ramen, and hers are the best I ever had anywhere. Grandma, aunt, uncle all are excellent cooks, which makes my mom spoiled, and an excellent food "critic." She doesn't know how to cook, but she sure knows what good food should be like. When we are not dining at grandma's, we are at restaurants and Mom will comment on how the dumpling skins are too thick, how the spinach salad is at its perfection. My mom can never teach me how to cook, but she did teach me how to eat.

KIM ALTER

I love her more than life, but she isn't the best cook. My favorite items that she cooks for me (taco salad and grilled cheese) comfort me, and I love and request and crave them, but when she cooks for guests it gets a little scary. Example: the first time she met my partner, she made "mayo fish." This consists of a coating of mayonnaise about ¼ inch thick around mahi mahi that has been seasoned with dill and Sriracha. It is then baked. It isn't awful, but you can't eat too much. My partner, Ron, asked for seconds—such a sweetheart . . . until he threw up the second we left her house. I love my mom.

THERESE NELSON

The truth about my mother is that she has become a good cook along with me. She was a marginal cook when I was growing up, which was understandable because she was a single mom and had a pretty demanding career. When I decided to become a chef and went to culinary school she became more interested in food, and we sort of learned together. It's an interesting thing to watch someone evolve as a cook over so many years. We still do virtual cooking classes sometimes, and she's actually a pretty adventurous cook now!

ANA SORTUN

My mother, Jennifer Johansen, was a stickler for good ingredients and quality. She never cooked anything too complicated, but she always respected the ingredients she used, ate, and served.

She loved butter and hated margarine, she knew the difference between store-bought and homemade. She was reading ingredient labels way back in the seventies before it was common practice. She developed her appreciation for pure ingredients growing up on a small family farm outside of Seattle, Washington, in the Green River Valley.

Her mother made her own bread and butter, milked cows for cream, and her father made ice cream with the cream, grew peaches, green beans, and more.

I grew up to be a chef, not because I was always cooking with my mother but because she taught me about good quality ingredients, and I knew that if I wanted to continue to eat great food when I grew up, I would need to learn how to cook and source ingredients. She set the standards that I use in my restaurants.

When I opened my first restaurant in 2001, my mom flew out to Boston every Mother's Day to celebrate some of her dishes included on a special brunch menu, with a half dozen others from the repertoires of staff members' mothers. Her crab melts and strawberry tarts were always a part of our Mother's Day ritual at Oleana restaurant for many years! We still make them today.

SARA LEVEEN

My mom raised three girls as a single mother in Upstate New York. She came from a family of dairy farmers in New Hampshire and ensured that her mother's approach to food and cooking was not diluted or lost on the new generation. From-scratch was a way of life! We picked, canned, pickled, and stewed all summer and fall . . . we had a "can room" full of Ball jars and a full-size freezer in the garage. We ate fresh from the garden or farmers market as often as possible and in the winter, breakfast was cereal and canned peaches, lunch was PB&J with raspberry jam, dinner was goulash with her stewed tomatoes. We were required to be part of the process, too; I can still feel the raspberries squishing between my fingers and remember how exciting it was to dump all that sugar in and watch it melt. I really, really want to hold on to this and pass it on to my kids.

ERIN MCKENNA

A woman who cares deeply about quality. When I was growing up she never put a meal on the table that was frozen despite the popularity of TV dinners and that she was raising twelve children. Every night was a meal with dignity: pot roast with twice-baked potatoes and vegetables, roast chicken with fresh corn. She even made fresh bread! When she needed cold cuts or hot dogs she went to Glenn's, the local butcher, because it made a better sandwich. She's the type that would rather not eat—even if she is starving!—if the food isn't up to snuff. As a mother of three I am still confused how she did it.

JEN AGG

She hated to cook and was terrible at it. I learned to cook because I believed there were more beautiful things to eat in this world than wildly overcooked Brussels sprouts and gray steak.

EMIKO DAVIES

Can I change this to my [Italian] mother-in-law?! She cannot cook, which goes against all the stereotypes of the Italian nonna— she is messy and haphazard in the kitchen, is known to take shortcuts (frozen pre-cut onion in a box!) and overcook meat and over-salt salad, but she can make excellent lasagne, which she does completely by eye. But I think this has also been great for me as there has never been any competition in the kitchen or about me feeding her son!

GINA HAMADEY

My mom grew up in New York City, one of the world's great Italian American food homes—first in Williamsburg, then in Floral Park. My grandmother and great-aunt worked at the local pizzeria, and when not working they were busy cooking up multicourse meals for like fifteen people every night. But my mom took it all for granted. She would trade frittata or sausage and pepper sandwiches for PB&J. When she moved to California, she was all too happy to open jars of Ragú instead of sweating over actual ragù. Visiting my grandparents, I got my fill of eggplant parm and broccoli rabe, and lasagna with tiny meatballs and hardboiled eggs, and stuffed artichokes. I am still trying to re-create those tastes. My mom does make an amazing and super simple blended zucchini soup starring frozen lima beans and grated parm on top. (Growing up the cheese was shaken out of the can; I've upgraded to freshly grated.)

NICOLE ADRIENNE PONSECA

My mom was the breadwinner, and my dad took on the role of cooking and maintaining our house. I was curious why my mom never cooked and asked her if she could make me a sandwich. While I was excited to have a lunch made by mom, when I got to school, the bread was just filled with mayo and lettuce.

CHANDRA RAM

My mom is an amazing cook, but at the top of the list of things she taught me to make and eat is a sandwich of soft white bread, smeared thickly with mayonnaise and filled with potato chips. It was a snack she and her friends ate when she was a nurse in London in the sixties. It's killer . . . and kind of a weird thing for her to have picked up while working in a hospital. But if I'm at home and have the makings for it, I make one and eat it, happily.

She made breakfast for me every single morning, something I never totally appreciated. Scrambled eggs with cream cheese mixed in (try it), Bisquick pancakes, an English muffin with jam! It wasn't fancy, but it was consistent and comforting.

SIERRA TISHGART

My dad is a highly skilled cook—he built a pizza oven in our backyard and makes incredible Neapolitan pies. He puts Thai curry gravy on our Thanksgiving table. My mom, though, did the bulk of the "cooking"—I put in quotation marks because she did a lot of heating frozen pizzas and microwaving mac and cheese—but even though her meals sometimes lacked in freshness and creativity, she made sure we all sat down together, as a family. That was sacred.

MASHAMA BAILEY

She only cooked on the weekends when I was growing up. I had no idea that she actually knew how to cook until I was in my twenties.

JORDANA ROTHMAN

My mom ties a small bell to her shih tzu's topknot so she can always hear where the creature may be hiding. The upshot of this is that the creature has spent years harrowed by the sound of a mysterious bell, a jingle that follows her everywhere she goes, the source of which she has never been able to understand. It adds up to a kind of practical torture and I have spent an equal amount of years unknotting the terrible bell and tossing it (or, occasionally, discreetly fastening it to my mother's jacket so that she may confront her own adorable brand of persecution).

Anyway, all of this to say is that my mom can be a little bit anxious, and puts a lot of effort into heading off any and all potential obstacles many miles before they become an issue. She will never not be able to find the dog (because bell!). And she will never not be prepared for a holiday meal because she cooks them months in advance and freezes their components such that they lose much of their flavor. The good news is this work frees her up to worry about other things on Thanksgiving Day, like, you know, where the dog has disappeared to.

Nerves notwithstanding, I have to give it to my mother for being game to learn and adapt to the inflexible predilections of her strange children. When my eldest brother decided to become a Hasidic Jew, she built a second kitchen for him so that he could feed himself the way he needed to in her home. When she read *Tacos: Recipes and Provocations*, the cookbook I wrote with chef Alex Stupak, she encountered a few ingredients she couldn't find in her local market. She grew cape gooseberries in the backyard to faithfully follow a salsa recipe in the book.

I guess I'm saying that the truth about my mother is that while I didn't learn about food at her knee, as an adult she did show me, time and again, that how we cook is how we are. That's a lesson that still rings true. You know, like a bell.

AISHWARYA IYER

My mom is a machine. She can cook four-plus complex Indian dishes in less than an hour. She can cook for eighty people without breaking a sweat. She can cook an extravagant breakfast after taking a red-eye flight. For years, I didn't think I could match any of her talents in the kitchen, and I avoided cooking in front of her. A couple of months ago, she visited me in LA, and through the weekend, I made some channa masala, jeera rice, avocado toast, and a simple pizza. I later overheard her telling my father, "Everything Aishu makes tastes so good." I was, and still am, overjoyed.

CAROLINE FIDANZA

Despite being a great cook, she served us Polly-O mozzarella sandwiches on toasted Sunbeam white bread for lunch everyday. Nothing else.

MONIQUE TRUONG

She, when she was a newly arrived refugee to the United States, loved Arby's roast beef sandwiches with their Crayola-yellow cheese sauce and any restaurant where there was an all-you-can-eat salad bar.

REBECCA FLINT MARX

She makes very, very good sour cream coffee cake; tortured me with tuna fish casserole but let us eat half-baked brownies straight from the pan and took us out to get ice cream for dinner when Dad was out of town; doesn't like spicy food;

can't eat potatoes, tofu, or corn; loves Diet Pepsi; has been drinking only decaf coffee for as long as I've known her; doesn't really care about restaurants; always has at least two kinds of ice cream in the freezer.

SOFIA PEREZ

My mother has never cooked from a book. Mom learned to cook from her mother and aunt, but she also has an innate sense of which ingredients to add and the best moment to add them. As an immigrant to 1960s NYC, she did not always have access to the ingredients she had used in her small farming village in northwest Spain, but she knew how to adapt a recipe to maintain its spirit—and often improved on the original in the process. The only time I ever felt tortured by her food was in elementary school. I'd sit down next to classmates who were eating PB&J or bologna, and open up my Scooby-Doo lunchbox to reveal a liverwurst sandwich. These days, of course, I love liverwurst and detest bologna, but back then, I felt mildly punished for a crime I hadn't committed.

CATHY ERWAY

She never used recipes to cook when I was growing up. As in many countries, she learned to cook by simply gleaning things from other cooks, verbally or by observation. She's from Taiwan and following recipes for everyday cooking was just not a tradition. Once

she moved to the States, she still continued to learn and expand her repertoire by befriending people of all backgrounds and learning from them. She got ideas from friends and fellow moms, and even from friendly chefs in our town, and made them work to her liking at home.

TAMAR ADLER

My mom has, unfortunately, totally missed out on the opportunity to be a wise older lady cook. She's an amazing cook instinctively and has even cooked professionally— for like a decade—but rather than gathering that around her like an accomplishment, like the pay-off for arthritis and aging, she pretends she doesn't know what she's doing. It's like she missed the idea that wisdom and experience are the reward for getting old. It's sad and saddening. It has everything to do with her being a woman. Or with being the woman that she is. Which is tautological. But it drives me and my brother a little crazy that she says things like: oh, how do you salt that chicken, or show me how you boil broccoli, when she's salted chicken and boiled broccoli for a lot longer than we have.

TINA ANTOLINI

It's probably my mom's fault (or to her credit?) that my love of eating feels sub-intellectual, as if it were something planted in me before I had the cognitive ability to choose my likes and dislikes for myself. When I was an infant and a toddler, she'd get so involved in cooking elaborate meals that, the story goes, I would fall asleep, strapped into my highchair, awaiting the meal. Then, after dinner was served, I would doze off again, face descending gradually into my plate. I suspect I absorbed something from putting my face in dozens of bowls of spaghetti al pomodoro or tagine.

My mom is a former recipe tester and cookbook editor for *Sunset Magazine* and Sunset Books. She left that career when I was tiny to go to divinity school and become an Episcopalian priest. Perhaps it's her familiarity with communion and its sacraments, but dinners at our house always felt like rituals of the most revered kind.

KRISTEN MIGLORE

She was a home ec major who secretly wanted to be a chemistry major, which meant she taught me how to bake like a scientist—always leveling measuring spoons and cups carefully, and looking at liquid measures from the bottom of the meniscus (the slight dip in the line), not the top. There was a scoop that lived in our tin of flour, decades before I'd heard of the "spoon and sweep" method for more consistent measurements.

DIANNA DAOHEUNG

The truth about my mom is she is an amazing Thai cook. From the minute I could walk, I was cooking with her. Growing up in central Florida, there weren't many options for finding Thai ingredients. So she would make everything from scratch, from coconut milk to curry.

ESTHER TSENG

She introduced me to the flavors and ingredients of Taiwanese food within our suburban Milwaukee home setting. She would give in to my and my three brothers' demands for American food, too, by juxtaposing her *bah tzang* (Taiwanese tamales made with rice, braised beef, boiled peanuts, wood ear mushroom, bamboo and tea egg inside) with a couple of links of bratwurst; fried rice with our Thanksgiving turkey; stir-fried snap peas, carrots, and chicken with lasagna; and turnip cakes with grilled steaks. The differing cultures for consumption on our table was a metaphor for our everyday lives: One foot in America, one foot back in Taiwan.

She taught the white ladies at our church how to make egg rolls in a sort of culinary exchange, acting as an ambassador of our culture by showing others how to make a food they actually really liked—having exposed them to these egg rolls first at a church potluck. It was one of the first times I remember being surprised that white people would actually appreciate something from the culture of my bloodline, rather than thinking it was strange.

I also used to watch her make the aforementioned *bah tzang* so patiently. She pulled up a chair next to the sliding glass door leading to our back patio and backyard, using the handle to hang strings of completed *bah tzang* wrapped in bamboo leaves. She'd fold the bamboo leaves into triangular cones, pack them with half-cooked rice, fill them with all the fixins, averaging a medium brown color, and then pack in more rice before folding the leaves on top and tying up the ends.

VIRGINIA WILLIS

She's a great cook and an adventurous one—always has been. I was the one taking leftover egg rolls and roulade au poulet to school the next day—which doesn't sound terribly odd, except it was the eighties in South Georgia. One key piece that I only learned a short time ago is how my mother became a Cajun cook. She moved to Louisiana from Georgia when she was twenty-nine years old with a three-year-old and a six-month-old—and a busy husband with a new job. She'd never lived outside her home state of Georgia and didn't know anyone. She recently explained to me that to get to know her new home and the people, she bought local cookbooks and started cooking the food. I grew up with gumbo, jambalaya, étouffée, and red beans and rice. This, too, may not sound all that exotic, but this was long before Justin Wilson or even before Paul Prudhomme became a nationally known chef. I grew up tasting cuisines from all over the world in addition to Southern classics.

JULEE ROSSO

My mom was a fifties mom who cooked tuna and noodle casserole, goulash, roast chicken, mac and cheese, smothered pork chops for family dinners. Salads were cottage cheese, Jell-O, or iceberg lettuce. That was our family's fare. She saved her creative cooking for testing desserts for the Bridge Girls. That was where she really shone.

Both of my grandmas were excellent non-measuring cooks who baked magnificently. My mom's mom regularly had to make the piecrust for her daughter, which was constant, because my dad thought that dinner wasn't complete without pie. I think that sweet tooth gene came to me from both sides.

One summer morning, my brother was asked at a family breakfast with our entire extended family of forty-plus, what Mom made him for breakfast at home. He answered, "Eat it and shut up!!" Mom was mortified. She never lived it down. Everyone else, hysterical.

We absolutely adored my mom. She woke every morning trying to figure out how much fun she could jam into that day while my dad made breakfast. She brought that sense of fun and an incredible wit to our family and to everyone she met. It made everyone love her! My dad would set her up, and she'd always come through with a punch line.

TIFFANY FAISON

She never met a container of sour cream she didn't love. She cooked delicious and soulful meals. The way she cooked created a giant barrier for me eating healthy as an adult; I crave the creamy delicious food I grew up on. She never realized how capable she was and therefore never realized how capable I could be.

EVA KARAGIORGAS

She is the best cook I know and no one can re-create her Malaysian dishes! I am the oldest child and therefore was the one asked to help most in the kitchen, so I have tried for eons to follow her recipes, but she adds her own love and energy into her curries, sauces, noodles, and soups, and that is just unmatchable. When I was young, she dragged me to Chinatown to buy all sorts of ingredients, from pandan leaves to kantan flowers to curries. It felt like she was in and out of dozens of stores (it was really just, like, three). She used to treat me to those moon cakes they sell on the street (which was a HUGE treat, my parents were very strict with what food we ate). Of course, being a temperamental, precocious child, I never valued this as an experience. But as an adult who lives blocks away from Chinatown and still frequents the same stores my mom brought me to, I constantly appreciate the experience.

MICHELLE HERNANDEZ

When I was little, the food on the dinner table was split. My mom often made two meals—one for my dad and my sisters and me, and one that she ate. The food that she cooked for us was a variety of different kinds of food, though much of it was Mexican cuisine; food that was familiar to my dad. Her food was usually rice, vegetables, fish, and maybe something fermented like kimchi or shrimp paste. My sisters and I did not embrace this food even though it was in our house.

It was only after college, when I started delving into cuisines I had never really engaged with, that I began to truly appreciate and crave my mom's island food. Living in the Bay Area, I was surrounded by people and food that reminded me of my mom. Ingredients started looking more familiar to me.

Now my mom's food is the emerging hipster food covered in every major food magazine, with ingredients that are also so healing. A return to and celebration of familial roots seems to be a common theme lately in the food industry. The kids of immigrants are now celebrating and cooking for others their food that was once only eaten at home. Today, I am a pescatarian and love bitter, sour, herbal, fermented foods. What my mom ate growing up is my ideal daily meal. My mom and I now share food and discover foods that are new to us, together. I am so grateful for the patience and openness that she has shown and taught me, two qualities that allowed me to embrace my food culture on my own timeline and terms.

ANITA LO

She wasn't the best mother, but she was a really great cook and instilled in me what it took to succeed in the restaurant business: a love of eating, a curiosity about other cultures and cuisines, a strong work ethic, and a certain amount of self-loathing that allowed me to persevere.

REGINA SCHRAMBLING

I have written publicly about her many times. She was mentally ill (schizophrenic, hospitalized repeatedly) but did her best to feed a too-large (thanx, popes) family with the knowledge acquired in the NYC public school system. She baked a sheet cake every single day she was among us and we ate half that night, packed the rest for school/work.

JULIA SHERMAN

I inherited my mother's penchant for acidity and bitterness.

YASMIN KHAN

She hates cooking. Throughout my childhood, she resented having to work all day doing a demanding full-time job, and then come home and cook for her family every night. Cooking was a real chore to her, another task to fit into her day. Remarkably however, given her disdain for it, she cooked us a homemade meal from scratch every single night. She worked in public health and had a PhD in nutrition, so we never ate any processed or ready-made foods. My mom made everything herself and made sure we ate healthy, wholesome, delicious meals. When I was six years old, she showed me a video of how pork sausages are made—it put me off processed meat for life! Instead, I got from her real love of fruits, vegetables, and wholegrains and the importance of cooking a homemade meal. Thanks, Mom!

CHARMAINE MCFARLANE

My mom hates food. Just the smell of oxtail braising sends her into spasms of revulsion that cause her to open all the kitchen windows in the dead of winter and light bowls of scented potpourri to cover up the smell. You can imagine her horror when I surreptitiously quit my Ivy League education and (potential) medical career to work as a pastry chef!

Priya Krishna

The first time I noticed Priya Krishna's byline was in an issue of *Cherry Bombe* where she wrote about living with a host family in Toulouse and fearing she had entered a horror-movie reality where her French father was an evil chef who was scheming to fatten her up for slaughter. When that story ran in 2014, she was working in the marketing department at *Lucky Peach* magazine. Now, she's one of the most respected food journalists in the country. She has written about meth addicts in Lexington, Kentucky, the demise of plastic straws, an Indian filmmaker whose videos of his father's village cooking became a YouTube megahit, and a Mexican take on the traditional cuisine of the Jewish New Year. Her first cookbook, *Indian-ish* debuted in 2019. I'm convinced she can write about—and do—anything.

 She and I talked about how profiles are written—who gets one, who gets to write it, and how it's presented depending on the subject's gender and cultural identity, and on the publication it appears in. Take a moment to consider those decisions—and who makes them—and then read Priya's essay.

Father's Day

One very hot July afternoon in Dallas, a sixty-three-year-old man named Shailendra Krishna drove down the I-635 highway. "Shelly," as his friends call him, was dressed in his daily uniform of a Hawaiian shirt (blue, this one), cargo shorts (gray, that day), chunky, well-worn brown sandals, and Bluetooth earpiece.

His car was full of laundry he had just picked up from his local dry cleaner (formerly run by his friend Sultana, but now overseen by a guy named Wade, a "huge, tall Texan, complete with cowboy hat, big belt buckle, alligator boots, starched denim pants, and white shirt," who loves to chitchat, Shailendra said). In his car's center console was a small composition notebook in which he had detailed every single instance in which he has gotten gas in the form of a chart, with columns for the odometer, the per-gallon price, and so on. He has done this for about two decades. "I just want to track gas prices," he reasoned. "And my dad maintained a log book, too."

His next stop would be Sam's Club, the discount wholesaler, and essentially the only place where he will fill up on gas—solely because it's cheaper than all the other brand-name gas stations (never mind that he has to drive out of his way to get there, thereby wasting more gas).

Then, it was onto Patel Brothers—potentially Shailendra's favorite store in the entire world.

Patel Brothers is a national Indian grocery store that, a few years back, opened its first location in Dallas—coincidentally, right next to a Sam's Club. This was a momentous occasion for Shailendra. "Patel Brothers revolutionized Indian grocery shopping," he exclaimed. And now he can fill up on gas in the same place where he fills up on mangoes.

Speaking of mangoes, Shailendra's first move when he arrived at Patel Brothers was wading through boxes of plump, yellowish fruit in search of the most promising ones. (It was peak season in India, which meant today's batch would be especially favorable.) In addition to Patel Brothers, gas at Sam's Club, and pizza, mangoes are a life passion for Shailendra.

He approached the mango display like a jaguar stalking its prey—focused, contemplative, ready to pounce on an unsuspecting Ataulfo. He removed various mangoes from their boxes, observed them for color and sap, then held them up to his nose to see if they were emitting any fragrance. He discarded several before settling on a box. "They'll be super," he said confidently about his chosen mangoes, and threw the box into his cart.

Shailendra knows the layout of Patel Brothers as well as he knows that of his own house. In general, he is a slow-moving man. But in Patel Brothers, he navigated the aisles with cat-like reflexes, grabbing boxes of idli mix and bags of green chilies as if his very survival depended on it.

"Persimmons!" he shouted, at one point. He had just spotted the endangered species of the Patel Brothers produce section. "What a treat," he said, his eyes lighting up as he gathered up a half dozen of the bright orange fruit.

He then quickly pivoted to the limes, grabbing about a dozen—he pointed out that he has a very specific strategy for choosing limes: he looks for ones with paper-thin skins, a characteristic that, in Hindi, is called kaagazi, or "paper-like."

And then, out of the corner of his eye, he spied his favorite vegetable, cauliflower, which happened to be on sale for only $1.19 per head. That's a dollar less than usual, he said. "I'm taking two," even though his wife wouldn't like it, he snickered. He reconsidered for a moment—there was already cauliflower in the house—and set the two heads down. Five minutes later, he made a U-turn with his cart back to the cauliflower to retrieve the fallen produce. "I'll make it today," he justified.

A quick stop at the samosa station to pick up a carton of snacks for the car ride home and he was en route again, spilling samosa crumbs all over the leather seat of his black car as he sped east toward the shoe repair shop for a final errand. As he got out of the car, he spotted his barber of over a decade, Mike, whose salon is right next door to the repair place. "Should I quickly stop in to get my haircut?" he asked, waving enthusiastically at Mike. But he decided against it. There were far too many other things on his agenda for that day.

*   *   *

This is about as typical as it gets for Shailendra. He has a wife and two kids—now adults. He is a principal at a sizable real estate investment company. But for the last twenty or so years, his day-to-day life has largely revolved around grocery shopping, cooking, and tending to the house.

In Texas, where he resides, and in India, where he's from, people like him—educated men of any sort of means—do not typically engage in any of these activities.

To fully appreciate the improbability that Shailendra Krishna cooks and does dishes (and rather enjoys both, as he'll openly tell you), consider his upbringing: He was born in Bombay in 1956, the youngest of four, to a father who was in the Indian equivalent of the navy and a stay-at-home mother. His parents were in their forties by the time Shailendra arrived, so childrearing was no longer a priority, he said.

When Shailendra was a teenager, he was shipped off to an all-boys boarding academy, The Doon School, in Dehradun, India, followed by the India Institute of Technology in Kanpur, which was not male-only, though men made up about 96 percent of the class. "They were probably sexist environments," he said. "But I just didn't think about it too much. This was the model taught to me: that I should have a wife, and she shouldn't work. It was ingrained in society."

But all that would eventually change for him—and quickly.

Shailendra arrived in America in 1977 to complete his master's degree in computer science at the University of Southern California in Los Angeles. It was the first time he had to cook and clean for himself, and he didn't particularly enjoy either. His favorite meal became "the taco guy who ran that taco stand on Figueroa." Tacos and burritos, he said, "reminded me of roti, so I liked it, all stuffed with spiced chicken and pico de gallo." He loved pico de gallo so much, he said, "I put the damn thing on pizza."

Pizza was his other favorite meal (and very much still is). He used to buy frozen pizza on a weekly basis and doctor it up with his own toppings—onions, cauliflower, Amul cheese (the Indian equivalent of Kraft singles). This was the extent of his cooking abilities.

He breezed through grad school, got a job as a programmer, and decided he would return to India to have an arranged marriage—the ages-old tradition in India wherein families match-make their children with their spouses. This is how Shailendra would experience the first major upheaval in his worldview. Her name was Ritu Elhence.

"She was young and open to adventure," he said of the first impression of the woman who would become his wife.

Of her first thoughts on Shailendra, Ritu had this to say: "He looked reasonable—like, I could get married to him."

But unlike her husband, Ritu grew up in a household where gender roles were far more fluid. Her father was a judge, and yes, her mother was a housewife, but her father helped with cooking and cleaning, her mother served as an informal advisor to her father, and the two treated Ritu with equal respect and care as they did her two younger brothers, Hemant and Sharad.

After their marriage in 1980, Shailendra and Ritu moved to New Hampshire. Ritu remembered that her first day in America, her husband cooked her a can of chickpeas and a frosted cake from a boxed Sara Lee mix. But for the next six months, she stayed at home while he went to work at Wang Laboratories, a computer company. Quickly realizing this life wasn't for her, Ritu told Shailendra she wanted to go to college and start a career.

This was certainly not what Shailendra expected from a marriage—but, he said, he was a pragmatist: He saw the benefit of two salaries instead of one. So he did everything he could to help Ritu build a career as a programmer, the only profession he knew.

Soon, Ritu was poached into management, and her job required her to travel to places like London, Capetown, and Sydney. The challenge was that at this point, she and Shailendra now had two young children, Meera and Priya.

This was around the time that Shailendra experienced yet another moment that would turn his life upside down (notwithstanding the birth of his kids)—the passing of his in-laws. The plan, he said, had always been for him and Ritu to bring her parents to America so they could help raise Meera and Priya. Ritu's mom, he recalled, "would always say, 'One day, I want for all my children to live in the same city, and in my old, retired life, I will cook for everyone all day long.'" Her kids would end up fulfilling their mother's wish for them to relocate to the same place, but not as she'd imagined it.

Ritu's parents died in a tragic car accident in India in 1992, when Meera was a toddler and Priya was barely a year old. "This is the only time in our lives where I felt dire and dejected and depressed," said Shailendra, whose parents had already passed away in the eighties. "We felt very lonely." So, they, along with Ritu's younger brother, Hemant (plus his wife, Sangeeta, and son, Hirsh), made the decision to move to Dallas, where Ritu's youngest brother, Sharad, had just landed a job at American Airlines.

In the meantime, Shailendra had realized that he didn't like the corporate life. After working for Wang Laboratories for a number of years, he had taken a chance and joined a specialized computer manufacturing business called Mercury as the first employee, and he quickly fell in love with scrappy start-up culture. He wanted to start a business of his own. But there were the kids to think about, and limited funds—plus, he and Ritu's childcare plan had now been derailed.

So, while Ritu continued to rise through the ranks of the software world, Shailendra made the decision to start his digital data entry company, Quadrant, out of the family garage, which meant he had a flexible schedule for taking care of his daughters' needs. "I considered getting an office somewhere, but it was more convenient to run it out of the house," he said. "It enabled me to be a father to my kids."

At first, it was mostly carpool. He'd pick up the kids every day. He'd change them into their leotards and leggings for ballet class and drive their lunch to school when it had been forgotten at home. This was all new to him, he admitted. His parents never actually parented him, so he didn't have a strong reference point for what it meant to be a dad—much less a dad who did domestic duties.

He didn't resent having to take on these new tasks, but "it was hard," he said, shaking his head. "I would often lose my temper. Sometimes I would have a tough day at work, and the kids were being demanding and I would say, 'Shush!' and there would be crying." There were times when he felt defeated—his company wasn't growing as fast as he wanted, money was tight, and childrearing was far more difficult than he could have ever imagined.

It was an adjustment for the kids, too, who, in Texas, were surrounded by friends with stay-at-home moms and were well aware of their dad's presence (and their mom's lack of presence) in their school lives. "I remember whenever I was sick, the school nurse would ask for my mom's phone number," said Meera, Shailendra's elder daughter, "and I would correct her and be like, *Actually, you have to call my dad.*"

As for Shailendra, "I treasure that time," he said. "In the moment, I was so caught up in the mechanics you don't give it much thought. But it was great that I got to spend all that time with [Meera and Priya]. It made us a lot closer."

When Ritu was in town, she did most of the cooking. She was a self-taught cook—her own mom didn't much care for cooking, so she learned by watching PBS cooking shows, recalling memories of her grandmother's Indian dishes, and relying on intuition. Cooking became a passion of hers; but eventually, work was so busy that she decided she would need to delegate.

That's how Shailendra learned to pressure cook dal, chop vegetables, and make basic sabzis (vegetables sautéed in spices). It was tough, at first, for Ritu to boil her instinct-based cooking style down to teachable techniques, but she came up with what she called "algorithmic" formulas that she thought would be easy for Shailendra's mathematical mind to understand. "Like writing a computer program," she said. "Repeatable patterns with predictable outcomes."

That algorithm was this: asafetida and cumin, followed by turmeric and red chili powder, followed by whatever vegetable or lentil was on hand. "I cook everything in that," Shailendra laughed. "It tastes good, but it is boring. Someone who has a dish of mine and loves it soon realizes I cook everything in the same fashion." But he doesn't mind the uniformity. "For me, the variation comes in the vegetables. So what if the spices are the same?"

Slowly but surely, Shailendra mastered the basic northern Indian meal. "It was very simple: make rice, make salad, heat up the tortillas," he said, and on most nights, Ritu would come home and finish everything up. It wasn't complicated food, but it was nourishing and easy to execute.

When Shailendra's business eventually took off, it afforded him even more flexibility. Cooking extended into grocery shopping, which morphed into taking care of the house, coordinating playdates, and attending school track meets.

By the time his kids had graduated and left for college, he had exited the data entry business (which, in all those years, never moved beyond the house), and was enjoying the semiretired life, which involved some investing but mostly tending to the house, going on long walks, and cooking—while Ritu continued the office life.

Since Ritu taught Shailendra to cook, he's developed a whole line of signature dishes—most of which are just adaptations of her recipes that he has crowned with jazzy names. There's "Dad's from-scratch pasta," which evolved from his doctoring of store-bought tomato sauce with cumin and butter. Today, it includes fresh chopped tomato, garlic, onions, and olives. ("The kids really love it," he asserted.) Also, "Florentine soup"—a white bean stew inspired by one of Ritu's dishes, which was itself inspired by a family trip to a farmhouse in Tuscany. "I co-opted mom's soup, gave it a fancy name, and made it more formulaic, with lots of pepper," he said, proudly. He has also gotten into making omelets, and dreams of creating what he called a "Simon and Garfunkel tribute omelet" (with parsley, sage, rosemary, and thyme, obviously).

His latest creation is ten years in the making—a fluffy yet nutrient-dense bread that has gone through many name changes. Its current title is "Krishna's World Famous Satrangi Bread," *satrangi* means "seven colors," referring to the seven kinds of grains in the dough. He used to use a bread machine to make it, but now he does it freeform because he thinks it comes out better. "It's a nice, wholesome stress control," he said of the process, before quickly adding, "not that I am very stressed."

*   *   *

Back at home on that summer afternoon, true to his word, Shailendra cut up the cauliflower for sabzi (it should be noted: his knife skills are exceptional). He filled a wide-bottomed pan with avocado oil and an alarming amount of cumin seeds, and added potatoes, chilies, and after a few minutes, cauliflower. He let the mixture cook for exactly sixteen minutes (he set a timer), after which he spooned the aloo gobhi into individual stainless-steel bowls for sampling. It was a little wilted and soggy, but the flavors were spot on. "Not bad, right?" he said, devouring his share out of the bowl.

In between making the food, he would occasionally step out to take a call or respond to emails in his home office. Recently, he's become a partner at a Salt Lake City real estate investment firm called Millburn & Company. He advises on new properties, and builds relations with investors. But the best part of the job for him is that he can do it remotely, in the comfort of his own home office, without interrupting his domestic schedule.

After a thirty-minute string of calls, it was time to make the dahi. In Indian culture, making one's own yogurt—or dahi—is a common tradition, as it often accompanies Indian meals as a cooling counterpart. Shailendra has been making dahi for three decades now and has a yogurt culture that's just as old. He doesn't really remember much about how he started to make dahi—he said he thinks it was something that Ritu's mom made, and then was eventually handed off to him because it was formulaic enough.

But, like all of his other responsibilities, he takes dahi-making extremely seriously. He donned his apron—a bright-red garment signed by Justin Wilson, a Southern chef who was known for his catchphrase, "I gar-on-tee it!" (Shailendra loves doing an exaggerated imitation of Wilson saying that)—and poured a half gallon of milk into a pot and set it over a stove, watching for it to boil with his hand overzealously placed on the gas lever. He is very paranoid about his milk boiling over, he said, because hot milk is very hard to clean off the stovetop, even with a good sponge.

Once the milk boiled, he added some of the leftover yogurt from a previous batch, and swished it around with a tiny spoon for three full minutes in steady, undulating motions until the yogurt and milk had become one. Then, he placed the mixture into an oven with the oven light on (the ideal conditions, he has determined, for yogurt to ferment). He placed a wooden bookmark on the oven to remind everyone that there was something in there. One time, he forgot this last step, and Ritu preheated the oven, promptly turning his dahi into ricotta.

The dahi would be ready the next morning, and it would likely be incredible. Even Ritu admitted that this is a skill of Shailendra's that she could never acquire. "It is the best dahi one can get anywhere," she said. "So perfect and chuck." (Chuck is the word she and Shailendra invented to describe dahi that is exceptionally plump and creamy—it is the dahi gold standard.)

Despite the amount of time he spends in this kitchen every day, Shailendra said he doesn't consider himself a good cook, and he has never once cooked from a cookbook. "The measure of a good cook is creativity," he said. "I am not creative. I keep asking Mom to show me how to cook stuff and she says no, because I will make it formulaic and it will always taste the same."

To his kids, though, it's exactly this approach that makes their dad's food so special. "Dad's cooking is the closest thing I have to soul food," said Meera. "Every day I ate whatever dal dad had made, his from-scratch pasta on Tuesdays, his dahi everyday. Mom's food is amazing, but in some ways it feels like more special occasion food in my mind."

*   *   *

In hindsight, Shailendra's life bears little resemblance to what he expected—at least compared to how he was raised. "I grew up in a family where all my uncles never did any cooking or any household stuff—it was always the aunts," he said. Most all of his friends from his generation followed suit and fell into more stereotypical gender roles, with stay-at-home wives and sons prized above daughters. He had no choice but to go against the grain: He had a wildly ambitious partner, two daughters, and a deep sense of practicality, all of which superseded any preconceived notions about gender.

As Meera put it: "He taught himself to be woke out of necessity. It's like those studies about how when you force yourself to smile, you become more happy and positive. He forced himself to do feminist things and now he is a feminist."

When asked about role models, Shailendra immediately pointed to his own wife. "I can't think of anyone who is a better role model," he said. "Look at all the things she has done and all the achievements and where she is today. She is part of the senior management team of a big American corporation," he said. (Ritu is currently the director of professional tax software delivery at Intuit.) "And look at her outside interests, and how she raised her kids, how she dresses so stylishly." He owes a lot to her, he said. "I have a more solitary existence because of the way I have chosen to live my life," he said. "Quite honestly, if she weren't there, I wouldn't lead all that interesting a life."

Being surrounded by strong-willed women has completely changed his perspective. "I have become more understanding of the challenges that women face. It's tough for a mom to have a challenging job and raise two girls. It's a hell of a lot for women to have that burden—especially women who work," he preached. "Society doesn't place that same burden on men."

He raised his daughters to be ambitious and independent, and as a pseudo stay-at-home dad, "I was able to assume a role that most fathers take for granted," he said. "Now, both Meera and Priya have different relationships with me, but equally intense ones."

His kids agree. "Mom and Dad's situation taught me that you can find creative ways to enable both parents to lean in," Meera said. "Dad didn't have to work from home, but he made it work so he could run a business and let Mom work. Opening yourself up to breaking your mental model of how your work is supposed to be is part of his personality. He was always doing things his own way." Now married, she added that she has never imagined a world in which either she or her husband would have to sacrifice their careers for children: "I approach things very much like *We will find a way* just because that's what Mom and Dad did."

Since Meera and Priya have moved away—Meera lives in San Francisco and works for Facebook, while Priya is a food writer in New York—Ritu and Shailendra have embraced the kid-free life whole-heartedly. They lived in the Philippines for two years so that Ritu could set up a branch of her former company there. They traveled across New Zealand, Greece, Chile, Vietnam, Portugal. They made dozens of new friends. They both talk of retirement, but still seem to adore working.

Despite this comfortable existence and all he has accomplished, Shailendra still buys most of his clothes at Costco, loves his ancient, dusty IBM laptop, and if he had to choose a last meal on earth it would be the same one that he learned to prepare for his wife and kids on school nights all those years ago: dal, sabzi, and roti. "Yeah, I know about umami, *foomami*, or whatever you call it," he said, "but I love most what I have every day."

∗   ∗   ∗

On that particular scorching day in Texas, Shailendra's cell phone pinged—it was Ritu. She'd be home from work a little early, closer to 5:30.

He knocked a few more things off his list: he wiped down the counters, did the dishes and readied to go on his walk—his daily form of exercise. To offset the heat, Shailendra typically soaks his T-shirt in the pool before donning it for his constitutional. As the shirt dries, it cools him down. "Like natural air conditioning," he said. Actually, it's kind of genius.

Then it was a quick shower, dinner at home with Ritu (dal, the aforementioned aloo gobhi, roti), and a movie at the Angelika Film Center. The two watch at least ten movies a month—largely because Ritu helps run a film festival in Dallas dedicated to South Asian works, so she tries to stay on top of what's out.

The following afternoon, this time in a slightly lighter blue Hawaiian shirt, Shailendra was back at Patel Brothers. After pulling into the parking lot, he sat in his car, deeply focused on his cell phone for about fifteen minutes before looking up with a wide-brimmed smile. He had just closed out a major real estate deal for his company.

"Now that we've placed 19.2 million dollars in equity," he said, "let's go buy mangoes and roti." And in that moment, absolutely nothing else could have made him happier.

A Conversation with Cheryl Rogowski

I always thought it was odd that I hadn't heard about the first farmer to receive the MacArthur Fellows Program "Genius Grant" sooner. Odder still, the food media barely seems to have written about or mentioned her. When Cheryl Rogowski received that fellowship in 2004, it would have been a big deal anyway, just because that award is one of the most prestigious, but you have to remember that, at the time, people didn't think farming was cool the way they do now. The new generation of young gentleman (and gentlewoman) farmers had barely begun to crop up. Plus, the Rogowski family farm wasn't in the Midwest or California, areas recognized as agricultural hotspots; this was a property in Upstate New York of all places. Again, definitely not cool back then.

Cheryl was born a farmer—she comes from a long line of them, and she started learning the family trade and pitching in as a child. Today, at sixty, she gets up at 3:30 A.M. to load all the trucks with produce for various farmers markets and community-supported agriculture (CSA) clients. At 5 A.M., she's out in the field, making sure her employees have what they need to start their work. Then she fills her van with ingredients and heads to the kitchen she uses to make prepared food for the farmers markets. She's there until midafternoon when it's time to make the rounds of all the satellite kitchens where she has high-school students baking cookies for those same markets. After that, it's back to the farm to bring in whatever was harvested that day for the next haul. Sometimes she works the market stalls and handles the CSA deliveries—those days, she might not get home until 11 P.M. It's a grueling job. But it's who she is. She's also an activist—the two come as a package deal—and it's time everyone knows her name.

Can you tell me about your history with onions?

Yeah, I guess you could say I have a love affair with onions. I mean, I grew up on our family farm and our region [the Black Dirt region], we were the onion producing capital of the world back in the 1920s. The region was settled by Polish settlers. My great-grandfather on my mom's side, Leonard Filipowski, is one of the first folks who came over here. My dad, he was first generation. There's German and Dutch and now, of course, there's a tremendous Latino population present. Our roots are still deeply entrenched in Poland. To this day, we still carry on different traditions, and one of them is the Dozynki, the onion harvest festival. My great-aunt and -uncle, they were the Lord and Lady of the Manor back in, I believe, it was in 1983, and I was princess for the harvest festival.

CD

You're onion royalty!

CHERYL

Our life was onions. I've often said to people, you know, if you ever walk into an old barn that's been used for curing and storing onions, the sweetness that you smell is just incredible.

CD

Do you guys still do some kind of celebration for the onion harvest?

CHERYL

It stopped. Dad died in 1999. (Funny how you measure things in life with death.) It was after he passed, or the year that he passed, I believe, the last festival. It's a tremendous amount of work, and my hat goes off to all the people that do it.

CD

Did you always know that you wanted to run the farm one day? Was it just assumed? Did you think of doing anything else initially? Or try to reject it?

CHERYL

It's funny, because there was a point in time when I was thirteen where I wanted nothing to do with it. I remember I was so upset. I was at the point of tears, because it is very hard work to be a farmer. Regardless of whatever it is you farm, whether it's animals or produce, each one has its own specific, unique challenges. I remember, you know, thinking, *Am I ever gonna get off this place?!* And then we had the most hellacious rainstorm. And I felt so guilty that it was all my fault. That was the end of my rebellion.

After that, somewhere around 1979 or 1980, I remember, my sister was in competition for horseback riding and she had to go up to Canada to compete. And my mother insisted she wanted me to go, because she didn't like how I was working so hard on the farm. And I was kicking and screaming because I wasn't leaving the farm. The harvest was coming in. It had to be done and I was staying and I was working. And it was so funny to have that 180-degree flipflop.

CD

And you never regretted it?

CHERYL

I never regret being part of farming. It's so embedded in my soul. I said to my sister the other day, "If I don't do this, I don't know who I am."

CD

When you first took the acreage over from your father, what was it like?

CHERYL

Actually, there was kind of a segue in between, because I was working in corporate America and my brother took over the farm immediately after my dad died. I stayed involved. I was more on the marketing end of things.

What was the corporate detour?

I worked for a real estate development corporation. I was there just shy of twenty years.

That's definitely a transition—from being in a corporate environment and office every day to going back to physically being on the land every day. What was that like?

It was intense. It was fierce. I never really left. But I wasn't out there all the time like my brother was. I would actually change my clothes at the office and drive straight to the fields to go to work. And I was driving down to the market on the weekends and all because that's what I could do while I had the corporate life going on.

When I came home full-time, I threw myself into the field. Growing up on the farm, my grandfather would teach me things. My dad realized that I could do better than the guys, because I had the concentration for it. If I didn't know all these things that my family taught me just by working side by side with them and just living on the fields with them—that took some of the pressure off, and put other pressures on; because I realized, in spite of knowing all that, how much I didn't know.

Had you talked to your father about the fact that he wanted to pass it down to you?

Our parents were older. They got married in 1960. They were in their late thirties, when, back then, you didn't get married—and have kids, no less. I remember my dad being so upset—people talking to him about his grandson, and it was his son.

I remember my dad saying, "I can't use the *O*-word because I'm not certified Organic," but growing on the farm without chemicals.

And I remember sitting down and talking with him, and he was like, *I don't want to see you work as hard as we did.* Because they had no chemicals when they were clearing the land and building the farms in this area. They didn't exist until after the wars. So they had to work with nothing except their hands because they barely had tractors back then.

He had really prepped you for it. You knew that it was coming. So suddenly quitting your job in corporate America and coming back wasn't a shock.

No. No. It was expected, I think by all of us. Again, my parents didn't want to see us work as hard as they had. But they also knew that we couldn't deny who we are.

Was it you and your brother, Mike, doing it together?

I'm the oldest in the family. So it kind of says something right there in a lot of ways. He's the youngest. There's only three of us: my sister and him and myself. After Dad passed, it was mostly Mike, and my mom was still around. She was the one with more control of the checkbook. And my brother was the one who was doing the day-to-day management—choreographing and taking care of things, and setting up the markets and the field management, and just running everywhere. And I was doing more of the local management—the local hometown farmers markets. I was more in the background, in the shadows.

Then that shifted when you left corporate America and came home full-time. Was it an easy transition in terms of dealing with your family?

CHERYL

It was easy and hard all at the same time, because at that time, my brother was so knocked out. It's fierce. It's intense. We were told thirty years ago by our extension agent that, because of the diversity of crops on our farm, what we were doing on a hundred acres—eighty acres is what we had in production—was the equivalent of running a thousand-acre soybean farm in the Midwest.

CD

Whoa.

CHERYL

Back then, already, we were doing the different kinds of carrots and beets, and again, most of the guys in this region weren't doing what we were doing. I had sunflowers; I had zinnias; I had the fancy summer squashes, pumpkins, which, today, are so normal—people think it's weird if they don't see that at a farmers market. I was doing jalapeños. I was told you can't grow jalapeños in the Northeast. I said, "Watch me."

CD

Was there a small community of people who got it when you were first doing it?

CHERYL

Yeah. And I give my brother a lot of credit for that. Getting us into the neighborhood of East New York and Williamsburg. I give him credit for starting the first low-income CSA in the state of New York, and it was in Williamsburg. But again, there was the Latino population that was the presence then. The demographics have very much changed since then.

I can remember standing up in the room—I don't think there was a man in the room. I think it was all women, moms. And I excused myself and asked them if it would be all right if I spoke in Spanish with them. And they looked at me . . . You know? *Who does this white girl think she is?* I proceeded to handle the conversation in Spanish, and I'm

good now, but I was even better then, because I was living it; I was in the field all the time with the farmers, and studying it in school and college. That's what enabled us to make that connection, and to crack those doors open for us to be able to come in and then start bringing in the different greens and things. And then, in turn, our farmers helped us and taught us and showed us so much about the things that we considered weeds.

CD

I think you guys started doing it in 1998 and CSAs had been around for a little while, but it wasn't a commonly talked about thing. Tell me more about it.

CHERYL

Yeah. It was a lot of explaining as to what it meant and what it was to be. We did the first low-income CSA and that was with Just Food [a nonprofit organization] helping us blow open those doors to make those connections, and because my brother was in those markets, folks got to know him. It was that evolution of connecting all those pieces that were critical in making it happen.

CD

It sounds like establishing the low-income CSA allowed you to keep the farm going and to continue planting the stuff you wanted to plant. A lot of people might see that as counterintuitive. They don't tend to think of a low-income proposition as a source of profit. But it seems like it was symbiotic: You were able to support this community of people in New York and, at the same time, feed the farm's economy.

CHERYL

Yes. I think that's a pretty fair synopsis. As we got more involved and tried different things out, that model didn't work as well because people were more demanding of what they wanted. I think if we had tried to do that at a different time, I don't know if it would have worked as well.

CD

What changes, good or bad, have you seen in family farming since you first started to focus on it twenty years ago?

CHERYL

I guess I'll start with the positive: The good things are seeing the number of people who have begun to embrace agriculture—and the kind of agriculture that we do. Because the agriculture that we do is so different than what folks perceive themselves to be familiar with and knowledgeable about, which is Big Ag, out in the Midwest. And I think folks feel that they are pretty knowledgeable about what goes on in California. But I don't think they really, especially up until recently, have acknowledged and appreciated what goes on here in the Northeast.

I used to go to all the conferences. I mean, I was always at conferences and when I first saw Eliot Coleman [of Four Season Farm in Maine], and I learned about the high tunnel production, I came home and said to my brother, "We need this on our farm." We had the first high tunnel. We were the only ones with this kind of production fifteen, twenty years ago. And now when you look around the valley: greenhouse, high tunnel, high tunnel, high tunnel, high tunnel. Again, everybody thought we were the crazy ones—"What does that onion farmer's daughter think she's doing?" someone said. I guess that was one of the negatives. It was, and in many ways still is, a male-dominated occupation.

CD

Were you one of the only female farmers back then?

CHERYL

I was one of the only women in the community. The women were always out in the field working. Always. But they weren't running the tractors. They weren't running the equipment. They weren't stepping up to the forefront in the way that I was. I was sawing the doors off the box left and right.

And people have come to appreciate that. I end up with a lot of young women working for me. And one of my girls, she just used me as a reference for a job in the food industry. And she said to me, "It reminded me of when you used to make us go out and look at all the vegetables and research them so that we'd know about them." She's doing that for food labels now. Sometimes there's just a word, a look, whatever—and to have that kind of impact and to see that progress. I'm going off on a tangent here . . .

CD

I don't think this is a tangent at all. I think there are lots of different ways not just to have an impact, but to feel validated by the work that you do.

CHERYL

Thank you for that.

CD

Passing something along to someone else and seeing them take it and run with it is a remarkable thing.

CHERYL

I've been so blessed with the people who have come through my life. And these people, these young women and men—the impact that they have had on my life as well has been absolutely incredible.

CD

Yeah.

CHERYL

One of the negative things that we are facing now is a crisis of more farmers committing suicide than ever before. We just had a farmer in Goshen—down the road from us, twenty minutes away—commit suicide. It's horrific what is going on out there. How can you survive as a dairy farmer in New York State, when you're still making the same income that you were making fifteen years ago, but your expenses have exponentially ratcheted up? How do you survive?

CD

Do you guys talk, as a community, about how you can support each other? Is there any kind of support system for that?

CHERYL

One of the attributes of being a farmer is that, in so many ways, we are very much solitary animals. That's why we're farmers. We keep to ourselves in a lot of different ways. There may be different levels of support, but that link of getting the folks that need it connected to it may sometimes be missing.

CD

But what about what's happening to migrant workers now? Do you see any solutions that you're optimistic about? Or do you think that also looks like a worse proposition in terms of how they are being treated and paid and getting on?

CHERYL

It's like an onion. Not to be trite, but there are so many layers to that question. You know, growing up, it was my aunt, my uncle; my grandparents were still alive. And we were very family-oriented on the farm. That was the workforce. Then there were the kids that I was able to recruit from school going on through high school. There is a woman who's been working for me, and her mom worked for my dad, clipping onions. We were in high school together. Now her daughter who's just graduated high school has been working for me for three years.

So that's one facet of this. It's a continual evolution of *Where's the next workforce coming from?* When I was a kid, the farmers were from

Puerto Rico. They came over from the island. And they would work with us. That's partly how I learned my Spanish.

Then it became farm workers from Mexico—from different areas. My dad provided housing. It was predominantly a male workforce. Some of them would follow the harvest. They would do tomatoes down in Florida, and then work up the coastline to us up here, to the apples and the onions. Some of them came just for the onions. And it was much easier for them. They just hopped on a bus or came across the border and here they were, knocking on your door. *We're here. We're back. You've got work for us.* And now I have farmers working for me, and their kids and some of their grandkids are now working for me. So we've had three generations of the family working for us in our operation.

CD

Wow.

CHERYL

Oh god, I'm gonna be really honest with you. And these are conversations I tend to avoid because of the climate of this country, and what we have to face. But, you know, these guys, they don't travel back and forth; they stay here. Their lives are here now. This is their community. And we don't provide housing anymore. They commute back and forth to us. They carpool. It's such a different way of life now on so many different levels.

But my bigger concern, too, is once these grandchildren go on—and some of them have gone on and started their own farms, which is awesome, the parents and the kids—where is that next generation coming from? I don't know. What are we gonna do? Everybody's scrambling for labor. Somebody said to me the other day, "How do I get workers like yours?" I said, "I don't know. I've known these people twenty years. I don't know where you get workers like this."

I can complain about it in journalism, but you really see it a lot in the restaurant industry. People don't want to put in the work. They want the overnight success. They just want to post some pictures on Instagram and then be like, *I'm starting a farm. I'm having a pop-up . . .*

CHERYL

I was looking on Instagram the other day, and yeah. This person, she's carrying on and crying about what it's like to be a farmer. And I'm like, *Honey, you've only been a farmer for two years. You have no effing clue what you're talking about.* And I lose my mind. I'm like, *You haven't lived and breathed through the floods and the wind when it actually blew your crops out of the ground because you had blackout conditions in your region.*

The year 2011, that was my personal year from hell. In February, my mom was diagnosed with pancreatic cancer. I remember calling a friend of mine. I said, "My mom's not gonna be here come Easter. She's gonna be gone." And in March, we had a flood. We were under water in the springtime; April, my mom died; August was hurricane Irene. I had eighty acres of crops that I lost. This entire region—that was our version of Hurricane Sandy down there. It was horrible. We were under water for almost a month. Crops were destroyed. Anything that was even near the water, the way that water looked, there was just no way that you could even consider harvesting or selling it. It came within a hundred feet of my high tunnels and I was able to salvage and keep going. And then, in October, we had Tropical Storm Lee, which was that godawful snowstorm. Happened on my brother's birthday; it was a Saturday. I had to go to Chester, another town, and rescue him because the motor blew in his truck. And it crushed my heated greenhouses that I had by my home.

So tell me you're a farmer when you've lived through that and you're back up on your feet again and you're still moving. And you're still working and you're still farming. Then you can tell me you're a farmer.

CD

I want to go back to something you said earlier—that when you first started running the farm, people really didn't take you seriously because you were a woman. Do you think that's changed? Or you think that sexist bias is still pretty strong?

CHERYL

I'm gonna say yes and yes. I think it has lessened a bit. And again, I come from an incredibly strong line of driven women: My great-grandmother was the local midwife. Her daughter, my grandmother—my mother's mother—was five-foot tall and drove tractor-trailers for my grandfather in his milk truck business. My mom, she went on later in life to become a registered nurse and a school nurse—and again, doing what she did, and surviving and guiding my father, and my family, and all of us in the way that she did. I have a huge legacy of female influence behind me. I'm so proud of these women, of what they have done and what they accomplished. And sexism, I think we're going to find it, unfortunately, in different ways, for a long time yet. I think it is dissipating; I think we're very fortunate in being located in the geographic region of the Northeast, because I think that forces different issues to be brought to the forefront, and the different types of farming that we do allow us to overcome a lot of these challenges.

CD

Something I was wondering is what was it like to win a Genius award?

Oh my god. I'll never forget when I got the announcement about it. I was standing in the barn. It was raining. We were getting under water again. Joan Dye Gussow [an environmentalist and food policy expert who is considered the matriarch of the sustainability movement] was supposed to come out and do a farm visit. And then the phone rang, and for once I was totally, completely alone, which pretty much never happens. And it was Dan Socolow from the MacArthur folks, and he's calling to tell me Joan's not coming. And, again, I was in the throes of, *This is a disaster. What am I going to do? How am I going to fix this?* He proceeded to start talking about the MacArthur grant. And he wanted to know if anybody was around. I said, "No. I'm alone." I'm like, *Who's this weirdo asking me if I'm alone?* And then he started to explain to me and did I know what it was. I was like, *No, I have no idea. I've never even heard of it.* And he proceeded to inform me that I was a recipient of the grant, and would I accept it. And he explained to me what it meant and different things. *Yeah, of course I'll accept it.*

CD

Who wouldn't accept it?

CHERYL

Exactly. And I said to him, "You have no idea what this means." I said I had just come home to the farm full-time, how much I desperately needed the help and support and all these other things. He's like, *We know. We know.* And I'm like, *How do you know?*

CD

How did they know?

CHERYL

Well, they keep it very secret, which is one of the reasons why it's such an implosion on society when it happens. You don't know. You don't know who nominated you. I've had people ask me, "How do you apply for it?" You don't.

You are nominated by someone. And then from what I understand and what I've learned, they reach out. They dug into every aspect of my life. They have to because you're representing them, even though you're representing your field of study and whatever it is you do. They said to me, "You do whatever you want with the money. You can go live on an island in Tahiti for the rest of your life for all we care." But they're really choosing you because they're hoping that you're not gonna do that.

CD

Why do you think that you were the first farmer to win it? Did they ever give you any indication of why they had decided that *you* should get this grant? And why to give it to a farmer?

CHERYL

Well they never really told me. But from what I have learned, I didn't receive it because I was a farmer; I happen to be a farmer who received it. It was more because of the social outreach and all of the other work that I had been doing for, basically, civic rights and just to make damn sure that somebody got fed that night. That's what I was all about and that's what I'm still about. I don't care if I feed you from my kitchen or from my field. I just want to feed you. And because of the strong activism that I had been doing at that time, and because I did it in this arena, and I used food as a vehicle to make it happen, I really think it was more that than *Let's pick this farmer.* Because I wasn't creating new vegetables . . .

CD

What impact did that award have? Did it change things for you?

CHERYL

Oh my god. Did it ever. There's the opportunity for speaking, people want you to write books. It was so overwhelming; it was ungodly. Even though I'm out there and I'm speaking on a public platform, my basic personality is a shy one. So to be thrust into that limelight like that was just unbelievable. It was intense and overwhelming. But the biggest thing that came out of it, it gave me a platform. It opened doors. It gave me the ability to be out there and speaking in ways that a farmer never could have been able to speak before.

CD

How do you think the public perception of farming has changed over the past two decades?

CHERYL

I remember someone talking about their family and how, when they would go to the grocery store—and this is right here in our hometown; they were animal farmers—their father would not let them go to the store unless they were absolutely spotlessly, immaculately clean-clothed, showered, the whole nine yards, because they were considered the dirty farmers.

And there was very strong perception of that. When we're harvesting onions, you can't even tell what color hair you have, what color your skin is because you are so covered in black dust. You look like you stepped out of a coal mine. In many ways, I think farming was considered work done by a dirty, stupid person—an unintelligent or inarticulate person. And I think that has changed. Some of the smartest people in my life have been the farmers I grew up with. You have to be a mechanic, a scientist, a lawyer, an accountant, a meteorologist. You have to be the community interpreter. You just have to be so many things to so many people all the time. And no one can be perfect at any of those skill sets. But yet you have to tap into all those skill sets, always. I think that there's more of a respect for farming, a much greater respect for farmers, which is awesome.

CD

You've been doing this for more than twenty years. What is your daily life like now?

CHERYL

It's changed a lot. And, again, it's something I don't talk about. I lost the family farm, because I didn't get the property tax in time. I missed the notices somehow. We've been going through a massive lawsuit that—yeah, it's ugly and gory and whatever. I have had to totally reinvent myself. From running a hundred and fifty acres with a full-blown café restaurant on the farm and all the different markets and like that, I'm now working on ten acres of land. It's fierce and intense in a different kind of way because I'm doing more myself. I'm really downsizing the amount of workers I have, downsizing the amount of markets I'm in—keeping things more slow, intimate.

CD

You seem so resilient. But I have to imagine that losing the farm was—I don't know how you would get through that.

CHERYL

It was one of the most horrifying things. I wouldn't wish it on anybody. Emotionally, it was just—and the outpouring of support from the local community around me as we were going through that, and we're still going through it. I don't know. It's like I said to one of my market managers, "Somehow you just have to find a way." Because all of a sudden, something will come up, and you just have to find a way to dig through it.

Evelyn Hockstein

Evelyn Hockstein and I have been friends since college. She knew she wanted to be a photojournalist from the day she arrived. When we met, her camera was strapped across her body, like a beauty pageant sash, only way cooler. She took it everywhere. When we were housemates, she was never home. She was out shooting life, as it was happening.

As soon as we graduated, she did what any hungry, committed reporter would: She got a job at whatever local (read: small-town) newspaper would take her. Two things I can tell you about Evelyn: She is not a small-town kind of person, and she doesn't like sitting still. At the end of 1998, she sold her stuff, bought a plane ticket, and up and left her post (in New London, Connecticut) for Jerusalem. Once there, she got hired as an intern at Reuters. Her timing couldn't have been better—or scarier. The Israeli–Palestinian conflict had re-erupted, escalating into what would become known as the Second Intifada. Her career took off. Soon she was covering the entire Middle East—including Iraq under Saddam Hussein.

After four years away, she returned to the United States for a journalism fellowship, then moved to Nairobi, where she began freelancing for the *New York Times,* traveling across the African continent and around the world on assignment. She has won awards and been nominated for a Pulitzer. Through her lens, when she catches you, she *sees* you. Her portraits of people—whether of white supremacists marching through the streets of Charlottesville, Virginia, or a female mountain rescue team in Pakistan—are hauntingly expressive and alive.

Ev stayed uncharacteristically close to home for this essay. It might make you think about the kinds of dining establishments—or coffee houses—that get media attention and awards, and those that don't. It might make you ask yourself what "hospitality" means and how a restaurant should be.

Community Cup

I grew up in Silver Spring, Maryland, and left for college three years before Kefa Café opened its doors on a shabby street called Bonifant, among a strip of local businesses. A gun shop, thrift boutique, and framing store are what I remember from my childhood. More than two decades later, when Charlotte suggested I check out a café she'd read about, it seemed I was destined to meet the Tsegaye sisters.

I spent nearly seven years covering the African continent as a photojournalist, making numerous trips to Djibouti, Sudan, and Ethiopia, the country Abebe Tsegaye and her younger sister, Lene, fled in the 1980s to escape violence and political upheaval. They traveled separately to the United States; Lene's route via Djibouti, Abeba's five years later, from Sudan. In 1996, they opened Kefa Café in Silver Spring when the downtown area was an economic desert, and when the city started its redevelopment boom, the business endured amid the influx of commercial coffee shops.

On my initial visit in 2018, I perused the thank-you notes, gifts, and postcards from customers, dotted around the shop. *Not once,* I thought, *have I felt the inclination to send a postcard to my local coffee shop when vacationing on another continent.* I saw the hugs and grins, and familiarity between owners and clientele; everyone who came in was treated with one of the sisters' beautiful smiles, or, more often than not, an embrace and a chat to catch up. I was smitten.

In 2015, a fire ravaged its interior; it survived that, too. "When it first happened, people were coming to say, "Can we help you with the cleaning? Can we move stuff for you? What can we do?" said Abeba. "There was a woman who used to work at the museum who helped put the art back on the wall. Other guys fixed the back wall and bought the supplies with their own money; they cleaned the place, put things together, and helped Lene prepare the place for opening. Isn't that beautiful?"

That same year, as the downtown area continued to expand, a new state-of-the-art library opened at the end of Bonifant Street. The ground floor houses a second outpost of the business that took a village to develop; a GoFundMe campaign started by three customers raised the necessary fifty thousand dollars in capital. "Of course, we couldn't come up with the money to build it. The community wanted us to be in there," Abeba said. "That shows us how much they support us and believe in us."

Perhaps because Kefa was initially one of the few places in Silver Spring where you could hunker down over a cup of coffee, it quickly became the neighborhood hub for late-night community organizing, a meeting place for local politicians to strategize, and a source of wall space for local artists to share their work. When the sisters needed help rebuilding after the fire or adding another business to the local downtown scene, they became the beneficiaries of the activism they fostered as their neighbors rallied around them.

There are two words repeated over and over by customers at Kefa, *community* and *family*. Their meaning is felt throughout the space, from the hundreds of photos of neighbors' kids gracing the walls and the mini shrines to patrons who've passed away, to the children's artwork decorating the bathroom and the regulars I saw on every return visit. The sisters cultivate this sense of kinship in their own interactions with customers and their concerted efforts to build relationships with those who come in frequently, and by encouraging everyone to talk to each other. Don't bother asking for the Wi-Fi code. Connecting is done in person, not virtually. Do order coffee, though. Get a cup of the Yirgacheffe house brew and introduce yourself to Lene and Abeba, and stay awhile. If you're lucky enough to return, you'll be well on your way to having two more sisters in your life.

"We became sisters because I've been coming here for so long and we know about each others' lives. I've gotten to know their mother. The last time Abi went to Ethiopia, her mom made injera for me, and Abi brought it back and it was specifically for me. How amazing is that? It's like family."

SUZANNE MINTZ

"For me, it's really personal. Lene and Abi opened this place when we were brand-new parents of an adopted baby boy, and we became a part of their family and they became a part of ours. When our kids came in here, they would go behind the counter and get an orange, but they'd have to give a hug first. Now they are 21 and 23, and they still give a hug first thing when they come in here. To me, it's exciting with the next round of changes in Silver Spring, to think that new families are going to discover this place and join the family."

DOLORES MCDONAGH

Dear ladies of Kefa,
We are now in our third
month of living in Montevideo,
Uruguay. There is very good
coffee here & them are friendly
people. But there is no
place that feels as warm
& welcoming & friendly as
Kefa. It may not be until
January, but we look forward
to being with you again.
Tia Westmoreland + Nick Olcott

Lena + Abeba
Tsegaye
Kefa Cafe
963 Bonifant St
Silver Spring, MD
20910 USA

"When I think about Lene and Abeba, the first word that comes to mind is 'community,' and the second one is 'welcoming.'"

SUSAN PETERSON

"They visited us in the hospital and brought us food and flowers. They always bring something. It's more like family, it's not casual. They call us to invite us to the Friday-night events at the café. Its a long-term relationship."

MARY THOMAS

FAILING UP...
AND DOWN

Have you *experienced*
a "FAILING-UP"?
What about a
"FAILING-DOWN"?
Please explain.

People keep talking about "failing up." The term originated in the tech world and is defined as per Kate Losse's op-ed in the *New York Times* as "to fail with an immediate career upside." I suspected this ability to achieve by stumbling was yet another luxury afforded to men and not something women were so familiar with, especially not women of color.

Women are expected to fail, men to succeed. When we meet that expectation, we're not given another chance; we were only being tested to see if we might be the exception that proved the rule that we couldn't cut it. When (white, usually) men shit the bed, though, a funny thing can happen: They can be upgraded to a bigger, more comfortable bed, with nicer sheets. A story in the *Wall Street Journal* last year (October 2018) summed it up in a headline—and sub-headline: "Women Managers Have Little Margin for Error. One mistake can stall a woman's career, while men's flaws or bad ideas are minimized."

Although Joann S. Lublin's article deals with corporate climates and executive-level jobs, it speaks to cultural behavior at large. The reason, Lublin wrote, women in managerial positions are unable to advance is that their "weaknesses are overplayed or punished excessively, while men's shortcomings often are ignored." Although "men are able to make multiple mistakes and not suffer career consequences," Joelle Emerson, the chief executive of a consulting firm that specializes in inclusion strategy and diversity, was quoted as saying. One on-the-job error can destroy a woman's professional reputation.

I'd imagine that if you work with the constant fear of fucking up, you wouldn't be likely to take risks or assert yourself—the kinds of actions that men are rewarded for; that male chefs, for example, have been praised for, and that bring them media attention and financial backing. But, as the piece notes, women who display bravado can be chastised for being too harsh, "not acting feminine enough."

It's confusing. Failure is something assigned to women. But because men get a pass for the same thing, they've been able to claim it for themselves in a new way. They call it "failing up," give it an underdog narrative, and present it with a self-deprecating humility perceived as charming and refreshing. I think this means there are two kinds of failing now—failing up and failing down. But I'm not totally sure on what the difference is. It might just depend on *who* is doing the failing.

To get some clarity, I asked some chefs and entrepreneurs to share their own failings-up and -down. I'm still not clear on the distinction between the two, and I find myself wondering if we (women) don't have the tendency to confuse a failure with a mistake. Maybe that's what happens when society has put the fear of God in you—like your entire livelihood rests on it—about doing even the slightest thing wrong.

JENI BRITTON BAUER

All failing is failing up.

NAOMI POMEROY

I'm not sure what this means, but probably. I've been around the block, shut restaurants, had a bankruptcy, landed on my face—and then rose "like a phoenix" (said by a reporter—not by me).

ALISON CAYNE

I feel like graduating from college without debt is the ultimate fail up.

ERIN MCKENNA

UP: I used to joke that I should write a book called *Failing Upward Faster*! I believe almost every failing makes you even more competitive, if you learn from it. I've hired the wrong people over and over again and have been scorched by trusting them. I would never take the experiences back because I'm sharper and more focused than ever. These experiences have made me a better boss and businesswoman.

DOWN: I've put an obscene amount of money into a location in downtown LA before the boom, closed the location, and then found out a couple years later that it's a highly sought-after location. That hurts.

CHARMAINE MCFARLANE

UP: I would say that my experience as pastry chef at two Michelin restaurants—A Voce and Dovetail—both of which are now closed, are great examples of me failing up: having landed both positions while having zero experience as a line cook or sous chef in a Michelin restaurant. Although qualified, I was wholly unprepared for the workplace politics at A Voce and the brotastic kitchen culture at Dovetail and my tenure lasted only a few months in each restaurant.

DOWN: One of my first pastry chef positions was as the executive pastry chef at Hotel Sofitel Philadelphia in 2008. The company had just begun outsourcing its bread program, laid off the entire bakery staff, and my only employee was six months into a high-risk pregnancy. To this day, I wonder how I landed that job except to say that at 50K, I was cheap, immediately available, and too inexperienced to realize that I was set up to fail.

MARISSA LIPPERT

I think the closure of my restaurant in some way has a silver lining—a "failing-up" . . . I'm just not sure exactly what it is yet, but I believe that what I'm meant to be doing—something that dovetails with what I truly want in life—is right around the corner. I had to close Nourish in order to allow the next thing to come into existence.

JOANNE CHANG

When I started at Harvard I had never really failed in school before—I had been at the top of the class in my high school in Dallas. In fact, I took sophomore standing—I skipped my freshman year because of all of the credits I already had. I fell flat on my face. I learned very quickly that I was now at the bottom of my class and I didn't know what to do with that. It took about a year to come to terms with being surrounded by really brilliant minds and I gave up my sophomore standing. And with it, I learned the value of being the best I can be, which is different from the best.

TIFFANI FAISON

UP: I waited a long time before taking an executive chef role with my name on it. When I did, I didn't know the questions to ask of the restaurant owners for whom I was working. I didn't know to ask about the financial health of the business, cash flow, viability of long-term success. Ultimately, I was brought on as a "last ditch" to keep the restaurant alive, which I didn't understand at the time. The restaurant closed later that year in a really painful way. I had to go on unemployment, which killed me. I used it as a time to gather my ducks and open my first restaurant; I refused to ever let that happen to me again.

DOWN: I took a giant job in New Orleans a year after Katrina. My ego and desire to stay in New Orleans and do good lead me into a job I just wasn't ready to handle. I felt so overwhelmed and so alone. This was just after a stint on *Top Chef* where people (very kindly) wanted to meet me and take pictures. It compounded my feeling of failure. The rabbit hole of my failure manifested in the oddest and most hilarious way as I look back. I remember seeing a case of mini Tabasco bottles in the room service kitchen and melting down about what would happen if we ran out. I literally started to freak out and tear up. Obviously, it wasn't about the Tabasco, it was me being in so over my head—but can you even imagine running out of mini Tabasco bottles and the chaos that would ensue . . . I still chuckle about that.

KIM ALTER

Every day I feel like I fail. Whether it is something small, like forgetting to order something we needed for service, or bigger, like not making enough time for my partner or myself.

OLIVIA WILSON

A few years ago, I moved to Richmond with no job and ended up working in a not-so-great bakery, then my appendix burst, then I got a tumor, and then I ended up working at a sandwich shop. I was willing to work and do whatever and eventually, I found a spot on the line at Metzger Bar, which led me to owning my own restaurant.

HOMA DASHTAKI

Oh man, I'm an expert in quitting and in failing. With every success, I don't celebrate because it usually just means more work, which is great, and I'm grateful for it. But the failures—those are a reason to party. To pour a drink, to really let it wash over you and learn from it.

UP: I make yogurt the old-fashioned way, which is illegal in California—so after two years of fighting the law, they kicked me out. I scoured the world over, from Oregon to Tanzania, to find a home for myself and ended up in Brooklyn, New York. I have no idea why I didn't just quit; I didn't really see it as a roadblock, but just as a stepping stone to getting to the right place.

DOWN: In spectacular fashion, I ordered two pallets of packaging . . . all in the wrong size. And there was no way I could make it work, so we had to forfeit them back to the manufacturer to recycle. Total waste of time and money.

The thing about making failure a positive thing is to turn it into an opportunity to flex your perseverance muscle. Success tests your perseverance because it entails a lot of follow-through and raising of expectations for the next milestone, and failure tests your perseverance in getting back up and moving on stronger and more determined.

ANN CASHION

It's complicated. I had two "nervous breakdowns" for lack of a more clinical term, twenty-five years apart. They were very similar. Both were restaurant openings for which I did not feel adequately prepared. Both were situations where I was in charge and the person who should have been providing all the leadership and guidance to the staff. In both cases my anxiety level was so severe that I stopped sleeping and eating. I experienced an overwhelming flight response whenever I set foot in the restaurant. And in both instances, I believed— really believed—that I could not cook anything worth cooking and that I was a total fraud. Twenty-five years ago there were no SSRIs so the condition lingered for many months, during which time, after I quit, I hardly left my house. The second one was briefer, a matter of weeks, and I couldn't quit because I was the owner. Thankfully, while I recovered my partner, Johnny, had my back and the public was none the wiser.

JAMIE KANTROWITZ

I used to work at Myspace. You remember that, right?

Korsha Wilson

Even though I'm not from Boston and have never lived there, I found myself reading Korsha Wilson's articles in the *Boston Globe* regularly. She was practicing the kind of food journalism I wish we saw more of—one with a social conscience. The reporting was done fairly, as it should be, but it got at the messy stuff: race and class, issues that have everything to do with the way we eat—which mainstream lifestyle media tends to gloss over in favor of feel-good stories about an up-and-coming pizzaiolo or a new grilled-cheese hack.

Korsha has no problem taking her colleagues to task for that, either. She's able to dig deeper on questions of representation and power on her weekly Heritage Radio Network podcast, *A Hungry Society*. Food is the thread that runs through each episode and every piece she writes. It also connects people and holds communities together, and I sense that this is why Korsha is drawn to it. Ultimately, what's she looking at is infrastructure and at the individuals who support or challenge it. Some loom large, while others remain unseen. Most of us food writers often feel pressure or are encouraged to focus on the higher-profile people or those deemed "newsworthy." But it's by virtue of assigning, writing, and publishing these stories that "news" is made. Journalists like Korsha believe that a society's invisible contributors are just as valuable—if not more—to its survival and success, and should be considered equally relevant for or "worthy" of news coverage. That's why I wanted her to contribute an essay. And it's why her choice of subject—and treatment of it—didn't surprise (or disappoint) me.

"Survival Pending Revolution"

n Montgomery, Alabama, on a street that's a five-minute walk from the house Martin Luther King Jr. and his family lived in, sits a simple, tan, single-story family home. The exterior is completely unremarkable save for a dark-brown placard emblazoned with gold lettering on a post at the end of the gray driveway.

It reads: "Georgia Gilmore, cited as a 'solid and energetic boycott participant and supporter.' Lived in this house during the days of the Montgomery Bus Boycott. Once arrested on a bus, Gilmore was ardent in her efforts to raise funds for the Movement and organized the 'Club from Nowhere' whose members baked pies and cakes for sale to both black and white customers. Opening her home to all, she tirelessly cooked meals for participants including Dr. Martin Luther King and Dr. Ralph Abernathy. Her culinary skills continued to aid the cause of justice as she actively worked to encourage civil rights for the remainder of her life."

Dozens, if not hundreds, of people, hungry for change and for Gilmore's Southern food and hospitality, passed through this modest house during the civil rights era. Despite intense uncertainty and fear, she opened the doors to her home and welcomed Montgomery in, offering a bit of shelter and respite from the discrimination that lived outside, in the city and beyond, across the country.

Georgia Gilmore, known around Montgomery as a "firecracker," ran a makeshift restaurant with a humble dining room that offered members of the community a place to organize, to fundraise, and to dine. It was a de facto center of operations for hungry civil rights leaders and the headquarters for the Club from Nowhere, a network of women led by Gilmore, who cooked and sold hot plates of food to raise money for the Montgomery Improvement Association. The name of the club was a reference to the fact that when people asked where the money came from, Gilmore and her fellow members would respond, "nowhere." It also acted as a reminder—it wasn't about one person being singled out as a leader of this endeavor; it was a collective pooling of resources. Gilmore was the president of the cooking club, overseeing bake sales and going to weekly mass services that doubled as community meetings with hampers full of food to sell to black Alabamans. "We would collect five, six hundred dollars a week," Gilmore said in a 1979 interview. In her kitchen, Dr. King and white and black community members strategized over plates of stuffed pork chops, baked macaroni and cheese, cakes and pies.

Pushed to the margins of society because of her race, gender, and class, Gilmore co-opted her stove to help create a future where everyone could be treated equally.

"There's something subversive in that," says author and Southern foodways historian John T. Edge. "She fed her family and raised money for a movement using skills that she had learned at the behest of whites." For Gilmore and for many black women at the time, the ability to cook well meant being hired by white families, their employers' pleasure paramount because it created the promise of a paycheck. What it never ensured was the promise of equality. Gilmore made full use of what white people would see as a valuable asset for themselves and flipped it, channeling her skills into an act to empower herself and support her community.

Before Gilmore was the president of the Club from Nowhere and ran a restaurant out of her home, she was a cook at Montgomery's National Lunch Counter. Confined to the kitchen, she and a team of mostly black cooks prepared a menu of Southern dishes for lunch service. The dining room, where white people could work as servers, held a seven-foot high partition to keep black and white diners from eating together. To make the two-mile commute to and from the restaurant every day, she relied on the Montgomery public transit system that required her to sit in the back of a bus so white patrons could sit in the front.

Through a careful and intricate manipulation of language, Jim Crow laws had put segregation into effect and made it a way of life in many Southern states; they codified wording that deceptively implied the goal was to keep black and white people from mingling. The actual goal was to make black people feel helpless in their own communities and inferior everywhere else. But the lawmakers underestimated the resilience of their targets. Instead, their legislation and the indignities that black people suffered as a result acted as kindling for a movement.

In October 1954, on her way to work via a Montgomery bus, Gilmore moved toward the back of the vehicle after paying her fare. As she searched out a seat, no doubt tired and hoping to sit down before spending the rest of the day on her feet, the bus driver yelled at her for using the front door. (Black riders had to pay their fare at the front door and then disembark, walk to the back door of the bus and get back on again to take a seat.) She realized her mistake and disembarked immediately, as dictated. As she headed to the back door, the driver drove away, leaving her stranded. What could she do? What recourse did she have in a city and country that didn't afford her the humanity of sitting where she pleased on a bus? "I had always asked the Lord if it would ever be—become possible for me to be able to just go around and not have to worry about going in the back door or getting up, giving somebody else my seat," she said in an interview after the incident. Less than a year later, with the embarrassment of that incident still fresh in her mind, Gilmore marched right up to Dr. Martin Luther King Jr. after service at her local church and offered her help. She couldn't be on the front lines—she needed to keep her job and feed her family, but she could raise money selling baked goods. As the plans for the bus boycotts came together at meetings around Montgomery, she thought about how she could contribute.

On December 5, 1955, four days after Rosa Parks was arrested because she refused to give up her seat on a Montgomery bus to a white rider, Dr. King delivered a speech at Holt Street Baptist Church to kick off the Montgomery Bus Boycott. As he spoke from the pulpit, Gilmore and other women from the Club from Nowhere combed the aisles, selling sandwiches of chicken, lettuce, tomatoes, and white bread. While her neighbors, family, and friends sat in packed church pews, listening to sermons and testimony for bits of hope that they could store in their hearts and take home like souvenirs, Gilmore offered nourishment of a different kind: simple food prepared in her home and sold cheaply to fill the stomachs of a community coming together to create change at any cost. The funds they raised were applied to supporting the boycott and paying for alternative forms of transportation like carpools for people to get to work, school, or wherever they needed to go.

When we think of the civil rights movement, we think of Martin Luther King Jr. and Rosa Parks and marvel at their courage and tenacity in the face of hatred. Their faces are in our schoolbooks and their stories are told as examples of what we can accomplish when we truly believe in something. What we don't hear are the stories of the Georgia Gilmores, the armies of nameless volunteers and foot soldiers that dedicated time and energy (and sometimes their lives) to supporting causes and fought alongside these leaders. History is filled with these overlooked women whose work was absolutely crucial.

Cooking, often seen as women's work, has long been a tool they deployed to fuel social activism. Community-driven events such as bake sales, potlucks, or repasts, have raised funds or comforted and sustained those engaging on the front lines, those engineering a strategy behind the scenes, and those who, like Gilmore, keep a movement running from day to day in other ways. They did work that's so vital—so elemental, it can easily be taken for granted, but it renders them just as valuable as the leaders they stood beside. What also goes unacknowledged is their commitment to the cause without knowing what its success would mean for them and if success would come at all.

Today we'd call these women food activists, a term acknowledging someone who uses food to create social or political change. The Club from Nowhere harnessed food's nourishing power to keep a movement alive. More than a decade later, the Black Panther Party offered a more radical version of this form of activism by treating food itself as a corrective for social injustice, and, once again, women did the heavy lifting to keep the operation running.

In the late 1960s, the Black Panther Party, a black organization originally founded to combat police brutality, launched social initiatives for communities across the country, including the Free Breakfast for School Children Program. Monday through Friday, neighborhood volunteers collected groceries donated by local merchants to prepare meals for children in a church kitchen. "It was simple," says Judy Juanita, a former party member who is currently a writing teacher at Laney College in Oakland, California. "We got in there, cooked breakfast, and served it to the kids." A study had recently been released that showed how important a healthy breakfast was to schoolchildren and how food insecure kids fell behind in classes, so the Black Panther Party created a policy to address the issue, says Juanita. "We made really simple stuff like eggs, grits, toast, milk, orange juice." Juanita, a young mother herself, garnered the ire of her new family when she started volunteering to take part in the project because it kept her away from the house and from them. "I wanted to do it, so I did." Like many of the other volunteers, she wasn't a skilled cook. "I remember some of the kids saying, 'there's egg shells in these eggs,'" she laughs.

Many women joined the volunteers for the breakfast program, seeing a cooked meal as a tool that furthered the advancement of the black community by making sure black children weren't hungry before they went to school and could bring the necessary focus and confidence to their studies. "The Panthers were never called food activists, but that's what we were," Juanita says. She refers to the initiative as one of the ways in which the party questioned the government's function in an unjust society and demonstrated how solutions to problems like hunger could be simple. "There's no reason why, in a country as wealthy as America, children are starving," she says. "It was survival pending revolution."

Revolution is never welcomed by those in power and the Free Breakfast for School Children Program was no different. Despite the fact that it supplied "stable meals" to black children dealing with food insecurity, J. Edgar Hoover, then director of the FBI, called the project "the greatest threat to efforts by authorities" in an effort to stop the Black Panthers' progress. Hoover instructed FBI agents across the country to go door to door to tell parents that the free breakfast program was a conspiracy to indoctrinate children with the party's ideology. In Chicago, police raided a future breakfast program site destroying the food and urinating on it. For Juanita, this is further proof that the initiative was effective and influential. "It was a powerful tool because it brought all sorts of people together and they realized that we were fighting for rights that had been denied," she says. The free breakfast agenda lives on today as a government program enacted by the USDA in the mid-seventies.

The lasting image of the Black Panther Party—black men with fists raised, Afros, and dark sunglasses—is an enduring part of the iconography of the seventies; what we don't see are the women involved. Just as, a decade earlier, Gilmore and many others in her community were part of the civil rights movement, using food to help advance their cause, Juanita and the volunteers that worked with the Black Panthers turned to cooking to substantiate their mission.

Juanita is encouraged by the calls to action from movements like Occupy Wall Street, Me Too, and Black Lives Matter and hopeful things will get better. As she sees it, "We're all Black Panthers now." We're all fighting against the unjust things we see in society, and food and cooking will always be a part of that. "All of these movements, they put something on the line to stand up against oppression," she says.

And just as she and the rest of that organization used food to underpin their objectives, women across the country continue that work today, using food to establish fairer and more equitable systems where they live.

Shakirah Simley, a food activist and legislative aide, grew up not far from the same churches where Juanita and other volunteers cooked as part of the free breakfast program in Oakland. Simley is the founder of Nourish/Resist, an event series that engages citizens in the California Bay Area through action-based dinner programs. Over a meal, diners write letters to their legislators, listen to a presentation about ballot initiatives in upcoming elections, or organize a protest. "Nourish/Resist is a democratic food space that centers the voices of people of color," she says. "It's about camaraderie, but also about doing something meaningful together." Simley sees her work as a part of a long legacy of black and brown women who have used their stoves to send a message. "Black women always find a way and food has been one of the few resources that we've had access to," she says. "Food is a gathering tool, but it's also a tool for justice and we've had to use it as both."

This may seem novel to younger generations. But Simley says it's one of the oldest tools activists and black women in particular have relied on. "Some of the most powerful organizing that has ever happened has happened around a kitchen table, in church basements, and in home kitchens," she says. Nourish/Resist is simply building on the past. "This is not a new thing," she says.

When I look at pictures of that placard outside of Georgia Gilmore's home, I know that the inscription doesn't say enough about the woman it's honoring. In a video interview recorded on the porch of that small house in Montgomery in 1979, Gilmore is fifty-nine years old, her gray hair arranged in a loose updo on top of her head. She's sitting in a small chair and her hands are folded in her lap as she talks about the Club from Nowhere and feeding architects of the civil rights movement, including Dr. King. "I served them food and everything and Reverend King was one of [them]—and Reverend Abernathy and Reverend Powell and all," she says casually, never letting her eyes leave her interviewer, who is sitting across from her just off-camera. "But Reverend King, most of all, was just like a member of my family, because the very things that I needed, he helped me to obtain 'em. And nobody, but he and I today know about them." This clip lasts only six minutes and there's not enough time for her to talk about the courageousness required to participate in the movement the way she did and lead a team.

When I see that placard, I also wish there was a guestbook of all of the people who visited that house: The members of the Club from Nowhere, cooking in their own homes, organizing and planning with Gilmore to help their community;

neighbors who just wanted to have some of Gilmore's food or heard about and wanted to support the cause; leaders who passed through town road-weary and exhausted. That information and the records of those volunteers are lost to history, but the collective efforts of those women are part of the infrastructure of the civil rights I have today.

And although I'm glad to be aware of their contribution—and inspired by it—I wish I could see those kitchens full of unpaid helpers who took time out of their day to cook for children as part of the free breakfast programs. How this project helped so many has been documented but, again, the architects of the program and the volunteers haven't.

I wish I could say that I'm surprised that Gilmore and Juanita aren't household names, but I'm not. I've come across many stories like theirs that make my eyes well with angry tears on behalf of the women who, for centuries, have done the hard work and continuously been marginalized. The act of a black woman using one of the few gifts that society told her she could have (and still, with conditions) to uplift a community is so beautiful and has been generously performed by so many.

Their faces and names aren't known, but the lesson—that each of us can apply our gifts to create the changes we want to see in society—isn't lost. We don't all have to be the spokesperson of a movement, like Martin Luther King Jr. or Huey Newton; we just have to show up and contribute in any capacity that we can. Lending our talents to our communities in small ways helps achieve the same goals, and that's powerful.

Cooking, whether the work of women or not, is a revolutionary act that has the potential to nourish in the present while providing a foundation for the future. It's a means of survival, but it can also be used to build a more equitable society.

And it will continue to be. "One of the few universals that we have as a society is hunger, so we can tap into that to make things happen," Simley says. And sometimes satiating hunger isn't all that's on the table. "There's not much you can do on an empty stomach."

A Conversation with
Devita Davison

If only you could hear Devita Davison speak. I don't want to sell this interview short; there's so much to learn here, and it's impossible to read it and not get a sense of the tremendous force of spirit that drives this dynamo. You'll recognize her mastery of rhetoric, but what you won't get to appreciate is how it works in tandem with her oratory skills. Devita, a proud daughter of Detroit, grew up in the black church; spreading the gospel is practically her birthright, and that ability to speak as though from a bully pulpit, even if on a milk crate or the telephone, was inculcated from an early age. She borrows the cadences and rhythms of sermonizing to talk about everything from the local food movement in her hometown to the ongoing resonance of the Great Migration (the mass exodus of African Americans from the farmland of the South to the industrial cities of the Northeast and Midwest between 1916 and 1970).

It may seem like an odd combination—an ecclesiastical upbringing and years of experience in lifestyle branding and marketing, but it has rendered Devita a superhero who inspires through narrative. She knows how to craft and spin a story, and she knows how to tell—and sell—it. This might be why she has been able to accomplish so much as the executive director of Detroit's FoodLab, which, to quote the local nonprofit's own mission statement, "is a community of food entrepreneurs committed to making the possibility of good food in Detroit a sustainable reality. [They] design, build, and maintain systems to grow a diverse ecosystem of triple-bottom-line food businesses as part of a good food movement that is accountable to all Detroiters." This ambitious agenda relies on activism and infrastructural development, and taps into the city's rich history of urban agriculture, while seeking to provide those on whose backs that legacy was built with the tools to revitalize it and profit from it. And it relies on Devita—on her vision, her persuasiveness, and her knowledge; she always does her homework and she always comes prepared.

I wanted to start with religion because I know it played a big part in your family. I think your grandfather was a preacher, right? And then your father is a minister?

DEVITA

That's right.

CD

I wonder how much it has influenced you in terms of being an activist and a community builder.

DEVITA

It has shaped the woman I have become in a positive and a negative way. When you have grown up in the church like I did, sitting at the footsteps of preachers and ministers, one of the things that you begin to experience at a very young age is the power of the bully pulpit—how someone could galvanize or catalyze a group of people that could ultimately lead to change.

I think that is the most important aspect that I take from religion, to this day, for the work that I do, Charlotte: Any change that is going to occur—I don't care if it is a change as it relates to shaping a community; I don't care if it's change in your neighborhood; I don't care if it's change in your city, change in the nation, change in the world—it all boils down to people.

Mommy and Daddy always prepared me with three things in life and those are a scripture, a song, and a prayer. Because when you're a preacher's kid, you never know when you may walk into church and be on the program. You always have to be prepared.

Being able to be articulate in a way that is inspiring people to let them see that change is possible and to be able to paint a vision that we all can follow, that's the first thing that I learned very, very early in life. The second thing: As I got a little bit older and more involved and started to read and

research history, I found out that the church in particular was always a safe space for African Americans and our allies, who were white folks, to do what's called movement-building work, specifically in the 1960s for the civil rights movement. The churches used to birth movements.

When you do this work, yes, it's important for you to have, in many cases, maybe a vocal, charismatic, outgoing, very articulate leader who folks can be attracted to. But the reason why I mention the fact that the church was the foundation of the civil rights movement—I'm talking about infrastructure. How are you creating infrastructure within your organization? The church gave me that as well.

I think the last thing and how this intersects with food specifically is because my father and my grandfather may have had this very visible role in the church. (Many men in the Baptist Church have very visible roles. They serve as deacons. They are in the pulpit. They are seen as the leaders.) But let me tell you something: My mother, my aunts, my godmothers, my grandmothers, they, too, had important roles, because it's the black women who were commandeering kitchens, selling chicken dinners, selling fish dinners, who were selling dinners in banquet halls that helped fill the tithes and offerings in the plate that also helped to fund the movement. Their work as cooks was so very important. This role of food, to me, was always so much more than just feeding people. It was about how to use food as a tool to make change, and how food can be used as almost a conduit for creating a movement that could change and shape for generations to come.

CD

You were saying that church had both a positive and negative influence on you. What you just described sounds incredibly positive, so I'm wondering about the negative.

There is a lot of misogyny. There is a lot of sexism that plays out, too, in the church. No better place had that played out than at the funeral of our great Aretha Franklin and the eulogy that was given by Reverend Jasper Williams. That, Charlotte, is just a bird's-eye view of what some black women experience every Sunday morning when they go to church and are told how women are supposed to behave, and the reason why we aren't married, and the reason why our homes are broken or the reason why our communities are the way that they are is because black women are not doing X, Y, and Z. It's this talking down to, this degradation of black women, more specifically single black women. Oh my god, it's even more specifically single black women who are mothers! That is a negative that has now started to rear its ugly head and people are starting to have conversations about that.

Sometimes I feel that black women in the church are not treated as equals, but yet still do the work. Behind the scenes they're doing the work, but aren't allowed to sit in the pulpit. You see what I'm saying? My daddy won't have women preachers. That's what I mean by some of the negative, too. That's the whole religious story. But I will say that everything in life has a good and bad. It is how you deal with it and for the most part, I am still very much so spiritually grounded and very much so understanding that the same guy who got my ancestors through is going to get me through and will get our people through as well.

CD

What it was like to grow up in Detroit?

DEVITA

Growing up, for me, in Detroit as a little black girl, I did not realize it; it wasn't until I was grown and out of Detroit, until I appreciated it even more: it was, *What did it look like, Devita, to grow up in an entire city where the majority of people looked like you?* Not only did they look like you, Charlotte, but they were flourishing. What does it mean to be a part of a city where your mayor, Mayor Coleman A. Young, told you every single day that you are valued as a black person, to be proud of who you are, and, by god, not only said it, but created a budget, had a city, put resources, put infrastructure, put systems, put money behind making sure that happened?

It is profound to me. Detroit right now and other neighborhoods, specifically in New York, whether it be Harlem, whether it be Bed-Stuy, whether it be in some parts of Queens, they are gentrifying so rapidly and African Americans are being pushed out of those communities. By god, I didn't even realize what it meant to live in a city where I was amongst some of the brightest people; to be living in the city that created the black middle class; to live in a city where you, your friends, your entire ecosystem of people around you grew up in a home, had two cars in the garage, grew up with mommy and daddy in the household, went to private school, holy shit.

It was a special time. If you know history, you'll know this: Any time black people in this country have made progress, there has always been resistance. There has always been a movement to not only eradicate the progress that we have made, but to take us two steps back even further.

If you take a look at the response to slavery, what this government did, it was epic. They ushered in something that was called the Reconstruction years. That is when they were going through and they were reconstructing this country in ways that white folks had never seen before. What was the response to Reconstruction? It was the Ku Klux Klan. It was also Jim Crow. That was the result. Then we came back at them. What was the response to Jim Crow? The civil rights movement. Then they came back at us. What was the response to the civil rights movement? Mass incarceration. It's always been a struggle in this country. So, what my parents didn't prepare me for is that you have to understand that this is only temporary, and we have got to make the best of it while we can. What happened in the seventies when I was growing up in Detroit is totally different from what happened in the eighties when my brother was growing up in Detroit. That was ushering in what we call the crack cocaine epidemic.

That beautiful utopian neighborhood that I just described to you got ripped apart, dismantled, devastated. That was his experience. My mother and father's reaction to that was like, *We got to get the hell out of Detroit. We got to go. We got to move.* That ushered in something that's called black and white flight, where they left the city and fled out to the suburbs.

CD

But it's what Obama was referencing in his speech at the University of Illinois on Friday [September 7, 2018], when he called out Trump for engaging in fearmongering and exploiting the same resentfulness politicians have been playing into for however long. He said we are in the middle of another one of those shifts—that the status quo is pushing back against progress. That's what's happening right now.

DEVITA

Absolutely. What folks don't seem to realize is that African Americans tend to be the canary in the coalmine. What happens to black and brown people in this country is usually what happens twenty to thirty years before it actually hits white America. If white America was paying attention to what happened in black and brown communities twenty, thirty years ago, they would have seen this economic anxiety coming. We experienced it twenty years ago when they did what was called deindustrialization and globalization of the automobile companies. This opioid epidemic and crisis, we saw that fifteen years ago with the crack epidemic.

That's why it's so important—this is what I tell people about the secret sauce of FoodLab and why it works here in Detroit. The outcome and the impact may not be the same in other places, and it's simply because you have to look at who started the organization and the foundation of the organization. When you let black and brown people, who are the most oppressed sometimes in this country, lead, the outcomes are a lot different. FoodLab never started out as, *Oh my god, we want to create artisanal jams and do what we want to do. We want to raise our own chickens and then we want to hatch the eggs and then we want to turn the eggs into mayonnaise and then we want to want to massage the feet of cows and make these beautiful beef jerkies.* It really started out of, number one: *I know how to cook. My house is in foreclosure. I can't pay my bills. How can I turn this hustle into a real business?* Some folks were like, *You know what, I'm a farmer and I am growing produce. How can I turn that produce into an added-value product that I could sell and make some money?* It started out with the intentionality being a lot different.

Could we have created an organization that looked a lot like what you would expect to see in Brooklyn or an Austin or a San Francisco? Yeah, probably. But that wasn't the intention at all. You have to really look at, when you're starting these organizations, Charlotte, not only who's in the room but who's *not* in the room. Then how do you get those folks at the table? Then here's the kicker, how do you give them a voice? How do you provide them with the agency so they can be in power? How do you give up some of your power to somebody else and let them lead?

CD

I think the most important thing is being willing to cede power. I think it's the only way that you see any real change or progress made. I wanted to ask you why you left Detroit. I know that you were in New York City for nearly twenty years, but I don't know why you left. Was it when your parents were like, *We've got to get out of here*? Or was it a separate thing?

DEVITA

When my parents left Detroit, I actually was an undergrad in Michigan State University. Then after graduating, I went back to my parents' hometown, Mobile, Alabama, to go to University of South Alabama for my master's.

It was when I was seven years old that I fell in love with New York City. I knew then that wherever the light took me, that one day I was going to live in New York City. Soon as I graduated from the University of South Alabama, I met a boy who was from Brooklyn, and lo and behold, I moved to New York City. I lived there for about twenty years. I have a love/hate relationship with New York, but like Carrie Bradshaw said on *Sex and the City*, "Nobody talks shit about my boyfriend."

I left because of a hurricane. I had purchased a home on Long Island in South Freeport. At the time, I was married. I'm divorced now, so you can imagine the drama that that caused in my very religious household. It was Hurricane Sandy that brought me back to the city of Detroit as a result of losing that home to a hurricane.

CD

When you got to New York, did you know from the beginning that you wanted to work in activism and specifically food activism or was it something that you eventually got into?

DEVITA

Oh my god. Activism was the furthest thing from my mind. My undergraduate degree was in social science and my master's was in marketing. I only had two jobs in New York over a period of twenty years—my first and longest job, where I was for about eight years; my second job, I was there for about seven. Then the rest of the time, I had my own business. But my first job was working in marketing for a pretty big lifestyle marketer—Ralph Lauren was the designer.

CD

Oh my god.

DEVITA

I worked in marketing for Ralph Lauren Fragrances. Then I worked for a major magazine publisher, Hearst Publications. I worked in their branding and licensing division. The things that I learned from Ralph Lauren and the things that I learned from Hearst were about lifestyle marketing. Lifestyle marketing is all about narration. It's all about storytelling. It's all about imagery.

[Ralph] created an entire lifestyle after every collection that he launched. It taught me this experience around storytelling and narration. Then, I think Hearst, again, was really about how do you codify that? That was my job in branding and licensing specifically. This is how I got into food, because I worked in what we called shelter magazines; these were all home and lifestyle. It was like, *How do you take* Country Living, *how do you take* House Beautiful, *and how do you create an entire line of consumer packaged goods using those titles?* I would pair up these titles of these magazines with large corporate companies like, for example, you can blame me for something that we had called Good Housekeeping Pie in a Jar. Yes.

CD

Oh no.

DEVITA

I know, I know. We worked with a company in Texas and they created a pecan pie that was probably full of sugar and just probably a few nuts. They put that in a jar. They made a box that you could turn into a piecrust. You throw this liquid into this piecrust thingie and all of a sudden, you have Country Living Pecan Pie in a Jar. You could also thank me for something that was called Good Housekeeping Salad Dressing, Esquire Barbecue Sauce.

Here I am in the early 2000s striking these branding and licensing deals with Big Agriculture, where I'm leveraging these Hearst titles, and my friends are in Brooklyn. At this time, we were going through a financial crisis, people losing their jobs. They're like, *We're going to deconstruct candy bars and make them all vegan and organic.* I was like, *Fuck this! I'm selling out!* When Hearst decided to defund the department that I was in, they offered me a buyout. I took the money. I created this hyper-local market [the Southern Pantry Company] and all of my friends who were making CPGs—consumer packaged goods—I sold them in my store. I knew already how to tell a story. I knew the distribution and logistics that needed to happen. Hell, I was doing it for Hearst. I just did it now on a very small level. That's how I got into local food.

CD

That's incredible. How, once you were back in Detroit, did that lead to the FoodLab?

DEVITA

All of my friends [in New York], they were storing their products in a warehouse that was in Red Hook. That warehouse got washed away. Because the warehouse was destroyed with all of their products inside of it, it wasn't like I could call a mainline distributor and be like, *Oh yeah, I need some more ketchup. I need more hot sauce.* I was just like, *All right, I have no house. I have no inventory for my store. I'm*

out. I got to go back and rebuild and figure out what I'm going to do. I came back to Detroit and I met the founder of FoodLab. At this time, she was just starting to put this organization together.

I went to a couple of meetings, and I was like, *I love this. I love the fact that it is inclusive. I love the fact that it's older, black Detroiters that are in the room as well as younger, white, kind of resourced, new entrepreneurs that are in the room.* It was very, very intersectional. She was like, *We really can't begin to launch and scale businesses if they don't have any place to produce the product.* I go, *I lived in New York. We had commercial kitchens. We had incubators. Where are Detroit's incubators?*

She looked at me, and she was like, *We don't have incubators.* I was just like, *Are you all building one? Do you want me to oversee that project?* She was like, *No, Detroit is struggling financially. We're on the verge of filing for the largest municipal bankruptcy that the country has ever seen. There is no money.* I was like, *Girl, what in the hell do you want me to do?* She was like, *Well, Devita, what we've been doing, right now, for folks is that there are a couple of churches that let us use*—I thought to myself, *Damn it, that's all she had to say.* See how my background comes back into play?

CD

Yes.

DEVITA

She was like, *I need for you to galvanize the religious community and to see if churches in the city of Detroit will open up their doors to us and allow us to use their already licensed commercial kitchens.* I started calling. Detroit was a city that's 140 square miles. At its peak, there were about 2.1 million people that lived in the city and you had the infrastructure in the city to support it. Now you have a city 140 square miles, infrastructure still here and more than half the population is gone. Where the hell?

It was these underutilized kitchen spaces that were just lying dormant in the communities that the people weren't using. We went knocking on church doors. There were about three churches who said, "Yeah, you could use our kitchen." Here's the beauty: Didn't charge us a dime for it. We were able to launch twenty-one businesses out of three church kitchens.

CD

Incredible.

DEVITA

We took a very small grant that the Community Foundation of South East Michigan gave us to see if this thing called FoodLab could even work. We turned that ten thousand dollars to, now, this organization that has almost a half-million dollar budget annually. This is why I can never give up on my spiritual practice or belief. FoodLab is nothing but a miracle. It started from nothing to, now, an organization that supports almost two hundred local food entrepreneurs, in which the community, 69 precent of them, are people of color. It's just that.

CD

Things feel so bleak to a lot of people right now and you hear that and you just think, *Okay, you can actually do some good*. You have to do your homework obviously; you have to have the infrastructure, but you can do it. I have a question for you: I grew up in New York City. I really didn't know anything about urban farming at all. I'm curious about what it looks like in Detroit, and in general, the kinds of farming that people are able to do now in cities that they weren't before.

DEVITA

I talk about this a lot as it relates to FoodLab, because FoodLab is the extension along the supply chain that really came out of this urban agriculture, this movement around urban farming in the city of Detroit. It is really important. That's why people really come from all over the world to see what urban farming and urban agriculture look like in a Detroit context, because we have specific assets in Detroit that you simply will not find in other places.

Detroit proper is 140 square miles. What that looks like from a geography standpoint is that you can fit the island of Manhattan, you can fit the city of Boston, you can fit the city of San Francisco within Detroit proper and still have room left over.

CD

Wow.

DEVITA

Again, a city that was built for, at its peak, a population of 2.1 million people and now only has about 688,000 folks. At its core, professionals, industry experts have estimated that probably about a third to a quarter of the city is vacant land. What that means is that we have land in the city of Detroit to actually grow. You're not going to find that level of vacancy of open land any place else within an urban context, I believe, in the nation.

What urban agriculture looks like in Detroit, girl, it's actually tractors that come. You could be driving down a busy street and all of a sudden, you'll see people out in two, three acres of farmland actually putting seeds in the ground for harvesting or tilling soil. It's not inside. It's not on roofs. It's actually in the ground.

The reason I talk about the migratory pattern of the Great Migration and how important that is to the Detroit story is that you have what I would call a repository of knowledge and information from the citizens of the city. Farming, agriculture, is a part of who they are, because they came from the rural South, or they came from Mexico, to Detroit, looking for a better job in the form of the automobile industry, but that skill around farming had never left them. They know how to farm. Right now, there are fifteen hundred farms in the city of Detroit. They may be family farms or gardens—market gardens, community gardens, school gardens.

CD

How many farmers are people of color? How many black farmers are there?

DEVITA

I live in a city that's 84 percent African American, so there's a large portion of farmers in the community who are black and brown people. The age of the farmers tend to be in their mid-fifties, early sixties. The gender primarily tends to be women.

CD

Oh!

DEVITA

What's surprising to me is that even though there are a lot of folks who are farming, who happen to be black and brown in the city of Detroit, as they begin to scale up their farming practice and really want to turn this into a business, that means they want to turn it into a market farm; that means that they are growing produce specifically for the market. That demographic tends to skew, now, whiter, because they get access to the funding. They get access to be able to buy the land. They now have resources in order to buy the equipment that is needed so that they can grow more, grow faster. We feel we've got a lot of work to do as it relates to that equity piece.

CD

I would think for younger black and brown farmers, too, it's something that you want to see continue. That's a lot. That's a big challenge.

DEVITA

Absolutely. The importance of Detroit in the world is that the city sits on 20 percent of the world's—not the country's, but the world's—freshest body of water. Water is gold, baby; water is oil. If you don't think that the world is looking at Detroit, you have another thing coming, because you really don't understand the assets. Also, not only that, but we have an international gateway that connects Detroit to another country, Canada. We were able to move cars all around the world, so we have the infrastructure to move logistically anything on this planet. All of that is why urban agriculture is so important in Detroit. We feel that if a natural disaster were to hit the planet, is Detroit prepared to be able to be a sovereign city? Do we have the technology in place? Do we have the expertise in place? Do we have the infrastructure in place so we can feed our own people?

CD

How can people help? How do you get closer to where we need to be? What are some of the most pressing concerns that you have?

DEVITA

One of the things that keeps me up at night is that I know for sure that capitalism does not see color. Capitalism doesn't give a damn about somebody being white. It doesn't give a damn about somebody being black, brown, yellow, red. It does not matter. Capitalism will eat up its own in order to keep growing and taking over. One of the things that scares the hell out of me—and I saw it in New York—is that capitalism is going to destroy every single thing that these grassroots, community-based organizations were able to create. What scares me to death is all of that, all of that thinking, all of that work, will be destroyed because of capitalism.

You have to understand that the churches in our community are losing their power.

More and more, the younger generation, they are not being embraced by the church; the demographics of the church are getting older. That kind of community activism organizing and, more importantly, the aggregation of funds, is not in the church anymore. How do we fund the movement? Where are we getting the money from? This is what I do know: I'm telling you this as a woman who runs a nonprofit organization where a large majority of my budget comes from foundations; foundations are not going to get us to freedom and liberation.

CD

No.

DEVITA

How are you creating that kind of model where the work is being funded by the people? I want to create an organization and then be able to share a model for other people to create an organization that's funded by the people for the people.

YOU KNOW WHAT THEY SAY ABOUT PEOPLE WHO MAKE ASSUMPTIONS...

What are some MISCONCEPTIONS about women who *do your job*?

HANNA RASKIN

If we [critics] don't like a restaurant, it's because of a personal slight by the chef or publicist.

ALEX VAN BUREN

That we [writers] accept free meals; many of us, including this one, do not.

SOFIA PEREZ

That we [writers] are groupies for male chefs and other men in the culinary world. There are male chefs I admire (just as there are female chefs I admire), and some of them are appealing human beings, but I'm here to do a job, *not* to go to bed with you. Take me as seriously as you would any male journalist.

NAOMI TOMKY

That our size has to do with our job, that we [writers] all depend on our spouse for money/health insurance, that it's second fiddle to taking care of our kids, and it's what we do for fun while they're in school.

KRISTEN MIGLORE

That talented food editors and writers are replaceable simply because there's a line of hungry people ready to take their job at any salary. I've been on the hiring teams for a lot of positions that require a critical editorial eye, a deep love of food, and a gripping voice—and candidates who possess all three are nearly impossible to find.

CATHY ERWAY

That we write about restaurants and, worse yet, that we have a restaurant recommendation at the ready for any occasion. That we write for just one publication where we have a desk that we sit at every day.

LIGAYA MISHAN

Someone once asked me if I ever had any issues dining with women friends who were watching their weight! All the women I know eat like wolves. (But neatly.)

KLANCY MILLER

One misconception is that women who write about food or cook only care about food. There's a lot that makes anyone tick. I'm passionate about food but also music, politics, social justice, comedy, film, travel, and the arts. I'm interested in all the bits that make up any person's human experience.

NICOLE A. TAYLOR

I think the biggest misconception is that all we do is stand over the stove all day. As a freelancer, you're writing invoices, creating a budget, pitching ideas. We're not just going out to dinner, going to farmers markets, coming back and cooking. A lot about it is making a plan and executing the plan. It's not just cooking, eating, pleasure.

EMILY FARRIS

I'm a food writer and a recipe developer, and people assume I love to cook. I fucking hate to cook!

I love making drinks; I love the challenge of developing recipes for publication and then styling and photographing the dishes. But you won't find me in the kitchen on a Tuesday night preparing dinner for my family; that's my husband's thing.

ALI ROSEN

I think if you host food television—especially as a woman—there is a sense that you aren't a "journalist." I came up through the ranks of TV journalism and then switched over to food and I still approach it the same way. My show airs on public television so I get to be inquisitive and my show is all about learning and teaching. But there is still a mental block—especially, to be honest, from other food media people who work in print or writing in general—against television. I guess everyone wants to be taken seriously, but in that capacity, I feel like it's a constant issue.

I also am really tired of traditional media thinking that hosting video content is not a learned skill. Every brand that puts their editors in front of a camera instead of hiring someone who has honed their craft drives me bananas. Would you hire a writer for a series who had never had anything published? Of course not. So why is interviewing someone on camera and coaxing the best possible story out of them in a visual and auditory medium any different? It completely minimizes the thing I have worked my entire career for. And I guess it is doubly frustrating since these roles often go to men.

WENDY MACNAUGHTON

People think that illustrators who draw food simply mirror the words on a page with pretty drawings. A recipe for peach something = a drawing of a peach. I suppose that's true of some, and sometimes true for all—but for many of us, we're less interested in illustrating text and more interested in collaborating with a chef and/or writer to find a visual representation of an idea or process that words alone cannot convey.

MELANIE DUNEA

I don't think the misconceptions [for photographers] are gender-based. Since the advance of the phone camera, filters, and technology, it is easier to take eye-pleasing photographs and become a "photographer." But those tools do not maketh a great photograph. Like cooking, photography takes a combination of classical training, observing, practicing, learning the technical, intuition, an eye, and sensibility. You can't skimp on this formula.

JASMINE LUKUKU

People underestimate the amount of tech knowledge that goes into running a food website. It isn't just snapping photos and posting the recipe. I have a huge basket of technical skills that I learned in order to be able to do my job. This includes CSS [cascading style sheets], html, SEO [search engine optimization], photo editing, video editing, and graphic design. On top of that, you have to stay informed about marketing and social media trends. Things are changing every single day, so staying current takes vigilance.

ALISON ROMAN

I'm pretty sure there is a misconception among some people that I'm successful because I have an "Instagram presence" and not the other way around. That drives me insane. Being successful on social media should not delegitimize your accomplishments.

VIRGINIA WILLIS

Common misperception is that since I am not a restaurant chef, somehow I don't know as much about food or cooking; that somehow because I write about it, that I—or women like me—actually don't know how to cook. I write books for the mainstream, for home cooks and yet I have worked, at least for a short period, in Michelin-starred kitchens. There are many things I don't know, but cooking is not one of them.

BONNIE MORALES

That we [chefs] can't handle it. That we just want to take care of everyone and that's why we are cooks. Men are more often viewed as artists or having some sort of more noble purpose. Also, specifically regarding business ownership, there is an assumption that my husband handles the numbers or the finances, etc. The

truth is that I absolutely obsess over P&Ls probably as much if not more than he does.

TIFFANI FAISON

Where do I begin? That I should be a mommy to the men that work for me. That I have somehow gotten where I am through a path that made it easier for me—my job isn't as hard as my male counterparts' job. And because my restaurants do well financially, I'm thrown into the "money hungry" bin of clichés.

NING KANG

That we need to be tough, strong, badass to be in the restaurant world. I don't agree that women must be, or at least try their best to be, masculine in order to succeed in the restaurant world, or as a restaurant owner. Some women certainly are all of those things by nature, and that's a part of their personalities and its great. But some women are soft and gentle and shy, and I don't think that should be a reflection of our work style. We are able to succeed with our intelligence, attention to details, sensitivity to people's feelings, and more . . .

ANA SORTUN

A big misconception is that women have to be "tough guys" and operate on adrenaline and haste. I think you can figure out how to be Zen and run a restaurant with kindness *and* still have a sense of urgency, get things done, and crush it.

TAMAR ADLER

I never liked the badassery part of being a female chef, and I liked when, getting to Chez Panisse [CP], we (men and women alike) were encouraged to ask for help. Before that, I'd tried to lift heavy things alone, be as strong as I possibly could, show no pain. But I think that's a really big problem. Being able to show pain, vulnerability, need, and also be an expert, be a boss, be skilled, be good at your job—well, that's where it is. Neither women nor men should have to be invulnerable superheroes to be respected. I thought my burns—forearms mostly—were cool when I got to CP. After a couple of months, one of the chefs, a woman, told me she had taught herself simply never to get burned and never to get cut. Like, the badges of hard work and hot ovens were a bit tawdry to her. The real class was in being so good that they didn't touch you. She never lifted a heavy compost bin or a whole lamb or half pig alone, but calmly asked for help. She was never exhausted, never burned, never depleted, angry, dirty. She took care of herself and took care of the kitchen. I liked that.

RACHEL BOSSETT

That we're either weak, fragile little ladies or bitches. We aren't allowed to be truly human and complex, we're just either weak or a bitch.

DIANNA DAOHEUNG

That we are bitches and emotional. I am very even-emotioned and level-headed. I'm not a yeller; I am a teacher.

MASHAMA BAILEY

That we can't handle the pressure or that we cry in the walk-in when we have a bad day. Women aren't the only ones crying in the walk-in.

NICOLE ADRIENNE PONSECA

My existence is unusual and a novelty and, therefore, previously inconceivable, which is in and of itself a misconception. The result of my existence and my accomplishments pushes what's possible and disproves misconceptions daily. Who am I? I'm a woman of color who owns and runs two restaurants in a predominantly male industry, in NYC, which has a 90 percent failure rate after year one; I have ushered in mainstream recognition for a formerly marginalized cuisine; and I have an agent who was able to negotiate a fabulous publishing [cookbook] deal with a renowned publisher. On almost every one of these accounts, my existence is a misconception of what's possible. I know this and speak this as true because I am almost consistently reminded when I meet people who are surprised or congratulate me, or by my friends who remind me when I'm feeling down or lost.

CHARMAINE MCFARLANE

People think that women work in pastry because we can't handle the speed and pressure of cooking on the savory/hot line. They couldn't be more wrong. I initially pursued a career in pastry because I was bored with listening to my male cooks boasting about "the size of their knives" and later switched to pastry because the quiet discipline and precise nature of pastry work reflected my interest in creating culinary art with scientific precision.

UMBER AHMAD

Because so many people, both men and women, bake at home, there is an assumption that what we do in pastry is the same as baking brownies at home. There is a misconception about women in pastry that we are taking the easy route, the more female-appropriate position in the kitchen. In fact, what we do is as difficult, intense, commitment-heavy, and creative as any other role in the culinary universe. Even more insulting is when someone says they can do what we do better because they have read the back of a bag of chocolate chips. I invite every one of those people to build a multi-million-dollar enterprise on that fucking cookie. It is a Herculean task for any human being, male or female. Don't assume because I am a woman and I can bake that it somehow takes me out of the running to take the pole position.

ERIN MCKENNA

That we're nice, hobbyists, not interested in the business side of the job. That what we do is easy and fun.

CHRISTINA TOSI

That we know what we're doing every minute of the day . . . and that we don't know what we're doing any minute of the day . . .

That we have too much emotion or are emotionless.

That we talk too much.

That we like/need too much detail.

That we're too risk-averse.

JENI BRITTON BAUER

That we are crafters.

CAROLINE FIDANZA

That they are not supported and valued. I think plenty of businesses really value the work of women and seek them out. This story could use more attention.

Charlotte Druckman

Gael and Mimi

Everyone loves a good catfight. Talons curled, zingers thrown, vendettas pursued, reputations trashed. It's a death match that plays out on the public stage, ending in social or professional annihilation. Some prefer *girl fight*. The terms are interchangeable and equally demeaning.

No matter their appellation, female feuds are rarely portrayed in a positive light. While men make each other greater through competition, women wind up in a swimming pool, tearing each other's hair out—or wigs off—sodden, sequined gowns stuck to their bodies, high heels floating on the surface of the water. They have Hector and Achilles; for us, it's Alexis Carrington Colby and Krystle Carrington.* Men, we are told, are always only in competition with themselves; a rivalry helps each become his best self. Women, ever objectified, are in competition for the purpose of entertainment.

Catfights distract us from the talents or achievements of the brawlers. They reduce legacies to gossip items, and icons to the butt of a joke. Often at the expense of their significant cultural contributions, we continue to pit women against each other in service of a narrative that panders to its audience's worst inclinations. Which is why, when I heard about a feud between two of America's most important restaurant critics, who happen to be women, some part of me wanted all the salacious details, as I'd been primed to. Another part suspected it had been greatly exaggerated or manufactured. So, I pushed it to the back of my mind.

That is, until I came across a story written by critic Robert Sietsema for the *Columbia Journalism Review* on the history of restaurant criticism. Craig Claiborne, Sietsema acknowledged, is "generally credited with being the inventor of the modern restaurant review," which is true.† In 1962, Claiborne borrowed the model of the French Michelin Guide and "established an ethical and procedural framework for restaurant reviewing." Now, there would be a single reviewer assessing each restaurant; his byline would be attached to the work; he'd visit the establishment numerous times, with multiple guests, to get at more items on the menu; ideally, he would pay his own way (courtesy of the publication that employed him); and he would do his very best to stay incognito. A year later, again following the Michelin

---

* As played, respectively, famously, and deliciously, by Joan Collins and Linda Evans in the epic prime-time soap of the 1980s, *Dynasty*.

† True in the sense that he is so credited, and that his system for reviewing is still considered the official, journalism-approved one. But he did not "invent" restaurant criticism and was not the first to practice it in America.

tradition, Claiborne instituted the star-rating system, which the *New York Times* continues to use to this day.

The next critic to arrive on the scene, as set by Sietsema, was Gael Greene, who "made a splash" at the newly launched *New York* magazine in 1968. "Her previous experience was writing for such fashion magazines as *Cosmopolitan* and *Ladies' Home Journal*"—mostly correct (the full title of the latter, *Ladies Home Journal and Practical Housekeeper*, should tell you that this was not a publication about fashion)—"and she introduced a flamboyance of prose to restaurant reviewing"—a fair assessment. "After Gael Greene," Sietsema wrote, "the restaurant review would never be the same." This, too, is true. But then he continues: "When Mimi Sheraton succeeded Claiborne as the *Times'* critic in 1975,* it was clear that the paper was at least partly trying to clone Greene. Handy in the kitchen, she'd earlier published *The Seducer's Cookbook*, which had a sexual zing never before seen in a book of recipes"—I stopped reading. The idea that Sheraton would ever be described as a clone of Gael Greene was almost funny—almost, because of the underlying offense in it.

Somehow, as soon as there were two women in the game, they could only exist by comparison to, or in competition with each other. Anyone who has read Sheraton's and Greene's prose (not to mention their reviews)—and this includes Sietsema who, himself, goes on to describe Sheraton's brand of criticism and its lasting impression on that discipline—should call balderdash on this.

A few paragraphs later, he landed on the next critic—Ruth Reichl—to take Claiborne's blueprint in a new direction without moving its bearing walls. "So Craig Claiborne built the foundation of professionalism. Gael Greene and Mimi Sheraton gussied it up and infused it with sensuality. And when Ruth Reichl, a Greenwich Village native, came to the *Times* in 1993 after a nine-year stint as food editor at the *Los Angeles Times*, three of them spent as restaurant critic, she turned the restaurant review into a bona fide literary form." We are in agreement on Reichl's towering accomplishment. Once again, though, there's the cursory bundling of Greene and Sheraton, and related claim of "sensuality" (not to mention the effeminate and trivializing overtones of the expression "gussied it up").

Still, these were minor violations. I clocked them and moved on. I was reminded of them while reading yet another essay outlining the history of restaurant criticism by yet another man. This time it was Kevin Alexander in a piece for *Thrillist* titled "Finding Pete Wells: A Search for America's Restaurant Critic." He summarized Sietsema's overview and covered Greene and Sheraton in the following three sentences. "In 1968, Gael Greene became the restaurant critic for *New York* magazine, and wrote with voice. People seemed to like that. The *Times* took notice

---

*Sheraton filled in for her predecessor, John Canaday, when he went on vacation in 1975, but she wasn't officially hired as the *Times'* restaurant critic until 1976.

and hired Mimi Sheraton in 1975, and she changed the game again, jumping off of Greene's more flowery, descriptive style to do longer reviews that sought to give context as well as describe all the foods she was eating." At least he removed the "cloning" reference, although the insinuation is there, and he saved space—and sidestepped my outrage—by not attempting to suggest that these women were hired for their writing sex-appeal.

Neither Sietsema nor Alexander alluded to a rivalry, but both implied they were vying, if not for selling sex in the name of restaurant criticism, then for appealing to a readership less through professional expertise than a shared manner of writing. It's an oversimplification that overlooks how distinct their styles were to each of them. Worse, it offers a limited and limiting view of their separate effects on a genre that hadn't actually changed much since Claiborne had instituted the system and its parameters.

To see their contributions reduced to a couple of sentences in the next annotated timeline would be an insult to their talents, a major omission in the history of food writing, and a loss for those who might wish to follow in their footsteps.

So let's go back to the beginning and set the record straight.

Craig Claiborne had, as William Grimes (the *New York Times* critic from 1999 to 2003) said, "found himself writing about restaurants as his journalistic mission and then formalized it." He did not, it has been noted, relish the task, which is something you might pick up on if you revisit his write-ups. They're what my grandmother would call dry, what I call boring, and what Grimes calls "straightforward and unadorned." (To be fair, it was a different era and food hadn't yet become a cultural fetish the way it did later, in the eighties.) Claiborne "ticked off boxes in a lot of cases and tended to just tell you what was on the menu. He'd say good, bad, or indifferent, but he didn't spend a lot of time trying to get across the experience or what the flavor was like or any of that. It was more like he was doing a tour of inspection," Grimes said.

Looking beyond food coverage, journalism, in general, had been plodding along on a "straightforward and unadorned" course. But, at around the time Claiborne began ticking off his boxes, a group of writers (male, with few exceptions) began to push against the established, stilted manner of reporting news. Norman Mailer, Hunter S. Thompson, Gay Talese, Tom Wolfe, and the rest of their literary brat pack freed up the language and the constraining structure of reportage by introducing narrative techniques associated with fiction. "They liberated journalism from the gray slog that caused the *Times* to always be referred to as 'The Gray Lady,'" Grimes said. These slog-bound correspondents, he explained, "all came out of the same school of writing for the Associated Press, which has its great merit—they tend to be accurate, thorough, they were dogged, all those things that are good for journalism, but the sort of color and character and scene and dialog, all those? Sort of the pleasure principle was totally ignored. They didn't really care about that, but this whole generation came along that chafed at the restrictions. They opened it up."

And *now*, enter Gael Greene. Born and bred in Detroit, she discovered her lust for life—and lust, period—at an early age. She was, and still is, a woman of boundless appetite. "I am certain I was born hungry," she wrote in her perfectly titled 2006 memoir, *Insatiable* (it was a double entendre; Clay Felker, editor in chief of *New York*, named Greene's column Insatiable Critic). "I could never get enough attention, enough love, or enough peanut butter." Unable to find a New York newspaper to hire her out of college, she stayed at home and began writing for the United Press International, convincing the higher-ups to let her do things like cover Elvis Presley's press conference (spoiler: she ended up sleeping with him and, before leaving his hotel room the next morning, ordered him a fried egg sandwich, which is the one thing she remembers from the entire episode).

Finally, she was granted a tryout at the *New York Post* that turned into a job on the rewrite desk. From there, she freelanced for *Ladies' Home Journal, Cosmopolitan,* and *McCall's,* writing profiles and the kinds of service-driven articles that are the backbone of women's lifestyle magazines, like "How the World's Great Beauties Stay Beautiful." But she also filed a piece on Henri Soulé (the owner of the famous fancy French restaurant La Côte Basque), for Felker, before he relaunched *New York* as an independent publication, when it was still the Sunday supplement to the soon-to-fold *New York Herald Tribune*. It was, she wrote, "a long, juicy, play-by-play" of what was going on behind the scenes of the restaurant's reopening. This was why, Greene presumes, once the magazine was reborn in 1968, Felker called her up and persuaded her to be its restaurant critic.

In her memoir, she claimed, self-mockingly, the reason she said yes was Felker's casually mentioning that the magazine would pay for all the critic's meals. But she wasn't sure she qualified as the "food person," let alone critic, he believed her to be. "I cooked and entertained and read food criticism. I was interested in food," the still-coquettish, eighty-five-year-old forever-blonde told me over lunch at the café above the original Fairway Market on the Upper West Side, a stone's throw from her apartment. "I was a newspaper reporter, so I didn't think of myself as a restaurant critic until Clay Felker called and asked me. . . . I never thought of it." What made her accept his offer, in truth, was the prospect of what the job would allow her to do as a writer. She didn't have a clear vision of what restaurant criticism would become in her hands, but she knew it would allow her to develop a *voice*. "When I agreed to review restaurants for *New York* magazine," she said, "I just liked the idea that I could write in any way I wanted to, and I could do something like Tom Wolfe—unique, and in my own voice." There have been legions of writers who have tried (badly) to imitate that Wolfian style. But Greene is no copycat. She wanted to enjoy the same freedom he had and that he and his contemporaries had afforded others.

Claiborne was her benchmark, and she insisted on playing by his rules—remaining anonymous, visiting a reviewed establishment at least three times, and footing the bill. She was also influenced by *Women's Wear Daily* and its publisher, John Fairchild. In his Eye column, printed "in the days before professional gossips multiplied like gerbils," he was the all-seeing, all-knowing, all-telling chronicler of the life and times of the fashion world's movers and shakers, she wrote in *Insatiable*. Greene didn't have the corresponding knowledge (yet) to apply his strategy to the denizens of the restaurant industry, but she "was a reporter after all" and she "could write the who, where, what, and why." And she knew the "sociology of Manhattan dining" thanks to her years of reading Fairchild.

The food and its underpinnings would always come first, but providing a sociological context would be one of the defining aspects of her criticism. It was a stroke of genius, not just in its entertainment value, but because it was so perfectly attuned to the magazine in which it appeared. *New York* instantly became the must-read of the cognoscenti. The response to Felker's reboot, Greene wrote, was "staggering." The title had "only a few hundred thousand readers, but they were the most outspoken, influential readers in town." A dining column that rated a restaurant while also providing a kind of culinary map of the stars might not be what you'd expect from the *Times*, or from anywhere else, really. Greene invented a form of restaurant criticism that was as much a reflection of her as it was of what, today, we would call *New York's* "platform."

For all that, it's her literary voice—with, she described, "all the pauses, the verbal acrobatics, and the tics and parenthesis"—that stands out. Sensuous, tongue-in-cheek, and anything but concise, with a quickening pulse, it was crammed with social commentary, pop cultural references (high and low), and, yes, detailed observations about the kitchen's output. As in her infamous 1977 review of Le Cirque, the one titled "I Love Le Cirque, But Can I Be Trusted,"* she could render a scene so vibrantly (and teasingly)—"A soup kitchen for the anguished orphans of the late Colony"—that we might imagine ourselves in it:

> The limos lined up outside 58 East 65th Street—the two-tone Rolls, the Cadillac with white mink carpeting. And inside were those old familiar Colony faces—Jean Vergnes, its chef, and maître d'hotel, Sirio Maccioni, Le Cirque's co-owners now—clicking heels, kissing hands,

---

* The doubt cast on her credibility was a coy reference to her "new friendship" with the chef, which she owned up to in the piece. Nearly thirty years later, when her memoir was published, we'd learn that "new friendship" was a stand-in for "occasional boyfriend."

doing headstands. The nibbling fashionables and the displaced rich felt comfortable in the beige-and-peachy dowager elegance with its witty monkey murals.

And then, with the same zeal, she could attack her plate:

> Forget about consistent refinement. Here, when the kitchen is good, it is very, very good, but when it is mediocre, you are not entirely surprised. Still, when it is brilliant you are dazzled. Todeschini's spaghetti primavera is as crisp and beautiful as a Matisse. I have called it the best pasta in town. Now, having tasted the spaghetti aux fruits de mer—an astonishing concerto of clam, mussel, scallop, and crab meat in a thin sea-scented cream—I'm wavering. The côte de beouf villette—a thick cut from the ribs aged three weeks in the house's own cold box—rivals the greatest steakhouse beef. And even a dish as humble as lamb steak (fussily called "selle de pre sale desossee" on the menu, without any accents) emerges impeccably grilled—gently charred and rare, with its kidney tucked inside.

Or, as in her 1989 review of Brian McNally's short-lived hotter-than-hot spot known only by its address, 150 Wooster, that had in its previous life been a body shop and sat in a deserted stretch of SoHo, she might drop all the necessary names, while folding in the pertinent facts about the chef and give you the lowdown on the food:

> Friday night. Mary Boone, tanned, in white. Behind me, I hear *Time*'s art guru, Robert Hughes, explaining the barley dish. "It's halfway between a risotto and a couscous." And it's good (though it was better before the chef decided to smithereen the sausage). "It's a bar, and you don't expect to eat as well as you do," notes restaurant consultant Clark Wolf. "The food's fabulous," says publicity tigress Peggy Siegal. "Surprisingly good," says Billy Norwich. And it is good, though chef Ali Barker, whose concoctions were hyperactive at the Union Square Café, still gets carried away. Rack of lamb is lost in eggplant sludge. His gnocchi, celestial in cognac cream, are less blessed in portobello-mushroom sauce. The tuna fish in one big chunk was bold. Sliced, it's a compromise. I miss the beer nuts in his sublime chocolate-caramel sundae. He needs an editor, and Brian, he laments, is too busy to sit down and talk.

If you didn't recognize all the New York socialites and muckamucks, you would have wished you did and felt you should (and probably wouldn't make that mistake again), and you would itch just to set foot inside the place. I've always thought that if Candace Bushnell (or her on-screen stand-in Carrie Bradshaw) had been a restaurant critic and had written her column, Sex and the City, for the *New York Observer* twenty-five years earlier, it might have looked something like Greene's. Though one wrote about sex and relationships, and the other dining and cuisine, their shared subject was New York City. It's not just me. Devra First, the *Boston Globe*'s resident critic said Greene "was very like the Carrie Bradshaw of food or something."

I hesitate to make the analogy because, one, their literary styles are so different, and two, people are all too willing to cast Greene as a cartoonish Jessica Rabbit–esque femme fatale whose primary interest was sex, and for whom the whole restaurant criticism gig was merely consequential—the backdrop against which she could write about her true passion. That tendency, in some part, may be blamed on the conflation of her *New York* magazine work with her memoir. Insatiable Critic, the column, vibrates with sensuality and titillating innuendo, but it's wordplay; she's manipulating language to get you excited about the food and the room. And *Insatiable*, the book, spells it out for us—she understood that "the same sense that registers pleasure at the table measures the delights in bed: the eye, the nose, the mouth, the skin, the ear that records a whimper of joy or a crunch of a superior pomme frite." In the memoir, you'll also find the details of her sex life, ergo the confusion. "Her stuff was so sexy. I mean, she made food sexy," Reichl said, drawing the important distinction. "She brought a whole new voice to it."

Bill Addison, critic for the *Los Angeles Times*, said he respects her "individualistic streak" and because, after arriving in New York from the Midwest, at "this moment of feminism and sexual liberation,"* she invented "this voice that still influences how restaurant critics describe food. How they think about food, how they contextualize what's in front of them." It would stand out in 2019, but try to imagine what it meant in 1968. No one would have seen it coming. Addison also credits her with recognizing restaurants—and reviewing them—as a "social medium, and we're talking not just about 'social' like who she's having the meal with, but what is happening in society around her; what's happening at the table next to her; what's happening around the room, what's happening in the city; what's happening across the pond in France and Italy where so many influences were coming from."

Her tenacity and timing allowed her to bear witness to, and document, a major shift in American restaurant culture marked by the rise of the celebrity chef and of dining out as a form of entertainment and performance. Grimes noted that, while most restaurant critics are only able to endure the frenzied pace and forced feeding for a few years before petering out, Greene is one of few to make a career of it. She stuck with it and never flagged. In 2008, *New York* ended her forty-year run, but she took her column with her, launching it as a website where readers can find archives

* A couple of reference points: NOW (National Organization of Women) was founded in 1966. The first issue of *New York* magazine arrived in April 1968, the same year that the WLM (Women's Liberation Movement) began rapidly spreading across the United States and beyond.

of her old work along with current reviews. That's over fifty years' worth of tracking every opening, every up-and-coming chef, and every new trend—along with every recycling of an old one.

Even if you don't love her style, you've got to acknowledge her impact. "Gael did make much of sex and it was a little forced, but she certainly wrote in a new way for food," said Phyllis Richman, who served as the *Washington Post*'s dining critic for more than twenty years. Ligaya Mishan, who writes the Hungry City column for the *Times* Food section, told me, "I think Gael Greene is underrated. Her criticism is so alive, and genuinely fun to read." Every venue had a life that was integral to a diner's experience of it, and, in documenting that, she gave restaurant criticism a life, too, which, let's be honest, it didn't have much of before.* She covered the menu with the same fervor and thoroughness as she did the crowd, understanding that when we dine out, it's not just for the *quenelles de brochet*; it's the action in the room—the scene, and how we feel in it.

Mimi Sheraton, meanwhile, homed in on those pike quenelles—whether they'd been correctly executed, whether the crayfish-infused *sauce nantua* was up to par, whether the dish was an accurate, exemplary version of the original. She was an eloquent stickler who went into great, vivid detail about the elements on a plate, if the service was up to snuff, how comfortable the chairs were. Claiborne defined the criteria against which a restaurant was judged, but his reviews didn't get into the nitty-gritty of how it met or didn't meet those standards. That's what Sheraton did, and she did it with just as much vigor as Greene brought to describing the gestalt of a venue. Her methodology may not be what editors—or readers—deem "sexy" in the twenty-first century, but it let diners know exactly what they'd get for their money, and it demanded that restaurants know their stuff—quenelles, decanting, and the rest—and perform consistently. And her writing, along with her fearlessness (some might say delight) in delivering a bad review, made her strictness entertaining.

"The last thing the *New York Times* wanted was a sex expert," Sheraton declared when asked what she thought of Sietsema's casting of her role in the history of American restaurant criticism. "At that time, you couldn't even say menstruation in the *New York Times*." (She couldn't resist following it up with "I mean, Robert Sietsema has a lot of imagination.") We were in the living room of the preppily uniformed, straight-backed ninety-three-year-old's brownstone in Greenwich Village, which, while spotless, is inviting, homey, and full of personal effects like the antique furniture and decorative objects she and her deceased husband collected

---

* Coverage of restaurants was patently dull at that time, with one noteworthy exception: an eccentric crank named Seymour Britchky, who was prone to making fun of the customers and whose work should not be forgotten.

on their travels around the world. If anything, her gender was a roadblock to getting the *Times* gig. She initially applied after Claiborne first relinquished the post in 1970. Charlotte Curtis, the editor of the section at the time was "a blazing feminist," according to Sheraton, but "wanted a man to replace Craig. I don't know one woman interviewed for that job." She was outraged and telephoned the National Organization of Women and complained to its cofounder Muriel Fox about the discrimination. Finally, in 1976, she got the call. That was after the newspaper cycled through a series of three men—Raymond Sokolov, John L. Hess, and John Canaday—in five years. At that point, she said, "Nobody ever said anything about a woman or a man, they just hired me."

In the meantime, she'd been reporting on food for *New York*, including "I Tasted Everything in Bloomingdale's Food Shop" (everything, comprising 1,961 products) and "The Burger That's Eating New York," about the resistance of the city's residents to the proliferation of McDonald's franchises. But Sheraton had started writing restaurant reviews in the mid-1950s, for a local New York rag called *Cue* under the pseudonym Martha Martin, and after that, for the city's Village Voice, using her real name.* Born in Brooklyn, she knew she wanted to be a food critic early on and gave up covering decoration and home design, her original beat, to do so.

Once at the *Times*, she would file her weekly assessment of two venues to run in the Friday Weekend section of the newspaper. That's where the restaurant column appeared in those days. To a large extent, that placement dictated the format and function of Sheraton's write-ups; she believed it was her job to provide readers with information and ideas about where to dine, now that the work week was over and they could enjoy a night out. "I made the restaurant critique what I would want to read if I were gonna decide, do I want to go to this place?" she said. "I made it a very, very straight service. It had some humor, it had little cuts, it had digs . . . Every one is what I want to know—I mean, a little bit about the décor, a hint of, for a woman, what she might wear, and then the service—and you know I went many times." She considered the Claiborne three-visit rule a bare minimum and claims to have eaten at one restaurant twelve times.

But that humor—the little cuts and the digs, and then those particulars about the design of the space and the appropriate dress—was distinctly Sheratonian. The most prominent characteristic of her reviews was the vast amount of knowledge she brought to the job and the enlivened, precise language she used to convey that information. It was service journalism with expertise and voice.

She kept her readers' means and interests in mind, rounding out her coverage so that she didn't only endorse expensive places, and she made sure she doled out entertainment and useful advice in equal measure. She considers her inclusion of

*See second note on page 160.

lower-priced venues, which tended to be those specializing in "ethnic" (her term) food, her standout innovation. "I would try to balance, if one was gonna be fancy," Sheraton said. "Or if one was coming up bad, and it was an important enough restaurant to be reviewed . . . then I would try to come up with something that was good."

I've often thought Sheraton's decision to make restaurant reviewing "very, very straight service" was a direct response to and pushback against the "New Journalism" of Wolfe, Mailer, et al. that so heavily influenced Greene and other writers who came of age in the sixties and seventies (and on, up until the present day). She's always embraced her inner contrarian, but she also seems to believe, unwaveringly, in telling the people everything they need to know, and nothing more. "We had very different views of what a food review should be," she said of Greene's work. "Well, she did something that has become a very popular way to do it that I don't like, and that is to make it a story—to make it a feature. Ruth Reichl made it a feature. I don't really like that." Sheraton is not a storyteller, and when she was reviewing, you didn't need to be.

Although Greene's and Reichl's "feature" writing set the tone for restaurant criticism going forward, Sheraton's old-school approach has its fans. Despite the stylistic sea change, Grimes can still see her fingerprints all over the *Times*' reviews. "She took over and, I think, turned it into something like its present form," he said. "When people think about a *Times* restaurant critic, certainly, she's the one who epitomizes—even though [Claiborne] was the pioneer, she really brought it to full flowering."

Bill Addison believes Sheraton's commitment to prioritizing the diner's needs is, in fact, her real legacy. "Mimi's lasting contribution to restaurant criticism, which is something that I sometimes argue with people over, is that I take pride in being a service journalist," he said. "It is not always about the heavily contextualized think piece or the cultural analysis. Sometimes it really just is 'the duck was overcooked and the French fries came out limp and cold.' I stand gratefully on Mimi's shoulders in that way, and her work validated my own interest in being that kind of critic, or in exercising those kinds of muscles as critic."

Sheraton may have shunned all narrative effects, but she had nothing against total annihilation. Go back to Friday, March 3, 1978, to read her thoughts on the then-new spot from the Hungarian-born restaurateur and cookbook author, George Lang, and see how quickly and effortlessly she thrusts—then twists—the knife:

> Gypsy violinists, colorful, if cheap, tourist-level folk art, white walls and a centerpiece sausage tree give the new Hungaria in the Citicorp marketplace a certain cheerfulness, brightness and air of fun. It doesn't take long, however, to realize how deafening the noise level is, once the musicians start to play, and how crammed together the tables are.

At dinner there are seatings at 6 and 8 o'clock, a regimentation we deplore. But at least one should expect to be seated after complying with the management's schedule. When we arrived at 8, we waited 10 minutes, then were shown to an awful table that should not exist, pushed into a corner in a front window opening onto an unattractive utility section of the kitchen.

Add to that a door to the kitchen that almost hit the table when it swung, and you'll understand why we chose to go the bar and wait a bit longer. Half an hour later, we asked the manager if there would be a table soon, and he answered: "You have eyes, don't you. You see the tables are full. I can't throw people out: You can leave if you want to." Under normal circumstances we would have, of course, but for the sake of this review we stayed.

Are we having fun yet? I think you can tell Sheraton is, especially in that last line where she winks at her readers. The food, she goes on to relay, is hit-or-miss, and she seems to get more specific, and vivid, when recounting the fumbles.

Compare, if you will:

Some of the food was delicious, especially such appetizers as the delicate brains or milt scrambled with eggs and heaped into patty shells. A pungent pickled pepper filled with sauerkraut, an interesting assortment of garlic-and-pepper-laden Hungarian charcuterie and a really marvelous gulyas soup à la Szeged, fiery with paprika, all promised a most satisfying meal ahead.

To:

Mousse of chicken liver stuffed into a hard-cooked egg that was capped with a tomato slice to simulate a storybook mushroom might have been good, had it not been ice cold. Something called double herring consisted of two pieces of undistinguished herring, and Fehervar, a fried, stuffed pancake, was greasy, almost burned, and about as appetizing as a frozen egg roll, which is what it most resembled.

Although she granted that the "fascinating and enticing menu" introduced New York City to a number of dishes otherwise unavailable, and "food buffs" might be "willing to put up with the unevenness of the cooking and the uncomfortable surroundings," she found the service "fast and careless at night, slow and careless at lunch." She gave Hungaria only one star, causing an outraged Lang to write a personal letter to the newspaper's executive editor, Abe Rosenthal. It was of little help. Hungaria didn't survive. Aside from her review, few records of it remain, although, in his memoir, *Nobody Knows the Truffles I've Seen*, Lang wrote, "Unhappily, one of the negative and mean-spirited reviews was from the *New York Times*, which can close any show on 54th Street or on Broadway. And close we did, after twenty-four months."

Sheraton didn't court controversy, but she didn't avoid it, either. She seems to have recognized its power early on. What she relished was upending expectations in the name of news. She didn't care how talented or well-respected someone was or about their track record; if the restaurant was a stinker, she was going to tell you, and if everyone was primed to like it, all the more reason to disabuse them. To be fair, she was equally disposed to ruffle feathers with a positive write-up.

Sheraton had unshakable faith in her convictions—and the stars she bestowed, or didn't. "Mimi Sheraton is magisterial and brooks no argument; I would love to go through life with her sense of authority," Ligaya Mishan said, and I agree. What we're responding to is a kind of swagger that, frustratingly enough, we tend to associate with male writers. "I'm not sure if gender plays a role in restaurant criticism—sometimes I think that men tend to write more declaratively, while women give more benefit of the doubt," Mishan posited. "But then, look at Mimi."

Ironically, Sheraton finds confidence lacking in her criticism and, rather alarmingly, prefers the writing of male critics. "I feel men have a different way of writing about food than women," she said. "The men are more sure of themselves. There's something in the thing that's hard-cut or punchy that you don't usually see a woman write . . . I'd say I'm very confident, but there's a way of showing it. There's a harshness that comes through." Whatever that "something" was, she's convinced it's "why it was considered better to have a man at the *Times*."

If anyone truly believes that men are better suited to the job, let's remember that the reason we're here, that you're reading this right now, is that the critics who made the most enduring marks on this discipline happen to be women.* "They weren't influences so much as they were these voices in my head," said Alison Cook, a veteran restaurant critic who has been at the *Houston Chronicle* for the last seventeen years. "What I did get from [Gael] and incorporated, I think, some, in my own writing . . . was almost like, *Oh wow! You have permission to do this and be considered a serious writer* . . . I think I used it as permission to have as much voice as I wanted." Sheraton represented the other extreme: "That Donald Dresden† model of rectitude" and provided a counterpoint to Greene's "extravagance."

This is where that insidious coupling of Mimi and Gael as two critics with the same agenda falls apart—and why it rankles: They looked at the same thing—the

---

* I imagine a number of you are wondering where the late, inimitable Jonathan Gold is in all this. Please note the name of his column: Counter Intelligence. It's one of the better puns, referring not just to a counter you sit at for a quick meatloaf sandwich or bowl of tripe (no white tablecloths or dessert trolleys here), but to Gold's MO as a countercultural critic. He went outside the system or off the establishment's eaten path. His may end up being the greatest and most lasting influence on food writing, period. But the Pulitzer-winner would not have had anything to write against, were it not for a Greene or Sheraton.

† Donald Dresden was the *Washington Post*'s restaurant critic from 1969 to 1976.

task of surveying a restaurant and, really, a restaurant itself—from completely different, but complementary points of view. Most critics who've come after them have borrowed from both, to varying degrees and in different proportions.

I said I was going to set the record straight. There's something I left out. Sheraton and Greene don't get along, to put it mildly. They never have. Was it a feud? A rivalry? Those don't seem the right words for it. Each is aware that her work can't be compared to the other's. The slights—on both sides—appear more personal. The baiting—some of which they participated in themselves, while a few outside instigators willingly stirred the pot—offers a few cheap anecdotes whose initial entertainment value is fleeting, leaving one with a regretful inkling that, under other circumstances, these two characters could have made a very funny comedy duo. The ill will didn't affect the reviewing process of either. And whatever their conflict, it was never as compelling as the world they commented on and chronicled. To leave it out would not yield a crooked record. To include it, however, might.

"A jerk is someone who competes with the wrong guy," the artist Alex Katz once said.* You know who else is a jerk? Someone who, deliberately or not, reduces a woman's legacy to her competition with another woman. As a society, we're still all too willing to buy into that story. As soon as we catch even a whiff of hostility, we'll attack, like sharks detecting a drop of (bad) blood. Then, of course, that story and our thirst for more ends up turning our protagonists into the jerks they weren't. Greene and Sheraton couldn't be bothered with competition; they both knew better than that. They simply chose to ignore or, at worst, take a minor jab at each other.

We might just as easily write about the animosity between male restaurant critics, which, if you look for it, isn't too hard to find. But we don't. And we don't need to; although, I suspect we might have, if any of them had been writing at the same time, in the same city, and with as much clout and skill as both Sheraton and Greene. Then, one imagines, we'd have had ourselves a clash of the Titans. It's just, I guess, the talent pool wasn't there. If it was, there would certainly have been room in it for more than one man (there always is), and if there'd been a toupee or necktie left bobbing in the water, we'd never have heard about it.

* This always amused me, because I have it on good authority that he's a jerk.

THANK U

SOFIA PEREZ

Dear Amanda [Hesser]:

Back in 2002, you shared a cup of coffee with a broadcast journalist who was looking to transition into food writing. You did not know me from Adam, but you took time out of your day to answer my questions about the industry and were kind enough to refer me to someone you knew at *Gourmet*, who hired me shortly thereafter as a freelance research editor. That was the toehold I needed to break into a field where I knew absolutely no one.

Over the years, I've worked with my share of women who tear other women down (likely prompted by insecurity and fear of losing their own standing), but you and others have served as role models—for the way that you carry yourselves and for your willingness to lift up those who are lower down on the totem pole. I am forever grateful.

Gracias, Sofia

JULIA BAINBRIDGE

Thank you to Christine Muhlke for her time, again and again and again.

MAISIE WILHELM

Dear Lili [Lynton],

Working with you for seven years at Dinex was very inspirational to me as a young woman. Before then, I had never seen up close a woman who had trained in finance do her thing. It was impressive to see your approach to business and watch you determine if deals were beneficial, if there was potential, and how to navigate situations whether they were positive or not. Thank you for being a role model for how to be a nice person while also being a badass (excuse my French).

PS Thank you so much for letting me stay at your flat in Paris!

JULIA TURSHEN

Dear Nicole [A.] Taylor, thank you for opening my eyes a little wider. Love, Julia

---

FOR NICOLE A. TAYLOR, FROM KRISTINA GILL

Dear Nicole,   Roma

Meeting you through DesignSponge has been one of the most rewarding connections I've made on the interwebs.

Thank you for your friendship – for putting down your laptop for an afternoon each time I come through New York, and for treating me and my family like your family.

You've demystified food media for me and helped me through tough times by showing me how you keep your chin up through yours. You're TRULY my inspiration!

Kristina x

ANA SORTUN

Dear Alice Waters,

I remember vividly, a Sunday in 1998 still in my pajamas at 4 P.M. and getting a call from Corby Kummer. He told me that you were in town, that he couldn't take you to dinner and that he thought we should meet. Could I be at your hotel in an hour and pick you up? WHAT? Pinch me.

I met you at the Charles hotel in Harvard Square and I took you to where I was cooking back then— Casablanca in Harvard Square. We talked about the Farm School and this really cute farmer that worked there (now my husband, Chris Kurth). I think you flirted with him when you eventually met! I told you about my Farm School experience where the children were collecting eggs and awareness of where their food comes from was forming in their little brains. We both cried. You told me to ask THE farmer out—so I did. You told me many years later that we should have a big greenhouse, and so we do . . .

Following our dinner, I spent the next afternoon in a limo with you and we went to visit a school garden in Cambridge. I eavesdropped on your conversation with the mayor of NYC and was in awe of how persuasive you were in convincing him to change all the food in the public school system. I was sure he was going to do it.

You changed things for me that day. Of course I should have a greenhouse, of course I should date a farmer, of course I should open a restaurant of my own, of course I should. Your strength and your clarity for what you believe in continue to feed my soul and encourage me to follow in your footsteps. I adore you.

TAMAR ADLER

Alice W[aters]: We had a meeting a few days after I quit my job cooking at Chez Panisse. I was considering going to law school, from which I'd deferred years earlier, I was considering going to policy school, to journalism school, and you dissuaded me, saying: "I'm worried that if you go to any of those schools, they'll teach you their language, and you'll speak in it and use it. And that's fine. But you already have your own language, and I wonder if it's worth all the time and money to replace yours with another. Plus, you can cook, which means you can always make money cooking." Because you said that, I decided I would just make a living speaking in my language. And other than for the regular (and I think universal) moments of crippling self-doubt, and worrying about my longevity, I've been grateful for that advice every day. Thank you.

LIGAYA MISHAN

Dear Anita [Lo],

The first time I ate at Annisa was a New Year's Eve. I've since learned that this is the worst night to try out a restaurant (well, second-worst, after Valentine's Day), but I was still relatively new to New York then, and new to the idea of food as an artform, capable of transcendence. All I remember is the scallop: I don't know what you did to it, but its whole autobiography was on that plate, a life unspooled in wild shallows, every ring on the shell accounted for. That dish told a story, and every dish at every other high-end restaurant in New York has had to live up to it.

Your admirer,

Ligaya

ALISON CAYNE

Thank you, Laurie Colwin, for speaking my truth better than I ever could, and I'm sad you left us too soon.

MARION B. SULLIVAN

Thank you potfuls of grits and stacks of biscuits, Nathalie Dupree, for being a teacher, mentor, and coach. I am profoundly grateful for all I have learned from you.

VIRGINIA WILLIS

I don't think I could put into words what Nathalie Dupree means to me. I love her beyond measure.

ALI ROSEN

To Melissa D'Arabian, Nathalie Dupree, Dorie Greenspan and Carla Hall:

Lending your name to someone for their benefit to promote their career is one of the kindest and most affirming things you can do for someone. Asking directly for help is hard, but boy did you incredible women come through and show me that women are our own best supporters. I will be forever grateful for the affirmation that our community has incredible people who want to lift up other voices even when they don't have to.
—Ali Rosen

HANNA RASKIN

I'm grateful to Christiane Lauterbach for acclimating Southerners to the notion that women can have strong opinions about food.

KRISTY MUCCI

Dear Susan Spungen,

Thank you for taking the time to check up on me. Thank you for giving me opportunities and encouragement, and moral and professional support. I feel lucky to know you as a food person and as a regular person, and I don't have enough of the right words to express my gratitude.

Xoxo

km

SARA LEVEEN

Thank you, Melissa Scully. In my first year as a manager, I asked you for advice on how to handle an issue with a guest and an employee. You said, "Sara, you know what's right. Do what's right." It was so simple but it gave me confidence to make decisions going forward. You taught me how to balance the guest, employee, and business, and when it's appropriate to favor one over the other.

AISHWARYA IYER

Dear Kerry [Diamond],

Eleven years ago, I would have never imagined we would cross paths in this way—I was always in awe of you, as a college student/Lancôme intern and still am, now as the founder of a food company. Thank you for just being you—it helped me see that I could have a multitude of passions, goals, and even careers. You are a shining force and I am lucky to be in your orbit. X

ANN CASHION

Dear Phyllis Richman,

It has been twenty-three years since your first review of Cashion's Eat Place. It was in the autumn, five months after opening and we were fighting for our lives. Robert Shoffner of *The Washingtonian* magazine had published a mean-spirited and very personal review that August that was designed to kill business and it was doing just that. And so, your thoughtful review of Cashion's was just in the nick of time. To the observant reader, your review was almost a point-by-point rebuttal of Shoffner's hatchet job. You complimented the menu, written in "my beautiful hand"; he referred to it as "illegible." He called me "the most overeducated chef in Washington DC." You called me one of our most intelligent chefs, etc.

Twenty-three years ago it would not have been appropriate for me to express my deep gratitude for what you wrote, but I can do it now. I imagine you know this but I want you to hear it from me. You absolutely, single-handedly salvaged, not only a restaurant, but a career.

Warmest regards,

Ann Cashion

CATHY BARROW

Dear Susan Edgerley,

Thank you for taking a chance with me. You schooled me in constructing a story, moved me from third person to first person, and always provided both an insightful, generous edit and a perfect hed.

KLANCY MILLER

Dear Ellen [Yin],

I want to thank you for allowing me to apprentice at Fork all those years ago. Because of you I had my first experience working in a beautiful restaurant kitchen—that apprenticeship let me know that I wanted to attend culinary school, which led to so many other rich adventures in food. When I connect the dots and look at formative experiences that made me who I am and shape what I do now, your restaurant, your generosity and friendship are an important part of my foundation and I am deeply grateful. Thank you.

Sincerely,

Klancy

CHARLOTTE DRUCKMAN

Dear Ruth [Reichl],

Thank you for making me a food writer, twice.

The summer before I started my graduate art history program, I broke my leg and had to spend the following few months cooped up at home, teaching myself how to translate German. To break up Die Monotonie, I read a lot (in English), including your first memoir, *Tender at the Bone*. I loved it—and I don't usually choose to read nonfiction for pleasure. I noticed you'd gone to graduate school for art history, too, and I remember thinking—and then trying to pretend I hadn't—that writing about food seemed like a path I wasn't taking and might be missing out on. I ended up getting my M.A. and being accepted for the doctoral program . . . and leaving. I missed pop culture and the real world too much.

After grad school, I went back to what I'd initially planned to do before getting sidetracked by dreams of becoming a professor and living among the tweed and libraries of academia, and entered the editorial world of glossy magazines. But I did not cover food. It was only after I decided to go freelance, and focus on writing, that it occurred to me I could write about *anything*, or at least try. I liked it right away, and more than writing about anything else. And I thought back to your art history background and realized that maybe there was a something to be said for having to describe all those paintings in grad school (it used to bug me, because you'd always include an image of the work you were discussing, but then still have to describe it, in great detail); maybe you'd had to do that too, and maybe, you'd applied it to writing about food . . . because your descriptions were always so

lush and vivid and poetic—the physicality of the food seemed to almost manifest, emanating from the text. I've always wondered about and assumed this to be so; it's helped justify those extra years in the ivory tower.

Not long after I had these epiphanies, I blind-pitched you a story at *Gourmet*—a profile of a chef who was relatively unknown outside Paris and didn't even have a restaurant at that point. It seemed like the longest long shot. But you said yes, and you did so immediately and with so much kindness. Writing that story for *Gourmet*, it really was the moment I began to believe that I could be a food writer. You gave me an opportunity to write for a magazine that wasn't only revered for the depth and scope of its coverage of the world of food (and the world over), but also for its writing. More than that, though, you gave me the confidence to pursue food writing seriously and to never look back.

Thank you, for planting the seed, and for sprouting it.

CD

REGINA SCHRAMBLING

Thank you, Leslie Revsin, for meeting with me in 1983 when I was considering leaving the top-of-the-dead-woodpile *New York Times* to become a chef; your advice that it was a man's world and would not be easy was spot-on. Also, thank you, Michalene Busico, for hiring me back at the *NYT* as your deputy in Di/Do [Dining In/Dining Out] and then letting me write even though it made your job much harder (so many wilted carrots needing to be converted into soup). Also: Thank you, Anita Leclerc, for publishing me in *Esquire*, always with only the gentlest of touches, and for knowing the turkey had to more than get off the ground but fly; revisions would not work.

KATHLEEN SQUIRES

Thank you to my friends Julie Besonen and Andrea Strong, who were my first food writing community. I would not have had the encouragement to forge ahead without your inspiration and camaraderie, and my chosen profession would have been so lonely without your constant support.

ANDREA NGUYEN

Dear Irene [Kuo],

Yours was the first Chinese cookbook that my family bought in America. It was through a Cookbook of the Month Club membership that my sisters and I shared; we'd cancel and get new memberships to avoid the sell-up pricing. We are frugal Asians.

My mom read and cooked from *The Key to Chinese Cooking*. I now own four copies, just in case the first one falls apart. I didn't know who Judith Jones was when I first read and used your book, but now, as a cookbook author myself, I know her name.

When I was writing my first cookbook, *Into the Vietnamese Kitchen*, I studied *The Key* to wrap my head around how a masterful, timeless Asian cookbook should sound and should be presented, to make a complicated and foreign cuisine seem doable.

A few years ago, I met your son, Jim. He shared glamour photos of you during your career as a celebrity chef and restaurateur. Why your legacy was forgotten kills me. It underscores the deprioritization of non-Western food from Western minds as well as the myths and mysteries that cloud Asian foodways, despite our long histories in America.

Jim gave me a copy of a 1982 letter you wrote to Jones and a proposal about a new book. Your address was on Vermont Street in Los Angeles. You died in LA in 1993. Turns out I wasn't far away, having lived in San Clemente and then attending and eventually working at USC.

I wish we had the opportunity to meet.

Yours,

Andrea

JULIA SHERMAN

Dear Norma [Listman],

When you invited me to be a chef in residence at your restaurant/slice of paradise in Mexico City, Masala y Maiz, you gave me a one-way ticket out of a prolonged period of blah. I never told you this, but earlier that year I had an ectopic pregnancy, a rather dramatic life or death experience whose aftershocks just kept coming. All this happened in the wake of an extended high that came with the publication of my first book, and I was blindsided by how swiftly the experience sucked the wind out of my sails. As someone who is generally thrilled to be alive, I didn't even realize what a stupor I was in until you pulled me out of it, without even knowing you were doing so.

Cooking and shopping alongside you in Mexico was like having a bucket of cold water thrown in my face (in a good way!). After eating barbacoa with your family, harvesting a thirty-foot-tall edible agave flower, and cooking alongside you and Saqib in your restaurant kitchen, I was reminded that I am still, and will always be, creative. I remembered that food, travel, and community are my north stars, that I am a lover of life, and that there will always be great things still to come.

Thank you Norma: The grace with which you deal with the everyday challenges of running your dream restaurant, the way you welcomed me into that sacred space and honored my ideas, made me feel whole after a year of falling to pieces.

Love,

Julia

KRISTEN MIGLORE

I'd love to say thank you to Irene Sax—my food writing teacher in grad school, and a deeply experienced, prolific, and talented journalist, who was more generous with her talents than most. For making me care—a lot—about writing well and relatably about food. (The A– in her class crushed me.)

TINA ANTOLINI

Dear Kitchen Sisters:

Tupperware made me want to tell food stories on the radio. In fact, Tupperware made me want to tell radio stories, period. I was in my last year of college, and just starting to learn about the joys of wandering the world with a microphone. Someone played me your Tupperware party story from 1980. It was a cacophony of voices, layers of them, of Tupperware burps, of women sounding like women, the way they actually sound, not the formal, contained version I'd often heard on air. I was entranced.

When your Hidden Kitchens series started, I was primed to love it, but even so, it surprised me. These were food stories, yes, but more than that, they were people stories, all of them presented with a dignity and humor not always afforded to such a wide swath of humanity: homeless folks cooking on George Foreman Grills, Lebanese immigrants crafting kibbe in the Mississippi Delta, the Ojibwe harvesting wild rice from their canoes, inmates making pralines at Angola State Penitentiary in Louisiana, the foods Japanese American families concocted at internment camps during World War II. This was a version of America that was complex and beautiful, both fraught and filled with hope. It taught me that food could be a vehicle to all the corners of life that sparked my curiosity as a journalist.

Thank you, Nikki [Silva] and Davia [Nelson], for the gift of your nimble attention and listening ears, and for sharing what you hear with all of us.

REBECCA FLINT MARX

Dear Gabriella Gershenson,

Even though you didn't hire me as *Time Out NY*'s food writer back in 2007, you did tell me that you liked my ideas and asked if I would write for you. It is in large part because of you that I began this long and odd journey, and it is because of you that I found my way back to journalism after abandoning it for a brief and grueling fling with professional baking and then culinary school. You were my first real (food) editor and the first person to believe I had something even remotely interesting to say about food, and for this I offer you my sincere and ongoing gratitude, as well as a Superheeb (fine, Superheebster) the next time we find ourselves at Russ & Daughters. Thank you, always and forever, Rebecca

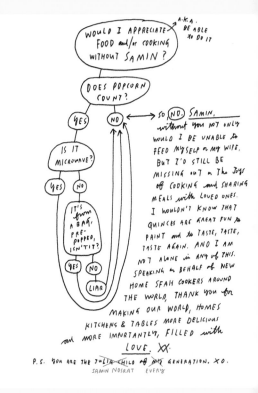

THERESE NELSON

Dear Dr. [Jessica] Harris,

I was rereading *Hot Stuff* a few days ago and it struck me how you have been the example of excellence and audacity that has made room for countless women of color to think and breathe in the food space. Your work is the foundation on which so many of us do our work, and because you had the vision and the insight to think critically about our foodways, they have space at the table in new and exciting ways.

I want to say thank you for highlighting the wonder of our culture in food and for adding dignity and grace to the discourse with your brilliant scholarship.

FROM JORDANA ROTHMAN TO
HELEN ROSNER

Dear Helen,

Helen fucking Rosner how you do intimate and delight with your PRODUCTIVITY Charlotte says you are productive "in a Capricorn way." and I am productive "in a Gemini way." which is a nice way of saying you are more productive by many orders of magnitude (which really was clear enough without sending in the stars). when something must be said you say it first but also best and most beautifully and with that wit and that occasional ripple you have of perfect. sparkling RAGE. In these you provoke and change minds. in language you noodle and luxuriate and backhand flip. You write more than the rest of us do and better than the rest of us could. And since that time years ago when you wrote about the trees and the leaves. I simply can't get through one of yours without muttering quietly to myself "GODDAMN YOU HELEN ROSNER." Turns out. you are the leaves.

With thanks,
Jordana Rothman

HELEN ROSNER

Dear Sheila Lukins,

Sometimes, when I'm in a certain snippy kind of mood, I flip through cooking magazines and websites counting how many stories open with memory: "Ever since I was a kid," or "For as long as I can remember," or "When I was younger." There are always a lot. Too many. I'll roll my eyes, and indulge in a mild performance of despair, and flip to the next page. But really, what else can our stories about food say? They begin where we begin. We learn the smells and tastes and colors of our own small world of childhood, and no matter how wide that sphere expands in the years that follow, the time-capsule sense memories of childhood will always be at the heart. Maybe not always in the very first sentence, and maybe not nearly so often under the same cover, but sometimes you have to start where it starts, and go from there.

Where it starts: On January 4, 1982, *The Silver Palate Cookbook*—your first book, written with Julee Rosso—was published, and two days after that, in an entirely unrelated event, I was born. A little over two decades later I ended up in an office at Workman Publishing, saying yes to a job offer that would involve running coffee and making photocopies and generally basking in the wise and creative glow of Suzanne Rafer, the legendary cookbook editor who had brought your books into the world. "We've got big plans for the twenty-fifth anniversary of the *Silver Palate*," I remember Suzanne saying, or something like that. "Are you familiar with the book?" She may as well have asked me if I knew the pattern on the sheets of my childhood bed, or the name of the cat I used to stare at through two windows in the apartment across the airshaft from ours. The blocky Marimekko cars-and-trucks print. Snowball. A white cover with an oxblood-red windowpane check and a photo of a storefront overflowing with greenery; pages full of stippled, slightly off-kilter black-and-white illustrations; recipes that felt louche and worldly and grown-up. By the time I sat there in Suzanne's office, the book had sold nearly three million copies, though I didn't know that at the time. All I knew was that ever since I was a kid, for as long as I can remember, we had *The Silver Palate Cookbook*.

Soon enough, I met you. You'd whirl into the office in a blaze of red hair, a tiny human flame, with your wide grin and patrician drawl, and you'd talk about your other books—*All Around the World*, the *USA Cookbook*, all the big, big, big ideas that you put into action after the *Silver Palate* era ended, after you sold the little shop in Manhattan where it all began, after you and Julee split up, the Simon and Garfunkel of the spice aisle. There was such fanfare when you reunited, briefly, for the *Silver Palate 25th Anniversary Edition*—"Chicken Marbella, now in full color!"—the two of you back together, still crazy after all these years. Julee signed my copy of the book at the launch party (the Central Park Boathouse, of course, the ideal time machine to bridge the early eighties and the late aughts), and in the flurry of festivities I couldn't quite track you down. A week later your assistant, Laurie, almost indescribably kind, handed me another copy of the book, with your signature and a lovely personal note.

The history of American home cooking is measured in unruly women who win book contracts: Irma Rombauer gives way to Julia Child who gives way to you. It was a tectonic shift from Francophilia and staid Americana to a sort of flirtatious Mediterranean epicureanism: pesto, raspberry vinegar, sun-dried tomatoes, capers, fancy olive oil, brie, chilled fruit soups. Everyone in the eighties bought olives and prunes and made Chicken Marbella, or had been to the dinner party of someone who had. "That page was covered in stains," my mother recalled, when I asked her to verify my memories. Like Julia Child, you'd taken classes at the Cordon Bleu while overseas for your husband's job. Like Julia, you became food editor of *Parade* magazine, shifting almost imperceptibly from a cook of accessible aspiration to one of accessible populism. Like Julia, while your later books were watertight— someone once told me that you were the only cookbook author who *really* tested her recipes, you and Laurie, both of you with sleeves pushed up, in the kitchen of your apartment in the Dakota, going at it with fierceness and rigor, making sure not a single teaspoon of flour went amiss—they still never quite captured the world-shaking magic of the first few volumes. History keeps moving: the *Silver Palate* era gave way to the next extraordinary women: Martha Stewart, Ina Garten, Edna Lewis, Nigella Lawson.

When you died, in 2009, it was the first time I experienced public mourning for a person I had known privately. I didn't know how to grieve. I had moved on from book publishing, I was making a go as a writer, sort of, and someone who knew that I'd known you asked me to write an obituary. I couldn't; I didn't deserve to. I wouldn't pretend that we were close—to you, I was probably the thousandth in an endless string of young editorial assistants, and to me, you were the surreally human and actual embodiment of a time and a memory I had once thought belonged only to me. It meant so much to me that you shaped my life in so many of its chapters, starting from the very beginning. You still do. It still does. Thank you.

JULEE ROSSO

This should go to many: *Joy of Cooking*'s Irma Rombauer, Perla Meyers, Paula Wolfert, Maida Heatter, Irena Chalmers, Barbara Kafka—but most of all, to Julia Child:

Dear, Dear Julia!

When you said, "People who love to eat are always the best people," you were oh so right! I've taken poetic license and often say, "The world is divided into people who love garlic and those who don't." Those who don't love garlic also don't seem to laugh much, are usually quite important, and are just not my cup of tea. Today the division that starts with garlic runs true and deep.

Oh, if you could only know how much the world misses you and your wit, Julia, especially the women in the food world. And, me! There just isn't as much fun without you as so many people are trying too hard to impress and forgetting that good food is simply supposed to bring joy and laughter

around the table. You made us feel at home in your kitchen and in our own.

You taught me how to cook in 1968, recipe by recipe as I worked my way through *The French Chef* over the course of a year. It was as if you were always right there beside me. When I finally met you decades later as we shared a "loo" at Pat & Walter's Chanteduc and laughed like crazy, while picking arugula, at the women in *W*, discussing whether we needed computers, and while making the ganache for Pat's birthday cake; it was as if we'd known one another forever.

I loved your before 6 A.M. and after 11 P.M. calls when over the line would come JULEEEEE!!!! it's JULIA!! As if I didn't know. You always left me laughing. I loved the roast you did for us in NYC with Irena, Barbara, and Florence, but mostly our late arrival (we'd been snow delayed in Aspen) when you leaped across the room of four hundred to greet Bill and me because you were so anxious to meet him! He, at six foot one loved that he had to look up to you.

I think fondly of our time together at the AIWF Board meetings, our side-by-side book signings when you'd warble, "Just how many cookbooks *have* you sold, *Juleee*?," our dinners in NYC and at Chez L'Ami Louis, and our gossiping. Oh, gossiping was the best!

But what I remember most is when you gave me the devil for writing a "healthy cookbook" and then you became my greatest defender, both privately and publicly, to both the industry and the press. Those late-night phone conversations, amidst the well-orchestrated, as you called it, "nonsense," helped me laugh it away and you got me through it.

You were there for me every step of the way and I adored you.

But then, you never ever let any of your friends down and we all loved you for that! You were a real broad in the best sense of the word. You did your homework, worked hard, earned great respect and justifiable acclaim, and you took it all without an ounce of pretension. I always wanted to ask you to do a cooking class with me "The Julia and Julee Show," but I felt that your time was being spent in more valuable and meaningful ways for such shenanigans. But boy oh boy, would it have been the show!

Julia, I can only once again thank you from the bottom of my heart for starting me on my food journey, for your incredible friendship, and for showing me that if you follow your passion, you'll love every day of your life. What wonderful memories you've left all of us!

CHRISTINE MUHLKE

Dear Judith [Jones]:

So Simca's cassoulet didn't turn out as planned. Thank you for your honest feedback—and for saving it for until the day after. I don't know why that final step of crisping the breadcrumbs wasn't in the recipe either!

And thank you for bringing along your correspondence with Mme. Beck from that time. I can't imagine editing a book with someone when it took several weeks just for your queries

to wash ashore—and another few for her arguments and refusals to reach you here. Your dedication to the process—no, craft—of both editing and cooking is an inspiration. No one has bothered to teach me the intricacies of the former. I wish I had been able to work under you. Or do you, like so many women I've encountered in my field, prefer to keep your work secrets to yourself? Given how many dedicated writers you have in your stable, I would think that you wouldn't. Who are your protégées?

When I look at the breadth and depth of the writers you have edited, I feel so insignificant in having chosen the magazine path. And when I look at the cookbooks of the writers you have so closely shaped, I am humbled to see how you have shaped American food in the process. Thank you for bushwhacking that path. The men at Knopf may have thought you were in a "women's" role—minus your occasional forays into, say, Updike or Gide—but you've certainly had the last laugh.

Above all, I'd like to thank you for showing us what happens when you make your passion your life. You chose food, and all the learning it entails, and it has borne a lifetime of fruits—not just in your remarkable career, but in your marriage as well. How incredible to be able to work and create together, to feed and nourish generations, and to still be madly in love!

Teach me, Judith Jones.

With gratitude and admiration,

Christine

Osayi Endolyn

In 2014, California girl Osayi Endolyn, now an adopted daughter of the South, penned an article for *The Bitter Southerner* on singer Ruby Velle and her band, The Soulphonics, in which the writer broke down the history and psychology of the blues. "If you're doing it right," she wrote, "you cannot help but tap into some personal, vulnerable place. But the blessing and irony of the blues is that the blues actually make you feel good." Osayi's work does something similar: her stories tap into personal—or cultural—vulnerable places. But her writing makes the read cathartic; it makes you feel good.

Two years later, she introduced what would become her award-winning column, Missed Cues, in *Gravy*, the magazine published by the Southern Foodways Alliance in Oxford, Mississippi, where she also served as deputy editor. Each installment deftly dealt with the complex, often painful truths of food and identity in the American South. Anyone who'd read that story about Ruby Velle and the Soulphonics would have expected as much.

According to her records, Osayi has "had dinner, lunch, or drinks in thirty-six US states and twelve countries, and counting." Some of those have been eaten as a solo diner. As a tiny subgenre of food writing, Women Dining Alone has functioned as a romanticized defense of the practice, featuring a (white) woman in a (cosmopolitan) city, who talks up how nice it is to take oneself for a glass of wine and a small plate or two to "nibble on." I hadn't thought about how much of a trope it was until Osayi told me she wanted to write about what it's like to be a black woman dining alone at local chains in the middle of nowhere or even at some of the world's most celebrated restaurants. Her essay raises a lot of questions about dining out and, more important, about race in America.

Trapped In, Dining Out

I.

I wish I could tell you when I first noticed that I'd become part of the act. I've considered so many dinners and lunches and beer sips and quiet cocktails of my adult life and no singular moment stands out. It's curious.

I remember my first taste of a West Coast pale ale and the moment when I realized bright Belgian IPAs would quicken my newbie palate's adaption to more biting, American versions. I recall awkward servers who'd seat themselves at my table while taking the order in some bizarre gesture of interest. I know the exact smirk of recognition when a bartender, trying not to encroach, overhears an excruciating admission that only your companion should know, and you hope the secret stays wrapped in the unofficial bartender code of silence. I've marked many dining firsts. But I cannot tell you about the first time I noticed I was part of someone else's show. I can't even think of the first time I got pissed off about it, that's how insidious the ordeal has been. But I *can* tell you about a recent time when I'd had enough. Because that's when I finally decided that if a fellow diner was going to ruin my evening and squander the hope that buoys any budding dining experience, then, I've come to feel, they best be prepared to tolerate a shitty ride home, too.

II.

She could not stop looking at me. Every couple of minutes her head twisted left, her eyes scanning, her lips pursed. I swirled a Sonoma pinot noir and breathed in its aroma. This was going to be one of those times. I surveyed the room for an escape hatch, yearning for retreat. But there was no available space to decamp. Moments before, I'd taken a bar seat at Hillstone in Winter Park, Florida, a suburban neighborhood of Orlando. Barely six P.M. and the dining room was already deep in the throes of dinner service—possibly related, the vast majority of diners were middle-aged or older. And like Winter Park's population itself, they were predominately white.

A deep-seated craving for the chain's French dip had brought me to this outpost of the namesake restaurant group, held up among indie enthusiasts for its consistency and attentive service. If you choose to eat at a chain, even an upscale one, you might choose a Hillstone or Houston's or Bandera, a handful of the restaurant group's multiple names in different US markets. I have often come to Hillstone seeking the Thai-inspired noodle salad, its crisp greens, filet mignon slices, and fresh herbs mixed and mounted into a pyramid. Other times, for the rib-eye steak, known as the Hawaiian, a hefty slab marinated in a pineapple-soy blend accompanied by a massive baked potato. This day, after work and errands, I wanted the straightforward simplicity of the French dip—a buttery French roll baked in-house with hot prime rib shavings served au jus, side of shoestring fries. I came for the sandwich, and I did get it. But I ordered an appetizer of seasonal grilled artichokes, too, charred halves served with a remoulade. It was this last-minute, almost cavalier indulgence that became one of several decisions that shook my dinner that evening.

I go out for hundreds of meals each year, and still, I'm amazed at how quickly a dining experience can change, how fast my world has repeatedly become so much smaller and strapped-in, and how often that shift has nothing to do with my behavior. Increasingly, I wonder if the truth about dining out in America is that, like many things in this country, it was only ever intended for white men, and, although it may distress some to acknowledge, yet another reality that contradicts our purported progress, that it's perhaps still not my demonstrable right to sit at a bar, a woman, a black person, and feel entitled to enjoy my meal in peace.

III.

In the years that I've spent dining out as an adult, particularly as a writer who thinks about food, drink, and eating spaces, preceded by about five cumulative years working as a host or server's assistant in casual and fine dining establishments, I've grown attuned to the many ways a meal can be corrupted. They comprise the parts of the show that is an active restaurant.

There is the food itself—its taste, its composition and presentation, its cost. Is it *good*? Do the dishes served deliver on the menu's promise? Are beverage options in line with edible offerings? There's the question of location. Is the venue's façade visible from the street or tucked away like a secret hideaway forcing you to endure a pre-meal scavenger hunt? Is there ample parking or must you valet, and if you valet, is it complimentary and, if not, how much is it, and do they only take cash? Can you pay the person who retrieves your car or must you queue to pay a cashier? You consider ambience. Is the restaurant flooded with fluorescent lights bouncing off faded linoleum in the manner of a 1990s driver services office, or is it the moody lighting of a PG-13 love scene, meaning you can hardly tell an eye socket from an elbow? Is the playlist so important that you cannot hear your companion speak? Can you hear your server or bartender? To that point, can you hear too much of them? Sometimes, if seated near a service station, you're left finishing your meal mindful that so-and-so missed their shift. What are the bathrooms like? I've lost track of how many times I've gone to wash my hands in fancy places only to learn there is no soap. When I notify the host they're always wide-eyed with shock, and I think of all the flatware and bread rolls in the dining room laced with human essence.

It's a wonder anyone leaves a restaurant smiling—when all those pieces fall into place, it's a joyful feat. And yet, there is the gamble of other people. Sartre tried to tell us. That is, even when the menu is award-winning and the music is so right, and the lighting flatters, and the room temperature is comfy—you might have a fellow diner insert themselves in your bubble of an evening. My black-woman experience has been that, collectively, white people are under the impression that when I'm out there in the wild, unpredictable terrain of a restaurant bar or dining room, I am in need of help and oh god, oh god! They must save me.

IV.

Energy was buzzing at Hillstone that evening. Young women huddled around the host stand, poring over the floor map while walk-in parties collided with late reservations. The bar was slammed. I was seated next to the service well, and servers from the dining room cycled back and forth to fetch martinis and wine for their tables. Two thirty-something men in crew cuts and collared shirts with no ties crammed into the opening. One noted the Negroni on the drinks menu and asked the other to explain Campari. On my right, a party of three had seated themselves at the bar. Two women and one man in animated conversation, maybe late sixties to seventies in age. I'd already placed my order and was fiddling with my phone, reviewing the day's news. The open kitchen sprawled behind me, so I did not see the young food runner approach, who was perhaps jarred by the two men standing where customers technically don't belong. I couldn't catch her eye as she headed to my right and, perhaps counting people instead of seat numbers, set the plate of beautifully charred artichokes slated for me in front of the trio who'd just barely ordered the same dish.

There are rules in upscale dining and an oft-upheld one is that once a misplaced dish lands in front of a diner, it belongs to them unless they reject it. (And if they do reject it, it goes in the trash. No guest wants the snapper amandine that rested even briefly under the nose of a stranger four tables over.) The bartender lobbed a sideways glance at the food runner to convey she'd erred. The trio was in disbelief at the speedy service given the hubbub of the bar; their artichokes had appeared faster than if they'd ordered ready-made chips and salsa. But they were delighted nonetheless. The bartender apologized to me, her ponytail bobbing to one side as she tucked her head to softly say the kitchen would rush a replacement. It was fine, I told her. I was fine.

But proximity being what it is at a busy bar, my right-side neighbor, part of the trio, picked up mid-chew that the artichokes melting in her mouth belonged to another.

"Were these meant for you?" Her tone was aghast.

I looked up from up my phone and offered a reserved smile, already sensing an interaction that could go on too long. There was no issue for her to resolve. "They're on top of it," I said.

"Oh *no!*" she responded. She turned to her companions and said, loudly, "We stole her artichokes! These weren't even ours!" The man and the second woman peered their wrinkly heads around the harried friend to view me, wine in hand, devoid of artichokes. Their mouths hung open in true uncertainty; I couldn't tell whether they were personally mortified by the restaurant's error or if they were made uncomfortable by their friend's rush to personal accountability. I returned to the safe space that was my phone screen. The woman roused me to apologize and I reassured her, it was all good. We held each other's gaze for a moment. I wonder now what she thought of me in the thick of that very white bar—a round, brown face often mistaken for nearly half my age, kinky coils of black hair framing amused, dark eyes. She had long, straight white-blondish hair that hung past her shoulders. I remember dangly, fringe earrings and bangs that obscured a face suffering under too much makeup—smudged black eyeliner clung to droopy lids, her faded lipstick revealed an ill-fated attempt at plumping her mouth with pink lip color. She wore a black, velvety blazer that hunched around her shoulders. Maybe she was going for a Stevie Nicks vibe, but that could be giving her too much credit; so, after it all ended, in my mind, I simply named her Donna.

It was from this point onward that I felt Donna staring at me. She stared while my artichokes arrived and I tried to enjoy them. She stared while the bartender poured me two samples of by-the-glass pinots. The stares would continue, eventually escalating into action. Donna leaned toward the bartender and asked if she could pay for my artichokes. The bartender gently informed her that the restaurant would be taking care of them on my behalf. None of this was meant for my ears, but tight quarters meant I could hear. Not to be outdone, Donna turned to me and asked if she could buy me a drink. I imagine an outcome where if I'd accepted, that could have been the end. But something about her insistence made me uncomfortable—she was not actually trying to make *me* happy. Donna seemed undeterred by my being in a lovely mood. She was trying to dislodge whatever feeling was making *her* unhappy, and the conduit to that serenity was me.

While I waited for the French dip, Donna turned to me and said she "felt like a dumbass." I opted not to resist because I knew now my ideal dinner was a wash.

"Why do you feel that way?"

"Because! These were your artichokes and we took them!"

I said again, with what I hoped was an air of finality, that no one stole anything and that Hillstone was handling the mix-up to my liking.

While I waited for my sandwich, Donna interrupted me, suggesting that I try the iceberg wedge salad, a dish the trio was sharing. She used her hands to explain to me that the iceberg wedge salad was a wedge of iceberg lettuce and that it had beets. Beets!

"I don't need dish recommendations, ma'am," I said. "I just want to enjoy my dinner quietly, if you don't mind."

Her head jerked back in surprise, and for a moment, I felt badly about the tide turning between our snug seats. But I'd earned myself a respite, at least for the moment, and when I bit into my sandwich the only sound I heard was the happy, muddled buzz of a hundred simultaneous dinnertime conversations.

V.

A strange logic is at work here. I've seen it too many times, I've written about it before, and I've complained to family and friends more often. I've experienced it in Asheville, North Carolina, at Cúrate, a tapas bar, when a young white woman overheard that it was my and my now-husband's first time there and presumed that it was also our first time in a place that sold tapas. From a couple seats down she lodged unsolicited recommendations toward us and widened her eyes with empathy at how "overwhelming" the menu could be. After multiple failed attempts at trying to end the interaction, her interjections feeling a bit intrusive during my birthday meal, I finally told her that my partner and I had both been to Barcelona, a true statement. We'd find our way, I said, and while she appeared bruised and unmoored, she let us be.

It happened at Pujol, the award-winning destination restaurant in Mexico City. As I was being seated for my multicourse solo lunch, an older white woman wrapping up her meal next to my table announced with grand authority that I was "in for quite the tasting." You'll have to trust me that she didn't say this as a giddy buddy in cahoots, or even as a star-struck fan exiting the latest Marvel movie while passing anxious ticketholders. She said it like you warn a child to look both ways before crossing the street. My butt had barely grazed the banquette in a Mexican restaurant, in Mexico, led by a Mexican chef, and yet this non-Spanish-speaking white woman was prepping me for what to expect—even though I too had to reserve my table with a credit card far in advance and had approved a temporary hold on my account for the coursed meal to follow. Which is to say, I knew quite well what to expect, and even if I didn't, why unveil the magic prematurely? Why she felt that I was any less informed than she about the provenance of chef Enrique Olvera and his much heralded talents is a question I don't need answered. I already know. I barely glanced her way when I replied, "I'm aware." I wasn't surprised when she took her end-of-meal coffee outside on the patio. *Adiós, señora.*

I've perceived this twisted logic at bars in Atlanta when ordering bourbon. Once, at Hartsfield-Jackson airport, an older white man complimented me on ordering Woodford Reserve, which, for the record, is no underground sensation. He wasn't hitting on me, as some feel compelled to counter. He was bemused and believed I'd feel honored by his observation.

I recognized it in Washington, DC, at the Kimpton Carlyle on Dupont Circle when I browsed the bottled wine list at the in-house Riggsby while waiting for my take-out order. It was during a ridiculous lapse in scheduling infrastructure, when room service was technically over, but the restaurant said I could order in person and a server would accompany me with my food back to my room. The white bartender came over and name-checked wine varieties, which, if I'm being generous was maybe to help me manage the list. I gently dismissed her unsolicited recommendation of a pinot grigio for a quirkier roussanne and two white women seated nearby tried to persuade me to enjoy my meal at the bar rather than in my room, because, now I realize, this was part of *their* show. They were so fervent in their goading I had to declare that this wasn't a group decision. I actually said those words and was thankful when a server appeared with my moules frites. "Well excuse me," one of the women said. Indeed, I thought, and I trailed the tray-touting man to the lobby elevator.

I am made aware of it when I ask a white, often male, bartender to tell me the style of a locally brewed beer that's referenced on the menu by an esoteric name like Blissful Kittens or some craziness that reveals nothing to even the most seasoned beer drinker. I have rarely had a bartender respond with the name of a beer style such as doppelbock, Berliner Weisse, gose, or my favorite, saison. Instead they opt for more "accessible" information like tasting notes (*it's fruity; it's hoppy; you might like this one instead*—"this one" is always a lager). I think about the way white men servers at Zuni Café in San Francisco and Chez Panisse in Berkeley interrupted me while in mid-sentence. I've noticed other white male servers pause to allow my white male dining companions to finish a thought before breaking in to explain the provenance of the mushroom dish. I think about the white woman server at GW Fins in New Orleans' French Quarter who walked me and my husband through elusive menu sections like appetizers, salads, and entrees. And while I'm sensitive to the likelihood that in a tourist capital like the Vieux Carré, such a speech is probably part of her job and even helpful to some, I swiftly but politely cut short her intro because I sensed if she explained to me what a "side" dish was, I might take my butter knife (for the butter, maybe!) and jab it up her nostril with years of pent-up frustration.

This is the part where, in retelling such encounters, a few friends, more colleagues, and at times, even my husband, jokingly try to help me "understand" what I misunderstood about a particular exchange.

> *You're at a bar, people talk to each other! Don't be so standoffish.*
> *She was just trying to be nice.*
> *She was an old lady. Be sweet to old ladies.*

The defenses, usually from men and white people, typically wane as I counter with a series of now-standard inquiries. My men friends cannot recall the last time a fellow customer—not staffer—walked up to them in a liquor store to help them with their selection. My white men friends often realize they've had to explicitly state that they're first-timers before a bartender gives them the Welcome to This Bar, Surprise, It's a Bar speech. I reject the idea that I'm colliding with common standards of dining. I reject that I keep finding myself under the thumb of white people who can't contain their enthusiasm for the food or drink about to be served. I can't even convince myself that people are weird sometimes and maybe I encounter more weirdos than others. Rather, I now believe that what I experience as a diner is inextricably linked to the racialized and gendered history of eating out in the United States. I believe that too many white people, still figuring out that they are in fact white and not de facto normal, struggle with what to do with themselves when in the vicinity of blackness, when they are neither the authority figure, nor the host or hostess, nor the most important guest in the room.

VI.

I know. It bothers many of varied ethnicity to think that people's behavior today in the early twenty-first century has roots in the genocide and displacement of indigenous people on this continent and the enslavement of Africans and their descendants in the Americas. That annoyance doesn't make the fact any less true. I can empathize, to a point. Nobody wants to cede that much power to history, to admit so little self-determination in the land of actualizing dreams. It's frustrating—disempowering even—to realize how much of our lives this country yields to tradition. Americans in particular have a tendency to believe we're governed only by the Now, that we're a forward-thinking culture with our gaze on the horizon. But that's a myth. Last winter, I drove down a highway in Santa Fe, New Mexico, counting cordoned-off Native American reservation signs and cheeky billboards for the state's Native-owned casinos. There's nothing wrong with cash flow and entertainment, but when it comes to ideas of freedom, I've gotta believe those ancestors had more than blackjack in mind. Manifesting destiny sounds great unless you and your culture are perceived as an obstacle in someone else's military-fueled dream fulfillment. Many of us avoid the truth, maybe for different reasons. Facing the devastating missteps of this country can feel like admitting too much wrongness, or it can feel like absorbing too much pain. But those who are willing—or have been forced—to confront our racial reality know we live in the imprint of vicious ideals. Parts of the etching linger.

I think of it like this: In order to manage the forced labor of a mass of people at once resistant, vigilant, terrified, and traumatized, all hailing from their own distinguished and varied cultures, jumbled together in grotesque and inhumane ways, then subjected to violence-induced work in a new land that was inspired and governed by the rights of man and individual liberties, white male property owners required the creation and enforcement of unique and particular laws.

Those laws criminalized blackness. Those laws were the legal foundation for using race as a divider and as a determining factor in how people got to live. Those laws created the framework to police the bodies, movement, education, and treatment of anyone visibly identifiable as African or of African descent. The pathway to this criminalization of blackness is an exercise in state statute hopscotch. When a person of African descent claimed for themselves the expectations of liberty ascribed to the Constitution's authors, sometimes successfully, the law poured in to fill what was subsequently seen as an unintended loophole. Other jurisdictions would catch wind and preemptively address their own loose ends, much like waves of similar state legislation permeate the country today. Slave codes confidently governed blackness while affirming derogatory stereotypes held by many whites that either aided their justification of slavery or rendered them blameless for a social experiment too big to undo. These codes and the people that implemented them tarnished every region of the United States.

Among them, black people shouldn't have the right to hold weapons; enslaved people are liable to their masters; the occurrence of death upon an enslaved person by an owner or overseer cannot be deemed a felony (and often fetched an insurance claim—among providers, Aetna and others); an enslaved person is the personal chattel of the master and not entitled to any rights such as the option to sue for new ownership; newborn blacks inherit the legal condition of the mother in perpetuity (this was, I might add, a cunning way for white slave owners to legalize the rape of black women and profit from the inherent enslavement of their own progeny—hi, Thomas Jefferson). Even as the practice of importing humans slowed—those trans-Atlantic voyages could get pricey—the domestic trade and ongoing enslavement of American-born black people encouraged authority-yielding whites to generate more constraints through which they could retain power, particularly in areas where an involuntary workforce of black people outnumbered them. This is how you get the Fugitive Slave Act, where any black person without documents (and even those with proper papers) could be hunted down, questioned, captured, detained, by anyone white with a stated claim. Such laws and countless others like them created social tiers of existence tied to the rightness of whiteness and the wrongness of blackness. Any black person who appeared misplaced in a white person's view required their intervention. It was the law!

While these legalized social stratifications buckled under the weight of Lincoln's proclamation, we never emerged from the cultural mindset they inscribed.

Proximity of people of African and European heritage was always dangerous for black people, but you could argue, not precisely the issue. The status of black people, however, was. It was one thing, for example, for an enslaved black person to prepare food and serve it to a white person, even while the domestic enslaved lived at great risk in their closeness to white people. Still, it was another thing entirely for a newly freed servant and an ex-owner of humans to find themselves stripped of labels from the preceding two hundred-plus years, but still burdened with the legacy of their skin color. Need it be said, this shift in power was only problematic to those accustomed to unchecked authority?

This upending of tradition is what triggers a white reaction to the Reconstruction Era: after more than two thousand African Americans are elected to local, state, and federal government, there's suddenly a social void only the KKK can fill, when lynched bodies of young men and women, sometimes whole families, sometimes children, double as punishment and warning. Here's what happens when you step out of line. This is how not addressing a white person honorifically, or trying to leave town in search of work disentangled from field labor and sharecropping, or attempting to register to vote become perceived crimes. This is how you eventually get the Voting Rights Act of 1965, to protect the voting rights of racially discriminated groups, and this is also how you get its invalidation by a conservative Supreme Court in 2013, because black people were never supposed to get that choice. This is how you get the Thirteenth Amendment, leaving the option for unpaid labor on the table in cases of criminal conviction. So now, at the whim of any white person, being a black person breathing can land you with a lifelong sentence as a leased convict. A consequence of state-sanctioned vigilantism, whether on the street or in the courtroom, was the white self-assurance that even if slave codes were gone, white authority was permanent and safeguarded.

This is the social climate in which the country saw the introduction of restaurants. Be they coffee houses, oyster houses, boarding houses, dining rooms, dining halls—the terminology and nuances changing with region, locality, industry, and proprietor preference—dining establishments in name and number thrived in urban centers in the mid- to late nineteenth century, an outcome of an evolving middle class. These were places that often hired black workers and catered to white men—and, only occasionally, white women, who typically required white male accompaniment to enter. Even through the early 1900s, unescorted white women were often identified as prostitutes and outwardly dismissed from respectable establishments, with select restaurants permitting solo white women or white ladies' groups to dine in private rooms, usually only during the day, and always out of men's sight.

There is more I'd like to say on the subject of women's history of dining out in America, on the pervasive inconsistencies in how black and white women engaged in that pursuit of pleasure, especially during so-called "women's" suffrage. For now, let's understand that the cultural space allotted for dining out, the social practice of eating at ease in public, was not created for the enjoyment of black people or other persons of color. But the practice was often expected to be upheld by the service of black people and non-white immigrants. And while white women advocated politically and socially to be afforded a seat at the table and handed the same menu as white men (with published prices, thank you), it was predominantly black people's courage in the face of mob violence, sit-ins, litigation, civil unrest, and relentless protest that granted me, an African American woman, the confidence to walk through any restaurant door with the expectation of service.

We are many decades departed from images of young, black college students being hauled off by white police officers for protesting, for daring to ask for a cola float and tuna melt in whites-only diners. But then, in the of spring 2018, twenty-five-year-old Chikesia Clemons was wrestled to the ground and detained by three white police officers in a Waffle House for questioning the charge of plastic flatware with a take-out order. Her bare chest is exposed in a recording widely circulated on the internet; the indecency shown her and countless others like her in recent days eerily similar to Jim Crow–era conflict—white patrons continued their meals and appeared unflustered by the ordeal.

This is the thing that unnerves me most about unwittingly becoming part of the performance of going out to eat, of being dragged into somebody's showtime. You're only part of the act when the white viewer summons you—if they don't want to bear witness, they don't have to. Being white means you can engage if you so choose, or you can leave well enough alone. Being white means you can watch an outnumbered, unarmed black woman be manhandled by law enforcement and stripped of basic dignity while enjoying your waffle and hash browns; it means you can harass a young black woman seated at the bar for no other reason than that you can't quite account for how she got there, same as you.

VII.

By the end of our respective meals, Donna remained unsettled by the artichoke snafu. She interrupted me again to explain how things transpired, blow by blow, as if I had not also been present. She capped off her speech by saying that all she tried to do was make up for taking my artichokes by recommending a dish. We all know that recommending a salad doesn't make up for anything, but this is the degree to which an ignorant, unchecked white person will go to justify their othering of you—salad as détente. Donna's patronizing of me inherently challenges the idea that I am equal. Her othering of me challenges the power I exert by taking a seat at the proverbial bar.

After Donna got done with her noble speech, I set down my wineglass, which I'd continued to swirl throughout this unnerving exchange. I said, "Hey, you know what—it wasn't your fault. It was the food runner's, and the restaurant was on it. But you couldn't let it go. You interrupted me several times and when you finally began to make the recommendation—"

"I just!—" she cut in.

"I'm talking now," I began again, in my best impression of my third-grade teacher, Mrs. Pavich. "When you made the recommendation, I told you I didn't want your opinion. You'll have to think about why you assumed I'd never had an iceberg wedge before."

"No, it was the beets!" she said, her pitch higher, her voice louder. She was increasingly flummoxed, her expression, drained. This is the moment I hoped she'd remember on her shitty ride home if, for no other reason, than to be miffed by confusion.

"Well," I offered, "when you sober up tonight, you'll have to consider why you think beets would be new to me. Beets."

Maybe it was unkind because she was a bit of a dingbat. But I took pleasure in the way her lips sucked in, what was left of the pink shade wearing off with frustration. I didn't mind playing antagonist. I had not initiated any of our multiple interactions. I believe even if there had been no artichoke-gate, Donna would still have found a way to implant herself in the crux of my evening. Her dimness notwithstanding, I knew that had I been the obtuse interloper troubling a white fellow guest in Winter Park, Florida, my meal would have been on the house because I would have been excused from the restaurant.

Donna's mouth opened and closed silently, twice, before she settled on a response. "You are righteous!" Her whitish-blond head whipped around with finality and she leaned toward her fellow diners who, this time, avoided my gaze.

"Just let it go," I said, almost soothingly. The three scooted their barstools away from the bar.

"I'm letting it go," Donna says. And they trailed off in a single-file line toward the exit.

If the audience leaves, is the performance instantly over? Or is it, as the jazz musicians say, that the music never ends, you just have to stop playing? In the absence of my makeshift dining companions, I was left with an empty wineglass, a mostly eaten French dip, and a dinner bill less the cost of one artichoke appetizer. My attempt at a quiet solo meal had been thwarted and I had nothing to show for it but more evidence about what doesn't work in America. Even if Donna left frazzled by my reactions to her, no lesson was learned. In her mind, she was not an obsessive woman harping on another guest for reasons nestled deep inside; I was an ungrateful visitor in her terrain, and how uncouth of me to deny white kindness that was so generously extended.

When recurring incidents like this take place, ones where it's hard to see a new future emerging, people rely on a time-worn sentiment: These kinds of perspectives are dying out. Don't worry! The old folks who continue to behave this way will take such actions to their graves. That's bullshit, and folks from all backgrounds are guilty of saying it, including me. While I can relate to the intended optimism, I know it's simply not true. Behaviors that uphold unjust systems based on race—also known as racism—are alive and embedded in the habits of plenty of youth. And since this is where we came from, it will always be our beginning. Racism is our American genesis.

Of more concern, the inaction of hoping for a brighter day absolves people—white people—from being accountable for excising their biases, from doing the complex, intergenerational work of self-education that can only have lasting impact through ongoing political and socioeconomic corrections that acknowledge the vast disparties built into our culture. If, one day, we wish to finally end the social devices that evolved from our legal foundation, we must address the existing framework that keeps injustice thriving.

I'm saying to you that dinners aren't going to get better for me until we also deal with our disproportionately black prison population, the joke that is our voting rights landscape, and the systemic lack of access to housing and land free of environmental harm that victimize people of color. Eating out is going to remain a spotty experience for me and others like me as long as white-led organizations continue to congratulate themselves for making one-off, symbolic diversity hires without questioning the patterns that keep putting the same types of white people at the top. We must look at our movies and streaming TV shows, our magazines and publishing outlets, our politics, our classrooms, our living rooms, and our food and restaurants. Donna was a fool, sure. But part of why she left Hillstone indignant is because she has a cultural legacy with all its laws and customs, unabashedly backing her up.

VIII.

I do what I can. My involuntary appearance in the dining performance tends to occur in places where I am in the minority, but patronizing restaurants owned and frequented by people of color is no failsafe, either. And although it's not my intention to eat meals in public purely as an act of protest, I'm starting to embrace that, for a black woman in America, that might be the way it is. At least for now.

The white gaze is constant. I can't control it any more than I can control where a food runner delivers a plate of grilled artichokes. But I have noticed something about the gaze—it's not necessarily a one-way act. I don't know if it will ever truly matter, but sometimes I respond to the intruder with a silent, steady look. In that quiet moment, even if the show goes on, I sense we are both clear—the whole thing is their own futile masquerade.

HORO-
SCOPES

By the bestselling authors of SENTIENT GRILLING,
PICNICS FOR BROS, and BOURBON IS A LIFESTYLE (Christopher
Kimball, Hunter Lewis, Adam Rapoport, and Sam Sifton),
whose new book, DO YOU EVEN ASTROLOGIZE?, is due out
at the next transit of Mercury.*

* The following horoscopes are composed of phrases and sentences taken, very much out of context (and very deliberately), from the Letters from the Editor or online newsletters of Christopher Kimball (founder, *Milk Street*), Hunter Lewis (editor in chief, *Food & Wine*), Adam Rapoport (editor in chief, *Bon Appétit*), and Sam Sifton (food editor, *New York Times*). There was a time not so long ago when jobs like those belonged to us, when people thought of food as the lowest form of "fluff" in the realm of news, or at best, relating to domestic matters and therefore only of use to housewives. Let the women write of such stuff, they said, throwing us a bone they did not wish to gnaw on. So write we did. We built an entire genre, and for a while, were mostly left to oversee it. Women held the highest editorial positions. Then a funny thing happened. Food took off in a big way; it became a pastime and legitimate form of entertainment, which made it a viable source of ad dollars marketable to men. And then, the men saw that it was good, and wouldn't you know, soon the names at the top of the mastheads of the country's major food magazines and newspaper sections weren't women's. What will they take from us next? I asked myself. What is left for them to pillage? "Horoscopes," the stars answered. The signs—and memes—are everywhere—on social media. Astrological content is ripe for the monetizing. For all we know, the guys who dictate cooking trends today may be predicting our futures tomorrow. With apologies to Christopher, Hunter, Adam, and Sam, I have only tried to forecast what lies ahead.

Scorpio

The call issues forth from a child: you've got to move fast and in the moment. We're moving forward. It will get better. But not yet. Last night with the accountant you met at CrossFit wasn't actually all that good. The suburbs are a study in industrial chaos, buildings and companies sprouting up in a grubby free-for-all. It's riveting strange and awful. Look today to a battery of tinctures, juices, extracts, and herbs: Concoct a cure-all. It is a way to make you feel better. Don't forget to wash your hands. Don't fall down a rabbit hole. Make sure to reach out for help if something goes wrong.

Capricorn

Time of wonder: A New Orleans riverboat pilot, a total noob who never even had to lift a finger, instead of being rich, swam in the ocean, ate a lot of BLTs, grilled and grilled and grilled, and managed a few rounds of golf. If that doesn't seem fair, you can publish from beyond the grave. And it's not as if you'll be alone. As people travel from one place to the next, they change their shape, introducing new civilizations to old ones. They are cultural ambassadors without borders; it's the new immigration. Because this is the modern world, and that is a fact.

Sagittarius

Who knows what boiler-room marketing shenanigans gave rise to these National Days. Whatever you think of the kazoos who herald it, singing loudly along to "Old Town Road" over and over and over again, you should address the fact: Curiosity is more powerful than divisive, isolationist jingoism. Curiosity opens the door to cultural exchange and understanding. One wants to experience the unfamiliar. It's central to our experience as humans who care for one another. Let's open our doors to others, set sail in that sea of cream cheese frosting. You'll make partner. You'll gain friends. You'll make someone happy.

Aquarius

If you're extremely bored and looking for any kind of serotonin hit, do yourself a favor: escape. Sometimes it's those impromptu trips, the ones you least plan, that you end up treasuring the most. Put down the cameras and credit card to experience the scents and flavors of foreign shores. Welcome tradition as a paean to the soul—a connection with the pageant of human history. Collect memories instead of things. Live through taste, and the world will start to live within you, where the bison graze on a special sweet grass. The place awaits.

Pisces

This is the quiet season now. Imagine walking down a street, stopping on the sidewalk, taking a breath, holding back tears. It's all about scent, an exhalation of steam through the nose. The city smells alive. One looks to a friend, who gets mixed up with drunken beggars and murder. It's a lesson worth learning—even if it does take you a while: It's nice to have nice friends. But when you depend on the kindness of strangers, you quickly realize that service is a way of propagating goodness in a world where goodness can appear to be in short supply.

Taurus

Luxury lives cheek by jowl with poverty. That outfit you thought was going to work is totally not going to work. If you're the type who's a visual thinker, you could spend the afternoon fantasizing about it, just sitting in darkness with a goblet of bourbon, worrying. You'll be futilely reaching for clothing as stylish as anything along Rue St. Honore in Paris. Remember how your mom always told you good lighting is everything? Well, she was right. At the end of the night when the votives are flickering, you will be very, very proud of yourself.

Aries

The long slog started a few weeks back, the sun having long since gone down. The day that follows will be hard. It can leave you a little wistful, which is depressing and a useful illustration of the malaise that greets a lot of us. When things go wrong in the world, if you can't fix it, just let the fire do its thing. You might stay employed. Go out and make a living in a liminal zone. You're armed and ready. Because, not to get all *Game of Thrones* on you, but it just keeps getting worse. Enjoy the dissonance.

Gemini

Did you grow up driving all over the suburbs all summer long, bored and kind of free, chasing adulthood? The routine was always the same: A mother set on murdering her own children, which has a lusty, suggestive ending. If you spend enough time with locals, you hear stories. You stop trusting yourself. If you go to the hospital to give birth, you need to bring your own sheets and pillows. Go there just to get out of your skin, to let go. It's not hard. You could give someone a smile of understanding. You just have to trust the technique.

Cancer

Lest we forget, children engaging in what's called patriotic education have to leave the house. But please don't take this as a formal endorsement. It's always better to have too many guests than too few. Hundreds of thousands have left their homes to seek shelter and millions more sit tensely, watching the storm models, looking out at the sky, wondering what's going to happen, how bad it might be—shades of the old Harry Potter days. We could, you know, just order pizza. Maybe that's a good lesson for this twenty-first century.

Virgo

In this age of the new and the next, nobody is marching in step. Then the bureaucracy kicks in. Of course, so does the dopamine rush of a tightrope act, brave and scary, ambitious almost beyond measure. You should set yourself up to see the whole plan unravel. Work on yurts and with wheelbarrows and chairs. You don't want to find out, too late, that there are none available, leaving you with sawhorses and plywood. When the sun disappears and you're like, *Well, what do I do now?* Keep it simple. Read a book. Build a fire. Make some soup.

Leo

After a seven-year stretch, beginning with a preponderance of Francophilia, it seems pretty clear everything's impossible. Honestly, if you make a pot of beans under glittering stars, it might blow minds. Smell the air here, not three hundred feet from the bowels—from where *Point Break* meets Bikini Bottom. If you give it time to mellow, here's where the flair comes in—a wonderful thing, a message to the universe that you have your act together, that you are properly buttoned up, that you come correct. The secret to a happy life—both past and present: All beans are magic. Is that all too dude?

Libra

We can banter all we want in the coming weeks about the merits of soccer and backgammon. But every now and then, take a deep breath and think about your plan for coming days. If you're really serious about retiring, you're going to need to start saving pennies that'll turn into dollars. Be ruthless about it. Strive for red-splashed communist "Worker of the Month" posters. That's something that anyone who labors his or her day away in an office can appreciate. You can roll up all boss-like on your colleagues, just like Lumbergh in *Office Space*.

Mari Uyehara

An alumna of *Time Out New York* and the only person to hold the title senior editor emeritus at *Saveur* magazine, Mari Uyehara has written—and edited—many notable food stories. My favorite, if I had to choose, would be "The Pickled Cucumbers That Survived the 1980s AIDS Epidemic," for *Taste*, about a friend of her parents and the gift he left behind. But she has also become a prolific op-ed contributor to—and now, the cultural editor of—GQ.com, and she addresses politics, head-on. She is fearless—even if it means questioning a popular, righteous-seeming party line. Or the media. In her essay "Women Politicians Should Swear More" concerning the uproar caused and criticism incurred (from both parties) when the House representative from Michigan, Rashida Tlaib, referred to POTUS as a "motherfucker," Mari wrote: "The only 'gift to Trump' here is the journalists and Democrats who join in with hypocrite Republicans to browbeat women over a made-up standard that craggy old white men are never held to. This isn't a mere double-standard; it's this kind of coverage that got us the most embarrassing president in living memory . . . In effect, the attitude of many in the media is that 'boys will be boys,' flawed but real, while women must be prim and proper in the face of the most grotesque of realities."

Sing it, sister! I wanted to see her apply her bold, forensically analytical line of reasoning to food culture. And she did.

How Fashion Hijacked the Food World

I n the 2016 US election, as the country's first viable female presidential candidate battled its toxic male id, deep and lingering societal inequities were laid bare: A sneering phalanx of male media types, many of them later exposed by #MeToo, gave Donald Trump a back-slapping pass on major deficiencies while hammering Hillary Clinton on minor ones, and a majority of white women helped vault the grab-'em-by-the-pussy candidate, with nineteen sexual assault allegations to his name, into the highest office in the land. It was an apotheosis of ongoing battles over sexism—still firmly lodged in our culture after various federal civil rights laws banned more explicit institutional expressions—that had, for years, been roiling all corners of American life: college campuses, tech, and entertainment. Even the glossy world of food media had its own moment of gender-bias reckoning when we were forced to examine the dark underbelly of fluffy feel-good restaurant coverage.

It was November of 2013. *Time* magazine ran the now infamous "Gods of Food" issue, with America's David Chang, Denmark's René Redzepi, and Brazil's Alex Atala in their chef whites on the cover, along with the enticement to "meet the people who influence what (and how) you eat." Inside, the editors listed thirteen deities of the culinary realm with an accompanying family-tree infographic of four more chefs and their supposed culinary progeny, as well as six more "influential outliers," altogether highlighting the world's purportedly sixty most relevant chefs. Pastry aside, not a single female chef was named.

For many, the underlying problem was obvious: sexist male editors. But there was something else at work. Food media, once dedicated to the prosaic domesticity of home cooking, had taken a sharp turn in the past couple decades, increasingly besotted with new restaurants, celebrity, and the all-important quality of hotness. The value system of fashion magazines, with a greater emphasis on trends, beauty, and consumerism, displaced the old practical ethos of cooking ones.

In the wake of *Time*'s Gods of Food issue, repudiations of gender bias came fast and furious. The *New York Times*, the *Los Angeles Times*, the *Boston Globe*, and many more weighed in on the controversy, bringing in women chefs and writers to dissect the matter. In an interview with the food and dining website *Eater*, *Time* editor Howard Chua-Eoan defended the choices. "We went with the chefs with the most name recognition," he explained. "There was no attempt to exclude women, we just went with the basic realities of what was going on and who was being talked about." I'd rather not slander some of the nice-but-not-exactly-talked-about male chefs that Chua-Eoan and his team chose to include over more prominent female chefs, but this claim was demonstrably false.

There was no mention of Alice Waters, godmother to America's farm-to-table movement, whose vision at Berkeley's Chez Panisse portended a generation of seasonal-cooking devotees and reshaped the American grocery long before Dan Barber, one of *Time*'s subjects, appeared on the scene. Neither was there anything on Ruth Rogers and her late partner Rose Grey of London's enormously influential River Cafe, which spurred a global trend of breezy regional Italian and helped jumpstart the city's moribund dining scene, nor of Barcelona great Carme Ruscalleda, who has scooped up seven Michelin stars across three restaurants between Spain and Japan. And nothing on Gabrielle Hamilton, who displayed a prescient hyper-personal whimsy, like serving canned sardines on Triscuits, with the opening of New York's Prune in 1999, which came to define the playfulness of many of America's best restaurants. Ambitious American chefs today cook much more like Waters, Rogers, and Hamilton, than they do like cover star Atala, whose anthropological Brazilian approach hasn't been a blip on our screen.

Time's family-tree infographic was ultimately a half-baked conceit offering little in the way of understanding how and why we eat as we do. Aside from snubbing female chefs, there were other deficiencies, too. It was inordinately white, tilted toward European chefs and exhausting tasting-menu restaurants that have since become démodé, giving way to coolly casual Australian-style cafés with healthy twists—pioneered in this country by women, most notably Jessica Koslow of Los Angeles's Sqirl. It also bafflingly excluded the entire Japanese culinary ecosystem—except two Japanese chefs who had worked for European chefs—an enormous source of influence and inspiration for Western chefs at nearly every level, and neglected African American chefs despite their shaping much of the country's culinary canon. But African Americans and Japanese don't make up the ranks of American food media, and the Japanese, at least, don't put much, if any, weight into one US news magazine's assessment of their food. And so, the lack of women was the main focus of outrage.

Now, of any industry, food media was particularly well equipped to deal with, as Chua-Eoan put it, "who was being talked about." Unlike Silicon Valley or Wall Street, the upper ranks of most food publications are stacked with plenty of women and plenty in positions of power. At the time, white women held positions as *Bon Appétit*'s executive editor, special projects editor, and associate restaurants editor, and *Food & Wine*'s editor in chief, executive editor, deputy editor, and restaurants editor, with many more across the country in prominent perches as restaurant critics or food section editors in major cities, popular recipe columnists, and television personalities.

This was no new development, either. While women were once barred from entering professions like law and medicine, lifestyle media was one of the few areas in American industry long open to white women, now with living legends like Anna Wintour dominating the scene. In 1828, almost one hundred years before American women were granted the right to vote, the writer, poet, and women's education advocate Sarah Josepha Hale started editing *Ladies' Magazine;* she also wrote *Early American Cookery* (1841) in between putting out collections of poetry and championing progressive feminist ideas. Long before the iconic *New York Times* restaurant critic Ruth Reichl took the reins at *Gourmet,* the magazine's first editor in chief, in 1941, was Pearl Metzelthin. And, at various stages, women, among them Jane Nickerson in the mid-twentieth century and Susan Edgerley more recently, ran the *New York Times* food section.

For twenty-one years, Dana Cowin edited *Food & Wine,* helping usher in the celebrity chef era with the magazine's annual Best Chefs issue, while, over at *Bon Appétit,* Barbara Fairchild launched its own annual Best New Restaurants issue in 2009. In the world of business, it's been said that women CEOs are only given a chance once a company is failing; the opposite pattern has been true in the world of food magazines in which titles led by powerful female editor in chiefs were handed over to men after print media was declared dead. As the industry started switching over to digital-first outlets, women dominated there too, with figures like *Eater's* Amanda Kludt and *Munchies'* Helen Hollyman running the show or Amanda Hesser and Merrill Stubbs launching the venture capital-backed Food52. And while niche culinary magazines, like *Saveur* and *The Art of Eating,* have had male editors, major media conglomerates consistently tapped female lifestyle editors, like Maile Carpenter of category leader *Food Network Magazine,* for big launches of ambitious new titles.

After the falling out over *Time's* Gods of Food issue, many of these power players were jolted into action. *Food & Wine* dedicated their January 2015 issue entirely to women, and *Eater* started enforcing representation quotas for their up-and-comer lists. *Cherry Bombe,* a new twice-annual magazine on women and food, debuted its own conference, Jubilee, which became a glamorous hobnobbing event, drawing almost every major female food editor for its empowering talks. With all this female firepower on mastheads and an energized fight against misogyny, you would have expected to see broader coverage of women chefs. Surprisingly, it seemed to have narrowed and converged around a particular type: young, hip, photogenic, and often working outside a traditional restaurant.

This development went largely unnoticed, as many took to focusing on percentages of female representation and some took to assailing the mere presence of male editors, particularly new appointments at the top of the masthead. "It's very rare for us to write a major feature-length national profile of a white male chef," Kludt of *Eater* told *Esquire.* "I'm just guessing, but I think a male editor wouldn't have a problem assigning a high-profile white male writer to cover a high-profile white male chef for a major national feature, and I'm just not going to do that." Perhaps that is true. But it didn't explain or solve why these patterns in coverage also arose under female-led titles.

From 1995 through 2015, while Cowin was overseeing *Food & Wine,* 15 percent of its Best New Chefs were women—lower even than the national average, 21 percent, of female head chefs—with one year (2003) completely male. Also during those two decades, exactly zero black chefs were bestowed with the honor; it wasn't until 2016, after nearly twenty-eight years, that the magazine named the first. Maybe it was unsurprising that the unquestioning celebration of a restaurant segment largely catering to a wealthy white elite automatically reflected institutional inequities. In a 2010 interview with *Eater* on gender imbalance—though not, notably, the exclusion of African Americans—Cowin asserted that: "There just are not that many women who have chosen to be executive chefs." She noted that only one in twenty of the nominations for Best New Chefs were women, seemingly incurious about the pool of people they called upon to make those nominations, as well as what effect rampant sexual harassment, an abusive boys-club kitchen culture, and the often discriminatory process of securing investors might have on the makeup of executive chefs as a whole. Apparently, it was easier to flog the hypothetical thinking of male editors than a fellow white female editor with a majority female staff reinforcing white patriarchal norms. The scapegoating of male editors also left prognosticators blind as a malignant form of lifestyle media started taking over food, one that has never been particularly kind to women: fashion.

In December of 2017, The Cut, *New York* magazine's fashion section, featured chef Angela Dimayuga in an extensive spread, sporting five different outfits, including a funky $3,950 off-the-shoulder black ball gown with tiny white polka dots and a prominent back zipper. Her satin gloves were hot pink, and her hair dyed egg-yolk yellow and coiffed and curled in waves around her soft features. It was almost a couture reimagining of the sartorial stylings in Willy Wonka's Chocolate Factory, turned into something more elegant and enviable.

In that year alone, Dimayuga was also the subject of a lengthy profile in *Eater,* a big entertaining feature in *Bon Appétit,* and a Fashion & Style article in the *New York Times.* Dimayuga is a considerable talent, with the kind of unbridled creativity that typically marks rising culinary stars. But she also left her post as executive chef of Mission Chinese Food before her profiles in *Eater* and *New York* were even written, and it is unusual for this dizzying amount of press to be bestowed on a chef who has not yet opened his or her first own place, rarer still for someone in between gigs. She is, however, young, stylish, and able to pull off a polka-dot ball gown with dramatic poof sleeves. It seems to be the standard, more and more, to which female chefs are held. In the same year, other American female chefs, whose own bodies did not fit fashion dimensions, were drawing lines out the door for their über-popular and locally acclaimed restaurants; they were not treated to the same high-profile coverage. While restaurant kitchens typically demand that female chefs compete in hypermasculine environments, media outlets have increasingly demanded that they conform to the fashion ideal of feminine beauty.

In addition to Dimayuga, Christina Tosi, the baking whiz behind the Milk Bar empire, and Rosio Sánchez, a former pastry chef of Noma who opened a renowned taco stand in Copenhagen (she now has a restaurant), also drew heaps of coverage—they were the names always on the tips of the tongues of both male editors and female ones, including my own. In addition to their youth and talent, all three female chefs had been anointed by former famous male chef bosses: Danny Bowien, Chang, and Redzepi, chefs at typically world-famous restaurants, gods of food, so to speak. They were also photogenic and exuded a kind of urbane cool. Ditto Sqirl's Koslow—although she trained under Atlanta's Anne Quatrano—another favorite of both food and fashion magazines who has appeared often in *Vogue* and *Nylon*.

What you won't see as often in food and travel publications, regardless of the gender of the reigning editor in chief, are older women chefs, particularly those who have successfully come out on top of the fine dining model. While their male counterparts, like Redzepi and Massimo Bottura, are endlessly fascinating, granted interviews and dramatic portrait shots ad nauseam, female European chefs of a certain age are almost always dismissed as *old* news, even if they've never been in the news. Ruscalleda has racked up more than twice the number of Michelin stars of Bottura for her (now closed) three-star restaurant and a pair of two-star restaurants. Only a handful of other chefs on the planet have the same number of Michelin stars as she does and an even smaller number have more. Yet she has never been profiled in a major American publication. Attempt to pitch story on Ruscalleda, who is in her sixties, and most editors will demure for someone more "fresh" and "up-and-coming"—read: young and more likely to fit into a fashion spread—a standard entirely absent for the balding and rumpled Argentinean chef Francis Mallmann, also a sexagenarian, who has been profiled in *Bon Appétit*, *Esquire*, *Saveur*, and *Food & Wine*.

Even more curious is that all the mentions of Ruscalleda, who is self-taught and the sole public face of her restaurants, come from mostly men: a nod from José Andres in *Food & Wine;* another from Mario Batali on Saveur.com; and even one from Chua-Eoan via *Eater*. Fellow female chefs running three-Michelin-star restaurants, like Annie Féolde of Enoteca Pinchiorri in Florence and Nadia Santini of Dal Pescatore in Lombardy, are also somehow completely absent from American coverage. These chefs should be a layup for female-centric food media looking to correct Chua-Eoan's narrative that decorated female chefs are not being "talked about." But they're ignored by American female editors, too. In the United States, only two female chefs have garnered two stars, and, coincidentally or not, both are European too: French chef Dominique Crenn of San Francisco's Atelier Crenn, who earned a third in 2018, and Swede Emma Bengtsson of New York's Aquavit. While there is often grumbling about Michelin not awarding stars to enough women, it was the fusty old organization that discovered Bengtsson, previously ignored by American media, and whose coverage now, for the most part, seems rather muted given her achievement, perhaps because the aged restaurant she oversees is hardly a design hot spot.

Part of the problem is that American food media, once the unglamorous domicile of the hilarious and witty Julia Child, has been hijacked by fashion types. Over the past couple decades, the top ranks of mastheads have steadily been filled by editors who honed their skills at fashion outlets: *Food & Wine*'s Cowin started out at *Vogue*; *Bon Appétit*'s editor in chief Adam Rapaport was previously style editor at *GQ*, while its former executive editor Christine Muhlke came from *T: The New York Times Style Magazine*; and the cofounders of *Cherry Bombe* met at *Harper's Bazaar*. To that end, *Bon Appétit* throws glitzy "Feast or Fashion" parties, and *Food & Wine* partnered with Bravo for the original *Top Chef*, for which Tom Colicchio, who earned his stripes in the kitchen, shares hosting duties with Padma Lakshmi, who earned hers on the runway. And while fashion media has progressively profiled more young photogenic chefs and designers started incorporating culinary installations into fashion week events, food magazines have increasingly made Hollywood celebrities, once more of a mainstay of *Vogue* than *Gourmet*, a regular Q&A fixture.

As the fashion world embraced a modern form of wellness, with ex-models in flowing caftans obsessing over exorbitantly priced spins on older hippie themes—dubbed "clean eating"—that, too, seeped into the pages of food magazines. They started featuring more crossover personalities like former model Jasmine Hemsley and her sister Melissa, who ran a wellness food company together, and Danielle DuBoise and Whitney Tingle, the twenty-something owners of the plant-based meal delivery service Sakara Life, approved by Victoria's Secret Angel Lily Aldridge. With female editors based out of style-conscious locales like New York City also filling out the ranks at most food publications, it may not be all that surprising that the female chefs they chose to highlight embodied their own aspirational lifestyle goals. The fashion-plus-food narrative is now the dominant one.

A high-fashion aesthetic has come to dominate food iconography too, replacing the workaday visuals of yore, as photographers with a fashion editorial sensibility and stylized imagery have co-opted the pages of major food and travel magazines, as well as cookbooks. In the last five years or so, as Instagram's noose has tightened around our necks, dictating how we portray what we eat, several motifs for contemporary food photos have surfaced. Most interesting are the recurring visual signifiers of masculinity and femininity: respectively, the meaty, tattooed chef arm and its corollary, the female hand with quirky nail polish designs—the kind found backstage at New York Fashion Week, not at the stove of any high-intensity kitchen. The fingers are always slender, and the skin is always taut and fair, never wrinkled and rarely dark. The nail polish is usually something edgy like a lime green or steel grey, not something boringly classic, like a red. Even disembodied, women in food, whether they are holding a dripping ice-cream cone or avocado toast, against a high-contrast background or in a high-design café, are uniformly a vision of young coastal cool.

There has, perhaps, been no food magazine more vocal about its mission in fighting misogyny than *Cherry Bombe*. It markets itself as a corrective to "interesting women . . . being left out of the food conversation," and online magazine *Taste* profiled it for its "war on food bros." Strange then that its covers overwhelmingly focus on subjects in line with the male ideal of a woman who eats: one who talks about food, but doesn't look as though she's indulged in too much of it. On the *Cherry Bombe* covers, the faces of the women over forty, like the serum-nourished Martha Stewart and Nigella Lawson, don't betray a wrinkle. Of its first eleven covers, five featured models or former models, and all within a range of a few skin shades—of the three women of color featured, all were Asian or South Asian and none black (the largest racial minority in the United States). Only two have been chefs running their own restaurants.

One of the few *Cherry Bombe* covers with a non-modelesque woman on it featured Lena Dunham, who is known for a particular type of feminism, the kind that mostly ignores the struggles of low-income women and women of color. In an essay for *The Hairpin*, Jenna Wortham reviewed Dunham's show asking: "*Girls* is good for girls. But which girls?" And the same question could be asked of *Cherry Bombe*'s credo that it "celebrates women and food." It certainly celebrates women, but which women? I can't help but wonder if swimsuit model Chrissy Teigen, hilarious as she is, and supermodel Karlie Kloss, both of whom have massive social media followings, and both of whom have been featured on the covers of *Cherry Bombe,* have been left out of the food conversation, or if theirs qualify as "the most vital voices."

The magazine seems to reflect the fashion world's recent adoption of feminism as "the new black," repackaging uncomfortable, perhaps unattractive, radicalism that confronts complicated societal issues in pretty, easy-to-consume parcels. For Christian Dior's Spring 2017 collection, the label lifted the phrase "We Should All Be Feminists" from the title of a book by Nigerian author Chimamanda Ngozi Adichie, for T-shirts. Models, such as Cara Delevingne, sport "The Future Is Female" sweatshirts and post about inner beauty on Instagram in between Victoria's Secret shows. There is an unavoidable tension when a beauty-focused industry, whose standards presume a white male gaze, invokes feminist creeds. And the sunny optimism of slogans and token representation can obscure harder entrenched realities, too. In an editor's letter for the first Cherry Bombe 100, a list of inspiring women, Kerry Diamond cheerily claimed that "things have changed dramatically" in female underrepresentation in kitchens and, perplexingly, media since the publication launched five years ago, as if the ratio of female executive chefs had just miraculously shot up. Just a month prior, McDonald's workers in ten cities went on a one-day strike in an attempt to force management to address on-the-job sexual harassment.

There is, of course, nothing wrong with a gorgeously designed, pink-tinged magazine that dedicates itself to beauty and food, and, to be fair, the weight of correcting food-world misogyny shouldn't rest on the shoulders of a twice-annual indie publication. Plus, *Cherry Bombe*'s interior pages and conferences feature a more diverse mix of voices, including the black Tennessee pitmaster Helen Turner and black chef Mashama Bailey, a Gabrielle Hamilton protégé, who scooped up a best-restaurant award from almost every publication for her Savannah restaurant, The Grey. Perhaps I just wish that it was Turner, Bailey, or Ruscalleda on a *Cherry Bombe* cover instead of a blond gluten-free baker, of which there have been two. And let us also not forget that some of Bailey's earliest boosters were white male writers and their white male editors, including the late Josh Ozersky, who named her to *Esquire*'s Best Restaurants in America, and Jeff Gordinier, who profiled her in the *New York Times,* in 2015—the same year Cowin's *Food & Wine* passed her over for Best New Chefs.

In this age of food-fashion fusion, I can't even see where my old female food heroes would fit in: the imitable Julia Child, the pioneering Chinese American restaurateur and television personality Joyce Chen, and butter-loving Brits Clarissa Dickson Wright and Jennifer Paterson of the archly funny BBC show *Two Fat Ladies.* Certainly, the formidable and rotund Eugénie Brazier—the first chef, male or female, to hold six Michelin stars simultaneously, all the way back in 1935—would not be any editor's first choice for a full portrait shot. Black domestic workers, as chronicled in Toni Tipton-Martin's *The Jemima Code,* were often the unheralded virtuoso force behind American cookery. But they didn't necessarily have the means to be on the cutting edge of fashion. When I flip through magazines and see the names of women chefs, ones who may not fit an ideal of beauty, get a best restaurant nod without their faces shown only to be rarely mentioned again, while style-conscious bloggers and lightweight figures receive a seemingly disproportionate amount of coverage, I wonder if amidst all this beautifully designed rah-rah food feminism we've moved forward or back.

In the past two years, as the fallout from Harvey Weinstein's grotesque abuses and pent-up release of #MeToo crashed down in the food world too, previously untouchable culinary titans, including chefs Mario Batali and John Besh, and restaurateur Ken Friedman, all accused of using their positions to sexually degrade women, were held to account. The first of those stories, on Besh, was broken by a white male writer at a local newspaper, Brett Anderson for New Orleans's *Times-Picayune*, after a yearlong investigation that started before Weinstein was outed; it goes without saying that stylized glossies avoid investigative reporting, particularly since the folding of *Gourmet*, which ran exposés like one on slavery at tomato farms. This again reignited conversations about gender representation in food media.

In a turn away from the cooking-teacher model, food media has asked that female cooks act as stand-ins for other forms of femininity that include not just the ideal of feminine beauty, but also that of female as helpless victim. This was another classic fashion trope—like the famously rapey 2007 Dolce & Gabbana ad featuring a woman in stilettos pinned down by one man and surrounded by four more, which drew a rebuke from the National Organization of Women, and many others in the same mode—with women presented in various motifs of abuse: tied up, choked, or lying lifeless. For *Bon Appétit*, then senior editor Julia Kramer opined on the subject of kitchen sexual harassment in a piece called "Dear Male Chefs: Talk Less," skewering those male chefs, like Daniel Patterson, for hogging the conversation, when it's a women's "story to tell." The assessment ignored what some female chefs have been saying for the years: that they wanted to be recognized for their food, not as mouthpieces for victimhood, and that male chefs should step up to address harassment in the kitchen instead of leaving the burden solely for women to carry.

After *Time*'s Gods of Food came out, Amanda Cohen, chef-owner of New York's Dirty Candy, wrote a *New York Times* piece, "Talented Female Chefs Are Invisible to the Press," complaining that the media asked for their opinions regarding representation and sexual harassment, but not cooking. And Hamilton, in the same roundup, questioned why she was being asked to answer for *Time*'s oversight and not leading male chefs. Four years later, after revelations about Besh's abuses, Cohen, writing this time for Esquire.com, declared that food media was only interested in women chefs as victims: "As you've made clear, it doesn't matter how well we cook. It only matters if a man wants to grab our pussies." In other words, women chefs have faced an uphill battle getting food media—even well-meaning female members—to treat them simply as chefs.

In another article for Esquire.com, "Food Media Is Dominated by Women. So Why Aren't We Writing About Female Chefs?," Kramer's colleague at *Bon Appétit*, food director Carla Lalli Music told writer Sarah Zorn that she's been in conversations where women were dismissed or prioritized based on how they look. "Yet no one ever complains about covering overweight, balding, sausage-fingered dude chefs," said Music. "That's a fact." It may very well be, but does that mean it's an immutable one and one which food directors are powerless to question or change?

Zorn's piece was a mix of partial truths and unsubstantiated theories, but little self-reflection. One editor claimed that the press is focused on newness, so therefore chefs with power and money could get more attention by changing the menu or opening a new restaurant. It is true that the media focuses on up-and-coming. But that doesn't explain why older male chefs who don't offer newness continue to draw coverage, while women chefs of the same age are completely ignored. Zorn went on to hypothesize that "it's certainly worth noting that while women hold top editorial positions at multiple influential media outlets, publishers themselves, particularly of national consumer magazines, are primarily male, a fact that could drive the notion that male chefs are more salable." This was quite a stretch, particularly when publishers at major cooking magazines have been women, recently including Pamela Drucker Mann at *Bon Appétit*, Christina Grdovic at *Food & Wine*, and Vicki Wellington at *Food Network Magazine*.

It also doesn't seem correct to claim that male chefs are perceived as more "salable." Of the few *Bon Appétit* covers that feature people, instead of food, most are women. But they're women of a certain type: fresh-faced and flaxen-haired Gwyneth Paltrow on the June 2011 issue; a red-lipped mezcal maker holding an icy pink pop on the May 2017 Travel issue; two dark-haired beauties, servers from Washington, DC, Filipino restaurant Bad Saint, laughing and slurping noodles on the March 2017 Generation Next issue. None major chefs. By contrast, the unfashionable *Food Network Magazine*, the country's most popular cooking title, consistently features both beloved women chefs and home cooks like Alex Guarnaschelli, Anne Burrell, and Ina Garten, none of whom is a size 0, as well as African American personalities, such as Sunny Anderson and Patrick and Gina Neely, on its cover. If there are differences in the aesthetic standards for women between the male-led *Bon Appétit* and female-run *Cherry Bombe*, they are hard to decipher. What the two have in common is fashion DNA that prioritizes female beauty, not culinary chops, as the determining factor for salability.

Female chefs have been breaking down barriers, for decades, many of them ignoring the norms of how women should present themselves. They have racked up Michelin stars in Europe, ignited long-term dining trends around the globe, and won the hearts of diners and critics, male and female, across the country. The question I have is whether this new pink-hued breed of food-fashion feminism serves them, too.

A Conversation with Carla Hall

The actress Busy Philipps calls certain people "sparkly humans," because, as she's written, "they sparkle from the inside out." According to her definition, they tend to be late bloomers—their inner magic not recognized or understood by their peers in the early years. "The secret is, if you're truly sparkly, you survive all that bullshit . . . at some point, you start to get rewarded for it." If you're not sure you've met one of these magical souls, spend a few moments in Carla Hall's presence, and you'll know. She has an electrified presentness; her joyfulness, uncontainable warmth, and intuitive understanding always come through. You can see it when you watch her on television. It's why she won the fan favorite title on Bravo's *Top Chef All-Stars* and why so many of us rooted for her when she competed on *Top Chef* the first time around. It's why she was picked to co-host ABC's food-centered talk show *The Chew* and why, after that program was canceled, she has continued to enchant viewers and make them want to cook whatever she's serving up as a correspondent on *GMA Day*.

Sparkle can only get you so far, though. Carla, who began cooking in her mid-twenties, didn't hit her stride—or get on the public's radar—until she was well into her forties. She spent those two decades in the kitchen, putting in the work—a lot of it. And since being recognized for her talent, and sparkliness, she's seen as much failure as she has success. She hasn't let that stop her from taking risks and saying yes to new opportunities, no matter how great the challenge. "I truly believe that frustrations are the ability to do work. When you are frustrated and you are being pushed out of your comfort zone, you're either going to rise to the occasion or you're gonna go backward and set yourself back," she said at Cafe Luxembourg, a neighborhood institution on the Upper West Side in Manhattan, where she lives part-time (Washington, DC, is home proper) and where I got to bask in her sparkle for a couple of hours.

Can you talk a little bit about how your childhood in Nashville set you on your path?

CARLA

It's interesting because the answer to that question at fifty-four is very different than what I would have answered even ten years ago, because Nashville set me up but I couldn't appreciate what it did for me until the last decade. That's the case with so many people. I think in terms of the warmth, and the people, and the joy; the friendliness, that Southern hospitality, that *do drop in*; my grandmother's Sunday suppers, church, hair salons—all of that made me the person that I am. I didn't realize it even when I was on *Top Chef* and I started doing comfort food. I realized after that I was making that food because I was homesick.

CD

That's so interesting.

CARLA

This is all hindsight, but when I was in France, I was homesick and I met these girls who were having this brunch on Sundays, and they would start making macaroni and cheese and Buffalo wings and all these things, and I had no idea how to make those things; I was just one of the people at the table and I started thinking, *This feels good to me*. It's because I was homesick. Whenever I've been homesick, all my life, I have gone back to that food. It was about comfort and emotion and just this connection and I couldn't appreciate it. I was running away from it as fast as I could get.

CD

Do you think that's because there was that idea of what you needed to cook if you wanted to be taken seriously as a chef?

CARLA

Absolutely. I wanted to be taken seriously so that meant one track: French cooking, culinary school. It's like dancing and ballet. It sets up the boundaries and the structure for success, and what you know and what you don't know.

CD

Yeah, it's true. You were probably combating that on *Top Chef*. You had the double hurdle of being like, *I'm a caterer. I'm already being boxed into that particular role, which people don't take seriously.*

CARLA

Right. Every time I make this food that to me is comforting, my castmates are looking at me like, *There she goes again. Carla's making not serious food, home cooking food.* Why would you ever associate it with homesickness? Do you know what I mean? There were too many other layers to get through. I actually felt that. People can say now, "She was great." But I absolutely felt like an outcast. I wasn't from a pedigreed kitchen. It has actually changed on *Top Chef* where I think that they look for that pedigreed chef so that people come from this world and are respected.

CD

It was not that way at first. It was how you got respect, by doing *Top Chef*. In the first seasons especially, the casting seemed so deliberate. It was like they wanted you to be an underdog from the start. They picked you to be one, which also sets up a very interesting dynamic and narrative. It's like you're already being considered someone who is other and lesser and scrappier and *Let's see if she can do it and wouldn't that make for good television, but probably she's gonna go home.*

CARLA

I was forty-four. I was a caterer; I was from the South; I'm a black woman. There were so many *isms* in that. Interestingly enough, I never thought of myself in those boxes.

CD

I think that's why you succeeded; because you didn't play into it and you didn't let them do that to you. Amazingly, because you persevered, it ended up being a launching pad for you to actually come into your own and be yourself, but also to become a representative for a lot of other women who might have felt like they couldn't do it. It had an upshot, but that's because of you. I think the way it was set up, no one imagined that you would do everything you did.

CARLA

One of the things that Padma Lakshmi has said to me post *Top Chef* is that the thing she liked about me as a contestant was that they would give me notes at the judge's table and I would take those notes and turn them into something for the next challenge. I went on that show; my intention was to challenge myself and to grow as a professional. It wasn't to shine, it wasn't to get to use that show as a platform for the next thing. It was really to be the best that I could be.

CD

I decided that you're a like a cat except, instead of having nine lives, you've had nine professional lives or careers and some simultaneously. Tell me if I got them all:

First, you went to business school at Howard University and then you were an accountant. That's one. Two, fashion model. Three, you're also a professionally trained chef who has been a caterer. Four, a reality cooking show competitor, which is like a thing some people do for the rest of their lives, even though you do not, thank goodness. Next we have cookbook author. After that, a talk show host. Then an entrepreneur: You had your lunch delivery service really early on and then you had the cookie company, too. Oh, and then you've been a restaurateur. What have I missed, because that's nine. I'm very proud of myself.

CARLA

That's amazing. I would add my next life would be actor. That's actually what I wanted to do as a child.

CD

All right, okay. We're going into ten! How did you get from being a *Top Chef* contestant (twice) to starting your cookie company and then to cohosting *The Chew*?

CARLA

It was *Top Chef* Season Five [2008 to 2009], the catering, *Top Chef All-Stars* in 2010–11, the cookies, and then I won Fan Favorite [of *All-Stars*]. *The Chew* came from that; they were casting at the same time. I had auditioned for it right after I finished *Top Chef*, before I went back for the finale, and they didn't choose me. Then, that summer, they were recasting and then they ended up calling me.

CD

What made you want to do it?

CARLA

They had people come in and we were talking about food. It was kind of like *The View* but with different food perspectives. I was like, *Wow, this seems really fun*. When we came back for the chemistry test, it was the five of us, Mario [Batali], Michael [Symon], Clinton [Kelly], Daphne [Oz], and myself. We were only together for twenty minutes and there were other people who we had chemistry tests with, but six days later they announced us as the cast.

CD

Did it feel right? Could you tell when you were sitting there?

CARLA

I think that was the thing. I've always been very intuitive about what my next step was. It wasn't necessarily then, but it was when we got together for the promos that I felt it. I was like, *Wow, this feels really good.* It was like I'd known those people all my life.

CD

Were you nervous at all about it?

CARLA

Yes. I was so nervous: I'm around two Iron Chefs; Clinton Kelly, who had done *What Not to Wear.* All of them, Clinton, Michael, and Mario had a load of television experience and they had been hosts. I am shifting from being a contestant on a show where they just film you doing what you do to being a host and it is a different perspective. You created this three-ring circus from cooking, engaging the audience whom you don't see, telling a little about yourself, and making it look it very easy in five to six minutes. It's really hard.

CD

It's very different from the *Top Chef* thing where you didn't have to play to the camera because the point was to capture this very real moment of you suffering in the kitchen. I want to ask you, not about the specifics of your cohost Mario Batali [who was accused of sexual harassment and abuse by numerous women] and *The Chew*, but about how you dealt with being in that situation knowing you can only say so much but probably having a lot of feelings about it.

CARLA

It's interesting. I've thought a lot about it just in general. When you read something about somebody in the newspaper and you don't know that person, that story becomes 100 percent of your perspective and view of that person. When you know the person and you have a personal relationship with that person, that story becomes 5, maybe 10, percent of your perspective of that person, which means you have 90 percent that is not that story. It's tough because when that happened, all of a sudden, I'd look at these stories not just

in the #MeToo movement, but I'd look at mothers crying over their children who were demonized in a very violent act in the news. In a way, I can relate when you hear this mother saying, *But they were wonderful* and *They were this* and *They were that,* because what the media wants you to believe is that story is 100 percent of that person.

Also, I have seen my job taken away because—and this may seem very dramatic— but people are being tried in the media in a way that it's like being tarred and feathered and lynched without a trial. It hurts me and it's not about the person, but it's how things are being done, and people get very righteous about all of this and they have no idea all of the people that are being affected, and there has to be a different way. There has to be.

CD

I had a similar thing where a friend of mine was written about and called out for harassing and assaulting women. At first, it's just the shock of it, because I didn't know. But second, there is that thing where my friendship with him was something that meant a lot to me and I really valued, and it became this really strange cognitive dissonance as I tried to figure out what to do about this person.

I think one reason that we're seeing the media do that is that the legal system has made it so hard to incriminate the people who have been abusive.

CARLA

That's true.

CD

In that sense, I think maybe part of the reason that it feels like people are being tried in the media is that we don't know how to get to a place where we could try them in court and know that justice would be done. That part of me understands it, but yeah, there's the part of me that saw one of my friends go through this and still honestly does not quite know how to deal with him. I know, you're entirely right, that's not all of him, but yes, also he did those things. Where do you put that?

CARLA

Right, exactly.

CD

For you it's harder because it's *where do you put that?* But you're also on camera, part of this team—of a show—and you still have to go out there and do it.

CARLA

That was probably one of the hardest to do and the other show, honestly, was after the election where we were like, *Oh, we have to—* what we call—*fake up.* (Instead of waking up, *fake up*, because there are people who are expecting us to do the service of lifting them up in the day.) The joy was always very honest with us, but it's tough and I appreciate you sharing that perspective because there's always two sides to the coin. You know that regardless of what happens with somebody, when you see the things that they're doing behind the scenes—the good stuff that people don't know about—and then you're looking at a situation and saying, "Whoa, I had no self-awareness around this so let me move to a place of ownership," and moving through it, I'm not sure that this format allows for that.

CD

So you had the restaurant in Brooklyn, Carla Hall's Southern Kitchen, and it closes and then you have *The Chew* and it ends. How did you deal with those things? Did they happen around the same time?

CARLA

The restaurant was the previous summer [2017], so August like in the beginning of the season. Honestly, it was such an amazing learning experience. It really was. It was my first restaurant and I loved it, I absolutely loved

it. I would do it again. The difference is, I had my first restaurant very publicly. A lot of people have their first restaurant on the DL. Mine was just very public and I'll tell you, the one thing that *Top Chef* allowed me to do was to be comfortable with being uncomfortable.

CD

That's great.

CARLA

It really did. It was great training for that. When people try to remind me that I failed, I remind them that there are no failures. I learned about my food. I feel like from that journey came this passion about my food and this reconnection with the South that I didn't have, the reconnection with Nashville.

CD

When you look at it in hindsight, what do you think caused it not to be able to do what you wanted it to do?

CARLA

One, the location. My partners and I could not afford a location where we needed the foot traffic to take advantage of this national presence that I had. When people say *location, location, location,* that was that. Also, even though I'm on television, in my mind, I'm still somebody who is a hard worker and willing to pay my dues and work hard and not skip lines. But I think that in my partners, they probably thought, *Because we have Carla, who is on television, it is going to be part of our success.* I actually would have told them, "No, child."

CD

Okay, you have that happen and then you have *The Chew.* What do you do in that situation? How do you collect yourself? Were you like, *I'm going to take some time for myself, I deserve it anyway?*

CARLA

I work really hard during the year. If I'm going to work eight hours, I may as well work twelve or sixteen. I would tend to do that while *The Chew* was taping so that I could take the summers off. We don't get paid over the summer; I take everything that I can so that, financially, I am ready to take the summer off. This year [2018] was very different in that, *Well, shoot, now I need a job.* That said, I thought, *Wow, my next job will probably be in television*, and I'm very grateful for that because I didn't expect to be a television host. For me to think this will continue, it wasn't lost on me. My gratitude for that wasn't lost on me. But, as shocked as we were that it happened, it was also not lost on me that it was seven years, fifteen hundred shows. I probably missed maybe six of the fifteen hundred. That's also great training.

CD

It is, and, also, you may have been ready to do the next thing and you didn't even know it. Okay, on to the cookbooks. You've done three, right?

CARLA

Yeah, three.

CD

There's *Cooking with Love: Comfort Food That Hugs You* [2013], *Carla's Comfort Foods: Favorite Dishes from Around the World* [2014], and then *Carla Hall's Soul Food, Everyday and Celebration* [2018]. How did the experience of doing the first one inform the second and then how did that inform the third?

CARLA

The first one was like birthing a baby. The first one, I was thinking, *Do I know enough to do a cookbook?* Because I know all of the people whom I admire have cookbooks and I would not have put myself in that category. It's like this impostor syndrome that you have going on. I was living outside of myself when I did that cookbook and really relying on the publisher and Genevieve Ko, who was the writer.

CD

She's great.

CARLA

Genevieve is amazing—and my literary agent, Janis Donnaud, who was very honest about the whole thing. It was a lot of recipes. The first cookbook felt almost like a food journal. It was like the food that I was doing and having, growing up with my grandmother, when I was catering, and then on *Top Chef.* Those are the recipes that are in that book.

The second book though . . . It was a two-book deal, so I knew I had to do another one. I remember thinking, around the presidential election, and you started seeing all of this divisiveness and this separation of people: *Does that happen around food?* I don't think it does. I really wanted to tell the story of how, with food, you can sit down and talk to people and they wouldn't question why you did certain things with your rice, or why you did certain things with your spinach or your chicken. It would be very accepting. That's what that book was about. It was really about showing how every time you're doing dinner, you know that you can relate to somebody not only in your country, but somewhere in the world.

Also, that book was about sharing some of the other cuisines that are my favorites. I love Indian food, I love Thai food, and I wanted to share that and it's all comfort food. It came at a time where the people were seeing me as the comfort food chef. I'm like, *We all have comfort food.* Comfort food doesn't mean soul food.

CD

No, I was going to ask you about that distinction because I think that people do not understand that there is a difference, which brings us to your third book. But first, quick question: Did you regret doing a two-book deal?

CARLA

I did and I did it because I felt like I had to do it. It didn't have this purpose behind it. It was more like homework. It felt like, *You've made this promise and you have to do it.* However, I was glad that I got that out of my system and had more experience. I think because of that experience, I knew exactly what I wanted for this [third] book. I also knew for this third book, I didn't have to do a cookbook and I was prepared not to do it.

CD

You wanted to do it.

CARLA

Right, I wanted to do it. My first book went up for auction two days after the announcement that I was going to be on *The Chew* and they bought the book based on that. I think, again, it was the perception that just because I was on television, and the show hadn't even started, that this was going to be amazing and *We don't have to do as much work because you're going to be on television*, and that wasn't the case.

CD

Publishers don't want to market the book, so they go after people who have built-in audiences and they assume that they'll just sell it to their audience and everything will be hunky-dory, and that is not how it works.

CARLA

For this [third] book, I said to Janis, "I don't have to do a book." When I was talking to people [publishers], she said, "Don't bring up the first two books." I got on the phone, I said, "Okay, let's talk about the first two books." Because they didn't do as well, and my question was: "The first two books didn't do as well and why would you want to represent me for this book and what would you do to overcome what happened with the first two books?" That's a real question. *How are you marketing? Don't make any promises that you can't keep because I will hold you to them.* It

was all about that. I love my publisher; I love my editor because I honestly interviewed them like it was for a job.

CD

Yeah, you have to do that.

CARLA

But I didn't know that. And it's why I have to catch myself. I didn't like the first two books, but without the first two books, I wouldn't have this book. Without the restaurant not succeeding, I wouldn't have learned those lessons. I am very grateful for all of these lessons. They're life lessons and, yes, they're public, but what I get to do with being in public is to model to somebody that this is what happens when you learn. When I failed at the James Beard Awards [tripping and falling on stage while hosting], it was very public. I'm like, *So what? I failed.* But what do you do after the fall? This is what I'm trying to tell people. This is how I really try to live my life.

CD

I think it's especially important for women to see, and for women of color, because most of the time when we hear these stories about succeeding from failure, it's men. If you have the confidence and self-awareness to do that and put it out there, it is the most positive thing. I want to go back to soul food and your third cookbook. For the first two cookbooks, you put the phrase "comfort food" in their titles. Then you decided to shift and make the next about "soul food." How do you go in and define that?

CARLA

What inspired the book were two things: One, I had the restaurant and I was actually doing recipes at the restaurant from my first book, and I wanted to show people—it was hot chicken and sides, and all the sides were vegetarian, and all the sides were very meticulously chosen and great ingredients sourced. I wanted to show people that soul food, which is delicious and our heritage and I loved it, was not the source of death. It wasn't gonna kill you. You could still do it and still honor everything that it had to offer in terms of culture. It was one, to teach people in the community that you could really honor this food and it can be quality, and two, to teach people outside of our community what it was.

Then I had my DNA done [again]. I had it done it some time ago, then I continued to do my mother's side and I found out my family was from the Yoruba people from Nigeria and the Bubi people from Bioko Island. All of a sudden, I kept thinking, *Wow, if my ancestors came over today, what would they be eating?* It's a connection to my ancestors from West Africa. It really became this journey.

Then I started thinking, *Okay, if soul food that we know is about celebration foods, what were they eating when they weren't celebrating?* I know my grandmother and mother talked a lot about grains and sweet potatoes and no meat. With my grandmother, my grandfather had high blood pressure so she didn't have a lot of fried foods, and everybody had a garden. What were they eating? I started getting back into this discovery where I wasn't sure that I knew what it was. Over the summer, I went with Genevieve and Gabriele Stabile [the Italian photographer] on this tour through the South to really rediscover the South and talk to farmers and restaurant owners and go to churches and really see my culture through the eyes of people who hadn't been there. It was magical.

CD

It sounds incredible. I do want to talk about this idea of audience, because that was something that really struck me in the *Eater Upsell* interview you did [August, 2016]—that moment where you mentioned your publisher being worried and presuming that your book would only be for black people.

CARLA

That whole thing, that I can't do a soul food cookbook if I am black and I'm giving you my perspective. Why do you think I'm isolating other people by writing about my culture when you don't do that with other disciplines? You don't do that with Italian food, Korean, Japanese, Greek, but you do it with an African American. That alone says something is broken with our system.

I think sometimes we have to check ourselves. I have to check myself too, because sometimes I think that we're the only ones who are experiencing this, but we're not. We experience things in a different way—but we have a very unique experience in this country that has been systematic and, quite frankly, it's hard to overcome. What I wanted to also do with this book, when I read people like Jessica B. Harris and Michael Twitty and Toni Tipton-Martin, there are all of these culinary historians; all of these people who are on the fringes of pop culture—I wanted to shine the light on the work that they're doing. Because I am in pop culture, I have the ability to basically shine the light on them. It's not for me; it's just to say, "Look at all of the work that they're doing and they continue to do to uplift this appreciation and the history of our culture." That was another inspiration for this book.

CD

I feel like there are two answers to that question that you were asked about making sure your book was going to appeal to white people. Why wouldn't it be enough to say, "I want to sell a book to black people," and it could be a huge seller? People who decide—I think, especially with cookbooks—there is still very much this presumed white reader.

But I think about how many other people live in this country. What would be wrong in saying, "It would be nice if white people buy this book, but really I just want to sell it to the millions of black people in this country?"

CARLA

Yeah, absolutely. Just for them to be proud of it. Exactly, to your point, the disposable income that black people spend on beauty products, hair products, on supporting each other is huge.

CD

If you think about the fact that most cookbooks written for white people over the past however many years have been about trying to teach them how to cook their food. Why wouldn't you think that black people in this country might have lost touch with recipes that they would like to get back in touch with?

CARLA

I think, and to this point, it's been proven in movies and in television that this discounted audience is financially viable.

It goes back to who is at the table. It goes back to when I was at *The Chew* and I kept saying, "You need different people as producers, because if you're telling me, a black woman, for this daytime show, that African Americans and Hispanics are the ones watching, why don't you have those people as producers? Because they have to be able to tell the story to these people; because it says, 'I see you, I care about you, and I hear you.'"

I think the other part of it is—and this may be where we are—people of color are a little cautious because we're "in" right now. We don't want to be that trend where people use us because we're the flavor of the month—no pun intended—for their financial gain. Because, if that's the case, I'd rather have the financial gain for somebody in my community.

CD

You have done so many things and you've been asked to do so many things, how do you decide when to say yes or no to something? Has that changed? Did you used to say yes more? No more?

CARLA

My six words of advice are: *Say yes. Adventure follows, and growth.* I say yes to things when they scare me. I say yes to things when it's about giving back. I say yes to things when it's about learning. I have started to say no because the busier I get, even with giving back, I realize that if I say yes to everything, I'm not making a difference anywhere. So I really try to focus on the few organizations where I really want to make a difference. That's been really hard because everybody could make a case for the wonderful things that they do and I am that person. I looked up one day and I was like, *I don't have any time left to actually make money.*

CD

I don't know how you are one of the few people who seem to stay really un-jaded despite the success. Maybe because it came later in life?

CARLA

I'm fifty-four, so it's only been in the last ten years. What people don't see were the twenty-five years that led up to that. Maybe not twenty-five, whatever; I started cooking like at twenty-five. It's hard work and I'm very grateful and appreciative of everything that has happened. If I could just model what happens when your dreams come true or whatever it is—it doesn't mean that it's roses and champagne all the time. I'm just grateful.

Rebecca Flint Marx

Rebecca Flint Marx doesn't spend a lot of time on social media shit-stirring or drumming up assignments (which are related, if not the same thing these days). She's more of a writer's writer, and although her work has been nominated repeatedly for—and won—awards, she remains somewhat under the radar outside the food media. With Rebecca, if you know, you know—it's really all about the writing and the research that goes into it. Her personal essays are deeply affecting; her investigative pieces, equally hard-hitting, and thoroughly reported. In 2013, I assigned her a series of the former; I believe she's proudest of the one about her unlikely and lasting friendship with a fishmonger at the Jewish appetizing shop Russ & Daughters on Manhattan's Lower East Side, but I'm partial to the one about her time at one of the city's few remaining SROs.

As is said of Beyoncé Knowles, Rebecca's got range. You don't need to follow her on Twitter or Instagram to figure that out, although you can (she's pretty funny). Instead, I think you should go to her website and read through her archives. But you can start with this.

"Oh God, a Waitress"

The 1996 film *Basquiat* is about the all-too-brief life and times of Jean-Michel Basquiat, the painter who found celebrity and dissolution in New York's downtown art scene of the 1980s. It boasts exceptional performances, most notably from Jeffrey Wright in the title role, art world–insider knowledge from its director, the painter Julian Schnabel, and David Bowie in brilliant Warhol drag. The film is about art and fame and exploitation and commerce and self-mythology, but when I think about *Basquiat*, more than twenty years after seeing it for the first time, I still think about the three-minute scene where Basquiat meets Gina.

Gina, played by Claire Forlani, is a waitress at an anonymous SoHo restaurant (actually the real-life future location of Café Habana). She is as unforgettable as the restaurant is unremarkable: when we first see her, in slow motion, from Basquiat's point of view, she wears an improbably spotless white T-shirt that functions as a blank canvas framing her beautiful face.

Basquiat, immediately besotted, opens a jar of maple syrup and dumps it on his table, smearing it with the back of his menu. He's then joined by his friend Benny, who openly carries a beer into the restaurant. When Gina comes to take Basquiat's order (pancakes), she gently chides Benny about the beer before grinning conspiratorially and telling him to hide it. Meanwhile, Basquiat uses a fork to draw Gina's portrait in the syrup. "Pretty good," she says. "It's me." But one of the cooks isn't having it, and tells Basquiat to leave. So the artist dumps a fistful of change onto the sticky table and starts for the door, but not before Gina hands him back his change and apologizes. She's too cool to care that a customer's objectification of her has translated into a mess she has to clean up; what matters is that he's an artist, a wild genius whose vision won't be compromised by something as mundane as basic table manners. He creates, and she (willingly) accommodates.

Gina the waitress eventually becomes Gina the long-suffering girlfriend, and, for me, that queasy synthesis of service and sexuality has always summed up Hollywood's general view of waitresses. If you watch enough movies that feature them, whether they're protagonists or ancillary characters, you'll start to notice certain organizing principles, most of which are correlated with the character's age and degree of perceived sexual attractiveness.

If you're a young waitress, for example, you get to be plucky and/or still hopeful about life (see: Forlani; Haley Lu Richardson in *Support the Girls;* the cast of *Mystic Pizza*; Liv Tyler in *Heavy*). If you're older, say thirty-five-plus, then you're a world-weary alumnus of the school of hard knocks (see: Karen Black in *Five Easy Pieces*; Joan Crawford in *Mildred Pierce*; Eileen Brennan in *The Last Picture Show*; Helen Hunt in *As Good As It Gets*; Debbie Harry in *Heavy*; Virginia Madsen in *Sideways*; Michelle Pfeiffer, Kate Nelligan, and Jane Morris in *Frankie and Johnny*; Frances Fisher in the television show *Fargo*'s third season; and, perhaps most spectacularly, Susan Sarandon in *White Palace*). But no matter your age, you most likely have a heart of gold—if you don't, you get Jack Nicholson commanding you to hold an order of chicken salad between your thighs, as he famously did in *Five Easy Pieces*. And your fortunes, more often than not, are intertwined with the whims of the male gaze.

Hollywood has a tendency to portray waitresses, in other words, much as it does prostitutes: fetishistically and narrowly. Both are there to be objectified by men and to take care of them. The movies have historically viewed waitressing the same way they do prostitution, as something to be done as a last resort, and often as a source of shame. Perhaps the earliest onscreen depiction of a waitress can be found in the 1934 adaptation of W. Somerset Maugham's *Of Human Bondage*. Bette Davis, in a star-making role, plays Mildred Rogers, a coarse tearoom waitress. Mildred is a hot mess: She's cruel and manipulative, and more or less destroys the life of the man who loves her. She ends up sick and destitute and—the film implies—working as a prostitute. And then she dies of tuberculosis.

So a precedent had been set, albeit perhaps unconsciously, and as the years went by, movie waitresses continued to get short shrift. As a case in point, consider the 1945 *Mildred Pierce* (another Mildred!), in which the title character turns to waitressing to support her family. "My mother, a waitress," her bratty older daughter, Veda, says disdainfully to Mildred after finding her uniform hidden in her closet. "Do you have to degrade us?"

Waitressing is also frequently used as shorthand for both a character's identity—"Carol the waitress, Simon the fag," says Jack Nicholson, making an introduction in 1997's *As Good As It Gets*—and for what has gone wrong, or could go wrong, for that character. Like prostitutes, movie waitresses are there to be dressed up—in both societal assumptions and clothing that makes them inseparable from their line of work. Hollywood loves a waitress in uniform, particularly if it's pink; Susan Sarandon spends so much of *Thelma & Louise* in a tank top and dirty jeans that it's easy to forget that she begins the movie in an Arkansas diner, wearing a paper hat and a ruffled white apron. Louise's profession, though it is incidental to the film, marks a convenient starting point for the character's trajectory: She begins the movie catering to other people's needs and gradually becomes a woman concerned solely with her own survival—until she decides to end her life on her own terms. The fact that she started the movie as a waitress could be said to make her final act—albeit tragic—seem even more transcendent.

Movie waitresses, like movie prostitutes, are almost always portrayed as women in need of salvation—from an outside source. If it should arrive, it typically takes the form of the love of a good man, though sometimes, as in the case of *Waitress*, it can manifest as a baby. The question of a waitress's own agency in the matter—or of what her desires or ambitions might be—often goes unanswered, if not unasked. Similarly, it is usually a given that gratification—from her job, life, or both—is an outright impossibility.

Rarely do we behold a happy, fulfilled waitress in a movie, much less one who makes six figures a year in the rarefied world of fine dining. To be fair, twenty-five thousand dollars, the mean annual wage earned today by the country's almost 2.6 million servers, is not conducive to contentment, in either life or fiction.

But it's worth considering the specific way Hollywood sees waitresses and their work, and how its portrayals dovetail with or diverge from the way they are presented in real life, meaning in the news and/or food media. If you do a Google News search for "waitresses," the majority of results tend to fall into the following categories: Area Waitress Receives Enormous Tip from Good Samaritan; Waitress Fights Back Against Sexist Boss/Patron; and the Broadway musical version of *Waitress*. In the news, at least, real-life waitresses get put into the same narrow boxes as their fictional counterparts.

And although there are numerous depictions of waitresses on TV and in fiction, I'm keeping my focus on films because they have historically reached more people and are unmatched in their ability to simultaneously reflect society's fantasies and inform them. Movies tell us who we think we are, or want to be, as much as they tell us what to think about other people, particularly those whose lives exist beyond the limits of our imagination and biases. And what they tell us to think about waitresses often carries an unpleasant aftertaste.

Before embarking on any exploration of the subject, it's likewise worth noting that in both film and food writing, women who work in the food industry rarely show up as anything other than waitresses. Sometimes they get to be bartenders, and, more recently, female chefs have been getting more real-world coverage as part of the food media's attempt at gender-based reparations. But that coverage usually carries the caveat that the chef's gender must become as much a part of the story as her profession.

In real life, waitresses (again, like prostitutes) are so often diminished that they become all but invisible, but when the movies grant them visibility, they give us ground rules that instruct us on how to see them. I'm looking at three examples that exemplify waitress tropes while offering more nuanced and complex portraits, and, in doing so, say a lot about what (and who) we expect women to wait for (or on, literally) and tolerate, as well as the push-pull between accommodation and agency, and how that plays out along gendered lines.

Any discussion of onscreen waitresses can't help but start with the obvious: *Waitress*, Adrienne Shelly's 2007 comedy-drama about an unhappily pregnant small-town waitress stuck in an abusive marriage. The movie's release was overshadowed by Shelly's brutal murder several months prior, a tragedy that colored *Waitress*'s critical appraisals. "*Waitress* is, by any reasonable standard, a fairly mediocre movie," Dana Stevens wrote on *Slate*. "But the two facts, of Shelly's death and of the movie's release, are inextricable from one another."

Jenna, *Waitress*'s protagonist, is played by Keri Russell in a performance marked by both gravitas and the same inexplicable, unreliable accent employed by every other actor in the film; it can best be described as Ambiguous Yokel. Jenna is married to Earl (Jeremy Sisto), a childish, insecure lout who makes his wife promise not to love their baby more than she loves him. We see him hit Jenna, control her comings and goings, and coerce her into having unwanted sex.

Earl also pockets Jenna's earnings from her job at the local country-style restaurant. There, she dons a baby blue, white-aproned uniform alongside Dawn (Shelly), a mousy young woman who hides behind a pair of thick black glasses, and Becky (Cheryl Hines), a sassy older (meaning in her early forties) woman who repeatedly bemoans "the dreadful misplacement of my bosoms." Like Jenna, Dawn and Becky have man troubles: Becky's husband is described as a "senile fruitcake," while Dawn would "do anything to meet a man."

All three waitresses must answer to male authority figures: There's the boorish chef who calls Becky a heifer and tells her to "get back to work or I'll fire your ass," and the restaurant's owner, Joe, whose portrayal by Andy Griffith evokes the folksy Mayberry-like charm that the film seeks to capture. But Joe isn't exactly what you'd call charming: He's a curmudgeon who vexes his employees with his idiosyncratic orders and subjects them to readings of his horoscope.

Jenna is only happy when she's making pie; she makes twenty-seven varieties of them each day, and we watch her dreamily stir their batter in the restaurant's improbably spacious kitchen. The kitchen's size and Jenna's total lack of urgency sum up how the movie presents the work of waiting tables: unrealistically. While the waitresses aren't exactly in love with their jobs, the film gives us a version of restaurant life that is so simplistic and inaccurate that it most closely resembles a domestic goddess fantasy—but at the same time asks us to believe that waitressing is a dead-end gig. That lack of nuance (and the contradictory messages) extends to the characters—the shrinking violet, the brassy broad, the downtrodden wife with no self-esteem—and to the movie's overriding theme of female empowerment.

Numerous critics touted *Waitress*—both the film and its 2016 musical adaptation—as a "feminist fairy tale," but while it centers on the lives of women, calling it feminist anything doesn't smell quite right. To begin with, there's Jenna's unwanted pregnancy: When she learns she's pregnant, she moans, "I ain't never gonna get away from Earl now," but the word *abortion* is never uttered, much less presented as a way for Jenna to secure some degree of agency in her unhappy life. There's also Ogie, a man who appears at the restaurant the morning after his first date with Dawn and refuses to leave, despite Dawn's increasingly desperate requests that he do so. "I can't leave you alone because I'm in love with you and you're going to be my wife," he says, and wouldn't you know it, Dawn's clearly unhinged stalker ends up becoming her husband.

And then there's Jenna's happy ending, which relies on a highly convenient miracle and keeps her in almost exactly the same place where she began the movie. When her baby is born, she is so overcome by love that it gives her the strength to tell Earl to get lost, which he does after putting up an unconvincingly brief struggle. She then finds an envelope from Joe, who has just died: It contains a check for more than two hundred thousand dollars. Joe, it turns out, is the only one who really *saw* Jenna: In an earlier scene, he tells her, "You don't even know what you are deep inside. You're not just some little waitress." His check buys Jenna's happily ever after: She buys the diner and revamps it, right down to the new (but still formfitting, classically feminine) uniforms.

But the thing is, Jenna does remain "some little waitress" (albeit one who owns the restaurant) as do Dawn and Becky. Even with a way out, this is the fixed identity the film gives the women—we see them stay in place, both literally and conceptually, from beginning to end. This choice makes *Waitress* one of the few movies to suggest that waitressing can be a sustainable and fulfilling profession that isn't something to run away from, but it would be easier to believe that idea if the film didn't operate in such a frustratingly inconsistent alternate universe where twists of fate and the wishes of deeply flawed men are often prized over the agency of its titular heroines. Sure, Jenna does get rid of her husband, but it's in the most gendered way possible: She only finds the strength to do so when she becomes a mother. And she gets to fulfill her dreams of making pie all day, but it's only after a man has given her the means to do so.

As Jenna (literally) walks off into the sunset with her toddler daughter at the end of the movie, you're left wishing that her happily ever after didn't come with such traditionally gendered caveats—and that the film's idea of a fairy-tale finish could be compatible with the reality of service work. Because you never lose the sense that you're in a fantasy, waitressing never seems like a "real" job. Instead, it's an idealized distraction that functions largely as an excuse to make some really cool-looking pies.

The trope of the waitress working a dead-end job in a dusty, dead-end town is a Hollywood favorite: Aside from the women of *Waitress*, two of its most memorable embodiments are Eileen Brennan as Genevieve, one of *The Last Picture Show*'s world-weary inhabitants of a dying north Texas town, and Brooke Adams as Nora, a single mother who waits tables at a rural New Mexico truck stop in *Gas Food Lodging*. It's a testament to both Brennan and Adams's talents that neither character becomes a stereotype; disappointment with life hasn't whittled them down to one dimension.

But the dusty-dead-end-town waitress to end them all is Alice Hyatt, the headliner of Martin Scorsese's 1974 film *Alice Doesn't Live Here Anymore*. The movie shares some commonalities with *Waitress*: Alice, played by Ellen Burstyn, begins the movie stuck in a bad marriage and eventually finds work in a diner alongside two other women, one of whom is sassy, the other, mousy. She also has dreams that are continually thwarted by both her spouse and her lack of money. Alice has always wanted to sing, and after her deeply unpleasant husband's untimely death, she decides that she's going to take her son, Tommy, and return to her hometown of Monterey to pursue the career she gave up when she married.

In her 1975 review of the movie, Pauline Kael described Alice as a woman "fighting for consciousness, after a long married sleep." The reality Alice wakes up to is portrayed as alternately brutal and unfair, thanks largely to men who run the gamut from sexist to downright violent.

When Alice approaches one lounge owner for work as a singer, he asks her to turn around so he can look at her. "Well, look at my face, I don't sing with my ass," she replies in one of the best comebacks in cinematic history. After she gets the job, she's wooed by a slithery charmer named Ben (Harvey Keitel, in one of his early turns as a psychopath), who turns out to be married; when his wife confronts Alice, Ben breaks into Alice's apartment, physically assaulting his wife and terrorizing Alice so badly that she packs up Tommy and leaves town overnight.

Alice's world nodded to the demographics of the real one: In 1976, according to a 1978 Census Bureau report, 11 percent of all US households comprised a single mother and her dependents. More and more women were negotiating how to live without a man, something unthinkable to their mothers' generation, and, like Alice, were beginning to voice a demand to follow their own dreams, rather than allowing them to be sublimated by someone else's. As Alice admits later in the movie, she was so scared not to please her husband, but also felt like he took care of her; now that he's gone, she says, "I don't know how to live without a man."

Alice eventually lands in Tucson, where she reluctantly gets a job at a roadside diner ("I'm a waitress, that's what," she says as she changes into her uniform.

"Oh god, a waitress.") The film's portrayal of taking orders from and serving (and cleaning up after) customers hews much closer to reality than that of *Waitress*: The labor is hectic and sometimes grueling, and the women endure their customers and, at the same time, find ways to take (financial) advantage of them. As a narrative device, this unglamorous, matter-of-fact depiction has the added benefit of allowing Alice to do the hard work of creating change for herself. In waiting tables, she stops waiting for a man to determine the direction of her life.

You can see the arc of this shift in her relationship with David (Kris Kristofferson), a rancher she meets at the diner. The first time she goes to take his order, he says, "First, I want a big smile," and she obliges. By the end of the movie, Alice no longer behaves submissively toward him; she stands up to him in a blow-out argument, refusing to back down, and when they reconcile in the diner, in front of all of the customers, Alice tells him, "I want to sing. I want to be a singer. I am a singer, and anything I do from now on has got to include that." "That sounds like one hell of a gamble to me," David says. "You sure it's worth it?" "Yes, *yes*," Alice replies. "I am definitely. Yes, yes!" With her declaration, she effectively gets to become an archetype rarely embodied by women in movies: the working-class hero. She's got aspirations, but she also keeps showing up to get the job done. Waitressing isn't her dream career, but also isn't a source of deadening drudgery, much less a profession incompatible with personal growth. We don't necessarily envy Alice, but we don't pity her, either.

Alice Doesn't Live Here Anymore was a critical success, earning three Academy Award nominations and a Best Actress win for Burstyn. It was subsequently spun off into *Alice*, a TV sitcom that ran from 1976 to 1985. In its portrayal of a waitress whose job helps, rather than hinders, her self-discovery and in its refusal to judge the profession—"what's wrong with being a waitress, huh?" her brazen, big-mouthed coworker Flo (Diane Ladd) demands at one point—the film is an exception to the rule of the Unhappy Waitress, but unlike, say, *Waitress*, it offers this revelation in the context of a recognizable universe, making it all the more radical—and convincing. More than four decades on, *Alice Doesn't Live Here Anymore* still rings true as a story of self-discovery and determination in a place, and line of work, where those things are often rendered moot.

The realities and banalities of the workplace, and the performative nature of transactional, low-paid service work, are at the forefront of *Support the Girls*, Andrew Bujalski's wry 2018 comedy about a day in the life of Double Whammies, a Texas sports bar whose motto is "boobs, brews, and big screens." "It's like working at Chili's or Applebee's," one character explains. "Except the tips are way better."

Over the course of the day we follow the bar's general manager, Lisa (played by the excellent Regina Hall), as she deals with a series of crises both small and substantial: There's a man who gets stuck in a ceiling vent while attempting to rob the bar; a customer whom Lisa kicks out of the restaurant after he calls a waitress fat ("I have a zero-tolerance policy on disrespect, so you're gonna have to go," she explains); a new waitress who takes the restaurant's "be sexy" mandate too far; a car wash fundraiser for an employee who purposely rammed into her boyfriend with a car; technical problems with the wide-screen TVs; the firing of a cook; the hiring of new waitresses; an appointment to look at a new apartment for her estranged husband; and a rat problem.

Lisa is seen as a heroine—an everyday heroine—both by the film and her staff, a collection of young women who report for work clad in short shorts and low-cut, midriff-baring tops. Double Whammies invites its largely white, male clientele to see the waitresses as decorative objects (and occasional targets), but Bujalski asks us to look at them as people who have a job to do and who have different approaches to accomplishing it. During an orientation for new hires, Maci (Richardson), a veteran waitress with a huge smile and relentlessly sunny personality, instructs on how to best exploit their customers' chauvinism for cash: laugh with your mouth open and place a hand on a shoulder when you're upselling the beer.

The movie is resolutely frank about the ways the women can accept and resist the conditions imposed on them by society at large and clueless men with power, the latter of which are embodied by James Le Gros as Cubby, the bar's owner. A temperamental bully, Cubby is seen making all kinds of threats, mainly to Lisa, who endures them with levelheaded resolve. But he's also ridiculous—a man-baby who wears white socks under his sandals. There's no question about who really knows how to run the place, but also who must bear the brunt of systemic unfairness.

The specter of Lisa, who is black, patiently dealing with an incompetent white man, nods to matters of race in a way that very few movies about waitresses do; save for Regina King's role as a plucky diner waitress in *A Cinderella Story*, or the character of Tiana in Disney's 2009 cartoon *The Princess and the Frog*, mainstream movies very rarely cast women of color as waitresses. If this lack of representation invites audiences to forget that low-paid service work is frequently done by people of color (and reinforces the assumption that audiences won't be able to empathize with a non-white protagonist), it also reflects the racist, if unofficial policies at work at many restaurants where people of color are often kept out of sight, confined to lower-paid back-of-the-house jobs. We see Cubby remind Lisa of the bar's unofficial "diversity policy," which limits the number of women of color who can be on the floor at any given time, and we see her take that in and breathe it out, just like she does the myriad other problems she must try to solve in the course of the day.

Lisa is unfailingly upbeat, but she is not an automaton: The film begins with her crying in her car, and as it progresses, we come to understand the toll that her job and issues in her personal life have taken on her. As it does with matters of race, class, and sexism, *Support the Girls* acknowledges but doesn't dwell: It's all part and parcel of what Lisa—and her staff—put up with daily, taken for granted as much as air and spilled beer.

Few films about waitresses have drawn such an explicit connection between the performative aspect of the job and what, exactly, is being performed. And in *Support the Girls,* neither the waitresses' performances of sexiness nor their efforts to accommodate their customers come at the expense of their dignity. They have agency, and if they have options, it's because they create them for themselves. In this respect, the movie's depiction of waitressing echoes that of *Alice Doesn't Live Here Anymore*: When Lisa describes the bar as "a mainstream place," she's by extension describing the work as mainstream, too—these are women getting by like anyone else, and trying to beat the odds that life and society have offered them. Like Alice, Lisa is the counterpoint to the male blue-collar hero, someone with both ambitions and boundaries, as well as the wherewithal and smarts to navigate the uneasy relationship between them.

What emerges from *Support the Girls* is a low-key but incisive portrait of a man cave that happens to be a hotbed of sisterhood. The men look at cleavage and flat-screen TVs; the waitresses look out for each other. (And it's worth noting that their most faithful regular happens to be a butch lesbian—played by Lea DeLaria—who looks out for them, too.) Sisterhood, for them, is a form of protection and a tool for perseverance.

In the last scene, Lisa, who has by now lost her job, goes to the roof with Maci and Danyelle (Shayna McHayle), another of her employees. All three women let loose with a primal scream, and that wild, uncorseted noise speaks volumes about what is required to get by as a woman in the service industry. Underpaid, underestimated, undermined, their identities made invisible or obscured by personas that play to societal assumptions, they have to find their own salvation—or, failing that, an escape route to the roof, where they can set themselves free, if only temporarily. It's a far, rallying cry from complicitly picking up the sticky coins a customer left in puddle of maple syrup.

Ultimately, *Support the Girls* asks us not to underestimate or pity Lisa and her employees even as it shows us their litany of everyday woes; they're not "colorful" or "tragic"—two adjectives that often get assigned to fictional waitresses—but instead average people with everyday problems. This, perhaps, is why it strikes me as the most realistic—and satisfying—film ever made about waitresses.

*   *   *

Where *Basquiat*'s depiction of Gina is memorable for how narrowly it defined her—as a waitress, she existed primarily to serve and be idealized by difficult men—*Support the Girls* shows what is possible when onscreen waitresses reach beyond the simple serve-and-accommodate paradigm. (To be fair, Gina was a secondary character in a movie about an artist, and her subservient role almost reads as commentary on the tendency of "great" artists to make sycophants of their admirers.) If Gina borders on an abstraction, then the waitresses of *Alice Doesn't Live Here Anymore* and *Support the Girls* (and, to a lesser extent, *Waitress*) are built of flesh and blood and nuance, and their jobs are shown as real ones, rather than as symbols or attempts at shorthand character development. Because they make us respect their protagonists, they encourage us to extend that respect to the work of waitressing, or at least deepen our understanding of it by giving it visibility.

MY BOOBS
GOT IN
THE WAY

Describe a time you were reminded you had BOOBS in the WORKPLACE (i.e., any moment where you were trying to be business-as-usual and you were made to feel self-conscious about being a woman).

JULIA TURSHEN

When a male chef touched them without my consent.

ANN CASHION

A notable French chef took me under his wing. He let me work in his kitchen when I had time and invited me to assist him when he did special events. I enjoyed being what I thought of as his protégé. Then, he hit on me and I understood . . .

VIRGINIA WILLIS

Once I was working in France in patisserie and the line had a huge rush and it killed the mise en place. Wanting to help out, I ran downstairs to the walk-in and brought up an apron full of something, I can't even remember what it was. With hands on either side, I held out my apron to offer it up to the *chef de partie*. He acted as if he were going to reach for my crotch. In my memory, I told him if he touched me, I would cut his hand off, but I am actually not sure that's what happened. I do know it made me feel more like a woman in a negative way than ever before or since. However, I have to say, when I am working with a group of women—and enlightened men—in a kitchen and it's all working great, the place is clean, the food is good, and it's not testosterone-filled energy, I appreciate my womanhood.

RUBY TANDOH

I worked in a restaurant kitchen for a short while as a pastry chef.

I went in there determined to pull my weight, get on with everyone, and mesh with the team. I was the only woman in the kitchen though, and it was pretty much immediately that I noticed the weight of that aloneness. One guy asked inappropriate questions; another always got changed in my pastry kitchen and would strike up conversation only once he was down to his shorts (I think that's American for underpants, right?). I became acutely aware that I was never going to be one of the lads as long as I continued to assert myself.

CHRISTINA TOSI

First job, first day, locker room. I shut it down. *Quick.* For shame! (I realize how lucky I am that I had a trigger I built in myself long ago to never allow for this.)

MARISA DOBSON

My first job was as a hostess at a seafood restaurant. I was fifteen. The manager chased me into the utility closet in front of other staff and held me in a full body hug. The "joke" was he was teaching me what to avoid from other staff members. Everyone laughed, including me.

TAMAR ADLER

In restaurants: The guy we'd hired as a "chef" in Georgia and I asked to train me on the sauté station used to tell me to bend over to pick stuff up in the middle of service.

In publishing: Two different people I sought as mentors either tried to kiss me or turned business meetings into tryst-to-be's despite my having no interest in anything but business.

KRISTINA GILL

Do you mean a time I was reminded I was a black woman in the food industry? Interestingly enough, with [the cookbook] *Tasting Rome*! My name was consistently left out of articles, pitches to media outlets, etc. Friends in different media outlets called and said, "Hey we got a pitch for a story/appearance for your book but your name's not on it, what's up with that?" The conclusion that those friends who were in executive roles at those outlets or who were in marketing reached most often was that it was much easier to market an Italian cookbook with the face of a white Italian American woman than to market it with the face of a Southern black woman in the mix. Who knows if that's the reason, but it does fit with broader considerations about how decisions are made about cookbook deals. Publishers need to earn their money back, so how they can market a book and who they think their market is are two big considerations. It's always about the bottom line and because 99 percent of people sitting at that table are white, that's the only demographic those decision-makers can relate to and are looking at. It takes someone white to "validate" a person of color before those decision makers will leave their "neighborhood" to look around.

ALEX VAN BUREN

A hand-job joke by a high-up executive in the middle of a book packaging meeting (when I worked in book publishing).

ESTHER TSENG

I was asked if I was on my period when I disagreed with something a man said. (I actually have small boobs so I get comments more about my butt.)

CAROLINE FIDANZA

When I was given a nickname that was an obvious reference to my ass.

CHRISTINE MUHLKE

The summer I was pregnant, I was wearing an uncharacteristically snug T-shirt and eating a bowl of blueberries during a meeting. As he entered the room, one of the men said, "Boob-erries!"

BONNIE MORALES

When I was pregnant with my second kid, Isaac. Our original location has this tiny narrow galley kitchen and one of my sous chefs pulled me aside and told me that all of my cooks were just terrified that they were going to run into their boss's ginormous belly with a hot pan or something. I was physically fit and able to work, but I had to start staying out of the way to make everyone else more comfortable.

After Isaac was born, I started coming in with him almost immediately (I think he was three days old). I felt so incredibly awkward nursing. And when I started leaving him at home and pumping at work, I was always afraid someone was going to be disgusted by my milk storage bags in the breakroom fridge. No one said anything to me, but it was constant paranoia anyway.

MAGGIE HOFFMAN

This is the same old song you'll hear from so many: Breastfeeding is both an amazing gift to the immune system and a huge inconvenience at work. I was largely working at home but needed to visit the office while I was still breastfeeding, and, at the time, the place wasn't set up for pumping—there was literally no private space. So I needed to pull a folding chair into the tiny office bathroom and camp out in there, with my laptop on the sink, and schedule my meetings around this terrible set-up.

NING KANG

I'm always aware of the fact that I'm a woman and I'm conscious about what my strengths are as a woman, and I'm not afraid to show my weaknesses as a woman. One time I was yelled at by a customer who waited for his food for too long; I couldn't hold it anymore and cried in front of everyone! The customer ended up understanding that it wasn't anyone's intention to make mistakes and even started comforting me. Later we just laughed about how the owner was crying and the servers were putting out fires.

At the same time, being a woman, I am always aware of everyone's emotion—if they are stressed out, content, passionate, or discouraged; the working environment is more encouraging rather than competitive.

JOANNE CHANG

I'm always conscious of being a woman—I wouldn't say it's self-conscious, but it's always there. I think about the world from a female perspective because that is all I know. I am aware that men and women sometimes think differently and I embrace that. I'm reminded that I'm female before I go into a big meeting and I always check to see if I have lipstick on.

MASHAMA BAILEY

When I first began cooking, I was reminded every day that I am a woman. I was also a few years older than everyone else so there was that, too. There were a few times I felt pretty low about that.

AMY BRANDWEIN

Most recently, when a national food event organizer approached me after signing on five male chefs to do a hunger event and told me, straight up, we need a woman chef. Note to organizers: If it's that important to you, ask me first and then get everyone else to sign on.

SOFIA PEREZ

On several occasions, I helped a good male friend organize some outings for chefs who were visiting New York City to cook for several public and press events. While my friend is like a father to me and has always been respectful of my intelligence, I cannot say the same for all of the chefs he brought with him. Most of them were great, but as with any group of guys, several were pigs, while others acted as if I barely existed. I was invisible to them and was not considered an authority on the food culture of the city and country in which I've spent my entire life; they were certain they knew more about every culinary topic than I did.

For another event, which took place overseas, we were shorthanded, and I was helping an American chef get ready for his presentation. I donned an apron and began prepping some produce. When two chefs I knew saw me in the apron, they burst out laughing, because they thought I couldn't possibly navigate a professional kitchen. What's even more ridiculous is that these guys are the same ones who, when interviewed by reporters, wax rhapsodic about their mothers and grandmothers and cite the cooking of their female ancestors as their culinary inspiration.

KRISTY MUCCI

It's often assumed that cleaning up is women's work. Lots of events in which people make equal messes, but the men don't ever bother to help clean up after themselves. "The girls will get it."

NAOMI POMEROY

Every food and wine festival and every after-party. #brozone

NICOLE RICE

Almost every meeting I was in from the ages of eighteen to thirty-six.

NICOLE ADRIENNE PONSECA

I attend meetings where the men say, "You seem like a very nice lady." What's nice about working sixteen hours or sacrificing my health or personal life? What's nice about not having health insurance and rubbing two cents together to make a dollar? What's nice about figuring out how to jump out of a plane not knowing if there's a parachute? Why aren't you calling me a formidable warrior woman with a mission and the nerve and moxie to see it through? I'm not a very nice lady—kind, yes. Nice? What does that mean?

ERIN MCKENNA

When a person I was entering into a high stakes partnership with literally only talked to my boobs.

MARION B. SULLIVAN

For more than a decade, I was the only female in a male-dominated food business. I had years of culinary experience and a prestigious culinary education, but when I suggested a change to a menu or the use of a different technique, I was ignored by the all-male cadre of chefs. Ten years of reminding me that I had boobs.

RACHEL BOSSETT

Every single time that a delivery driver or maintenance/repair man comes into the kitchen, they look or walk right past me as though I don't even exist. Even when I'm the only manager on duty, these men will constantly seek a man and assume that I have no idea what I'm talking about, or couldn't possibly help them. This has been a rare experience in regard to coworkers, though. But I've always been told that I'm "one of the guys," and that I'm "intimidating," so I seem to be bypassed on the boob-reminding shenanigans (which is a whole other trip).

EVA KARAGIORGAS

Am I lucky to not have experienced any of this? I guess the closest I have come is when it's a bunch of men in a room, at an event or in a meeting. One man—no problem—business as usual. Where there is more than one, something happens and it's like . . . they really try to dominate. Then what happens to me is, I get like ten times bigger because I'm an animal at heart so I puff up and it makes me roar.

JEN AGG

This is complicated for me, because obviously I've experienced so much institutional sexism, but in terms of sexual harassment, it hasn't happened to me in a long, long time. I'm sure some of this has to do with being the boss . . . But what would be even better is to raise our boys to not treat women as objects of desire so we could just exist, instead of react.

LIGAYA MISHAN

Aside from a few shy, bumbling flirting overtures from distant colleagues who were neither part of my regular work life nor in a position to wield power over me, nothing! Again, I've been very fortunate.

JULIA BAINBRIDGE

Believe it or not, I never felt this until very recently (i.e., twelve years into my career), after wrapping up an interview with someone and hopping on the train to head home. We had had a nice chat about his journey toward embracing his identity, his work, and his wife and child. After I texted him a final thank you for his time, he told me that if he weren't married, he would try to "make it" with me and asked if I would "let" him. Then he proceeded to tell me he would be in New York in a few months if I wanted to join him in his hotel room. He has since followed up to confirm, even though I didn't respond to any of these questions or comments.

It bums me out. We had had such a positive interview and what I thought was a nice professional connection; now I have a bad taste in my mouth and am troubled over to whether or not I want to share his story, even though it's so very powerful.

HANNA RASKIN

Nobody made me feel self-conscious, but I remember being keenly aware of what it meant when a managing editor slapped a fellow reporter on the back and said something along the lines of "good job, champ." Because there was no way for him to lawfully touch or nickname female reporters, the exchange made clear the closeness to power that women in the newsroom couldn't ever achieve.

DIANNA DAOHEUNG

Whenever I go into investor meetings or meet with an older demographic they always shake hands with my male counterparts but feel the need to kiss me on the cheek even though it's the first time I am meeting them and I clearly place my hand out to shake.

TINA ANTOLINI

This is a relatively small anecdote, and, I'm sure, a common one, but it's stuck with me. It gets at the embarrassment I felt because of the kind of harassment that was commonplace waiting tables as a young woman. I spent one summer working at a seafood restaurant and bar on a pier in Maine, which happened to be next to a park where they held a giant music festival each July. During the festival, the bar set me and other waitresses up with whole trays of shots to sell to the folks—mostly men—who gathered on our pier. The head bartender thought it'd be hilarious to send me out with a whole tray of "Sex on the Beach" . . . which meant that's what I had to offer to random strangers. We were required to sell them all in order to come back in and replenish our trays. It was one of the most agonizing stretches of time I spent in my years as a waitress, fending off comments from nearly every customer, trying to treat it like I was playfully in on the joke, while also not actually endangering myself around these guys, many of whom were drunk and getting drunker. Some part of me was furious, but it was subsumed by the part of me that was deeply embarrassed—as if offering these men sugary shots named after sex acts was some reflection of how I thought of myself, as if I was that cavalier about my sexuality.

MARISSA LIPPERT

Sometimes if I wore heels and a dress to work, I would almost feel out of place and less like the boss in a weird way. That and a handful of times when a vendor or workman would be in the café and refer to me as "hon." Maybe they didn't realize I was the boss, but I'm pretty sure they did.

KIM ALTER

Every single time I have a photo shoot. Makeup is expected; I am expected to look perfect even though I am normally running around the kitchen trying to get everything ready for the photo shoot and service. I am *always* asked to smile; you know they aren't asking male chefs to smile.

NICOLE TAYLOR

Well, when men particularly keep commenting on my dress or my clothes when I have maybe something a little tight on top. I don't work in a restaurant—usually, it's food writing, media, consulting; I keep receiving the same compliments on the same day from the same person.

ALI ROSEN

Every single time a man commented on my outfit, so basically every day.

CHARMAINE MCFARLANE

Once the warm weather hits and the whistles of appreciation when people see me in a T-shirt and jeans for the first time. The assumption that I'm on my period when my mood is off, the fact that I may have worked multiple double shifts without a day off or more than eight hours between shifts seems to be irrelevant. Uniforms—the bane of my kitchen existence—which are never sized for my forty-five-inch hips and D cups so I often provide and launder my own.

AUBRIE PICK

When I'm trying to sling a camera off of each shoulder and around my body and accidentally make a bondage-like bra.

JENI BRITTON BAUER

Every single day. I am a 34H (that's 5 Ds).

TIFFANI FAISON

I know you're not looking for answers this literal, but I worked for a chef that I actually had to remind where my face was located. He would just stare at my boobs all the time—and the grossness of that is compounded by the fact that I was always in a chef coat that was about two sizes too big for me. It was like, *Jesus—dude—there's nothing to fucking see here!*

SAMIN NOSRAT

Not so much boobs as a vagina. Working on the line as a woman is already a constant battle to prove you can hang with men. Then, add a period into the equation. I'd take all sorts of measures to try to minimize the number of times I'd have to go to the bathroom during a shift. The inevitable result: leaking tampons, stained underwear, and general discomfort just so my coworkers wouldn't think I was weak. Not to mention the UTIs I gave myself on several occasions because I refused to listen to my body and go to the bathroom. Every female restaurant cook I know has had to deal with this—thinking about it fills me with rage.

MICHELLE HERNANDEZ

Every day that I have walked into a kitchen since I started my career in the industry, I have quickly been reminded that I am a woman. Most of the time now, it is instinctual, but many times, starting out, there were ongoing daily reminders: When there was only one locker room or even no locker room to change clothes so I had to go before the rest of the staff, or wait to change, or change as fast and discreetly as I could next to all the male staff. When one of the fine dining restaurants I worked at only had a urinal for staff to use during service and service was long, I was very aware that I was a woman.

In some kitchens that have felt particularly hostile, I have tried to make myself as plain as possible so as to not attract any unwanted attention. It is an awful feeling to be on guard each time you go to work. To this day, I am not self-conscious but am conscious that I am a woman working in a male-dominated industry. Balancing the staff in kitchens would not change someone's awareness that they are a woman, but it would help to change someone's feeling self-conscious about it.

REGINA SCHRAMBLING

Odd as it sounds, my worst moments were in the "ladies'" rooms at newspapers where I was hired as a college dropout and had to deal with very angry women who wanted me to know they had master's degrees and I was not gonna get ahead of them. On the copy desk, I could very easily pass for one of the guys cuz I drank and swore and did what I liked to do and wasn't just allowed to "pass."

KATHLEEN SQUIRES

I was once told, by a woman, not to "write like girl"—that I needed to write more "like a man." I ended up working well with this woman, but I was offended and angry about the comment and it still irks me today. She thought I should be more "authoritative" in my voice . . . well, then, why not say that instead of insulting my writing and my gender? It was one of the most insensitive criticisms I have ever received. I write how I write. As a woman.

I feel like women aren't "allowed" to display anger in this industry—and in general, honestly—and when they do, they are trolled and publicly shamed in spaces such as Twitter. Not so for men.

I also wonder how often men have to chase down payments. Or if men are treated the same way when it comes to expectations for things like speaking engagements . . . I'm made to feel icky for asking for travel reimbursement, for example.

EMILY FARRIS

Oh, just the one hundred times I've been told to be less assertive, more polite, nicer. Fuck that. This is why I'm a freelancer.

EMIKO DAVIES

Well there was that time a well-known Italian-British food icon read my cookbook and referred to me as a housewife. Admittedly, in Italian, *casalinga* in reference to cooking is a good thing—it equates to authentic, good home cooking—but still. It is 2018 and I doubt a man writing a cookbook about traditional regional cuisine would have been compared to a housewife. It was belittling.

CHANDRA RAM

The last time a guy mansplained the #MeToo movement to me and remarked that the problem was that women were going to misunderstand men and claim they were being sexist or inappropriate when they were just kidding. I couldn't say anything, but was really shocked that it was the conversation in an office.

REBECCA FLINT MARX

Greatest hits:

The time when I was a twenty-one-year-old intern at the *Philadelphia City Paper* and the news room director celebrated his birthday with a tit cake from the local erotic bakery. I believe they'd somehow managed to frost pubes onto it, too.

The time when I went to shake hands with a man I'd just finished interviewing and he decided to hug and kiss me instead (on the cheek, but still).

The time when I was at my office doing an in-person interview with the (male) owner of a local absinthe company and he looked at all of the books lining my cubicle and said, "You know what they say: if she doesn't read, don't fuck her," and then asked me if I'd like to get lunch sometime.

The time when I was interviewing a cheesy Italian popera star at a restaurant and he kept trying to get me to eat his food. Pretty sure he wouldn't have done that if I were a guy.

The time(s) a male chef I was introduced to in a professional context would invite me out to talk about the industry and it ended up feeling more like a date.

The time I went to dinner with a (male) publicist thinking it was for business and then realized, after the fact, that I'd actually been on a date.

The time, during a job interview, when my interviewer (a woman, actually) asked me if I was married and/or had children, and if I liked to exercise.

A Conversation with Rachael Ray

I used to watch *$40 a Day* on the Food Network all the time. For anyone who hasn't seen an episode of the series, which was picked up for four seasons (2002–2006), it was based on the following premise: Host Rachael Ray has arrived in a city with only forty dollars to cover a day's worth of meals—can she do it? This was my introduction to Rachael, who had previously debuted another show on that network a few months earlier—*30-Minute Meals*, which launched her as a food personality and television star, and had an eleven-year run, followed by a reboot this past spring. In 2006, backed by Oprah Winfrey's Harpo Productions, Rachael expanded her reach beyond food television with her now-syndicated daily talk show. A year prior, she was given her very own magazine, *Rachael Ray Every Day,* which is still going strong. She has written too many cookbooks to keep track of, designed one line of cook- and tableware and another of home furnishings, and developed her own brand of food products for humans, and one for pets made with all-natural ingredients. Then there are her nonprofits—Rachael's Rescue, for animals in need of home and shelter, and Yum-O!, whose mission is to teach kids and parents how to cook, and eat, and help end childhood hunger in America.

How many celebrities—or people, in general—do you know who have done the same or similar? Oprah. Martha Stewart. Gwyneth Paltrow. Maybe Ina Garten. And yet, we don't seem to acknowledge Rachael's accomplishments in the same breath as those others'. Why? I think it's snobbism, tied to a fixed editorial bias. We (in food media) like to celebrate the aspirational. We say it's in the name of "service journalism," but we're usually delivering that practical information in a package that feels just out of grasp—or sometimes very much so—for the audience we're addressing. Rachael wants to offer people what's in reach, not sell them on a dream they can't afford that leaves them feeling inadequate. I think that's why I hold her in such high regard. Her humility might make you underestimate her; it should only increase your respect for her.

I want to know a little bit about your childhood and especially the role that food played, because I know there was so much of it and I wonder if you knew early on—if it was a foregone conclusion that you would end up in food.

RACHAEL

I think yes and no. I was born into it. My mom worked in restaurants. She's eighty-four. She's retired now. But she worked in restaurants for sixty years, fifty-seven, something like that. When I was very small, we owned restaurants in Cape Cod. But then the gas crisis—and the second gas crisis—made it impossible for people to go to Cape Cod. We went bankrupt and my mom started running restaurants for other people. My mom liked to keep an eye on her kids. So we were always on her hip as much as we could be in the restaurants.

My grandfather lived with us, also, when I was very little, 'til his death. He was my best friend and he had ten children—my mother was the firstborn. And my grandfather was always in the kitchen. He was a stonemason by trade but he'd stay up half the night, leave the family meals for the next day. He was the family cook.

When I wasn't with my mother, I was with my grandfather and I was always in the kitchen, all of my life. When I was real little, my actual first memory is of grilling my own thumb on the flat top griddle because I was reaching for a spatula. My mom had put me down to hang up the phone and I remember grilling that thumb. So I guess I was sort of branded to be in the kitchen.

CD

Were your siblings branded to be there, too, in their own way?

RACHAEL

Everyone in our family can cook something: My sister's a wonderful baker. My brother loves to cook game. I think I'm the only one who gravitated to it for the way it made me feel . . . when you work in food, even if you're working in a Howard Johnson's, when you give somebody a beautiful plate of anything—scrambled eggs or a hot flapjack or something—and you see that sense of relief on their face, or they take a bite of something that's really good and it looks like they opened a present, or you gave them a compliment when they think they look shitty; I love the immediate gratification that food brings people.

This sounds stupid because I'm on TV so much, but I also like being behind the scenes. I like work more than I like being a celebrity. I like what being a celebrity affords me. I'm very interested in people. As is any service person, I would hope. And I like talking to them. So I accommodate what I have to do in order to go make a TV show.

CD

Financial success aside, how do you feel about celebrity, then?

RACHAEL

I actually loathe celebrity. I hate having my picture taken. I hate being in front of a camera. I wish all those same people would just come over and hang out at my house. But they won't. So it's kind of a quid pro quo kind of thing. It's a wonderful and generous opportunity. I'm not complaining about it. But that's what I like about working in food. You're in the kitchen. And you're cooking and you're making things for people—to make them happy.

CD

What do you think, when you look now at the Kardashians, at people who are professional celebrities and they haven't worked in any particular industry or at a particular trade?

RACHAEL

I don't know anything about that experience. They look pretty happy, I think, by their standards. Everyone has to make their own barometer in life, you know? What they can bear, what they can't, what they can do, what makes them happy. None of that would make me happy. Getting my hair and makeup done for forty minutes makes me twitchy nervous. God bless the people who have to do it. I can't imagine the amount of patience you have to have, in a different way, to become the perfect-looking thing, and making that a goal every single day, at every age. I can't imagine that, but on the other hand, they look amazing. They seem to have a lovely life.

CD

You have multiple television shows, you have books, you have your own magazine, you've done all of this amazing not-for-profit work, now you're doing it for animals. If you look at the number of women who have accomplished all of those things, there are very few of them. And I feel like, and maybe I'm wrong, they've somehow gotten more recognition or respect, or we speak about them more as though they're moguls. And to me you're a mogul.

RACHAEL

I'm not a mogul and I hate that word. I love work. And I love to draw. I draw all the time. I have furniture because I drew furniture and it didn't exist. I have pots and pans because I drew a pot I wanted. People wanted to make them because I got on television, but I only got on television because my mother told me, "What are you afraid of? If you're not afraid of where you come from, you can't be afraid of where you're going. Therefore at least try, because the worse thing that can happen is someone says no."

I work very hard for what I have. I don't consider that being a mogul. A lot of people get license deals so they can put their name on things. That's not what I do. I simply keep working. That's all. And I think that anybody can do that as long as they make work the

thing and not themselves the thing. In fact, I try to make myself a smaller and smaller part of everything—like furniture, anything new—in case people hate me. I still want them to buy my sofa. I still want them to look at my kitchen island. If they don't like me, I want them to appreciate the design or the aesthetic of something.

CD

Even if it doesn't bother you, do you think that society rewards the people who are more interested in doing it for themselves than doing it for the work?

RACHAEL

I think they get different rewards. I think that people who work at being celebrities get more celebrity in that one vein. I call that notoriety; they may get more notoriety. They may get more magazine covers and red carpets and parties. They get invited to better places, but I don't care about any of that. I'm getting exactly what I like. I'm making a lot of money for dogs. I'm making a lot of money for kids. I can help people when there's a hurricane. I don't get invited to a ton of parties. Therefore I get to spend more time at home, which is where I want to be anyway.

CD

When you were in your twenties you came to New York City—

RACHAEL

Jesus, twenties . . .

CD

And we are across from the newer outpost of the Italian food store Agata & Valentina, where you worked—

RACHAEL

I was the opening buyer, the manager; I ran the whole shebang.

CD

So what made you—

Leave?

Well I was going to ask first what made you come, and then, leave.

My mom took us to New York when we were young. We lived check to check, but we weren't dirt poor. And New York was like living in a snow globe. I wanted to live in New York and I wanted to work in Macy's food hall, which I did. My boss left for a job in Washington, DC. (Michael Corsello, I still talk to him. I still talk to every boss I ever had.) And he tried to take me with him and I said, "I can't drive. I'll die if I have to drive on the beltway. I won't survive to work for you."

He said, "Okay, go see Joe Musco." I said, "Of Musco Foods? Why?" And he said, "Joe and [his wife] Agata are going to open their own market." I went to see Joe and I had a ten and a half-hour interview; he just wouldn't let go of me. And so Michael kind of gifted me. It was very *Godfather*, kind of patriarchal, creepy. You know? It's like right out of the movies—one Italian guy passes her off to another Italian guy. And I loved my job. I loved my life. We worked one hundred hours a week. They would go in at dawn, so would I. We'd go home at 11:30 P.M. or 12 A.M., when everything was mopped. We worked like this. I lived in Woodside [Queens] and they would drive me home so I wouldn't have to stand on the train platforms by myself. They had a Mercedes. But I would sit in the back; it looked like I had a car service. So I think kids in my neighborhood thought I was rich.

Anyway, I got mugged. I maced the guy, he got pissed, he came back a week later, and he beat the crap out of me, and that's why I moved to the country. Started my life over. I had to wait a year once I moved back to the country, because there was only one market;

it's called Cowan & Lobel. And I got a job there. I was their buyer. One of their senior managers, Donna—she is one of my absolute best friends—she fired the chef for taking kickbacks. She told me she liked my food better than his, why don't I take his job too? I said, "Are you going to give me a double salary?" She said, "Well, I'll try." She let me take over the kitchen.

And then I'm like, *Okay, everybody's buying my food, nobody's buying our groceries.* So she and I took a poll of our customers and asked them why they weren't buying the groceries. And they almost universally said it was because they don't know how to cook. So I started teaching thirty-minute meals with Donna every Wednesday night, a three-hour class. Six base recipes, five versions of each recipe. You could learn a month's worth of meals in three hours.

Incredible.

We played music and just had fun and served wine, even though we shouldn't. We got football teams, and girls getting married, and retirement groups. We became this huge, happening thing. We were our best-selling item. The local news gave me a spot. "30-Minute Meals" became a thing. Then people started writing in hate mail because they had to collect all the recipes; you'd write in on an envelope and they'd send you the recipe. People were like, *Can't she just print a book?* I went to a one-woman publishing house here in New York and I asked her if she'd print it. Well, we couldn't sell it at bookstores, because nobody knew who I was. I was only on local news. So she made a deal with Price Chopper to sell it in the grocery stores. And that was the first 30-Minute Meal cookbook.

CD

Which is amazing—

RACHAEL

Amazing. But on the other hand, not that amazing: got mugged, actually got a great job, failed, left, went back to the country. There's a lot. That's what I'm saying. It's not all like *poof*. I keep starting over and it's fine.

CD

It's also that, with you, it's very idea-driven and it's very service-related; it's usually rooted in a very practical service that you're giving people.

RACHAEL

I want people to be able to fend for themselves. The number-one thing for me is that a person feels good about themselves at the end of the day. As a waitress, I wanted them to get more than they ordered. As a cook or a personality—or a person who writes books or delivers content—I want people to be excited to try it, to feel that it's accessible and, more important to me, to be more successful at it than even I am.

It's getting a person excited about living a more adventurous existence. I know people all my life who were happy and poor. In America, you don't see a ton of that. You see a ton of, *I'm okay but I'm waiting for my weekend or my summer or my vacation or my retirement*. And I don't think it has to be that way. I think every day, even when you're poor, should be fun.

CD

There's some joy in it.

RACHAEL

That there's some joy in it and a little adventure. I did not have a parent that told me "Don't talk to strangers." I had the polar opposite. They said, "Be compassionate to strangers, and curious." Of course she worries, but my mom would literally take us on get-lost Saturdays or Sundays or Tuesdays or whatever her day off was. We would go get lost. Like, on

purpose. If, when we went to Vermont and we turned right, we knew we were going to hit Manchester, we'd take a left. My mom used to chase UFOs when I was a little girl. And wake us up in the middle of the night to take us with her. You know, she's a fruit loop but that's a sense of adventure.

CD

It is. [The TV show] *$40 a Day* is that exact same idea, right? Because there's the adventure, but it's the practical side of how can you do it and not spend too much. How long did it take, after starting at Food Network, to really be able to have autonomy over your work?

RACHAEL

Day one. In fact, I thought I should be more professional. I went in and left the meeting. I said, "I'm not a proper chef." And they said, "What do you mean? You've been working in restaurants since you were twelve." I said, "Yeah, but I don't have culinary, fancy degrees and a toque and all that . . . I'm beer out of the bottle, you realize you're champagne?" And they're like, *Yeah, that's exactly what we like.* And they loved the travel thing I was doing.

They're the ones that offered me both shows. They did a pilot and they said, "Would you be interested in trying both concepts?" Then again, I never pretended to be something I wasn't for them. And they never made a huge promise 'til they saw the pilots. Within a year I had 163 episodes. Within a few years, I did my personal high, which was 270-something episodes in one year, between all of the shows.

CD

How did the Food Network deal come about in the first place?

RACHAEL

Well, Food Network happened because I moved back to Upstate New York and Al Roker is from Upstate New York. Somebody gave him a 30-Minute Meal cookbook from the grocery store.

His producer (her name was Michelle) stuffed it in a folder because Al showed it to her, and when everyone canceled on the *Today Show* one day, they brought me in and it was the same weekend a friend of mine who worked on public radio in Albany, his guest canceled because of the bad weather. He asked me to come in and cook a thirty-minute meal on a hot plate in the radio station and I made *jambalike-a.*

Some guy named Lou Ekus, who was driving to the Culinary Institute [of America] at Hyde Park, he was lecturing on how to become a brand and how to work in food TV for the students. And he heard me on NPR. He called his friend Bob Tushman at Food Network and said, "You got to check out this girl." Well, two days later, I was on the *Today Show.* So Bob Tushman sees me and he calls Lou, and he's like, *You know that girl you told me about? She's actually on the* Today Show.

So Food Network thought I was somebody from somewhere, but really it was just a snowstorm. My life is a weird mishmash of like horrible accidents that turned out to be the greatest things that ever happened to me, and luck and hard work. It's a little bit of all of those.

CD

Tell me how the magazine happened.

RACHAEL

The magazine happened because a man named Tom Ryder—at the time, he ran *Reader's Digest*—he was a fan. He wanted to have a magazine that had my personality. He said, "You think we could put you in print?" I said okay. And then now we're with Meredith [Corporation] and they're lovely. We're still here.

CD

What about the talk show?

RACHAEL

Oh, my boss, Brooke Johnson, went to all of her co-bosses at Scripps [Network] and said, "We need to stop being cable and we hate syndicated. I think it would be better for this person that we work with if she was both." And she got them to think differently about the idea that somebody on cable could not be on syndicated, or vice versa. Scripps, Oprah, our company, and CBS distribution are our four partners in our daytime show. We all stayed together as a family. Oprah had me on her show and then said she wanted to be a part of whatever we were doing. That was thirteen years ago and we're all still partners and friends.

CD

I wanted to ask you about your marriage. For so many women, I think there's this idea that if the woman is more successful or shines, it doesn't work. How do you make it work?

RACHAEL

Broke up every relationship I had. I had a boyfriend that was the most handsome man I think I've ever seen in my life. He spoke seven languages. Gorgeous. Could've been anything in life, had absolutely no ambition whatsoever. Lost job after job. Amazing physical shape. He just had no ambition. Didn't care. And that's fine. That's great. But we were completely not compatible because of that. Broke up. I had a lot of boyfriends that were successful that wanted me to be with them at events and all that. It's just not my thing. I have to have work.

Through a variety of things that happened in my life, I helped my brother get through college; my mom and my brother ended up living with me at one point. I had a lot going on. Then the Food Network thing happened. My early thirties were really busy. I didn't care. It's when most women are getting really nervous and *Oh my god, I'm not going to get married*, or whatever. That's just not who

I was. I've been working since I was a little kid. The one thing that makes me feel truly threatened is if you try to pull me away from that part of my individuality. And the thing about John [Cusimano] is he's the same way. He's a lawyer by day, but he's a very frustrated musician. He has to live like a double life. If he gets a tour with Mötley Crüe and Alice Cooper and he's gone all summer, I'm not like, *Who are you not to be home? Blah blah blah. I'm going to crumble.* I like being alone. He likes being alone. It's great when we're together, but the only reason I married John is because we make sense. We're enough alike that neither person is threatened.

CD

If you were giving advice to women who are dealing with this now, because there's a larger number of women who are becoming more successful than their partners—

RACHAEL

That is the one thing I do not compromise on: You have to respect my independence and my need to be creative.

You have to follow who you are or you will become so resentful of the other person you can't be near them. I think women are finally learning to speak up for themselves, both in the workplace and in their private lives. And let me tell you, I have gotten in a lot of fights with female friends over the years, because I tell them, "You're never going to be happy with that man. He doesn't have enough ambition for you" or "He's going to become threatened by you. He's going to break your heart." It's cost me friendships with females, but we always come back to each other. Eventually they go out on their own or they find an equal. Me and my mom always said, "Water seeks its own level."

I wrote on a legal pad, right before I moved back home, what I liked about my life, what I liked about myself and what I didn't. And from the day I drew that line down the paper, I do not compromise on those things. Period.

CD

Do you still have the paper? Did you save it?

RACHAEL

Somewhere in my cellar, I'm sure. I'm a notebook person. Everything starts in a notebook. Everything. Every drawing of furniture. Every pot, every pan. Everything I make in my house. Everything I write for the magazine. Everything I write for the TV show. It's all coded. My house notebook is separate and it just has the dates of when I made certain meals. But yeah, I write down everything.

CD

When you first started, everyone loved calling you the girl next door. As you get older, how do you take that perception of who you are—or what your brand is, and how do you make sure it grows with you so you're not locked into that image?

RACHAEL

People are going to think whatever they want about me. I don't care at all. I think about the product first and how that product can be the best, smartest thing it can be. I think the magazine gets better and better, because we get better and better staff. I try to pick people who are fresh and have big ideas and are of the same motto, but can take us in newer avenues while staying true to the thing. And when it comes to design, I just think about the design. I don't think about me. When people are sick of watching me they'll tell me and I'll go away. Then I'll produce other people for TV.

CD

Which is a great thing to be able to do anyway.

RACHAEL

I'm fifty and I'm still here. Very few people in life can say they spent twenty-something years doing this.

Especially women. I'm curious about your relationship with your agents. I have discussed this with a lot of my friends, especially writers, because I feel like the way the system's set up, it's pretty exploitative. And I can't really figure out why we need to have them.

You're preaching to the choir.

Can you talk about why you got rid of yours?

I didn't feel that I was getting my money's worth. They had made dozens and dozens of millions of dollars off of my work. And for me, my husband took my drawings of oval pots, in his briefcase, on his day off, to the Javits Center [for a trade show], and went to the pots and pans people and said, "My wife likes your material that you make pots and pans out of. Would you make her pots and pans? By the way her name is Rachael Ray. And she has TV shows."

I felt that all of the things I'd done that matter to me—*30-Minute Meals, $40 a Day*—they came to me. And the things that they [agents] brought to me were not for me. They were for them to make more money.

My theory is you're better off having a really good lawyer.

Oh, ten thousand percent. You need to make sure the contracts are not taking advantage of you in perpetuity, which, by the way, the only bad contracts I ever had were because of the agents. You can go in and ask for more. Your lawyer can go in and ask for more. You don't need an agent to go in and say, "That's not reasonable." And quite frankly, people are way more scared of me than they were of my former agent.

I do think there is that thing—and it's true when you're in the service industry too—there's the likability factor, which I think women worry about a lot. You just want to be liked and so it often gets in the way—

I want my customer to like me. I want businesspeople to respect me. They're two very different things. And I think that people do like you more when you simply tell the truth and you're frank with them. I think that people don't really like doormats. They only like them day one when they're brand new and shiny and clean. After they get footmarks all over them, they don't like the doormat anymore. Doormat looks dirty and sad. Nobody likes a dirty doormat.

That's true. That metaphor is excellent. I'm taking that with me. I know that you do not like to identify label-wise as a feminist—

No I don't, because "female bully" is what that screams to me. I don't like to go into a discussion that's marked as a feminist-only thing. I love to talk about "like a boss," our hashtag for the magazine. I don't mind being in a room full of women that work in food and talking about that. I just don't like to wear a label any more than I'd like to go to something where a man is wearing a label.

It goes back to respect; that everybody's getting an equal amount of respect. I should be able to earn that on my own without shoving in your face a label. *You need to respect me just because I'm a woman* makes no sense. *You need to respect me because I did this, this, this, and this and I'm making this argument about that.* That's even to me. If I come to the table with a chip on my shoulder and I say, "You need to just give me more money because I'm a woman and you pay other men more," that's not fair to me.

You're a meritocracy person, too.

RACHAEL

Yes, I am.

CD

But I have to tell you, even if it's not something you want to do, just by virtue of being yourself and also talking about your experiences, it's so empowering to women. It's empowering to me to listen to you talk about not taking bullshit.

RACHAEL

Don't take crap. And stop apologizing for everything. You're allowed to have an opinion. Speak it. Be fair. You have to listen, too. And if you're working on a team, you do have to listen to a director. You do have to listen to a producer. You do have to listen to everybody. And then come in again where, *Okay, here's where I'm gonna meet you.*

CD

It's almost like, in this very organic way, you are a living example of feminism without being part of the ideological discourse conversation, if that makes sense.

RACHAEL

I don't need to wear a button for it.

CD

What you have done, which is achieve parity, and done on your own terms, and earned the same respect that is given to men, those things in and of themselves would be considered very—

RACHAEL

They are feminist. My mother was told when she graduated high school that she could get married or become a secretary. She ended up running a company for a man that she took from three million dollars to thirty million— from three restaurants to nine restaurants. (Back then that was a lot of money. Now you can make that with one place.) She did that because that was in her. And she worked

harder than everyone else and she didn't complain about it.

But she was also a woman. She would be very nurturing to these kids. If she had a couple stoners, if they were drinking too much, or didn't show up, she would go to their apartment, rip them out of bed, tell them to iron their uniform and get their ass to work. A man wouldn't do that. A woman would. She also fired a lot of kids who were just lazy. She'd say, "I'm an at-will employer. You just asked me for your break and I've been here since four A.M. Take your apron off. Get your ass outta here. I'll do your job for the rest of the day." It's a give and take. That's who I was raised with.

CD

It's no surprise.

RACHAEL

I'm a byproduct of a great, hardworking grandpa and a very strong woman.

CD

One of the things that I also really respect about what you've done is the giving back. You seem wired for it.

RACHAEL

Money makes me uncomfortable.

CD

When did you start actively pursuing nonprofit projects?

RACHAEL

Well first came the kids. Yum-O! came first. Oprah told me when I was a guest on her show—we had like a little sit-down—and she said, "I'm very interested in you. Let's get to know each other." And I said, "It's very important to me, now that I have a nice job and I make some nice money, I want to figure out my way to give back." She said, "Do it the way you make your money. It has to feel natural to you. For you, the conduit is food and service so something to do with that." I can feed kids, because I don't have kids of my own. I'm sick of people asking me when I'm going to. So that feels natural and great. Kills two birds with one stone. Sending the next generation into a better place, how do I do that?

And then the dog food people; we started recipes. I started writing recipes for dogs the day the magazine came out. I had a dog page, because I cook for my dog.

OD

I know!

RACHAEL

And I don't need money. I am happy poor. For me, it's very easy to give it away, right? Everybody in the family has a house, a car, college, whatever. I've ruled my land forever wild. We've given thirty million dollars to animals; I have no idea how many millions to people. And we keep a little fund so that when there's a hurricane we can dedicate one million dollars to Puerto Rico, one million dollars to Houston—just for clean water and relief for children. We also did a million dollars for animals in both places. It's amazing to have that power. That's the cool part of being a celebrity or whatever.

Bee Wilson

Bee Wilson is usually identified as a British journalist, historian, food writer, and author. She is all those things. But I think of her as a cultural anthropologist as well—or maybe that's what unites all of those other lines of work. What Bee is always asking and answering is: What does our relationship with food tell us about who we are (or were) and how we live (or lived)? Her first book, *The Hive*, looks at the history of humankind through our interaction with bees and honey. It may sound dry, or scientific, but Bee (no relation to her subject) brings in literary references—from Shakespeare to Sherlock Holmes—and connects hives to honeymooners. In *Swindled*, she acts as a culinary detective and investigates the ways in which our food has been tampered with and people have been hoodwinked about what they're eating, by individuals or corporations, since the dawn of civilization. Then we come to my favorite (apologies for having one), *Consider the Fork*. This one gets at our utensils and what impact they've had on our cooking and eating. Since then, she's tackled the origins of our diets—how our palates develop and what we might do to change our habits (*First Bite*)—and, tracked the globalization of ingredients and diets while questioning the psychology behind and validity of what we think of as "healthy" (*The Way We Eat Now*).

In *This Is Not a Diet Book*, a slender volume published in 2016, she wrote, "Children learn to eat better when the process feels less like a lecture and more like a game. The same is true for adults." I think the same could be said for learning how to cook—out of necessity or for pleasure—and, based on this essay, that she might agree. Maybe that will be the topic of one of her next books. She has so many ideas and they're all good; it's impossible to keep up, or guess.

Labor Saving

Cooking, it is sometimes said, is one of the highest forms of human self-expression. But tell that to the person who is trying to get dinner ready, children in tow, after work and before bedtime, with an imperfectly stocked pantry and nagging pings from unanswered emails.

The first time I used my Instant Pot, to make a vegetable biryani on a timer delay setting, it made me cry. This probably says as much about me as it does about this multifunctional electric pressure cooker. But still. "When we get home, there will be a piping hot dinner waiting for us," I said to my youngest son, as if announcing to a Victorian orphan that I had managed to buy him a goose for Christmas. He raised his eyebrows quizzically at the phrase "piping hot." As usual, he and I were at his after-school sports training, which annoyingly falls most days of the week during just those hours when—if only I were Michael Pollan—I would be at home, chopping an onion in a contemplative fashion. Often as not, our weeknight dinner will be food from the weekend, reheated, or a speedy omelet, or a random stir-fry foraged from the fridge. There is nothing so terrible in any of this (especially when the reheated leftovers are one of those spicy sticky stews that improve over time), but it's the sense of time-panic and compromise that I don't like. The first night with the Instant Pot was different. We walked in the house and smelled cloves and bay leaf and the warm scent of basmati, aromas that became still more intense when I flicked the steam valve, opened the lid and heard that happy little jingle that the machine makes when it opens or closes. Some thoughtful person had been cooking, and so many hours had elapsed since I sautéed the onion and spices and put the rice and vegetables in the pot that it did not feel as if that someone had been me.

Some say the intense devotion that this gadget inspires is due to its multifunctionality. It certainly isn't due to its looks, which are clunky verging on ugly. This appliance—invented by Robert Wang—can do "a ridiculous number of things" as Alex Beggs wrote in *Bon Appétit* in 2017. It is a yogurt-maker, steamer, warmer, and slow cooker as well as a pressure cooker. But in truth, how many Instant Pot owners ever get around to using it as a steamer, let alone as a yogurt maker? The real value of this machine, in my view, is not the multiplicity of cooking techniques that it offers but the fact that it enables its users to produce a home-cooked meal *at all* on days when that task seems insurmountable. My kitchen has seen many devices come and go. I have bought more gadgets than I care to remember that promised to make me a better cook, a faster cook, a healthier cook. I own other devices—the microwave being the most obvious—that assume I don't want to touch or handle food at all. The Instant Pot, by contrast, seems to understand I do want to eat and serve home-cooked food, but it also tactfully relieves me of most of the stirring and switches itself to "keep warm" mode without being asked to save me from burning dinner. It is that rare thing: a labor-saving device that factors in what a cook needs and feels.

I didn't expect to like the Instant Pot so much. As a rule, I am skeptical about labor-saving devices because they so seldom seem to understand that the most taxing work in the kitchen is brain work.

Women and machines have a complicated relationship in the kitchen. Myriad devices have been sold over the years on the promise that they would make our lives easier, and, for the most part, they have failed. "Labour-saving," says the *Oxford English Dictionary*, means something "designed to reduce or eliminate the work necessary to achieve a task." What the *OED* does not bother to mention is that—at least in relation to cooking—the phrase is usually an untruth of one kind or another. "Labour-saving" contrivances have created as many problems for cooks as they have cured.

The first shock about labor-saving devices in the kitchen is how long they took to arrive in our lives, relative to other technologies. In the year 1900, an American city-dwelling woman could ride efficient cable cars through modern streets brightly lit by electricity yet she would return to a home containing tin and iron pots, where she was still expected to haul fuel for the fire and water in a pail, and chop ingredients with knives that went rusty unless they were meticulously cleaned. In 1900, American food preparation "looked much as it had in 1800," according to historian of housework Susan Strasser: "Three times daily, women prepared meals for their families, using heavy iron utensils, first at fireplaces, later at stoves."

It wasn't merely that the makers of kitchen tools lacked the ingenuity to lessen the burden on a cook. It was more that they did not even try because, all too often, labor-intensive cuisine has been seen as a positive status symbol by those who did not toil over it. Perusing recipes aimed at wealthy households from centuries ago, I found that many of them touted the amount of work that a given recipe might require in a fetishizing fashion. (There's still a vestige of this labor-fetish in the cooking at Michelin-starred restaurants.) There is a pancake recipe in *Le Ménagier de Paris*, a household advice book published in 1393. It instructs us to get a quart-sized copper pan and melt in it a large quantity of salted butter. Next, it asks us to take eggs and warm white wine and "the fairest wheaten flour," and to beat it all together "long enough to weary one person or two." I was taken aback by this phrase "one person or two," which seemed to treat servants as if they were human eggbeaters. When one of them became exhausted, another would step forward to take their place. The relative lack of labor-saving devices in the premodern kitchen reflects the stark reality that rich households possessed their own labor-saving technology in the form of servants. In poorer households, a wife's labor fulfilled the same role.

The realization that cooks might actually like to be relieved of some of their grind seems to have dawned very late. It was only in 1791 that the phrase "labor-saving" entered the language—in relation to industry—and it would be decades more before labor-saving tools entered the kitchen in any significant quantities. In the 1850s and 1860s, a sudden rash of small mechanical cooking utensils came on the market in the United States, made of cast iron and tin. There were cherry pitters and apple parers; eggbeaters and butter churns; lemon-squeezers and ivory cucumber slicers. Many of these items were the subject of patents and were presented as great miracles launched on an unsuspecting world.

There can be something poignant about the labor-saving devices of the late nineteenth century because they bring home just how much work was once required to get a meal on the table—work that in many cases has now become obsolete because of advances in food processing. The meaning of "scratch cooking" has changed considerably over the years. Whether she was a servant or a wife, a nineteenth-century cook was often expected not just to bake her own bread and churn her own butter, but to grind and sieve her own sugar, skin her own almonds, light her own fire, and even to deseed her own raisins, one by one. In an era before seedless raisins, the mechanical raisin seeder was an object of desire, a profitable enough item that it was advertised in newspapers. Here is an example from San Francisco in 1866:

RAISIN SEEDERS!

The Latest Improvement.

FOR SALE BY LOCKE & MONTAGUE

112 and 114 Battery Street

A typical raisin seeder was a heavy cast-iron object that was clamped to the table like a meat-grinding machine. You would feed wet raisins into the hopper and crank the handle and—hey, presto!—out came perfectly deseeded raisins. The raisins were squeezed between two rollers, which forced out the seeds. One raisin seeder manufactured in Manchester, England, claimed it could seed a pound of raisins in just five minutes. The raisin seeder sounds like a marvelous invention, even if its time has long past. But it leaves me feeling wistful that it was ever needed. Think of the hours of manpower (or rather womanpower) that must have been wasted making raisins and sultanas fit to eat, especially in the weeks before Christmas when there were fruitcakes and raisin-studded puddings to bake. Imagine all those women who sat in a poorly lit kitchen attempting to remove the seeds from a pound of raisins, one by one.

In the context of such drudgery, the new labor-saving devices of Victorian times probably did seem pretty impressive, even if they barely scratched the surface of the work that a cook needed to do in a day. Everything was modern once and it's hard to remember that tools that today appear cumbersome were once the dernier cri. In fairness, a few of these nineteenth-century kitchen gizmos genuinely were marvels at performing a single self-contained task. The apple parer is a case in point. Before the contraption became common in the American kitchen, people in states such as Vermont, where that fruit is grown, used to hold "paring-bees" at which an itinerant apple parer would arrive with a machine and peel a few bushels' worth in an evening while the rest of the party got to work coring and chopping. This changed with the advent of the domestic apple parer.

The first apple-peeling patent was issued in Great Britain in 1802. By the 1850s there were dozens more in both the United States and United Kingdom. The earliest models were very basic, consisting of little but a rotating wooden fork on which the apple would be speared. The idea was to hold your knife against the apple as it rotated and thus remove the skin. It's questionable whether this was any less taxing than simply paring an apple by hand. But in the second half of the century, there was a great leap forward: Inventors started to design many varieties of all-in-one hand-cranked parers, corers, and choppers. Versions of these can still be bought in kitchenware stores. You attach each apple to prongs at the end of the apparatus—which attaches to a table—turn the handle, and before you know it, you have a piece of perfectly peeled and cored fruit, shaped like a slinky or a concertina. The effect is so clever that it can still make onlookers gasp, in my experience.

Yet this multitasker was an outlier in its brilliance. All too many of these early "labor-saving" tools were ineffective, trivial, or slightly ludicrous. There were peanut-roasters and automatic mustard-dispensers, horseradish scrapers, and biscuit breakers (the biscuit in question being a kind of rigid, matzo-like cracker). Looking back in 1890, a journalist in the *Los Angeles Times* recalled the strange flood of useless objects that arrived in kitchens a few decades earlier: "Among other patents which I remember are jar-lifters, bag-holders, fish-boners . . . and a thousand and one curious appliances for household matters." Writing for country-dwelling women in 1881, Helen Campbell noted that "many complicated patent arrangements are hindrances, rather than helps." The problem with most of these is that they were designed more with a view to profiting than meeting the needs of a cook. The same is true of much kitchen paraphernalia today. It is a rare tool that is any improvement over a pair of dexterous hands and a sharp knife.

Due to its coinciding with a radical adjustment in the division of labor between the sexes, the arrival of appliances did not necessarily make life any easier for women. This case was made, with scholarship and wit, by Ruth Schwartz Cowan in her groundbreaking 1983 book *More Work for Mother*. From around 1860 to 1960, the American household steadily shed its colonial character and became industrialized. That century saw countless new contraptions hit the market, from cheese graters to toaster ovens; electric waffle presses to blenders. But, at the same time, the whole workflow of household cooking changed, and not to the benefit of women. Cowan observed that in the preindustrial rural kitchens of the United States, men and women were forced to collaborate to prepare food. The housewife might stew a simple meal of meat and grains in a kettle, but her husband would have grown the grains, butchered the meat, and constructed the fireplace. He grew corn; she baked cornbread. Children would also have helped out their parents by carrying pails of water. By contrast, the advent of industrially milled flour and cast-iron stoves and running water left women alone in the kitchen, solely responsible for making dinner.

"There is more work for a mother to do in a modern home because there is no one left to help her with it," wrote Cowan. As late as the early 1980s, the author observed that the existence of large numbers of culinary contraptions could make some men feel unburdened of any obligation to help out. "In homes where there are garbage disposals, men give up removing the small quantities of garbage that still need to be carried to the curb; and in households where there are dishwashers, men cease providing whatever help with the dishes they had formerly proffered."

Another problem with the labor-saving devices aimed at women is that they have always come along at the same time as a rise in culinary expectations, so the net result was a cook who was more exhausted than ever. From 1850 onward, eggbeaters became a veritable obsession in the American household. From 1856 to 1920 there were an astonishing 692 separate patents issued for this tool, the most famous of which was the Dover with its two revolving beaters. When it came to getting fluffy egg whites, not one of these elaborate designs was an upgrade from the French balloon whisk (an unimprovable piece of engineering) or even on the old-fashioned birch twig whisk, which can do a surprisingly effective job if you don't mind the occasional fragment of bark in your meringue. It would not be until the electric mixers of the twentieth century that beating eggs became radically easier. The early patent eggbeaters, by contrast, brought only the illusion of ease, coupled with a sense that producing perfectly beaten eggs was something that women *ought* to do, and a woman in possession of a Dover felt obliged to make fancy cakes with it. The popularity of these whirligigs also corresponded to a new vogue for angel food cakes, which necessitated huge volumes of eggs to be beaten, the whites and the yolks separately. So far from halving a woman's work, this latest, greatest mechanism could actually multiply it.

To add insult to injury, many kitchen gadgets came with the message that now that she was being given so much help in the kitchen, a cook had no reason to complain about her lot. "Cooking a Recreation" was the headline of an insufferably patronizing advertisement a kitchenware company placed in the *Salt Lake Semi-Weekly Tribune* in 1898. "It is very foolish to make hard work of your cooking" advised the copy-writer, "when you can make the work in the kitchen a pleasant recreation by spending a very little money for a few of our labor-saving kitchen utensils." These alleged labor-savers included tea strainers, fruit steamers, and "favorite cake spoons," none of which would seem to offer any detectable alleviation of effort. Given that perfectly serviceable spoons have been around since ancient times, it was insulting women's intelligence to call these utensils labor-saving.

The great feminist worry about all this equipment—articulated by Betty Friedan in *The Feminine Mystique*—was that it would trap woman in the role of housewives, confining them to the home. Kitchen inventions of the early twentieth century did not just pretend to make cooking easier, but to transform women's lives by turning their prescribed headquarters into a gleaming enamel paradise. Strange as it now seems, in that era, one of these supposedly life-changing devices was a cabinet that became a widely coveted object of desire before it was supplanted by the refrigerator. Like other household contrivances, these early cupboards—which contained many compartments, from cutlery drawers to sugar-bins—sold themselves on the promise of order. How could a woman who owned so many interlocking drawers possibly be unhappy? In 1900, a full-page advertisement for the Hoosier kitchen cabinet insisted it "saves health, good looks, strength, time and standing." "The Happiest Surprise of her Life!" was the tagline of another advertisement for one of these miraculous pieces of furniture; the accompanying image showed a glamorous mother in a flapper dress standing in dazed rapture next to her husband, who presents her with the open cabinet as if it were a great prize.

The trouble with kitchen cabinets—as with so many other "labor-saving" tools—is that they did not get to the nub of what makes cooking so arduous. It is often not the doing itself that is or was so hard but the life circumstances of the responsible party. By the 1920s, an American housewife on a modest income might have access to a gas oven, a technology that is surely one of the greatest advances in the history of cooking. After centuries of building a life around the smoke and inconvenience of a fire, cooks could now switch the flame on or off at will. Yet, as Cowan observes, the truly labor-saving technology would have been effective birth control. "When there are eight or nine mouths to feed (or even five or six), cooking is a difficult enterprise, even if it can be done at a gas range."

You can tell that the "labor-saving" kitchen of the 1950s was a lie from the fact that so many women chose—if they could afford it—to have human servants as well as appliances. From 1940 to 1950 the number of domestic workers in the United States dropped from 2.5 million to 2 million. But then—in one of the great mysteries of American social history—the number of people working in service rose again, back up to 2.5 million by 1957, a growth of 31 percent over five years. As a journalist for *Time* magazine wrote, "Despite all the labor-saving new gadgets, the U.S. woman wants and needs a maid to help out." A maid might work a sixty to one hundred hour week for low pay and be required to do shopping as well as cooking and cleaning for the household. She would have to have been prepared to cook three times a day, but not make a sound while doing it. In July 1943 *House Beautiful* magazine noted that "noises of pots, pans, and dish scraping can ruin an excellent meal."

No high-tech mixer could have made the life of a maid easy because she was required to turn herself into a kind of machine. One of these domestic workers, an American woman, wrote about her life in *Ladies' Home Journal* in 1960. She complained that her employers simultaneously expected her to have the "kind of organizing and intelligence a woman uses in managing her own household" and yet treated servants like her "as though we did not have a brain in our heads." Maids of the 1950s—who were likely to be over the age of fifty and African American—were expected to be as mute and responsive as a refrigerator.

We like to believe in progress. But consider again that medieval pancake recipe from 1393 that asked for the batter to be beaten long enough to "weary one person or two." Was this mindset really so different from the affluent American households of the 1950s that expected their maid to cook in silence and stand around all night waiting for a party to finish so she could wash their dirty dishes and rinse their martini glasses? In both cases, tethered to it by marriage or the need to earn a living, humans in the kitchen were being treated as robots.

The whole concept of "labor-saving" assumes that the work of cooking is something that needs to be canceled out, or mitigated, or forgotten. When Julia Child burst onto the scene in 1961 with her French cooking "for the servantless cook," she offered a counterblast to the labor-saving mindset and its compromises. "This is a book for the servantless American cook who can be unconcerned on occasion with budgets, waistlines, time schedules, children's meals, the parent-chauffeur-den-mother syndrome, or anything else which might interfere with the enjoyment of producing something wonderful to eat," announced Child in her foreword to *Mastering the Art of French Cooking*. Whether they were making *quenelles de poisson* or Quiche Lorraine, she urged her readers not to take shortcuts: "A pot saver is a self hampering cook." To Child, the wonders of French cooking deserved—no, required—the correct vessels and utensils for the job. She was not interested in saving labor but in saving cuisine and in her own pleasure.

Child was part of a novel way of thinking about home cooking from the 1960s onward, at least among educated middle-class American women. What if time spent in the kitchen could be more like play than work? The postwar years saw the emergence of a completely new kind of kitchenware store that presented tools such as chicken bricks and asparagus steamers as toys, targeted at an emerging breed of hobbyist cooks. These expensive articles were designed more to enhance the luxury of being in the kitchen than to cut down on work. For those with the money and the leisure, it could be huge fun to spend time coaxing delicious scents in beautiful pans, relishing the suave texture of hollandaise or the lovely jolt of a lemon when it is zested. But for the average cook on the average income, the chore of preparing meals remained largely unsolved. Yes, there were those all-in-one food choppers advertised on home shopping channels—mince onions, whip cream, make salsa, all with a few turns of the handle!—but they were so fiddly to wash up that they were hardly worth the bother. Meanwhile, the microwave promised to make cooking a breeze—or reduce it to the zapping of a pre-prepared, store-bought frozen dinner—but this was only true if your definition of cooking didn't include rendering food crispy or brown or tasty.

Behind the disappointment of labor-saving devices lies a bigger problem, which is our collective failure to see the work of cooking as something important, and skilled, and worthy of our respect. "We simply do not value the most valuable thing in the world," says architect Carolyn Steel, author of *Hungry City*, on the topic of food. We like to imagine that dinner arrives on our plates as if by magic and we discount the work involved in getting it to us, whether it is the toil of a cook in a kitchen, or the punishing lives of tomato pickers and the chicken packers who enable us to feed ourselves.

In the end, it was the processed food industry, more than any wonder tool, that spared Western women in the twentieth century the labor of readying a meal. Marketers of packaged foods have spent a long time convincing us that real cooking is never worth the grind. Who needs a cherry pitter or an electric pastry mixer if you can stroll into a supermarket and buy a mini cherry snack pie anytime you feel like it? It won't be the same as a real cherry pie made from scratch, not even close. But what if you don't know the difference? We are now in an era where most of the meals we eat most of the time are not so much labor-saving as labor-forgetting. Around half of all food consumed in the United States and United Kingdom is "ultra-processed"; we no longer understand most of what goes into its production—or the origins of its ingredients, come to that.

At the opposite end of the spectrum, there are still places in the world where most cooking happens the slow and difficult way, without a single labor-saving apparatus. India is one of them. The country would grind to a halt without the unpaid labor of women producing delicious feasts from scratch three times a day, often in kitchens with the most minimal tools. In 2017, I spoke to art historian Prajna Desai who spent three and a half months running a culinary workshop in Dharavi, the largest slum in Mumbai. She documented the cooking and the lives of eight of the women she worked with in her 2014 cookbook *The Indecisive Chicken: Stories and Recipes from Eight Dharavi Cooks*, which is one of the most extraordinary food books I have ever read because it describes how cooking fits in with the rest of a person's life; among the interviewees, it was both an inescapable daily burden and form of solace.

The women Desai met did not think they were doing anything special, as they used the palms of their hands to flatten roti breads or painstakingly stuffed bitter gourds with a mixture of green mango, onion, and spice, sealing the edges with toothpicks; they saw these actions as part of a vital job, producing food that gives their families both health and pleasure. Many of them derived satisfaction from their craft. They took the time to burn an eggplant over an open flame to perfect silky smokiness. Yet the care that went into that task and so many others like it was somehow never given its due, because in the eyes of their culture and their husbands, they were simply fulfilling an obligation. Under these circumstances, no wonder people switch to packaged sliced bread, which is becoming popular in India, as elsewhere. It's also striking that cooks in that country have been among the world's keenest adopters of the Instant Pot, embracing it as a faster route to making traditional slow-cooked dishes such as butter chicken. This could be a sign that Indian women will not always be prepared to thanklessly devote hours of skill to the kitchen.

"We fetishize the scent of cardamom in rice pudding but the women producing it are forgotten," remarked Desai when we talked via Skype in 2017. She spoke of the deep ambivalence she felt about home cooking in India. She grew up eating her mother's food and saw Indian cuisine as something for which there was no substitute and no shortcut. There is no tool that can replicate a human hand when it comes to the making of chapattis and other flatbreads. But that being so, why are the hands and the women they belong to not given more respect?

Perhaps the real problem with the concept of "labor-saving" in the kitchen is that it tries to answer the wrong question. Instead of asking, "How can we cancel out this work?" we could instead try to ask, "How can we reward and recognize this work, and the person who does it?" Cooks have never been given anything like their full due.

I don't think we need to get too purist or too artisanal in our cooking. For something that can be prepared just as well by a machine, let a machine do it (unless you crave the sensory pleasure of doing things the slow way). As the chef Raymond Blanc has said, you can make sweet pastry by hand instead of in a Cuisinart, but it will take much longer and won't be any better. I am only too happy to delegate one or two work-night suppers a week to my Instant Pot. But there are those dishes whose production relies on the human touch and intellect, and it's time we gave the people responsible for getting them on the table some respect. We buy "smart" fridges and "innovative" egg poachers but no gadget has ever been half as clever in the kitchen as a person and her wooden spoon. As Mrs. C. S. Peel wrote in *The Labor Saving Home* in 1917, "The greatest labor-saving apparatus which we possess is the brain."

THE BEST THING SINCE SLICED BREAD

What's the
BEST THING since
sliced bread (in food)?

CHANDRA RAM

Unsliced bread that you can tear apart with your hands and dip into softened butter. And Cheez-its, for real.

CHRISTINE MUHLKE

The bread made by Pam Yung.

EVA KARAGIORGAS

Honestly, can we talk about how awesome Cheetos are?

ANITA LO

The Microplane. Soooo much better than a grater!

ALEX VAN BUREN

An acknowledgment that we should pay as much money for Chinese and Mexican cuisines as we do for Western cuisines at restaurants, because those foods are equally complex and beautiful.

NAOMI TOMKY

Though I fear that the current ICE movement is going to ruin it, the growth of high-end Mexican and Chinese food forcing Americans to stop dismissing entire cuisines as "cheap."

RACHEL BOSSETT

Soft serve ice cream.

CHRISTINA TOSI

French fries. Or soft serve. Or both, depending on my mood.

WENDY MACNAUGHTON

Heirloom beans!

ALISON ROMAN

I think Imperfect Produce is brilliant. I think there are a few kinks to work out for sure, but the idea has the potential to do insane amounts of good for the wild problem this country has with food waste.

MAISIE WILHELM

Prewashed lettuce by *far*.

NICOLE ADRIENNE PONSECA

Avocado on said sliced bread.

JOANNE CHANG

Sliced bread with some really great salted butter. Also, I recently tried some yogurt in Hong Kong filled with young coconut and it blew me away.

MARION B. SULLIVAN

I realize that this may be seen as a Southern cliché, but for me a summer tomato sandwich slathered with Duke's mayo is the best thing since sliced bread.

ERIN MCKENNA

Vegenaise. Am I gross?

KRISTINA GILL

Hamburger, rare. Only ketchup.

SOFIA PEREZ

Sea urchin. It was a revelation to me that this beautifully briny morsel was hiding in such an odd-looking and intimidating vessel. In hindsight, of course, it makes total sense that the species (like so many others) would rely on a form of natural protection from predators, but the first time I tasted sea urchin, I was walloped by the burst of flavor encased in the porcupine-like shell.

MONIQUE TRUONG

No-tipping restaurants; a living wage; health insurance and sick days for restaurant workers, front and back of the house.

HANNA RASKIN

The movement to reassess tipping and pay food workers a just wage for their labor.

ALISON CAYNE

Crispy roast chicken.

YASMIN KHAN

Pomegranate seeds sprinkled with golpar and salt. (It's an Iranian thing.)

MELANIE DUNEA

European butter.

JULIA SHERMAN

Bjorn Corn. I don't know what they put in that stuff. Also, Seed + Mill Tahini. I put it on/in everything.

KLANCY MILLER

Cookies.

TAMAR ADLER

Eggs. Being allowed to use eggs at lunch and dinner.

ANDREA NGUYEN

The food processor.

JASMINE LUKUKU

I'm a big fan of natural wines and craft chocolate—not together. I know this makes me sound insufferable, but I will live with that perception. I am not a purist—if you see me eating a Snickers bar and washing it down with a glass of boxed wine, don't judge me. What I love about natural wines and craft chocolate are the nuanced flavors achieved through a combination of agricultural practice and carefully considered production methods.

CHARMAINE MCFARLANE

Pastured eggs and grass-fed milk.

KRISTY MUCCI

Produce grown by farmers who care! It came before sliced bread, but nothing is better.

MARISSA LIPPERT

The rise and appreciation of heritage foodways/crops, farmers, greenmarkets, ethnic cuisines and more diversity. More sustainable, healthier ways of growing, producing, cooking, and consuming.

DIANNA DAOHEUNG

Being able to source more local and organic foods with ease. Almost every vendor now carries these options.

AISHWARYA IYER

I recently discovered date nectar through a new friend's company, D'Vash, and given my massive sweet tooth, I'm in heaven.

CLARE DE BOER

Carta di musica. It is the thinnest, crispest flatbread that hails from tiny Sardinia. It is a snack, it is an antipasto, it is a plate for salad, and can even double as a noodle in your lasagne. It is the most versatile of crackers.

ESTHER TSENG

Fried chicken. It's cross-cultural.

TIFFANI FAISON

The #MeToo movement.

ANA SORTUN

Hummus is the mashed potato.

CATHY BARROW

The return of white anchovies.

BONNIE MORALES

The availability of Kampot peppers.

JULIA BAINBRIDGE

Sumac. (Although that was around before sliced bread, I'm sure.)

REGINA SCHRAMBLING

Loaded question, 'cuz we have to specify we want our $$ bread left whole. But: The internet, which has made any ingredient accessible (for those who can pay), which has made cookbook editors less fucking timid, and which has opened up the world to multi-culti exploration that the old Time-Life series never could, with its white-guy limited perspective.

CATHY ERWAY

Sliced bread is not the best thing at all for anyone who cares about food—rather, it's a marker of our drastic turn from eating real food toward the industrially-produced, nutrient-deprived, heavily subsidized, cheap food that large conglomerates have fed to us in their interests and to the detriment of us and our environment.

JORDANA ROTHMAN

Unsliced bread. And Helen Rosner.

Emily Gould

Emily Gould had amassed a large archive by the time I "discovered" her work. Maybe that's because she began as a blogger and, to my detriment, I remained stubbornly resistant to the digital page long after it would have been considered acceptably skeptical or respectably old-school to do so. She had moved on to books (she's penned a collection of nonfiction pieces and two novels) and was contributing articles and essays to publications—online and in print—when I found myself gravitating to her writing. I also seemed to learn later than everyone else that in 2011, she and Ruth Curry founded Emily Books, a publishing house with the mantra "we make weird books by women." It's the best kind of weird—Nell Zink's, Jade Sharma's, Barbara Browning's, or Chloe Caldwell's—and I don't know if I'd have read any of it if I hadn't (finally) gotten wise to what Emily and Ruth were doing.

What I didn't realize was that Emily was leading a double life—as a food writer. In 2009, she set up a dedicated Tumblr blog—*Things I Ate*—where she posted regularly for seven years. She also started a cookbook club with none other than Sadie Stein (see page 12) that pays tribute to authors whose prose is often as memorable as (and sometimes better than) their recipes.

This essay incorporates aspects of both of those lives, and her (third) life as a parent and spouse. Motherhood and domesticity are two topics that come up repeatedly in this book. That wasn't intentional; it's a reflection of the issues that we continue to grapple with, even in the twenty-first century, and of the fact that food—cooking and feeding—is implicated in both housekeeping and, still, being a mom and wife. Emily tied them all together in a way I don't think anyone else could.

Who Cares?

Before I gave birth to my first child, I sent my husband, Keith, who doesn't cook, a series of emails with the subject line "new dad cookbook." I wrote down how to wash lettuce and the formula for vinaigrette. I codified, for the first time, the steps I took without thinking. "These are some of the easiest things I know how to cook, the first things I learned how to cook. Obviously I am not dead so you can ask me questions about stuff but I am still going to err on the side of possibly over-explaining," I wrote in the first email, which described how to make citrus-marinated pork chops with a side of sautéed greens. I even wrote down how to check the pantry for items like garlic and olive oil and where in the grocery store to look for the brands I usually buy.

I had written "obviously I'm not dead," but I must have thought that I would die, on some level. There's no other explanation for these emails. How could I not have understood, even then, that as long as I was alive and conscious and able to stand upright, I would be the one to cook? The first time I made a meal after giving birth—I had a home birth—was when our son was less than two days old. I know because I instagrammed it: scrambled eggs and toast with jam, all exactly the way I like them. Keith never prepared a single meal from the "new dad cookbook"—not the pork chops, not the Greek salad, not the many variations on the theme of pasta with vegetables, not the fish, not even the smoothies. Our friends brought food, that was part of it, but also I never gave him an opportunity. In the first months of our first child's life, I still cooked almost every one of our meals. Sleep deprivation and the brain-breaking love I felt for my child were a huge shock; I had lost the other parts of my identity, the ability to do even simple writing assignments—temporarily, as it turns out, but I didn't know that then. In the absence of the ability to produce with my brain the way I always had, I took refuge in my continued aptitude for cooking. It was a way back to creative expression, a way to accomplish something and provide structure on days that felt otherwise amorphous and wasted.

Somewhere around the time when my son started to eat real food and I started to return to full-time work, though, a subtle shift occurred. The distribution of household labor, which before children had always been almost even, became markedly skewed. Cooking and grocery shopping are inherently linked, and even if I made meticulous lists, it was hard to get Keith to buy exactly what I wanted—choosing cheese, fish, meat, and produce may not be rocket science, but it's also not that easy if you don't know how to cook. Buying food and planning meals had seemed to happen naturally in the background of my day prior to having kids; it always helped that if I didn't have spare time, it wasn't hard to run out and grab takeout, or throw something together from bodega ingredients, and besides, we each went out several nights a week, either together or separately. But a family, like an army, marches on its stomach. Peanut butter for packed lunch sandwiches and milk are either in the fridge or they're not, and it has to be one person's job to keep that inventory perpetually updated. Without ever really discussing or deciding that I was the head of household acquisitions, I took on that position.

Left to his own devices, Keith still refuses to make anything more complex than peanut butter sandwiches or boxed macaroni and cheese, even though I've pointed out a million times that regular mac and cheese isn't that much harder to make. Without kids to feed, he'll either neglect to feed himself (and wonder why he's tired, spacey, and out of sorts) or eat something less appetizing than Soylent, like this staple of his bachelorhood: a can of chickpeas and a can of tuna, mixed in a bowl and drizzled with olive oil and sprinkled with salt. That actually makes it sound kind of appetizing! But keep in mind that Keith made it, and he has no idea how to combine even the simplest ingredients in an appealing way; trust that the resulting dish is too oily and salty or maybe not salty enough. He makes rubbery fried eggs and burnt toast for our three-year-old on the mornings that our infant allows us to sleep in, and I'm grateful, honestly—who cares if he makes inedible food as long as I don't have to eat it? Plus, I'm not opposed to digging into a can of tuna myself every now and then. But if I have even five spare minutes I'll make it into tuna salad. Treating food as mere fuel, a distraction from the real business of life, makes me feel depressed and nihilistic. If cooking and eating are just something to get through so that we can focus on what's really important . . . wait, what's really important again? Anything?

Still, as much as I'd like to be able to cook delicious food for myself and my family and also work all day, I am forced to concede that I'm failing. More than once recently, I've tried to work a full day then come home and make dinner for guests while also simultaneously helping to keep two children on track toward their scheduled bedtimes. You will be shocked to learn that this hasn't gone particularly well. Both times the food turned out delicious—Ottolenghi chicken with clementines and arak to fête an out-of-town guest, latkes with lox and roe for Hanukkah. But I was either busy in the kitchen or sniping under my breath at Keith the whole time; I'm sure our guests felt super comfortable and welcome.

It has taken the arrival of our second child for me to realize how thoroughly the kitchen has transformed from a refuge into a prison, one that I have conflicted feelings about attempting to escape. Not long ago, I read two pieces of writing by women who found ways to elude gendered domesticity, after suffering under its yoke, and they made me question some of the presumptions I'd never thought to examine before. The first, by Lyz Lenz for Glamour.com, was an essay about cooking after divorce, in which the author realizes at the end of years spent trying to please an ex who rated her culinary efforts (never more than a four out of five, to leave room for improvement) that her love of cooking is less important than reclaiming that time and effort for herself; she currently lives "off of bagged salads, rotisserie chicken, and whiskey." The second, *Women's Work* by Megan Stack, a National Book Award-nominated journalist and author, was a book about waged and unwaged domestic labor worldwide, and how it is performed everywhere by women. She describes how the woman she and her husband hired in Shanghai to keep house and care for their newborn son practically saved the author's life—only to be nearly fired because Stack's husband didn't like their employee's cooking.

I can't afford to hire a housekeeper, and I don't want to get a divorce or live off bagged salads, even temporarily (especially now that there's an *E. coli* scare every few weeks). But casting domesticity as a pure distraction and a time-suck, as it was for these women while they struggled to shift their focus away from the constant demands of their households and toward work that is undomestic, or public-facing, feels to me like an evasion. During the last installment of the argument that my husband and I have on-and-off about housework, he told me I had to find a way to start doing less. He didn't, of course, mean that we should hire someone to help us with shopping or cooking or laundry or organization; he meant I should start caring less about what we eat and what our home looks like: the bagged-salads approach. It echoed something I read years earlier in an essay by a feminist writer whose name I can't remember about the wages-for-housework movement. The author wrote that she'd conditioned herself to accept untidiness in order to stop herself from using housework as a way to procrastinate and keep herself from doing her important work. I have thought about that essay intermittently for years now. Usually it pops into my head as I survey a wrecked living room and contemplate whether I'll feel less bad if I shave an hour off my morning to tidy it up before I leave for work or come home to it later on with kids who will immediately compound it. I'm up against it either way; it is my problem, because I'm the one who cares. And I think, *fuck you!!*

There's a third way, too, visible in the work of the food writers I've admired for years. It's not a coincidence that I've always gravitated to the pages of women who elevate domesticity to an art form, seeming to render "work" and "making dinner" one and the same, rather than distractions from each other. Though this is an illusion, it's a powerful one, in part because, for years, I didn't fully realize that it was one. I took Laurie Colwin's word for it that she made bread and wrote novels at home as her daughter . . . played, I guess, or napped. I skimmed right over Ruth Reichl's descriptions of her childcare arrangements and focused only on the moments in her memoirs when her young son was adorable at restaurants. And the bloggers and cookbook authors whose perfectly entwined interests I spent my twenties trying to emulate—their long, meticulously photographed posts and recipe testing were invisible to me. All I could see were the happy children helping to stir the batter.

My older son splatters batter all over the kitchen whenever he tries to "help"; I'm much happier cooking when he's nowhere near the premises. The baby is still invited to join me in the kitchen, but not for long; he recently rolled over, so crawling can't be far behind. Soon, we'll have to reinstall the baby gate to keep him away from the knives and oil spatters. But there is some truth to the domestic-goddess myth, mixed inextricably with its fundamental falseness: Beyond the pretense of effortlessness there is something unfeigned that strikes me as crucial. At a bare minimum, these writers are making the *work* of cooking and shopping legible, even when they present that work as expressive or fun. The trick is that labor *can* be fun. It's incredibly hard to decide where the fun stops.

The un-idealized reality, the cold truth of the current iteration of my domestic life, is that if I want to eat homemade citrus-marinated pork chops and sautéed greens, I will have to make them myself. But it is not necessarily my job to buy the peanut butter, an act that brings me no joy beyond knowing that this task has been checked off the list. I can't decide to care less; a lifetime of caring has not prepared me to turn caring on and off like a light switch. All I can do is care differently—and take care to preserve, for myself, how the version of me who wrote those "new dad cookbook" emails felt about food.

In the one I sent a week before giving birth, I described the difference between Kirby cucumbers ("bumpy") and regular grocery store cucumbers ("too watery") in a recipe for "a refreshing and super easy summer salad with three variations." Revisiting this email gives me the same heartbroken, self-indulgent pang that I'd get if I had the courage to revisit my high-school diaries. Has anyone ever been so innocent?

But look, cucumbers *matter*! Most of the readily available ones, even the newly ubiquitous mini European hothouse kind, have a strange fishy aftertaste; they seem to be bred for shelf-stability, which gives their insides a cottony denseness. Those are the cucumbers I buy these days, along with the chicken drumsticks and string cheese and milk that gets my family through the week. I can't teach myself to like this, or to feel less thwarted by it, any more than I can teach Keith to pay attention to what he puts in his mouth and what he buys at the store. All I can do is console myself with the hope that my children might also turn out to be the kind of people who care.

A Q&A with
Nigella Lawson

In 1998, at age thirty-eight, an established journalist named Nigella Lawson wrote *How to Eat*, a recipe book, sort of ("It is and it isn't, but it has got recipes," she has said). It was both a collection of opinions (on everything from not cooking when hosting a weekend lunch to the real reason anyone ever cares about low-fat food: because, she wrote, "they want to improve their ligne, not their soul") and a pragmatic manual for feeding oneself—and one's children, friends, or partner—without suffering for it, and maybe, while deriving pleasure from it.

With that first, career-changing cookbook, the ten that have followed, and the corresponding television programs she has hosted, the global "food personality" has told us, to paraphrase an oft-cited line from Helen Fielding' s 1996 novel *Bridget Jones's Diary*, that—as cooks—we are likable just as we are. "Home food," Nigella wrote in her cookery (one of the better Britishisms) debut, "should reflect your personality, not your aspirations." That's one of the reasons I find her so relatable. I also like her culinary sensibility—her combinations of ingredients and her mindfulness about reducing the number of steps you need to follow or vessels you need to use (and then clean). She keeps it doable, but not dull. As a writer, what I've always noticed and appreciated about Nigella is her unmitigated love of words and how she deploys them so lyrically, even in her cooking directions. I adore reading and—because of that—following her recipes.

Two other things I've observed from watching her and being lucky enough to talk to her: She has an impeccable sense of style (covetable wardrobe alert) and, much more important, she's a genuinely kindhearted person who's highly attuned to and concerned for the feelings of others. For someone so successful and well known, she is remarkably grounded—maybe because there's so much natural talent there. "I like to work with people who are incredibly talented because it usually means they have less ego involved and you can do something collaborative," she told me, which says a lot about her and is also a truth we should try not to lose sight of. This interview is a little different from the rest. Due my own technological failings and Nigella's rigorous schedule while on tour in Australia, I ended up sending questions, and her, answers, via email. She was a good sport, for which I send eternal thanks.

What role did family—or its absence—have on you as an eater, and a cook?

This is such a huge question, and such an entangled subject, that I'm not sure if I'm going to be able to unsnarl it completely. I have to start off by saying that I really didn't like eating as a child. Even so, I grew up immersed in food. But to backtrack, I suppose it is really more the case that I hated meals rather than eating. I didn't eat much and was brought up in a ridiculously old-fashioned way. I had to finish everything on my plate (and I feel it almost goes without saying that as children our tastes played no part in the choice of what we were fed), and if I didn't, I had to sit at the table until I had done so. When that failed (as I resisted), I would be given the plate back at the next meal, the food cold and congealed, and would be expected to eat it. So mealtimes could be fraught.

And, I think too, that when we did all eat as a family (which wasn't the norm at home), I'd feel anxious about my mother's volatility: It was easy to irritate her. Although, I have to say that that was probably one of the reasons I learnt to cook. My mother got me and my sister (who was sixteen months younger) to help her in the kitchen from a very young age: We were probably about six and seven; the services of my brother (who is three years older than I am) were not required. So I definitely learnt to cook more than I learnt to eat as a child. I think today parents often cook with their children as entertainment, as if they're children's television presenters; my mother just wanted help getting meals on the table. And she was very impatient: She'd show us what to do once, and then expect us to do it. And we did. So cooking just seemed an entirely normal thing. And this was cooking without recipes, without measures: I feel I just learnt to cook by cooking.

And I did, I'm glad to say, become an eater, too. As I got older, I had more control over what I cooked, and thus more control over what I ate. I think now that much of my resistance to eating as a child was just a way of holding on to myself as a person. I felt so impinged on. When I was in my teens, I was sent to boarding school, and although it did initially feel like a painful rejection, I do think that without having to struggle against the family, or to show I was a different person from the rest of them, I relaxed around food. I suppose it also made a difference that the food there was so bad. It made me realize how good the food was at home, and it turned it into a subject: something to fixate on.

So, rather as Diana Henry has written about doing in *How to Eat a Peach*, I used to read about food and plan make-believe meals and menus, and imagine what I would cook. I was very close to my maternal grandmother and would write to her every week from school. Soon, those letters contained ideas for recipes, or she'd send me a recipe she'd cut out of a newspaper or magazine, and I'd write out recipes I'd found for her. It was a recipe swap as conversation, and I think that has been a central tenet of my work. I should say that cooking from recipes was something my mother rather looked down on, but I loved my grandmother's file of cut-out and stuck-in recipes from all over the place: I flicked through it much more often than any of her photograph albums. It made me realize that cooking could occupy a whole imaginative world.

It occurs to me that just as not eating was my resistance when I was a child, eating became my resistance as I grew up. My mother had an eating disorder. I think I must have been about eighteen when I became aware of it, but I think it had started when I was about fifteen. Anyway,

I distinctly remember feeling that I didn't want to be in that prison. But I'm afraid I didn't feel that in any sympathetic sense. I just felt that I would show her that I didn't have to become that way, follow those rules.

So much of the daughter's rebellion against the mother is about insisting on being different, and yet I feel such a strong connection with my mother every time I cook. I don't necessarily cook the same food she did, but I think I cook in much the same way. I learnt from her to trust my instincts as I cooked. And I don't think I could have written *How to Eat* without having been brought up to have such strong feelings about food. But actually, I don't think I would have written it had my mother and sister not died young (when they were forty-eight and thirty-one, respectively). I had been very close to my sister, Thomasina, and so much of our daily phone calls were about what we were cooking, and so much of our time together was spent in the kitchen. And after such pronounced childhood difficulties, I did have a loving relationship with my mother from about the age of twenty-three, but I was only twenty-five when she died, so it was very intensely a relationship interrupted. I feel that in some part I wrote *How to Eat* as a way not just to memorialize their food, but to continue the conversation.

You have always believed in cooking's ability to empower the individual: What do you think are the essentials things a self-respecting (and -sustaining) human being should know how to cook?

I think cooking is such an important expression of the self (or it is for me) that I'm not sure I feel comfortable telling people what they should be able to be cook. Of course, I'm aware that that doesn't exactly chime with having written eleven cookbooks, but I will try and explain. I certainly have a chapter called "Basics, etc." in *How to Eat*, but even then I was insistent on there being no definitive list: "Your idea of home cooking, your whole experience of eating," I wrote, "colors your sense of what foods should be included in the culinary canon." And now, twenty years later, I feel that even more strongly. I have prejudices, it is true, and my books reflect them (and how they shift), but I have grown so weary of the "you're doing this all wrong" school of recipe writing online. There is no one way to cook anything. But we all find our ways, and I suppose what I want to do when I write about food is invite people to join me, make them see the pleasure in it, not bark instructions at them.

But when I reflect further on your question, I suppose it makes me want to emphasize the importance of cooking for oneself. I don't see cooking as a moral act—I don't think those who cook are better than those who don't—but I do think that being frightened of cooking is disabling. I always tell people, when they ask how they should learn to cook with more confidence, that the best way to learn what cooking is, is to cook for oneself. When you cook for yourself, there is no pressure to perform, and you can just concentrate on what you're doing: It gives you the space to learn. And, of course, you will worry less about things going wrong, which means you start off without that stress, and can allow yourself to enjoy it. And anyway, of course things will go wrong, and that's how you learn. So I think cooking for yourself gives you a freedom in the kitchen that I find very creative.

But it goes beyond that. I think that by cooking for yourself, you are saying something very important: You are taking care to keep yourself alive; and you are taking your own pleasure seriously. Cooking for others is an act of generosity and kindness, and it is no less important to be generous and kind to oneself. This sounds like I am getting dangerously near self-care! I slightly shrink from that bath salts and scented candle approach (not that I have any argument with either), but I don't see cooking for oneself as a hushed and reverential thing: The whole point is that it not be a special exercise. Cooking for oneself for me is rooted in the everyday and is not about nurturing foods or exquisite ingredients, but about acquiring an ease in the kitchen. I don't want to make a fetish out of cooking, though. And it certainly can't always be enjoyable: Sometimes you just need to eat something. But even on those days I feel exhausted, and don't feel I have the energy to peel and chop an onion, once I'm there at the chopping board, peeling and slicing, I begin to relax. But of course, cooking for oneself means that it isn't drudgery. I think over the years, many women have resisted cooking as it felt that it was an enforced act of service (which becomes servitude)—which it was—and I suppose I feel that by cooking for ourselves, we can reclaim cooking.

Did you have any hesitations about writing cookbooks when you started?

I don't think I'd say hesitation exactly, but I certainly felt a sense of shame (which in itself is shaming now). I wrote my first book almost by accident, and I hadn't even known it would have recipes, but as I wrote it, it became what it was, and I do remember feeling that because it was a food book, it wasn't a proper book. I remember someone who I'd worked with at the *Sunday Times*, where I had been a (non-food) journalist, saying: "But Nigella was always such a serious girl!" But it's true: Then, food and cooking were thought of as unserious, chiefly by men, but also, understandably, by women who wanted to distance themselves from a traditionally subservient role. It's complicated. I feel that cooking is such an important part of my self and how I experience the world. And even if this stems from the way I was brought up—as a female—it doesn't now feel limiting or undesirable. I remember someone saying to me, a few months before *How to Eat* was published, "I see you've got a book out soon." And I remember feeling embarrassed or awkward and batting it away, saying, "Oh, it's just a food book." I wouldn't do that now.

A big part of our job as food writers is to distill cooking and make it accessible for home cooks. But I'm not sure if people are aware of what that entails, work-wise, or how much work it is. What, for example, is the work of writing a cookbook like? And what do you think are the biggest challenges—and most time- or energy-consuming parts of your job?

Different parts of the process bring their own challenges, but I think I spend the most energy (and time) testing and retesting recipes, and editing them once they're written. Luckily, I have an obsessive bent—I think you probably have to, to do this—which means that I rather enjoy working on a recipe, making it simpler and simpler, and whittling it down to its essentials. Now, it's true my recipes are often long, but I don't think brevity has much to do with clarity or, indeed, ease. I find the testing and retesting quite exhilarating. Or rather, I have to admit, it's exhilarating when it goes well, and monumentally lowering when it doesn't.

But that's important because the same is true for the people who are going to cook the recipes. I'm not trained and I don't have any particular skills, so I am very sensitive to what could go wrong. And while that actually helps me write recipes, I hope, that readers can understand and have confidence in, it does also encourage what is anyway a pronounced negativity: I can't help but look for pitfalls and potential disasters. I think this is good for recipes, but not for life!

But I can go into a strange spiral when I actually write up the recipe and edit it. I never want to be too prescriptive, but I also want to be as clear as possible, and I sometimes write up a recipe that is so very detailed that actually it becomes claustrophobic. Then I have to edit so that it provides the reliable framework without taking away the reader's autonomy. In many ways, writing a baking recipe is simpler, because so much is mandatory. Precision is appropriate. But when you make a stew, say, it really doesn't matter whether you have two leeks and three carrots or two carrots and three leeks.

Since I write recipes by first cooking—often in a pretty slapdash way—and then looking at everything in a more rigorous way, I feel I am imposing an order that need not exist. And yet that's what I think people look for in a recipe: order and clarity. And until you've cooked a lot, you don't know what you can ignore and what you have to obey, so you need guidance. I think the greatest challenge for me as a food writer is to provide that order and clarity by being precise enough to be helpful without betraying the fundamentally anarchic nature of cooking.

As someone who had trained as a (print) journalist, how did you navigate TV— how did you learn to become comfortable with and express yourself on camera?

As a young journalist, I worked in print and on radio because I felt it was very important to exist in my words, not in my person. I was resistant to television, and although I had done bits here and there (as a talking head, or on a books program), I had no intention of making food programs. Not that I'd had any intention of becoming a food writer before that, so maybe there's a pattern. And I suppose there was: I'd really just burbled out *How to Eat*, and when I agreed to make my first food program, it was on the condition it wasn't scripted. I feel that is so important. Even were I to write the script myself, it would turn me into a performer.

When I make my programs, of course, I think a bit about what I'll say for the first sentence or so (though I do this on set, not beforehand), but really, the director says "action," and I have to fill the silence. So I have to think. And that's what fills my mind up, not the essential awkwardness of being on camera. When I'm filming, I have to concentrate on what is happening with the food, and what I want to say about it.

I can often feel comfortable on camera, but that doesn't mean I always feel comfortable about being on camera. I don't know that it's helpful to have one's physical appearance be so much a part of what one does, but I'm grateful I didn't start on television young. I think I was forty when I made my first food program. And what I love about it is the ability to talk so directly to people, to convey my enthusiasm and show how simple cooking can be. And I relish crew life. The camaraderie is so warming, and the connections run deep. It's very different from the necessary solitariness of writing, and that's interesting. I think I can say that I enjoy television, but its ramifications, what gets projected onto you, and so on, can be less straightforward.

Another part of our job, a relatively new one, and not one that we're inherently drawn to or that we planned on as writers, is self-promotion and the maintenance of "a platform." You are considered a "personality"—you do TV, you have a social media presence. What is the work and pressure of maintaining that like?

But I don't maintain it. I'm not a personality. I'm a person. Yes, it's true that I try to remember to post a recipe of the day—in that sense, I see it as work. But that's not very burdensome. I try to respond to people as much as possible, without drowning in demand. I really enjoy so many of the exchanges I have on Twitter, and I value the feeling of connectedness it can give. But on days when I feel vulnerable, I can stay off it without any further thought.

I think I have an easy relationship with social media, in the sense that I don't agonize about it. And maybe it's because I drive it that I feel so unweighed down by it. So much promotion involves interviews and generally having to be out there, that lying on a sofa at home tweeting a recipe of the day, or whatever it might be, feels relatively relaxed and natural. And of course, when you have a book out, you want people to read it, so tweeting about it, or posting on Instagram, is a good thing. And I love seeing pictures of recipes of mine people have made: It is extraordinarily touching. It's a real connection, and I value it.

How—negatively and/or positively—have social media and the internet affected the way we think about food and cooking? How have they affected your own work?

I feel I have answered this somewhat above. But I'd go further and say that one of the things I like about the internet is its ability to serve as some huge recipe share. Nothing will ever take the place of food books, and nothing can replace voice, but as a research tool, it can be fascinating. The downside of the digital food world for me is its clamoring for attention. By that I mean, the various outlets have to try and get clicks and the way they do it is so often by appealing to people's insecurity. Every time I see a post or an online article with a headline like "You've Been Making Scrambled Eggs Wrong All Your Life," (and this is just one that I've noted down) I despair. I find it so reductive. And just wrong. It seems so fundamentally anti-cooking.

And while I know that many lament the prettification of Instagram, no one who truly loves food would ever be taken in by this. We all know that brown food tastes wonderful and that some of the recipes that mean the most are the least photogenic. I actually have always taken photographs of what I eat, and I did so even in the olden days, when you had a camera with film in it that had to be sent away to be developed, so it would be a strange sort of hypocrisy for me to condemn it now. And I don't want to anyway.

What I do find interesting is that nothing erodes the value of the cookbook for people. Even those food bloggers who have a gazillion followers on Instagram want to bring out a cookbook. It still means something.

How do you separate what's private and what's personal in an age where the public imagines they know you and are entitled to know you?

I've thought about that differently at various stages in my life, but what I generally felt is that it is possible to be honest without having to open up about one's every secret thought. I do think I have got more guarded as I have got older, and I regret that as, in a way, the less guarded one is, the more one cannot worry about it all. But it's hard to be unguarded if any off-the-cuff remark can become a tabloid story. But maybe that doesn't even matter, even if one can get into the habit of thinking it does.

Over the years, I've jettisoned, whether willingly or not, a lot of privacy. And at times that can make me feel vulnerable. But when I do events which include questions from the audience, I always enjoy them. And I answer honestly. But I won't have these events filmed, because I value the intimacy of the room. It will take me a long time to work out what I feel about privacy in the age of publicity, but I certainly don't start from the premise that sharing one's inner thoughts is in itself a bad thing. But nor do I believe that because one invites people in to some degree, one then has a duty to divulge everything. I wouldn't feel that with friends in real life, so why would I with people I haven't met?

In what ways do you think well-being or "wellness" and food are related? What does that term mean for you?

I am so outside of the whole wellness arena and feel uncomfortable even writing the word. But if we are to talk well-being and food, I think that for me, that involves cooking for myself, for the reasons I gave earlier. I also think that I'm greedy for as much time with food as possible, and if I just ate and didn't cook, I think I would start to feel unsettled eventually: I wouldn't want to be reduced just to a consumer of food. But anyway, I wouldn't feel like myself not cooking. I'm on the road now, and will be for about seven weeks, and I won't be cooking in any of this time. I can feel how alienating it would be if it went on any longer. In a way, I am such an urban person that cooking is really the only way I interact with the natural world. And I do feel it makes me feel grounded in some sense. It also is probably the nearest I will get to a meditative act.

I'm sorry this is going to sound like one of the most idiotic questions, but it's something I've been wondering for so long and been embarrassed to ask . . . I always thought that English muffins as Americans know them (i.e., Thomas's) were a failed attempt to make crumpets. Is there an actual thing that is an English muffin? And, if so, what distinguishes it from a crumpet? (Again, sorry.)

Well, what you call an English muffin is what we call a muffin! And what you call a muffin, is what we called, when we first encountered them, an American muffin. Now we call both muffins. I would say, really, that English muffins and crumpets have no similarity other than their shape. I suppose you could call them both griddlecakes (though neither of them is sweet, so perhaps breads would be more accurate). But crumpets are made with a thick batter, and muffins are made with a dough. Their similarities are that they are both made with yeast (crumpets have baking soda too, to help make the bubbles or holes) and both are cooked in a griddle. You need to pour the crumpet batter into greased rings to make their shape, while you either cut muffins out of the dough, or form it into balls, which you then pat into fat discs.

Related to the above: What is the best way to eat a crumpet? And do Brits love and eat them as much as everyone imagines you do?

I think the best way to eat a crumpet is with butter and honey; an important part of eating them is having the butter drip into your hands, and even down your arms, as you eat, so there has to be plenty. The crumpet must be squelchy with it. It should go without saying that they must be toasted. Yes, we do love eating crumpets, but I don't think they are made at home much.

Whenever I read your books, I marvel at your use of language. Your love of words always comes through. Which writers or books have had the strongest hold or influence on you?

I don't know how to choose any particular writer. I think that reading in general gave me a feel for language, and I do feel I experience words as I experience food: When I read, I sometimes feel I just relish the taste of the sentences. But I don't think it has ever occurred to me to emulate a particular writer. I believe your question to be about all writing, not particularly food writing, by the way. But if I were to talk about food writing, just for one instance, I certainly feel that if I had read Laurie Colwin's *Home Cooking* before I'd begun work on *How to Eat*, I would never have felt able to write it.

What do you hope to do next? Is there anything you haven't done that you'd like to do?

I am almost pathologically not a planner. I can't operate except instinctively. Once I start trying to impose order on the ideas I have before they've taken proper root, I feel shut in, claustrophobic, and the fire goes out of me. And because I've been on the road for a while, I've haven't had time to tinker with ideas, to let them start to percolate creatively. It was a surprise to me that I started writing about food, really, and so I don't feel I should know what else I might do. I'm not sure I'm ready to turn my back on food though. I enjoy it too much still.

Carolita Johnson

Carolita Johnson's cartoons in the *New Yorker* would always make me giggle or smile in understanding. But the one she did a few weeks after the stories exposing Harvey Weinstein came out and the #MeToo movement surged, titled "This Is the Hand: A Response to Recent News," was disturbingly effective, and affecting. She sketched a series of (male) hands in black and white, identifying each with an inappropriate "handling" of her body—like the hand that brushed her breast "'by accident' while its owner asked about 'the pussy bow'" on her sweater. At the end of this catalog of groping paws is one that holds a pen. Its caption reads: "This is the hand of the cartoonist, me, who never forgot and who used her hands for better things." That was the cartoon that made me remember Carolita's name and begin actively seeking out her work; I wish I'd started a lot earlier.

Carolita's been writing, illustrating, and performing as a storyteller since 2002, when she returned home to New York City after spending the first twelve years of her adult life as "an on-again, off-again illegal immigrant, fashion model, student, and legal IT employee in Europe, exploring these different lives in Paris, Spain, and Italy," as she shared when I asked to her send me some important facts about her life so far.

She provided some other key intel: 1) She realized her life goal—"retiring early, working old"—at age nineteen, after seeing the movie *Roman Holiday* starring Audrey Hepburn and Gregory Peck. 2) She studied fashion at Parson's School of Design, and when she came back to the States to pursue her (revised) goal of being a writer and illustrator, she ended up with a day job in fashion and a side-gig as a *New Yorker* cartoonist instead. 3) She is, "of course," working on a book of her own. Thank god.

Comfort Dishes

My mom was a terrible cook. The success of her first attempt to prepare a Thanksgiving turkey was its comedic effect: She had left the plastic wrap on. Her inability to cook was a combination of lack of inspiration, lack of instruction, and, I suspect, a trace of defiance. She'd grown up in a South American country in a time when most people of any means had servants.

In America, she had to cook. She learned a few tricks from my uncle's wife, who had been the daughter of the cook in her wealthy uncle's house back home. This was a lesson in the equalizing force of democracy: in New York my aunt was no longer a servant or a servant's daughter. In fact, not only was my aunt the only woman in the family who knew how to cook well, she had also become my mother's financial superior.

There may have been some snobbery keeping my mother from acquiring culinary skills as well. It wasn't feminism, yet. She learned to cook a few loveless, easy, "modern" things from magazines like *McCall's* and *Good Housekeeping*. These usually involved using artificially flavored bouillon cubes, tinned vegetables, and cans of Campbell's Soup. Cream of Chicken was the key ingredient in a dish called Chicken à la King, which for ages I thought was an Ecuadorian dish. I hated it.

Since my mother was a terrible cook, comfort food, for me, centers on what my food was prepared and served in. My earliest example is a soft-boiled egg. I think it was one of the first meals my *mamá* cooked for me, once I graduated from jars of Gerber baby food. It wasn't just about the egg. Yes, it was a soft-boiled egg, but it was a soft-boiled egg broken up into a humble little Pyrex ramekin of clear, tempered glass. The gently scalloped lip and the little carved rings on its body were its only adornments. As a child, anything transparent fascinated me, and I loved looking at the spoon-cut chunks of egg white with the bright yellow yolk oozing over it through the glass wall. I was young enough that my mother still called me by a Spanish term of endearment, "Carolita," meaning "little Carol," while she fed me. I can still hear the dulled clicks of the spoon hitting the glass as she broke the egg up for me, and though I don't remember much about eating it, I do remember her offering me the spoonful, a classic gesture of motherhood, ready-made for nostalgia even with the most terrifyingly depressed and moody of mothers.

As an adult, one of the first things that made me feel like I was creating my own home was buying the same Pyrex ramekins I ate those eggs out of as a child. They're different from the updated version, which have a thicker, smooth lip above

The Pyrex ramekin and the teaspoon with the wooden handle that my mother used to feed me soft-boiled eggs. I took one of these spoons to Paris with me, too.

indentations that only give the illusion of a scalloped edge, a detail that's hard to spot unless you're looking carefully. It took me decades to perfect soft-boiled eggs. I still have to look at my recipe card every time I make one since I so rarely make them, but I can't live without those ramekins.

One day, in my twenties, having caught a cold, I craved something else my mother used to make when I was sick: chicken broth with white rice. It would be years before she learned to prepare *real* chicken broth, that is, from a chicken instead of a bouillon cube. Before, when she wanted to make it, she'd send me to the local supermarket called Associated's to go pick up a box of MBT (stands for More Better Taste). When I was sick, she'd drop a cube of MBT into a Pyrex pot of boiling water with white rice in it. I loved watching the rice in the simmering liquid through the clear vessel—even its handle was glass! The whole thing was see-through, like the magically alive Glass Cat character in one of my favorite Wizard of Oz books by Frank L. Baum.

Pyrex was the height of modernity when I was a child. Why? Imagine all the mothers of previous generations cooking in their opaque steel, enamel or aluminum pots and pans whose contents—and secrets—were kept hidden, mysterious. Then along comes Pyrex and you can witness every bubble form as the water boils. You see your food suspended over a flame and, thanks to the miraculous laws of physics, watch it become your dinner.

On a visit home from Paris, I found that pot in my parents' basement. I wrapped it up in my clothing and brought it back to my then-apartment abroad so I could cook (real) chicken broth with rice in it whenever I caught a cold. Even when I broke it, I kept the handle. I have it still. I have my eye on a potential replacement that I spotted at a thrift store a week ago. I've been trying to decide if there's enough room in my small kitchen to indulge that nostalgia. I know just what I'd cook in it, of course.

When I take ill, nothing else will do. I have a bag of white rice in a tin that I only break out for special occasions like a filthy cold or food poisoning. I cook the rice the way my mother used to: in a square white Corningware pot with a glass lid. At one point I may have had one I pilfered from her cupboard, but it's equally possible that the original broke one day and I replaced it with another midcentury casserole of the same brand just like it with its signature blue cornflowers on the side, found in a thrift shop.

It really doesn't matter. It will always be my mother's, either way, because of the memories it evokes. One, in particular, will permanently inhabit it, in any of its iterations. My mother had a habit of taking her gum out of her mouth to taste the water the rice was boiling in, to see if it needed more salt before she lowered the flame. She would remove the lid, placing it on the counter, then stick her gum to its interior as she took a little of the hot water in a spoon to sip. One day, she forgot all

The Pyrex pot my mother used to make MBT chicken broth in.

about the gum, put the lid back on the rice, and let it finish cooking.

My brothers and I all noticed immediately that the rice tasted like spearmint and said so. When I remember that moment, my mother's disproportionate exasperation with us is explainable if I imagine it widening to encompass her entire adult life, one she hadn't expected to live. Perhaps she saw cooking for three kids and a husband, in a small apartment, in a lower-middle-class neighborhood as a just penance for years of thinking that she, who had been educated and groomed for another life in which she'd be swept away by a rich man of her own social class and wear fine clothes, own at least one fur coat, attend ballet performances and concerts, and employ a nanny, was better than everyone around her . . . and thought that, in complaining, we were deliberately being difficult, as if to add to her punishment.

"Just eat it!" she said, "don't give me your nonsense."

"But Mommy!"

"Just eat!"

"But—"

"Eat!"

We tried to eat it (and I can still taste the minty rice as I tell the story), but it was such an unnatural taste. We poked at other parts of our meal, trying to buy time, and then, after a glorious second or two of suspense, watched our mother's facial expression transform as she tasted the rice herself. Humility took over while she slowly fished out her little green wad of gum from the rice and began to melt into helpless laughter.

I'll never pick up the clear glass lid of a Corningware pot without half-expecting—maybe even hoping—to see a wad of green chewing gum stuck to it.

My chicken broth with rice experience isn't complete unless the soup is served in a midcentury tempered clear glass teacup, with a chunky square handle and a clear, round-edged square glass saucer. Of course, the broth cooked in an invisible pot must be presented in a nearly invisible glass teacup.

This was how my mother served it to me whenever I was ill. To tell the truth, I never liked these teacups when I was a kid. I found them difficult to hold because of the square handle. It was uncomfortable for a child's fingers, and later, too small for an adult's. The only good thing about the cups was that they were stackable and looked great in the cupboard. I used to sneer at them, thinking the obvious favoring of design over ergonomics was more evidence of my mother's continued, vain aspiration to join a higher class.

And yet, I keep coming back to them. At one point I had a set of two in Paris that I brought over in a suitcase, stuffed into tube socks, further wrapped in pajamas. I ditched them as I packed for the trip home to New York after twelve years abroad. When I set up house years later with a husband, I found two more in my

The Corningware pot with the blue cornflowers, and the infamous gob of green gum.

parents' basement and brought them to Riverside Drive in New York. After his death three years ago, I abandoned these, too, as I pared down, packing up our belongings and putting them in storage to wait for me to go on with my life when I was able. For all I know, they may still be in that house, becoming part of someone else's memories.

So . . . If anyone who knows me is reading this, please see the drawing and feel free to gift me a set of two. I miss them. They're not expensive at all! I almost bought another pair at the local thrift store but came back too late for them. They're cheap midcentury artifacts, nothing special, except to me.

When I finally realized that being an adult meant knowing how to cook and feed oneself on a daily basis, as opposed to whenever the need for comfort food arose, I took home some Farberware from my parents' kitchen to work with. I have been known to say, "I'm a Farberware girl," as if that were a thing. Introduced in 1944, Farberware is stainless-steel cookware in a simple, utilitarian design, with black knobs on the lids. I use it for everything except eggs. I just can't manage to fry an egg on a stainless-steel frying pan. I have a Teflon pan in my oven that I bring out for that purpose alone.

My Farberware pan is used for one thing: "my mother's Bolognese sauce." I'll explain the quotation marks in a moment. This is the only thing I cook in it because it is the pan my mother cooked her Bolognese sauce in when I was growing up. My favorite part of that process was the stage where she had the ground beef simmering in olive oil with a bay leaf and powdered cumin and oregano. As soon as the meat was just cooked, she'd add a good dose of vermouth. That was when I would beg her for a little Pyrex ramekin of the meat, before she added the tomato sauce. I loved nibbling it in tiny spoonfuls while it was almost too hot for my teeth to bear.

Mom's Bolognese was terrible, and this was partly because, back when I was a kid, there was no such thing as "certified organic" anything, and as far as my dad (who did all the shopping) was concerned, meat was meat, so his choices were based on price, not quality. I dreaded the gristle I'd find in the sauce— there was always a bit of boingy gristle and I was always the one who got it (or maybe I was the only one chewing my food properly), and I'd often be caught trying to hide napkins full of the half-masticated beef in drawers of the credenza in the dining room. I spent many a long evening sitting alone, admonished not to leave the table till I'd finished my meal.

I began making this dish for my boyfriends in the early '00s, when I read in *Cosmo* that one of my most important duties as a modern woman (aka as the coolest girlfriend in the world), next to administering "mind blowing" oral sex, was learning to make "man food." The main ingredients of this cuisine are pasta, meat, and tomato sauce. My version of my mother's Bolognese was cooked with organic ground beef or sometimes, even, bison. The Johnson tradition calls for powdered

The tempered glass teacup for serving chicken broth with white rice.

cumin and oregano, but I used the whole, organic spice that I ground myself in a mortar and pestle, and when I could find it, I'd throw in some fresh leaves of the herb. I chose an organic, "smoked, crushed tomato" sauce rather than the pre-seasoned brand my mother used.

It was always a success, especially with a nice frisée salad, French bread, and goat cheese on the side, and, of course, the mind-blowing oral sex. It was also the last meal my late husband ate in the hospital before declining further treatment and not eating much of anything anymore. He took a spoonful with his eyes closed, threw his head back and exclaimed, "Oh, yummy!" It's a point of pride for me. But I haven't made it since.

My affection for vintageware is obviously all about the past I never had; the one that eluded me, that I didn't even know about till I grew up and saw other families—tasted their food, saw their interactions. It's my way of conjuring my childhood, of bringing back those moments of anguish and fear, and imbuing them, instead, with comfort. The trick is in making the food I place in the vessels now more delicious than it was then. By lovingly cooking in and eating serenely from them, I'm pretty sure I'm rewiring my brain to experience and generate positive memories, while undoing the bad ones. It's a therapy I came upon accidentally; perhaps all nostalgia is such a therapy. It's an apology to my child self; it's me, saying, *Here is the food you should have had, in a place where you can savor it, in safety, without fear or anxiety. I made it just for you—for me, little Carol, my own "Carolita."*

Farberware pan and pestle for making "man food."
I also took the pestle from my parents' kitchen, since my mother never used it.

A TOAST!

What is a
GOOD THING
to put on toast?

CHANDRA RAM

Please. Name one thing that isn't good on toast. I dare you.

CATHY ERWAY

Whatever's good in season.

MASHAMA BAILEY

Anything and everything.

CAROLINE FIDANZA

Almost anything. Toast is a perfect food. But top of the list: butter and tomatoes with sea salt, any kind of cheese, ham and mustard, sautéed greens, salad, on and on.

MONIQUE TRUONG

Salted butter from Brittany and honey.

CHRISTINA TOSI

Tons of butter and cinnamon sugar.

MICHELLE HERNANDEZ

Unsalted French or Irish butter, gray sea salt, apricot confiture.

On a warm tortilla, the same, minus the confiture.

OLIVIA WILSON

Butter and radishes and salt.

JENI BRITTON BAUER

Grass-fed butter, heavily salted summer tomatoes.

EMIKO DAVIES

Anchovies and butter. Proper Cantabrian anchovies and proper butter, ideally.

ALEX VAN BUREN

Butter and peanut butter.

TINA ANTOLINI

Peanut butter and crescent moons of perfectly ripe nectarine.

MARISSA LIPPERT

Peanut butter, tomato, and bacon (thanks to my grandmother!).

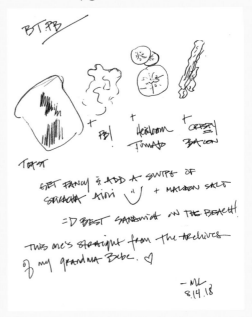

JASMINE LUKUKU

Peanut butter, banana, honey is my breakfast standard. I'll toss on some cacao nibs if I'm feeling fancy.

RACHEL BOSSETT

Labneh and honey.

TAMAR ADLER

Escabeche

Beans

Ricotta & marjoram

Butter and smoked fish

HANNA RASKIN

Pickled herring.

ALISON CAYNE

Excellent canned tuna with a little mayo and lemon.

Or butter.

Or cream cheese and tomato with Maldon salt.

WENDY MACNAUGHTON

Fresh salsa.

SARA LEVEEN

Pineapple jam! Purée a ripe pineapple and cook it in a nonstick pan for an hour over a super low flame. It develops flavors of vanilla and cinnamon that you won't believe.

A close second: chicken liver pâté.

CHRISTINE MUHLKE

Any jam that a friend has made.

UMBER AHMAD

Don't laugh, but I will take leftover buttercream, slather it on a piece of toasted brioche, and top it with slices of banana. It's a little French, a little childlike, a little Elvis. And completely divine.

ANA SORTUN

Dark Chocolate ganache, flaky salt and olive oil

OR

Good tahini and grape molasses

OR

Chopped spinach salad with yogurt, mint, and melted butter

JORDANA ROTHMAN

My feelings.

NAOMI TOMKY

Ricotta.

SIERRA TISHGART

Peas and ricotta!

KATHLEEN SQUIRES

Whipped ricotta with a touch of olive oil, honey, and red chile flakes. Or, whipped ricotta and zucchini flowers.

KRISTY MUCCI

Ricotta, chopped hazelnuts (preferably Italian and toasted), honeycomb (preferably local), and flaky sea salt.

BONNIE MORALES

Fresh sheep cheese, thin slices of peaches, and cocoa nibs.

GINA HAMADEY

Ricotta/honey/figs

Mayo/tomato/s&p

Avocado/toasted walnuts/salt

MARION B. SULLIVAN

Goat cheese drizzled with local honey.

NICOLE ADRIENNE PONSECA

Same answer for the best thing since sliced bread: avocado on said sliced bread, except the bread is toasted.

CHARMAINE MCFARLANE

Anything but an avocado. Just stop with this and give the avocado crops a chance to catch up so I can afford and enjoy my salads again. How about goat cheese and tupelo honey, or garden-ripe tomatoes and stracciatella di bufala?

JULIA SHERMAN

Butter, cinnamon, and sugar (can't beat it)

Tomato, garlic, and anchovies (pan con tomate)

Olive oil and flaky salt

Tahini, roasted banana, cinnamon

Tomato and aioli

NAOMI POMEROY

Rub of garlic and smashed-up sungold cherry tomatoes and salt.

EVA KARAGIORGAS

Feta cheese and a summer tomato.

SAMIN NOSRAT

Hellman's mayo and heirloom tomatoes sprinkled with flaky salt.

SOFIA PEREZ

Tomato, olive oil, and Ibérico ham.

On a separate (second) piece of toast, chestnut paste.

Eat the tomato-ham toast first, and the chestnut toast for dessert.

VIRGINIA WILLIS

Thinly shaved Vidalia onion, sliced ripe tomato, and sharp cheddar cheese all melted under the broiler until bubbly and brown.

ERIN MCKENNA

Same answer as for the best thing since sliced bread: Vegenaise. Again, am I *gross*?

CATHY BARROW

Hot-smoked salmon and goat cheese.

EMILY FARRIS

Super buttery scrambled eggs.

DIANNA DAOHEUNG AND ANDREA NGUYEN

Condensed milk.

REGINA SCHRAMBLING

Pimento cheese after a debauched dinner party.

HOMA DASHTAKI

Thick yogurt or labneh, cucumber, tomatoes, salt, pepper.

LIGAYA MISHAN

Something I learned while testing recipes for Priya Krishna's *Indian-ish* cookbook: almond butter and chaat masala.

YASMIN KHAN

Tahini, date syrup, a sprinkle of sea salt. Trust me.

AISHWARYA IYER

Maple tahini, extra-virgin olive oil, blueberries, pecans, sea salt.

CLARE DE BOER

The question you could be asking is: What is a good thing to put on *carta di musica*? [See page 267.] A recent favorite was warm peach jam fresh from the stove with equal parts cold butter. The two melt into each other and drip down your hands. On the savory side, again take cold butter, this time top with an anchovy fillet, black pepper, and olive oil. Tastes a lot like Marmite.

NICOLE TAYLOR

Mashed sweet potatoes with savory toppings, such as onions and sumac, or sweet toppings with cream cheese and cinnamon.

REBEKAH DENN

What *isn't*? Everything is so wonderful on toast. Maybe that should be the restaurant concept that hasn't been tried but should? [See Bright Ideas, page 384.]

HOW TO BUTTER YOUR TOAST

Butter, alone, was overwhelmingly the most popular answer to this question. But people were very particular in their responses. The most devilishly delicious buttered toast is in the details. Here are some essential tips: The butter has to be the best quality you can find. Generic products are not recommended. French is the gold standard, preferably salted (if you can find and afford it, Rodolphe Le Meunier Beurre de Baratte is a cultured butter, churned, the old-fashioned way, with cream from some very special cows in Normandy, and chefs are big fans). Let your butter come to room temperature for spreadability and don't skimp on it; apply copiously.

WHAT TO DRINK WITH YOUR TOAST

Alison Roman and Julee Rosso both offered veritable toast menus. You could make a meal of just one of their suggestions or create a brunch around their respective lists. I figured, if you're going to have a supper of toast, or throw a party in its honor, you might want to pour yourself—or your guests—a glass of wine. Megan Krigbaum, a wine and drinks writer in Brooklyn, has some thoughtful pairing suggestions, so we can properly toast our toast.

Alison Roman's Toasts

Cream cheese and Aleppo pepper

MK says: Aleppo pepper is such a transporting ingredient; you can feel the hot Mediterranean sun and the baked earth and groves of citrus trees. The spicy little flakes always steer me right toward *rosé*, preferably from southern France, like the one from *Chateaux Pradeaux*, which has ripe fruit to balance the heat and tang to stand up to cream cheese.

Yogurt and cucumbers

MK says: This combination is my go-to every summer when on vacation with my family. For me, it triggers soothing, sunny afternoons spent between the lake and the deck, when there's always a couple bottles of cold, intensely acidic, salty *muscadet* in the fridge. The alcohol's in check so that I can drink it all day and the wine meets the cool cukes in freshness. I love the affordable one from *Domaine de la Bregeonnette.*

Smashed eggs (soft-boiled) and caviar

MK says: If you're going to spring for caviar, you might as well spring for *Champagne*, too. Eggs can be tricky to pair with wine, but they benefit from some bubbles, as do fish eggs, for sure. Look for one that's a little toasty, but has some freshness to it, like the nonvintage *Bérêche & Fils Brut Réserve.*

Butter, salt, and pepper

MK says: Is there any food more perfect? The only way to up the ante is to bring in just a little dusting of sugar, and by that, I mean *riesling*. If you have sworn off riesling because you think it is too sweet, you are wrong. Stop it. For rich foods that need a laser beam of acid, but still a little weight: riesling. For salty, crispy snacks: riesling. For anything spicy: riesling. For this toast: riesling, like the *Von Hövel Feinherb.*

Almond butter with hot honey

I love *pet-nat*. Alison Roman loves pet-nat. So drink a fizzy pet-nat with this sticky spicy combo. Look for one with some good juicy fruit character. It will be the jam to your toast, if you will. A perennial favorite is the pink *Moussamoussettes* from natural wine great *René Mosse* in France's Loire Valley.

Julee Rosso's Toasts

Fava beans, garlic, Parmigiano, mint, and olive oil

MK says: *Vermentino*, a white wine from Italy's Mediterranean Liguria region is worth stocking up on in the springtime—for everything green, including favas and mint. It brings a little bit of citrus and its own herbal element and is compulsively drinkable. I love the *Vignaerta* vermentino from producer *Bisson*.

A PLT: Roasted prosciutto, baby arugula, roasted cherry tomatoes, and aioli

MK says: The last time I was tasting wine in Chianti, there was an important emergency sandwich stop made in Radda that involved thick white bread, tomatoes, and arugula with mozzarella (for me), and prosciutto (for my husband), olive oil, and an expert amount of salt and pepper. This sort of sandwich will, from here on out, indicate *Chianti Classico* for me. Try the organic one made by *Federica Mascheroni Stianti* at *Castello di Volpaia*.

Smashed avocado, lime juice, red pepper flakes, and great Tuscan olive oil sprinkled with ground black pepper

MK says: The great thing about the ubiquitous avocado toast is that it lends itself to basically any wine you happen to feel like drinking. If you have a really citrusy *albariño* in the fridge, it will play up the lime zest and the grassiness of the olive oil. If you've got *garnacha* from Spain, its juicy fruit and tannins will be so tasty with the fattiness of the avocado. If there's a glass of *rosé* left in a bottle from last night and it's 11:30 on a Friday morning and you're working from home, go for it.

Rogue Chocolatier's Sambirano 70% sprinkled with Maldon Salt

MK says: Don't drink red wine with chocolate—it's gross. Instead, get yourself a bottle of *madeira* like the *Rare Wine Co.'s Historic Series Savannah Verdelho*, for when you're having really good chocolate and need just a little sip of something. While often quite sweet, madeira also has this brilliant acidity—frequently in the orangey citrus realm—that's outrageous with chocolate and salty dessert. The wines stay well in the refrigerator once opened, so don't feel funny if you've had a bottle kicking around for months.

A Conversation with Preeti Mistry

Preeti Mistry is one of the most outspoken people in the food industry. She seems almost incapable of keeping her mouth shut in the face of injustice or plain old malarkey of any kind. It's made her something of a polarizing personality, someone labeled "difficult." But without the Preetis of the world, how would we ever get anywhere closer to fairness and parity? It's thanks to her that people who want to speak up, but just need a little nudge or someone to stick her neck out first, do. What's infuriating, to her—and to me, is how many people see all the bullshit for what it is, like she does, and stay silent, letting her be the big-mouth because they're too cowardly or "political" to back her up.

Born (and culinarily trained) in London with roots in Western India and reared in the United States, Preeti's an Indian American chef who first came to the public's attention, nationally, when she appeared as a contestant on the sixth season of *Top Chef*. Back on the West Coast, in Oakland, she developed her totally unique style of cooking—a mash-up of Northern California ethos and ingredients, traditional Indian flavor profiles, French techniques, and, always, an almost mischievous playfulness. She showcased this, in full, at her first restaurant, Juhu Beach Club (est. 2013), and then, in her version of an Indian pizza place, Navi Kitchen (est. 2017) in Emeryville, where proceeds from special dishes were donated to local nonprofits and which was designed to be a safe space for immigrants, people of color, and the LGBT community—customers and employees alike. A 15 percent service fee was included on every bill to provide her staff with a reasonable living wage. But restaurants don't allow for much progressive structuring. Finding it impossible to sustain those businesses without compromising their values, she and her wife/partner, Ann Nadeau, chose to close both properties in 2018.

A self-described "gay, brown person with a mohawk," Preeti hasn't given up. She's figuring out her next move. Don't expect her to back down anytime soon—not from her vision or her beliefs. She knows putting those things first comes with a price—one she's willing to pay.

You hear a lot of men talking about how they had a major failure and then they succeeded. And I always feel like it's a luxury to be a guy, and be able to fail, and then have people come back and invest in you. And when we talk about our failures, they're never as big as those failures—not on the same scale. And yet we still process them as failures. You refer to *Top Chef* as a failure. But I don't think it was; it's just that you didn't win.

PREETI

Did you see it? Pretty bad. It's all okay now. I think *Eater* called me the Jennifer Hudson of *Top Chef*.

CD

Which is good, I would think.

PREETI

It's great. Yeah. When they said that, I stopped talking about it, because it was kind of this ongoing joke with my friends—that I wanted to be the chef that had the largest chasm between how poorly they did on the show and how well they did in their actual career. That was my goal. So I was like, *I'm starting from the bottom . . .*

CD

I think you've done it. Similarly, I think that there's a difference when it's a guy's deal falling through. I don't think most men would think of it as a failure. I think they would just be like, *Okay. So that didn't work.*

PREETI

Not to mention, it wasn't like it [the initial deal for opening Juhu Beach Club] fell through. I was like, *This guy's an asshole, and I don't wanna be in business with him. And we have nothing signed. I just wasted a year of my life having fucking lunch and coffee with this person. And talking to the media about it.* I was actually the one who said, "I don't wanna do this with you anymore." One of the reasons I cut it off was he wanted 51 percent. I feel like I dodged a bullet. I could just tell. He was treating me more like an employee than a partner. And he therefore wasn't seeing the talent that I was bringing and what I was capable of. He was just blowing sunshine up my ass to get me to basically run a restaurant so he could come there and hang out—I mean, he was an Indian real-estate mortgage guy. He wanted a place to go meet all of his friends and hang out, and be like, *I own this restaurant. And I can fucking run it every day.*

CD

There are two things there that upset me. The first is the way restaurants became the new art collecting. It's the same thing where people who made a lot of money would want you to see how much they had by hanging expensive art on their walls. Later, it turned into, *Look! Come to my restaurant.* The second is that it was always exploitative for chefs. There've been so few partner examples that I can think of that were fair. Maybe it's changing, I don't know. Maybe you think it's changing. But for the most part, I think a lot of those partnerships start out where the chef is at a disadvantage. You had the foresight. I don't know how many people have the foresight to see it till it's too late.

PREETI

Well, my wife has an MBA.

CD

That's very helpful.

PREETI

And she's not about to let me make a stupid decision. When I first met him, this guy literally walked into my pop-up in a liquor store, and was like, *I wanna make Juhu Beach Clubs all over the country.* And I was like, *Fuck yeah.* And then all these people were like, *Preeti, what are you doing? Why do you wanna get in this with this guy? You don't know him.* And I was like, *Do you have half a million dollars?*

No you don't. So I'm going with that guy, 'cause I wanna open a fucking restaurant. And if I'm still in this liquor store three years from now, then this didn't work out right.

CD

Yeah. And if you had done that with him and it had been a failure, it's already hard enough to get backing as a woman or a person of color, let alone a woman of color . . .

PREETI

It would've just been a totally different place. So yeah, was there a failure? I was just worried at that point what some people expected from me. This little flash and then, oh it doesn't work out.

CD

I don't see any of it as a failure. But I see myself doing this. Every time I do something that feels like it's not quite right, or it didn't hit the mark, I interpret it in my head as a failure. And in the grand scheme of what a failure is, and who's allowed to fail, this is not right.

PREETI

I talk about this with my therapist all the time. Every single thing that I'm speaking at or I'm cooking for, the expectations that I have of myself are so ridiculously high. Whether it's making the speech at the *Cherry Bombe* conference, or making a speech at my parents' fiftieth wedding anniversary, whatever it is, I have to kill it, or it's like I failed.

CD

Is it that there is also something in us that's so acutely aware that we have to always be right, because people are just waiting around for us to not be?

PREETI

Yeah, I totally think that's true. I mean, showing any level of vulnerability—

CD

Because they already assume we're just vulnerable messes anyway.

PREETI

I think a lot of it is impostor syndrome as well—expecting people to look for that opportunity to discredit you. Sometimes I seriously still have moments where I'm like, *I'm not a chef, right?* And my wife will say, "Honey, you've been nominated for two James Beard Awards for best chef. You're a chef." I mean, it's just stupid things like that where you get this idea of what that thing is supposed to mean and be in the world. And then you also have so many people out there, who, I don't know, have a blog, and they went to culinary school for three months, and they're like, *Chef . . .*

I think it's also this idea that there's one way to be a chef or a writer, or whatever the occupation is. One thing I often say is that I've done a certain amount of butchery, and I can break certain meats down, or joints down, but it's not necessarily my forte. And for the past ten years, it's been all about the whole animal. I'm like, *Yeah, but how many of these chefs know how to use these thirty fucking spices that I fuck with every single day?!* There becomes this sort of arc of, *This is what it's about.* And it's like, *Yeah, that's just what we're currently valuing in our industry.*

CD

Yeah. It's the same with the standard of types of restaurants too, right? We're still looking at that French model of fine dining as the barometer for what makes everything else a good restaurant. But there are different ways you could have a restaurant. Does it change the idea of the impostor syndrome, too, when you have people who are like, *Well, you should be cooking Indian food,* and then you have people who don't understand Indian food in the first place?

PREETI

I have a great story. I was at an event for an organization called Kitchen Table

Advisors—great organization that works with small farmers, to help them with the business and marketing and all that stuff, and hook them up with chefs. And they do their annual fundraiser, where they get a bunch of different chefs and they match them with farmers. And everybody does a dish, and rich people walk around and taste things. The chefs get drunk behind the tables. It's all good. I was doing this event, and this very tall, straight, white chef, male, from San Francisco, who I won't name—his table was next to mine. And he showed up late. His two cooks were already there setting up. Everybody's asking, "Hey, what are you cooking?" and tasting each other's stuff. And he didn't know who the hell I was. And I was like, *Okay, whatever. You're in San Francisco, you actually should, but anyway, I'll let it slide.* I say, "I'm doing blah blah blah." And he asks, "Do you use good proteins? 'Cause I just ruined myself. I can't eat anything." And he started saying this, and in the moment, I was just like, *Yeah.* And at the same time, I'm questioning . . . Like, *I don't buy my meat at Restaurant Depot, if that's what you're asking. Whatever.* But then I went home and started telling my wife. And I was like, *So fucking racist.*

I started to unpack it a little bit: We were at a farmer-chef event. Does he really think they asked me to do this because they just needed a token brown person? And that I don't actually believe in these tenets of quality meats, vegetables, cooking seasonally, working with small farms, etc.? *You really think that? Think about it, first of all, buddy.* And then secondly, if this was not an Indian restaurant, he would've never asked me that question. And if I was white, would he have assumed that I was the white savoir of Indian cuisine? It was just all of those layers to me in this way of, *What the fuck?*

What I see a lot of in the Indian food industry, currently, in the echelon we're talking about, is a lot of copycatting. It's a lot of rich fifty-plus Indian guys, sitting around going, *How do we make this cool?* I feel like it's all my uncles sitting around like, *What do the kids want today?* And cherrypicking shit off my Instagram . . . but no one's actually gonna give me credit for it. They're all just gonna do it now.

CD

You won't get the credit.

PREETI

I focus on a quote from 2 Chainz—I follow 2 Chainz on Instagram—where he says something like, "When you're an innovator and a creative, people will copy your work and use it as inspiration. You just have to be okay with that." 'Cause I'll keep coming up with shit. I'm onto the next.

CD

That doesn't mean you still wouldn't appreciate the mention . . .

PREETI

Yeah, I mean, to speak specifically to the gender of all this (I have to self-deprecate for a second before I say it): There's a large part of me that feels, if I was a guy, that people on both coasts would be saying that I was the fucking David Chang of Indian cuisine.

CD

Where's my TV show? Where's my podcast?

PREETI

Right. Where's my million investors to open Juhu in New York like Danny [Bowien of Mission Chinese] did, within a year and a half? But, nobody wants to commit. I've heard people say shit like, "Where's our David Chang?" And I'm just like, *They're in California. They just happen to have a vagina,* which is why everyone's pretending they're not actually there. And they're still waiting for someone else . . .

CD

I'm shifting for a second. I want to talk about your family a little bit, about your mom. I loved that you wrote about taking those two trips to India with her: The teenager trip and the other, when you were older, doing research for Juhu. It seems like the food aspect of it definitely connected you. I was just wondering what that relationship was like. And what those trips were like, in terms of just dealing with your mother.

PREETI

It's complicated. But for me, definitely the food is a uniter. I was always my mom's favorite, 'cause I'm the youngest. And it was always like I'm her baby. And then things sort of shifted in puberty, in coming out, and things like that. 'Cause then my parents were like, *Whoa. I don't know how to relate to this person.*

CD

You felt the awkwardness, but it sounds like you didn't feel rejected.

PREETI

I mean, my parents are never gonna just reject me. They're gonna be like, *We love you. We want you to be around. And then we're just gonna constantly tell you how you need to be, and how we want you to be. We'll never just cast you out.*

CD

Were they psyched about your wanting to be chef?

PREETI

No.

CD

A lot of people talk about their parents not being psyched about that, especially, a lot of times, first-generation Americans with immigrant parents. Were they into your opening a restaurant?

PREETI

I think the main reason they were actually totally into it is that before, I went to college in San Francisco and was working for Frameline, which does the Lesbian Film Festival, and I made a short film which was very queer, and I think they were just really excited I wanted to do something that wasn't gay. I feel like they thought, *Oh my god, she wants to do something that's not gay! This is fantastic. Sure, go to culinary school.*

CD

Did they have opinions about what you should cook?

PREETI

Well, I never really told them anything about wanting to cook Indian food. I kinda always knew in the back of my head that's what I wanna do eventually. I just said, "I'm going to culinary school." And then I didn't go work in an Indian restaurant, mainly because I already know how fucking sexist the restaurant industry is. And the idea of working with a bunch of Indian men sounded horrible and frightening to me—especially not knowing what the fuck I was doing . . .

I worked in European restaurants. My desire was to work in restaurants that spoke to what I was into and I'd been living in San Francisco, so it was the whole California thing. Those were the kinds of restaurants that I tried to work at. I wanted the professional training of European restaurant cuisine. I wanted to be able to say, "I know how to do that, and I can do that," before I went and cooked Indian food.

CD

But also, back to that feeling of being an impostor, I think it's harder for someone to call you an impostor when you've had that training, regardless. Even if we're like, *What if that training didn't matter*? But it still does matter. I think it used to be harder to get the jobs in those restaurants if you hadn't been to culinary school. Now, it sounds like people are so desperate to get cooks who are committed. But I think before, especially for a woman and a person of color, you had to prove that you were that much more serious. And culinary school is definitely a way that you could do that.

PREETI

Yeah. And then working in certain places, and being able to say you worked here and there and whatever . . . I mean, I used to think that the kitchen was a meritocracy.

CD

I've seen a slow chipping away of all my ideals about a meritocracy. Seriously, just when I think I've made peace with the fact that the world is not a meritocracy, something happens where I'm reminded again. And I get just as upset. It does not get tired for me, the disappointment. My idealistic side thinks if we could at least have multiple meritocracies—if there were all sorts of different ways that you could measure or consider having merit . . .

PREETI

Well, I mean, I think that speaks exactly to what you're saying about the failure in men versus women. When a guy shows some expertise in something, everyone's like, *Oh my god, look at how great they are at that one thing!* And they focus on that. As opposed to the other way around, where a woman might be doing ten things amazingly, but look at that one thing . . . it's like the way I read Yelp reviews. There might be a thousand where they talk about how great my restaurant is, but I focus on that one . . .

CD

We're also considered scattered if we're good at too many things. Whereas, when guys have a cool hyphenation—like, you're in you're fifties and decided to take up the oboe . . .

PREETI

Right, Jack of all trades.

CD

If we do it, it's like we're dilettantes, like, *Oh, that's nice.*

PREETI

Yeah, *Oh, you're a quitter, moving on to the next thing.* They'll always think that way. It doesn't matter in the end.

CD

I admire your outspokenness, and what I think is almost a natural activism; that it's so deeply embedded in who you are, to just speak the truth when you see it, and to say it. It really is as if you cannot be silenced. So I'm wondering—

PREETI

What would it take to silence me?

CD

On Twitter, in a conversation with Jen Agg [Toronto restaurateur/activist] about speaking out you wrote, "Damned if you do. Keep quiet and you're complicit. Speak out and you're quote, 'making a career out of it.' Or maybe just speaking when no one else does and that shit makes people uncomfortable." I wonder what kind of pushback you've gotten, and how it has affected you? Do you think you've changed how you say things? Do you find yourself not saying things? Or do you find yourself provoked to say more?

PREETI

It depends on the situation—how much do I want to give a fuck about something or not. Part of it might be what mood I'm in that day, honestly. If you catch me on a bad day, and then some news breaks about something . . . some of the stuff's helpful, honestly. It gives me the gumption to be like, *I'm gonna fucking break this shit.* Yeah, I mean, it's always been who I am.

CD

I think when you see that spirit in other people, you're like, *These are the people we need to rally around.* They're not just wearing a "Feminist" T-shirt today because someone told them feminism is cool.

PREETI

Yeah, there is a certain chef I saw recently who had some Instagram post that said, "Activist." And I was like, *Oh really? Oh really, now you're an activist?*

CD

It's like, *It's cool now. You were afraid to speak up before.*

PREETI

Right. *For twenty years you've been famous. But now all of a sudden you're an activist.*

CD

One thing that I did not get the answer to in the cookbook was just the little gap between the not doing film and going to London and, while you were there, the decision to get into food. What was the thing that made you want to cook professionally?

PREETI

The part that is in the book is that I was cooking a lot—my wife and I were having a lot of dinner parties and stuff like that. I was really trying to figure out what I wanted to do with my life. A lot of people were talking to me about how this is what I should do. They were just really impressed with what I was coming up with. And this was eighteen years ago. Twenty-somethings were not having dinner parties the way they are now. It was a different world. The word *foodie* barely existed. People thought we were so weird. They thought it was awesome. We would tell people what wines they could bring and write things about what the dress code was.

CD

So when you enrolled in culinary school, were you thinking, *I may want to make this a career?* Or was it more like, *Oh, let me just see . . .*

PREETI

No. It was definitely a career decision.

CD

If it wasn't food, what do you think it would've been? Do you think you would've stuck with film?

PREETI

I don't know. I used to joke that I wanted to be the first cross-dressing weatherperson—not have to get a degree in meteorology, but kiss babies and go to the Sonoma County Fair and wear snappy suits—

CD

Like Willard Scott.

PREETI

Yeah, exactly. Totally. I wanted to be Willard Scott. I feel like I could do really well at that. And the Bay Area seems like the perfect place . . . I actually joke around sometimes about what if I went back to film? I don't know. I think about writing a screenplay.

CD

You could do that.

PREETI

Yeah, right? I could do that. I could spend seven years doing it. I feel like my family drama could be an amazing movie. I think it could be the Indian *Joy Luck Club*: three sisters, the lawyer, the fashion writer, the chef. One's queer . . . We have a lot of drama between us. I don't speak to one of them.

CD

That would be a movie I'd see or a book I would read. Just to let you know—to encourage you, in your copious spare time.

PREETI

Honestly, I feel like it [cooking] chose me. I really don't know what the fuck I would do. It's really just what I know how to do.

CD

I know when you hire, you're really hiring for people who feel like they're going to become part of the family of the restaurant. And you've said how important it is to recruit not for the sake of diversity, but because of what diversity can do to make a better food product. People talk about how it's so hard to get people to stay now; they just go to the next job and want to fast-track. But it's also hard, incentive-wise; there's not a lot of room for promotion within one space. Once you've built the family, how do you get your hires to stay?

PREETI

It's tough. Right now it's tough because of a lot of outside influences that make things really difficult. One, you have this extreme shortage of experienced cooks. Two, living in the Bay Area has just become so fucking hard. I don't know how people survive. Yet, there's only so much I can pay them. And a lot of times those financial issues get in the way of the personal. Because it doesn't matter how much somebody loves working at a place, whether it's because of the menu or the environment. Or for me in particular, where I've had people say, "I wanna work for *you*."

Sometimes those other things just supersede it. Sometimes those things get clouded in people's heads, and they feel like they're not appreciated. And it's not because they're not appreciated; it's because they're literally asking, "How do I survive? Doesn't my boss see that it's impossible to live on fourteen dollars an hour?" And I do. But I don't know what to do about it. I don't have all the answers. There's only so much I can charge. But I think that the retention part is really important.

CD

This is gonna be a really unfair question, I know that, because you can't parse your identity this way. You have all the odds against you, if you think about the stereotype of the restaurant industry: You're a woman, you're queer, and you're brown. When you look at people's experiences across the board, do you think any of those things is harder to deal with within the industry? Or do you think they're equally hard? Do you think right now that if you were a straight woman you might have maybe a little bit more of an easier time of it?

PREETI

You can't extrapolate them from each other. Because as much as I could say that, in some ways, it might've been easier to be straight, I also feel, for me, it's been really easy to blend in to just be one of the guys, which is a different experience than a lot of cisgendered women and a lot of gay men in the kitchen have. I mean, people would say shit. I've had sous chefs—when I was a commis chef—say, "You're such a dude." And they meant it in the most complimentary way.

CD

It's backhanded, right?

PREETI

Right. On one hand I'm sort of like, *Okay, my masculinity is being seen, and I appreciate that, I guess. And you mean it in a positive way.* But at the same time I'm like, *I'm not, but yeah. Basically what you're saying is that you like me and you wouldn't mind if I joined you and the other cooks for a beer after work. So, right on.*

CD

I'll take it. Does that mean *the other women aren't invited?*

PREETI

Yeah, exactly. Or, is that when the conversation shifts? Where I'm like, *I'm not okay with what you guys are talking about and how you're talking about women.*

CD

Everyone is talking about this idea that there are certain things that were so normalized in those contexts. It almost either didn't seem worth it to raise the red flag, or it changed your threshold for what a red flag was. It was like you get almost numb to a certain kind of banter, and then it's going take something really extreme for you speak up.

PREETI

Yeah. Well it depends who's saying it, right?

CD

Of course . . . I'm of the opinion that, if you can, you should always use your outsider status for good. It usually means having to trip the system or fuck with things. But I was wondering how *you* go about doing that? Because I think you're definitely someone who does it.

PREETI

Here's the thing, the way I feel about it is: I'm not gonna wait around to be deemed a great chef by fucking Michelin or this person or that person. It's just like, *You do realize that once you even get a seat at the table, those guys still won't give a fuck about you? So stop trying.* That's the biggest thing for me. I think that's why I take it as a responsibility as well. Whether it's doing a talk at the *Cherry Bombe* conference, or being on a panel, or being interviewed by journalists, it's really important to me that I do continue to say the shit that nobody else will say. Because somebody's gotta say it. And I don't care. I really don't care.

CD

To get back to what's happening in the Bay Area and the insane rate of gentrification— it's homogenizing and gentrifying, but rapidly; if Oakland were to change too much, would you still wanna be there?

PREETI

I have no idea. I mean, if someone had asked me that same question about San Francisco ten years ago, I would've been like, *You're fucking crazy. I'm never leaving San Francisco. I love this place. This is who I am. It's my identity.* And now I'm the fucking poster child for Oakland. So, who knows? Right now, I feel like it's big enough, in terms of square miles, as opposed to the island—that there's still room. But I don't know. I have hopes that it's possible. If not, at least, hopefully, we can make some money and at least live a happy life somewhere else after. I want my Juhu 3.0 . . .

CD

Yeah. You want your Thomas Keller retirement package. Where is it?

PREETI

Exactly.

Von Diaz

Von Diaz is a storyteller. She works in multiple media to build narratives that meet at the intersection of memoir, culture, tradition, and food; it might be a reported article, a personal essay, a radio program, a cookbook, or a dinner. Each of these stories will be memorable, not just for its content, but for Von's voice. Born in Puerto Rico, she grew up in Atlanta, Georgia, which makes the fact that she's the editor of a platform called Feet in 2 Worlds seems especially apt. (Through its online magazine, radio shows, and podcasts, it highlights the work of ethnic and immigrant journalists from across the United States.) Her focus is primarily on the Puerto Rican experience—both in the Commonwealth itself and here in the United States—and she takes a culinary tack to share it and educate others about her heritage. She also maintains strong, if complicated ties to the American South where she spent her formative years. In 2018, her first cookbook, *Coconuts and Collards*, came out and I fell in love with it immediately, as a home cook and a reader. If you read it, which I hope you do, you will understand just how meaningful and fraught the process of writing the following essay would have been for her.

Some stories aren't meant to be told right away. Some we need to sit with for a spell. Von knew she was going to share this one. She just knew she had to do it when she—and the story itself—was ready. I'm so glad to have caught her at the right time, and that she caught Bobbie Hart at the right time. And I'm grateful to both of them for this essay.

Sitting Still

Tension and silence are, for me, nerve-wracking. Which is why, in the midst of an incredibly somber moment, I started talking to a perfect stranger about banana pudding.

Her name is Bobbie Hart. It was May 2016, and she and I were sitting in the back of a roomy Town Car traveling through Alabama from Tuscaloosa to Montgomery. The driver, Ernest Ward, and his copilot, Wes Edwards, knew each other well and seemed perfectly comfortable with the stillness. Restless and awkward, I turned to Bobbie and asked her what she liked to cook.

"Banana pudding," she replied with a smile.

Jumping at the chance for levity, I asked, "How do you fix your pudding?" (*Fix* here meaning *make*, as it's often used in the South.)

"A lot of people use a box pudding, but I do it from scratch," she replied. "And I use a tablespoon of margarine that gives it a little kick," she told me.

Ernest chimed in, confirming that Bobbie's banana pudding is one of the best. Wes cosigned with a nod.

Bobbie continued to explain her process: evaporated milk, a bit of flour, vanilla extract, and what she calls "sweet milk," or homogenized whole milk. Crisp, buttery vanilla wafer cookies—Nilla Wafers, specifically—layered in a deep glass casserole dish, alternated with a half dozen thinly sliced ripe bananas, then topped with warm pudding. After resting, the final touch is a fluffy meringue, then the whole thing is baked until browned.

I grew up in the South, and banana pudding was among our dessert staples, up there with cobblers and layer cakes. It was frequently served alongside cole slaw and sloppy joes on my school lunch tray, or prepared by my friends' skillful mommas. Even though it didn't originate in that region of the country—New England staked that claim—it has been adopted and perfected by Southern cooks. Lately I've seen it everywhere from Atlanta diners with red-checkered tablecloths to upscale Brooklyn bistros, further showing how Southern culture and cuisine—once dismissed as backward and inelegant—are being celebrated.

In the roomy backseat, next to Bobbie Hart, I let the description of that warm pudding permeate the space. I imagined her preparing it for her grandkids, for a church gathering, or a community meeting in LaGrange, Georgia, where she'd lived most of her life. Ernest and Wes weighed in with their own family recipes, and Bobbie got sassy about her superior approach. We needed the distraction and clung to it until our thoughts returned to the experience that had brought us together that day.

A few hours prior, our group had driven three hours to an unmarked piece of land next to a gas station in Tuscaloosa to collect soil from the place where a young black man named Bud Wilson was lynched on December 27, 1889. Wilson was accused of assaulting a white cotton farmer's wife and, while he was being transferred to the county jail following a preliminary trial, a small vigilante group blocked the vehicle, overpowered police, and ripped Bud from the car. He was then hanged and shot to death, his body left dangling in plain sight, tethered to a tree by a steel chain locked around his neck.

My fellow travelers and I were volunteers for the Equal Justice Initiative, an organization that seeks to end mass incarceration, excessive punishment, and racial inequality. In addition to that work, EJI built the first-ever memorial to lynching victims in the United States in 2018. We had been sent to collect soil to memorialize the more than four thousand estimated hate-fueled hangings across the US, most of which have never been acknowledged, much less investigated or their perpetrators brought to justice. Together, using a few small spades and our bare hands, the four of us took turns cutting through grass and gnarled roots and filled a large glass jar with burnt-umber earth. Afterward we formed a circle, held hands, and prayed; a practice that seemed everyday to the trio, but not at all for me. This was how we made space for Bud Wilson and the thousands of other souls who were murdered in this way.

Like many who grew up in the South, I began wrestling with the brutality and aftermath of slavery at a young age. As a kid I was taken on field trips to plantations, watched episodes of the miniseries *Roots* in the classroom, and read the tales of Uncle Remus and Br'er Rabbit. But lynchings weren't covered much in my schoolbooks, and I always sensed I wasn't getting the full story. I felt surrounded by ambiguous shadows when the subject of slavery came up; enslaved people were rarely named or honored. Without the right words to speak about it, when I tried, I found myself mute—confused and frightened by this history without the resources or guides to truly comprehend it.

Years later, it seemed as if little had changed. Sitting in that Town Car, on the way back from Tuscaloosa, carrying this jar of earth—which felt to me as if it was Bud Wilson's ashes—I sensed the weight of Bobbie's experience on her. But I did not know what to say. The pain I felt, the discomfort it brought about in me, was so unbearable that I had to fill the space with my own noise.

And so I focused on the universal unifier—food—and investigated her pudding technique. Who taught her to make this? What temperature was the oven set to? Why margarine? She seemed relieved to put her thoughts elsewhere, but I could tell she was holding that space, and the pain, for all of us.

For months afterward, I thought of Bobbie Hart. I was surprised by how often I shared the story of collecting soil on behalf of Bud Wilson, and time and again I referenced her and her dessert. The memory crept into my consciousness like the melody to a song I couldn't quite recall. I think I knew there was more to her than she could reveal at that moment. When given the opportunity a year later, I traveled down to LaGrange, Georgia, to interview her.

*   *   *

"We were what some would call poor, but we didn't know we were poor because we were loved," she told me.

She was stoic as she shared the ups and downs of her life, her speech, a honey-eyed low Southern drawl, spoken in elongated words, often turning one syllable into three. *Was* became *wuh-uh-uhz*; *baby* became *bay-ayyy-bee*—these simple words suspended in air for just a moment before being absorbed by your ears. So when she spoke, you listened.

Bobbie Hart was born in 1952 in Hogansville, Georgia, just up the way from LaGrange. She lived in a small farmhouse with her mother, four younger siblings, and grandparents, who were farmers.

"Everything that you could grow in that garden my grandfather did," she said. "We had a watermelon patch. We had a cantaloupe patch. We had peach trees, pear trees, plum trees. My grandmother had a strawberry patch. We even had a pomegranate tree in our yard."

Her parents separated when she was young, and she began cooking for her family as a teenager. I, too, started cooking out of necessity to feed my younger sister and myself after my parents split, so I could relate. At Bobbie's house, they cooked everything on a woodstove and used as much as they could from their farm. She had a knack for sweets, often making pies and other desserts with the fruit they grew.

And while her family was warm and caring, she grew up in the shadow of inequity and racism. She was required to use the back door at the doctor's office and was in racially segregated classes through 1970 when she was set to graduate high school.

She'd grown up with stories of white men in white sheets riding up to black folks' homes at night and tried to grapple with her own family's disappearance. Because her parents were separated, she was largely estranged from her father and his relatives. And so she didn't learn until after he passed that, in the early 1930s, her paternal grandfather had gone to work on the railroad and never come home, abandoning his wife and four kids. It was extremely uncharacteristic; he had been a dedicated father.

Many black families across the South have stories of men disappearing suddenly; uncles, cousins, brothers, and fathers, many of whom were perceived to have slighted a white person, who were never heard from again. Mystery surrounds these vanishings: Some are chalked up to the thoughtlessness of men who leave their families, however out of character that might have been.

"That's just the way things were," Bobbie said, sadly. It was a phrase she repeated over and over again during our conversation.

Like many young women of her era, she got pregnant and married young. She didn't finish high school (though she later got her GED), and she and her husband, George, moved onto his family's property in LaGrange, where they bought a mobile home and raised their three children. She went to work cleaning houses for a white woman who paid her five dollars per day. They struggled to make ends meet, so her husband improvised.

"I came home from work one day and the bathtub was full of sugar," she recalled.

They lived in a "dry county" meaning alcohol could not be sold, and so George followed in his father's footsteps and took to making moonshine.

Bobbie didn't care much for George's moonshine business, and that, along with other factors, led them to separate for a period of time, though she said he was a wonderful father. Tragically, following a sudden illness, George died in 1986, and she was left to care for their three children alone.

*   *   *

At the time I met Bobbie, it had been nearly a decade since I'd left Atlanta for New York City. And I felt immediate affection for her, even though the South was not a welcoming place for me as a child. My name, however simple, was foreign to my teachers and peers, who somehow managed to fumble "Von Diaz." And it took a lifetime for my Puerto Rican palate to adjust to Southern fare. But distance changes things, and each time I returned home to Georgia, I became drunk with nostalgia for accents and turns of phrase, for cavity-inducing sugary sweet tea, and the richest, heaviest Southern food.

In much the same way, Bobbie was the embodiment of so many women who'd raised me. They were my best friends' moms and my mom's best friends. They were my principals and my teachers; they cooked the meals in my public school cafeterias. There were few Latino kids in the area where I grew up, but black folks accepted me in ways white folks would not—despite my white skin. And so, instead of the *tias*, or aunties, I might have had if I'd been raised in Puerto Rico where I was born, I had women like Miss Bobbie, who I credit with everything from my education to my manners to the way I make biscuits.

So I wasn't surprised, when I tried her recipe at home, that Bobbie's simple, elegant banana pudding made me feel a kind of longing for the South, for a Southern way of being. But my experience of the South and Bobbie Hart's experience of the South were two very different things. And the chasm between them could not be so easily bridged by pudding.

* * *

After her husband passed away, Bobbie moved to a double-wide trailer with her kids, a "marginal house" that she says was very nice and "looked just like a regular house." Around that time she started cleaning the home of Miss Mary Ellen Hill, a white woman in her late eighties from LaGrange. Bobbie went to her house once a week to clean, and also came by to help prepare luncheons on the weekends. One day, while straightening up Miss Hill's library, she came across a large antique book. Curious, she peeked in and was struck by what she saw.

"It had the names of slaves, and what they paid for them," she said. "If they were female or male, and a slight description of what they could do."

Bobbie had always known that she and her husband were both descended from enslaved people. She was captivated by the information in this book and came to notice a familiar, repeated surname: Hall, her mother's maiden name.

Curious, she probed Miss Hill for more information. Miss Hill confirmed that, yes, her family owned the Hall Plantation in Heard County, a half hour or so north. She mentioned that the Halls were "smart people," meaning they were intelligent and worldly, and then she pulled out photographs of the plantation that included a family cemetery. She also mentioned a family member named Frederick Hall. In that moment, Bobbie began to piece together the string of coincidences. She had a Frederick Hall in her family too; he was also known for having been very "smart." That, and the contents of the book, led Bobbie to conclude that it was very likely that she and Miss Hill were related.

"We have similar facial features—my face is rounded, high cheekbones. And hers are the same," she told me.

Some time later, Miss Hill approached her while she was working and said she wanted to visit the Hall Plantation cemetery. Bobbie drove her employer up there one day and had an uncanny sense of belonging; a deep feeling in her spirit that she was among her ancestors.

"We talked about it, and her reaction was, 'Well, you know Bobbie, that's just the way it was back then.'"

Miss Hill's response to the connection and its underpinnings was disappointing. Bobbie had hoped she'd be willing, as she herself was, to probe this history further, to acknowledge the past and make some kind of peace with it. While, to this day, Miss Hill hasn't been willing to discuss the topic further, that incident seems to fuel Bobbie's commitment to helping families get the resolution she has not be able to.

You rarely hear about activists like Bobbie. She's not organizing marches; she doesn't tweet. But she has continued to use the experiences that shaped her family to bring truth to those who seek resolution, and call on those complicit in violence to acknowledge their mired past. She cofounded a community group called Troup Together, named after the county she lives in, and their work gathering stories and searching for justice has spawned investigations in neighboring areas. Just one town over in Harris County, the organization is helping uncover the facts behind the 1947 murder of a man named Henry Gilbert, as well as the related murder of a man named Gus Davidson. They've held memorial services, spoken to interfaith groups from across the world about racial reconciliation, and are now turning their attention to helping people who have been recently incarcerated adjust to life outside of jail or prison. Because for many involved in this work, slavery and lynching are a continuum, not a dark moment of the past.

Bobbie still lives in LaGrange and now dedicates most of her time to her family (she has three children, five grandchildren, and one great-grandchild) and to making peace with the history of a LaGrange lynching. In 1940, a black teenager named Austin Callaway was imprisoned for allegedly assaulting a white woman, and—much like Bud Wilson—was ripped from the jail by a group of white men who shot him to death while local police stood by.

On the weekend that I traveled to interview Bobbie, the local police chief, Louis M. Dekmar, issued an apology to the Callaway family for the ways in which local law enforcement were complicit in Callaway's murder. I sat in the back of an old historically black church—as I had on countless Sundays as a child—tearful as I listened to community members, the Callaway family, and local police speak about what it meant to be coming together in this way. Quon Willis, a twenty-year-old blues singer with a voice like John Lee Hooker, performed two somber songs that were so resonant they seemed amplified by some higher power. This would be the place for that.

There, my thoughts turned back to the private vestibule that was our Town Car returning from Tuscaloosa, where I sat with the horror of what had happened to Bud Wilson. But sitting as I was now in the back pew of this place of worship, I felt a collective sigh from the group, many of whom were hearing their family history recognized for the first time. I grew up thinking these violent acts were rare. That day, I saw the ways in which lynchings impacted more than the families of those killed. This brutal vigilantism engulfed surrounding communities, forming a collective web of fear across the region, and beyond.

To this I could relate. My great-grandfather was assassinated in the 1930s during the era of Rafael Trujillo—the notoriously racist, misogynist dictator who reigned over the Dominican Republic for more than thirty years. Just as Bobbie doesn't know the truth behind her grandfather's disappearance, my family has only to guess what might have actually happened to my great-grandfather. He, too, was a doting father. His murder forced my family to flee the island. No one asked questions, no one called the police. And my family was forever transformed.

As a young person, I did not have the capacity to imagine the brutality that so many endured. But since meeting Bobbie Hart, I have been privileged to witness moments of defiance and consciousness, in a Town Car, in an old church. That evening, I went up to thank her for inviting me. Her eyes were crystal clear; her look was stern. She thanked me, in turn, for being there, and said little else. Unlike me, she was not bothered by silence, but let the gratitude linger in the air between us. I had the feeling she would occupy this role as many times as she could in her pursuit of justice. I hope, one day, to be able to move forward with such humility and grace.

My encounters with Bobbie have also forced me to think differently about my idea of comfort food. When I reflect on my childhood, particularly the rich, decadent dishes that, for me, exemplified the South, the joyful nostalgia I once felt is peppered with the knowledge of the pain endured by so many black and brown folks in Southern kitchens. Banana pudding will always have this resonance for me now. Perhaps it's the stark contrast between sweet indulgence and vile, bitter earth, but claiming the South and its cuisine requires a reckoning with the worst aspects of its history. To celebrate a plate of crispy, buttermilk fried chicken, a bowl of collard greens brimming with potlikker, or a pan of creamy banana pudding, one must acknowledge that the recipe was likely perfected by black hands forced to work in white kitchens. This simple Southern dish, like so many others, has become a reminder that sometimes my only role is to bear witness and help others tell their stories.

Bobbie Hart's Banana Pudding

Serves 6 to 8

Before I met Bobbie Hart, I'd never made banana pudding. I'd eaten many, and loved some, but desserts just aren't my thing. I was on the phone with my mom one day while testing this recipe, and she mentioned that my grandmother often made banana pudding. Except she called hers *isla flotante*, or floating island. Excited, I went back to her worn copy of the classic Puerto Rican cookbook, *Cocina Criolla*, and sure enough, there was a vanilla pudding recipe with a toasted meringue topping. But, there were no bananas, no Nilla Wafers. I deduced that my grandmother, who was born in the Caribbean but raised in the South like I was, blended a traditional banana pudding recipe with one from her favorite cookbook. This recipe is an adaptation that honors Bobbie's signature ingredients, combined with my grandmother's meringue and my own variations for quickness and ease. —VD

PUDDING

3 large egg yolks (reserve whites for meringue)

1½ cups (360 ml) whole milk

⅔ cup (135 g) white sugar

1 tbsp flour

2 tbsps cornstarch

½ tsp salt

1 (12-ounce/360 ml) can evaporated milk (see Notes)

1½ tsps vanilla extract

2 tbsps margarine or butter

1 (11-ounce/310 g) box vanilla wafer cookies

5 to 6 ripe bananas, sliced into ½-inch (12 mm) rounds (see Notes)

MERINGUE

3 egg whites

1 tsp lemon juice

6 tbsps (75 g) white sugar

Notes: One can of evaporated milk can be substituted with 1½ cups (360 ml) whole milk if desired. If you can, purchase your bananas a few days in advance to ensure they're ripe. If they need a little help ripening, place them in a brown paper bag and seal until use.

1. Make the pudding: At least an hour before you begin, take eggs and milk out of the fridge to let them get to room temperature.

2. In a medium nonstick saucepan, combine sugar, flour, cornstarch, and salt, whisking gently to incorporate and work out any lumps. Slowly add evaporated milk or whole milk, egg yolks, and vanilla, whisking well to incorporate.

3. Cook over medium-high heat for 3 to 5 minutes until mixture barely boils, stirring occasionally. Reduce heat to low and simmer for another 3 to 5 minutes, stirring frequently so pudding does not stick. Once the mixture thickens enough to thickly coat the back of a spoon, remove from heat. Add margarine or butter, and whisk once more to combine.

4. Assemble the pudding: First add an even layer of vanilla wafers to the bottom and along the sides of a 9 by 11-inch (23 by 28 cm) casserole dish. Next, add an even layer of bananas, then pour on warm pudding to cover bananas. Let cool for 1 hour, then prepare meringue.

5. Make the meringue: Combine egg whites and lemon juice in the large bowl of an electric mixer and beat on medium speed for 1 minute, or until soft peaks form. Slowly pour in sugar and increase mixing speed to high, beating for an additional 4 to 5 minutes until sugar is dissolved and stiff peaks form. Spread meringue evenly over top of pudding.

6. Heat oven to low broil, then place casserole dish on an oven rack at least 2 inches (5 cm) from the broiler. Bake on low broil for 2 to 3 minutes, watching closely so it does not burn. (If your oven only has one broiler setting, place the dish farther away from the broiler. You can also use a kitchen torch for this.)

7. Banana pudding can be served warm immediately, or refrigerated and served cold. Bobbie serves it warm.

<u>ASK ME</u>
<u>ANYTHING . . . ?</u>
What are some
QUESTIONS you
really *hate being asked*?
What questions
do you wish people
would ask you instead?

JENI BRITTON BAUER

That one about balance.

JULIA BAINBRIDGE

I don't hate being asked anything. I honestly encourage people to be inquisitive and unedited, and if I'm uncomfortable with a question, I can simply say I'd rather not answer it, providing the reason should I choose.

AMY BRANDWEIN

When are you going to take a vacation? When are you going to take time off? (Imagine a customer asking Eric Ripert when he is going to take time off . . . never!)

CHARMAINE MCFARLANE

Do you have kids? Are you married . . . no boyfriend? Why not?! These are the first three questions I'm asked when I start working in a new kitchen and I really despise them. The implication is something is wrong with me because I'm single and childless. Rarely am I asked about interests beyond pastry or how I managed to eke out a career in a male-dominated industry, starting first as a dishwasher, then line cook, then pastry cook, and now pastry chef. The inquiries into my career only happen after people take note of the scars on my arm, my kitchen presence, and my calm(ish) demeanor when I'm in the weeds. Only then does it dawn on them that I really earned my place in the kitchen.

DEB PERELMAN

How I juggle it all. How I handle being away from my kids when I go on a book tour. Men never get asked this. Nobody asks a man on a business trip if he's sad to be away from his kids. How I cook with kids underfoot (because I work from home, everyone assumes I'm a stay-at-home mom, no matter how consistently I've said this is not the case).

GILLIAN SARA SHAW

I would say that the question that starts with, *Have you ever thought of . . . ?* Or, *Why don't you make more of . . . ?* Or, *At X bakery, they do this . . . Why don't you do it like that?* I live and breathe this business and I am 100 percent confident there isn't an aspect of it that I have not scrutinized more than one million times. If we are sold out of something, I am already mad at myself for not seeing into the future and making more. I have been to every bakery and compare myself to the hundreds I see online and worry that I am not quite enough. I wonder how receptive people would be to strangers giving them helpful tips at their jobs. I *know* I am in an industry that is customer service–focused, but sometimes the *nerve* of people is galling and hurtful. I would like to be asked, how I am doing and what treat they should get.

JOANNE CHANG

I hate the question, *If you were a pastry what kind of pastry would you be?* I think I'm too literal for these types of questions.

AISHWARYA IYER

Do Indian people use olive oil? Because I, an Indian American woman, founded an olive oil company. I would love to ask many, many white men and women with certain businesses if their heritage/place of origin/culture used turmeric, ghee, ashwagandha, chai, yoga, meditation.

RUBY TANDOH

Something that lazy journalists love to ask me is whether I have any grudges against other people in the food world. They always ask it euphemistically and in a really roundabout way, but the message is clear: If you call out someone's bullshit, we will enthusiastically and wholeheartedly reframe this as a catfight. It's infuriating. Whether it's bad science, wellness fads, the elitism of the British food press, or unequal pay that I'm speaking out against, the story gets framed as me "lashing out." A lot of other women face this kind of scrutiny in the same way. Ideally, the question wouldn't be about personal grievances but about our ideologies, our food philosophies, or our issues with the food world.

KATHLEEN SQUIRES

I was recently asked to speak on a panel at an Ivy League university on the topic of "Writing While Female." What in the hell is that supposed to mean?? A completely boneheaded topic. Thankfully, after I and the other panelists voiced discomfort with the topic, they changed it to "The Power of Storytelling," a much more useful and relevant topic for the young women in attendance.

ERIN MCKENNA

How do you juggle motherhood and running a business? Would you ask a man, *How do you juggle fatherhood and your job?* It's a relevant question, because most career women who are thinking of having kids want to know what it's like. But I still don't like to answer it because the answer can vary depending on the day.

LIGAYA MISHAN

I know that some women hate being asked about how they balance work and family life, but I wish I—and my male colleagues—were asked about that more often, because it's a fantasy to pretend that there's no cost to what we do.

BONNIE MORALES

I hate being asked what it's like being a woman in kitchens. More importantly, I hate being complimented on being a woman in kitchens. Would you compliment your doctor for being a female doctor? It's absurd yet I get it all the time.

THERESE NELSON

I suppose I hate that women are still having to confront questions of equity and inclusion in our work; when we're asked about those issues almost exclusively, it diminishes the work. I wish more journalists were asking more culinary questions that allowed women to talk about craft and ethos more than identity and equity. It's novel when women wreck shop and, even when they do, they're still having to qualify themselves which is a big bag of bullshit. I think equity and identity are important issues that should be addressed by marginalized people on their own terms but the question is always posed to them as though they have the control to fix other people's isms. Instead of making women answer for misogyny or posit reasons for why it exists, how about being tougher on men and demanding they answer for it?

NAOMI POMEROY

I am actually tired of, *What is it like to be a woman chef?* I just want to talk about the business; I want to focus more on its general challenges and less on how it's hard for *me*. It's hard for everyone. I am interested in health, vitality, and the long-term viability of the industry as a whole.

MASHAMA BAILEY

How does it feel to be an African American chef? I really hate that one! It feels pretty normal to me because I'm not sure how it would feel to be anything else.

ANITA LO

All of these gender, race, and sexuality questions eventually get exhausting. And the answers end up feeling trite. But they have to be addressed or we don't make any progress.

MARISSA LIPPERT

I hate being asked, *How did you open your restaurant?* But at the same time, I really appreciate it. I also would love to open the conversation up more about the financials and realistic costs of opening and operating a food business/restaurant. I don't think most customers and consumers understand the costs and labor and love involved in sourcing and producing quality wholesome food and a memorable dining experience.

NING KANG

People always focus on food and the cuisine, which is great, but being a restaurant owner is not just about serving food. It's more about (for me, at least) creating a platform for the staff to learn about business (because most restaurant workers don't have a career choice in mind), making connections with industry people, making a difference in people's lives through influencing the way they eat. Sadly, these perspectives are often overlooked. It would be great if interviewers paid more attention to what a restaurant can bring beyond just food.

MICHELLE HERNANDEZ

How much money do you make?
Sometimes it is not as direct as this, but sometimes it is and it is almost always asked by men.

UMBER AHMAD

I hate being asked why I left my previous career to bake cookies. The question is asked in a way that insinuates I have taken a step back in my life; that I somehow decided that the intense investment career I had was too much for me. There is an automatic assumption that I am on some sort of consolation-prize path. The truth is that I have taken everything that I have learned in my career and life thus far, and decided to apply it to creating my own legacy. There are very few people, men or women, who dare to do what I have done. So don't ask me why I left investment banking.

JAMIE KANTROWITZ

Why would you go through all this hard work at this point in your life? What big food company are you planning to topple?

JASMINE LUKUKU

I don't have an answer that relates to interview questions, but there are two questions that are guaranteed to tick me off. The first one is, *Can I touch your hair?* No, I'm not an animal at a petting zoo. The second one is, *Where are you from?* These are classic microaggressions and they make me want to smash things.

JULIA TURSHEN

I hate being asked, *Which one of you is the husband?* in reference to myself and my wife.

JORDANA ROTHMAN

I get asked about my body with a regularity that I can't imagine existing in most other professions. Constant questions about my workout routines, about the way that I eat when I'm not working to achieve #balance, generally many questions about the terror of fatness, posed as though it is a malevolent warlock lurking, cackling, plotting 'round the bend of every goddamned sandwich. It's a lot and it's intrusive.

Something I tend to talk about with other people in my position, but that we are never asked, is the larger question of personal and emotional well-being (survival, at times) when we are on the road. Most people are fixated on the idea of glamour as it pertains to living out of a suitcase, eating multiple dinners at big restaurants every night, commuting in an airplane . . . but it can be a spectacularly disorienting experience. Over time, you end up flattening your own narrative into its most agreeable points, like a comedian polishing a tight ten, so when people ask you how you've been or what you've been up to, you don't have to do the emotional work to access it fresh every time. I'd like to have a more open dialogue about the complexities of this work, but I also know that most people aren't interested in knowing too much about the sausage.

KRISTY MUCCI

The most obnoxious thing, and it's come up so many times in so many ways, is being asked about working in food and my body.

These have come from men and women, strangers and people I know a little better (but no one who's uttered a line like this is actually my friend): *You don't look like you work in food. Do you really eat all the things you cook? You'd probably be much bigger if you did. Oh you work in a kitchen? It must be a real struggle to stay in shape.*

Before I took a job in the test kitchen at *Saveur: A job in a kitchen? That's going to be dangerous if you're eating all the time. Say goodbye to that figure of yours.* Do men *ever* get this crap?

I'd love to be asked literally *anything* but the above. Ask me about stories I'm interested in writing, products I love, producers I admire, ingredients I can't get enough of. Ask me about farmers and the greenmarket and the season's best produce. But, my god, please don't ask me about my body or my weight or anything like that.

ALISON ROMAN

I *hate* being asked, *How do you not weigh five hundred pounds!* Or, *Must be so hard not to weigh five hundred pounds doing what you do!* Well, guess what. It *is* hard to not think about my body image 24/7,

especially when I'm getting asked dumb questions like that (especially dumb when asked by other women, IMO). My lifestyle includes eating and drinking more than the average person. Partly because of my job, partly because I really love eating and drinking. How I regulate (or do not regulate) my eating and drinking habits for the sake of my physical appearance is literally nobody's business. It's especially insulting because overweight men are just called men and overweight women are called overweight women. I have a lot to say about this.

This is going to make me sound like a grump, especially because this question is never asked in a malicious way, but I really, *really* hate when people ask me, *What's your favorite thing to cook?* Or, *What's your favorite recipe in the book?* Nine times out of ten, one of those two questions will be asked in an interview or when meeting someone for the first time and they find out what I do. Maybe I find it annoying because I don't have an answer (how could I have an answer?), but especially when coming from someone interviewing me professionally, it feels . . . phoned in.

KRISTINA GILL

The last meal question I think is morally repugnant. People have last meal requests when they are on death row. I don't find anything romantic or interesting about it. It's just insensitive and offensive.

TIFFANI FAISON

I fucking hate to be asked what my signature dish is. Fuck that all the way up. I can cook almost anything.

I never mind real questions, questions that pry a little, open the lid on things—but I hate more than anything when that happens and people in our industry choose to answer untruthfully or avoid real conversations and, sadly, that happens all the time.

TAMAR ADLER

I hate: *What's your specialty?*

I never get asked what it's like to have left the kitchen after years cooking in one. I never get asked whether I hate sitting at a desk all day, whether I miss the high of total Zen flow that comes with a wood-burning oven and endless tickets and knowing you just need to keep moving and can't waste a single gesture and that every time you put a plate down, make a cut, turn a pan, it has to be efficient and precise. No one has ever asked me any of that. I miss it so much that when I lived in Brooklyn, right before getting pregnant, I started picking up secret shifts at Franny's just to feel it again. I didn't tell anyone, and no one knew I was there. I was a *Vogue* and book writer and then prepped and butchered and sweated in secret just because it makes me so happy.

EMILY FARRIS

I get irrationally angry when non-writers contact me to say they're thinking about changing careers and they want tips on how to break into some of the bigger food publications I write for. It's usually always men. Shocking, right?

You want my advice? Move to New York with literally zero dollars when you're eighteen. Take out student loans you'll pay off for the rest of your life while you go to college for six years and work at a bar until 4 A.M. serving cocktails and getting groped. While you're doing that, intern at a bunch of publications for no money and a few clips. Then write articles for twenty-five to fifty dollars apiece for years, but spend half your time chasing down those checks while your bank account sits in a constant state of overdraft. Have your pitches rejected from your dream outlets for years. Then get one picked up. Now it's time to start aiming higher. Go get 'em tiger!

But that would make me sound like a real bitch, so I usually just say, Start a blog.

NAOMI TOMKY

Are you still writing? Oh, so do you have a blog? How lucky is your husband that you do that? Do you get to go out to eat every night? Will you take me?

HANNA RASKIN

Do you have a blog? Do you eat for free? And my very favorite, which I've only been asked once: *When you take a man on a review visit, do you write about what you think or just go with his opinions?*

NICOLE TAYLOR

One of the questions people ask all the time is, *Are you a restaurant critic?* Or, *Are you a caterer?* The caterer one makes me cringe—there's nothing wrong with being a caterer; it's one of the easiest ways to break into the food industry and make money. But nothing online, on my social media, etc., would show I'm a caterer. But people still ask. Cooking for more than twenty people makes me crazy. When a food person asks me if I'm a restaurant critic, it shows they're not that deep in the food world. There are only a handful of restaurant critics.

MELANIE DUNEA

It would be brilliant if I never heard again: *You actually make a living as a photographer?*

JULIA SHERMAN

Who shoots the photos for your blog and book? This might be paranoid, but people always seem so surprised to find out that I am both a photographer and a writer. I began my career as a professional photographer working on film sets, where I was made to feel like a little girl with a toy camera. It disturbs me that the assumption is always that I hired someone to do the most important aspect of my project.

ESTHER TSENG

What's the best restaurant in LA? What's the best thing you ever ate? Best, best, best. These are annoyingly nonspecific.

REBECCA FLINT MARX

Hi! I'm going to be in [city/town/country] *tomorrow and need to figure out a place to have* [dinner/lunch/brunch/a wedding reception/wake/dog's obedience school graduation] *for twenty people, fifteen of whom have food allergies, both real and self-diagnosed. Where should we go?*

NICOLE ADRIENNE PONSECA

Hate:

1. *What's your favorite restaurant?* Or, *Where should we go tonight?*

2. *What is it like as a female entrepreneur?* (Why does this have to be gendered? It's actually quite great to be an entrepreneur, period.)

Like:

1. *How are you?* (So simple, but not a lot of people ask this! I assume it's because they don't care?)

2. *What's your sign? What's your sun sign? Your moon?* (Man, do I think this is telling!)

EVA KARAGIORGAS

No one asks me how I am doing. No one checks in just to say, *You okay?* Or, *Do you need anything?*

REGINA SCHRAMBLING

Question I'd love to be asked: *Would you like either of your unpublished, way-ahead-of-their-time manuscripts published for a nice chunk o' change?*

Dianna Daoheung can't stand it when you ask her what her tattoos mean, and she's sick of the one about being a woman in the food industry, too.

And if you see **Christina Tosi**, ask her, *What do you stand for?* She'd like that.

A Conversation with Jessica Harris

Applied to Jessica Harris, "admiration" seems like a tepid way to describe what is more like a profound, hushed respect. You don't go all fan-girl on Dr. Harris, and it's not because of that honorific, either. It's because her work—and her very presence—demands something more solemn and attentive. A scholar, educator, author, and journalist, and possibly the person for whom the term *culinary historian* was invented, Jessica laid the groundwork for the ongoing efforts being made to explore, define, and archive America's Southern foodways. She has done that through her own extensive study and documenting of the cuisines and foodways of the African diaspora, to which she has devoted most of her professional life. Her output, so far, encompasses twelve food-related books, a memoir, a translation, and several edited works, along with a radio show and podcast.

In her memoir *My Soul Looks Back*, she writes about attending the school of Performing Arts in New York City, where she grew up, and wanting to be an actress, only to learn she would "never be an ingénue," because she had "too deep a voice and too large a personality to be meek and mild or cute and cuddly." That voice is melodiously commanding and that personality the reason "admiration" was never going to be a suitable choice to sum up my regard for her. It's why, when she gives me any of her time, I feel like I'm back in the classroom shy and quiet, afraid to raise my hand, as a favorite, slightly terrifying teacher asks her students a question after delivering another riveting lecture. This interview wasn't much different, except that I got to ask the questions. It was still an education for me, and I hope it is the same for you.

CD

Is this still a good time to talk?

JESSICA

It's as good as it's going to get!

CD

Okay, I'll take it.

The first thing I wanted to ask you, and I know you wrote about this, and so magnificently, because I read it in *My Soul Looks Back*, but maybe you could do just a quick recap of your childhood, your parents, where you grew up, and how that set your life on its course.

JESSICA

Oh, good Lord. Jeez . . . Kinda once I write about something, then I figure that's what I've said about it.

CD

I know, sorry.

JESSICA

There's nothing to add to it; there's nothing different about it. I'm an only child. I grew up in Queens. My parents were aspirational, if you will. They gave me all sorts of advantages, partly because I was an only child, partly because that's how they were focused. I have been told I was the first non-UN child to go to the UN school, which was pretty amazing and set me on an international course from pre-kindergarten. Went from there to the High School of Performing Arts, majored in theater. Wanted to be an actress; went to Bryn Mawr; went to Sarah Lawrence on a junior year abroad; went back for a graduate year in Nancy, France, and came back and started teaching. I have just retired from teaching after fifty years.

CD

Oh! I wasn't sure if you were still teaching and one of the things I wanted to talk to you about was your life in academia and what drew you to it—not just to higher learning, but then to stay in academia and want to teach. What do you think it was that compelled you?

JESSICA

It's very simple! My parents.

CD

Yeah, I figured, but you could have gotten out, and you stayed.

JESSICA

Oh, I probably could have, but I've been told I'm a natural teacher. I enjoy teaching; I enjoy the students; I very much enjoyed the time that it gave me, because it gave me the time to do all of the other things that I loved. I think it suited me.

CD

It's not just that you took to teaching naturally, you've taught numerous subjects. You've been prolific—

JESSICA

Well, I mean, I've taught French, I've taught English, I've taught essentially food, and that's pretty much it.

CD

That's a lot! Didn't you found a department in New Orleans, at Dillard?

JESSICA

I was the first person in the Ray Charles Chair in Dillard. I don't think it exists anymore, as a chair; I think it exists as a program [in African American Material Culture]. I started some of that, but I don't know how much of what I started they're doing.

CD

You've really taught a lot. Based on that, how do you think academia has changed in the last five decades? I'm especially interested in knowing how many women were on the faculty and how many black women, or women of color, were there and if you've seen that change. Similarly, the student population— what kinds of changes have you seen?

JESSICA

Well I taught in a special program at Queens College and I taught in that same program for all fifty years. So it's really more about how *it* changed. Queens is the most diverse—ethnically, culturally—borough in the city of New York and that's because people tend to get off a plane and go to where Uncle So-and-so or Aunt So-and-so lives.

The student population where I teach has gone through all sorts of changes. When I started, it was mainly black and Puerto Rican—black and Hispanic I guess you'd say, but Hispanic was really Puerto Rican. Then it morphed through all sorts of other things, and now it's 43 percent Asian, meaning not just Chinese but also South Asian, and probably, if you count Indian among that, even larger.

CD

Yeah.

JESSICA

And that's a big change in just what you teach, how you teach it, and to whom you're teaching it. But along with that, I think that students have changed. I taught through the growth of the computer. What people do, what people read, how people get their information, how people research—when I started teaching, it was all about teaching the card catalog when you taught research. And no one's doing that anymore so it's all of those kinds of things. Those are big changes.

CD

They're huge and this is maybe overanalytical, but I think a lot about the distinction between fast thinking and slow thinking. And how so much of technology and social media favors and encourages fast thinking, and so much of what I think draws us to academia and that kind of research is really very slow; it's on the slower end of slow thinking. I would imagine that would be a very interesting challenge to get students to start with the fast thinking and

figure out how you're going to take them from there back into a more slow kind of thinking and analysis.

JESSICA

Well, *if* they go, if they can, if they feel the need, and a lot of them today do not feel or have the need.

CD

Yeah, it's interesting. You try not to judge it and just understand it, but I'm sure it would definitely affect the way that you teach.

JESSICA

Well, certainly, it affects what you teach. Students no longer really read, so.

CD

And you were teaching English literature, right?

JESSICA

No, I am actually teaching composition, which is a whole 'nother story because students no longer read, so therefore students no longer write.

CD

Oh god! That's really heartbreaking.

JESSICA

It's the nature of the world. And particularly when you're talking about students who come from other places, because reading is hard; reading in English is difficult, and so, in some cases there's resistance to it and in some cases there's inability. So all of those things count.

CD

Have your own ideas about composition changed because of any of this? Or do you think you're pretty steadfast in that?

JESSICA

I think I'm pretty steadfast in the need to be able to carve or cobble together a decent English sentence.

CD

Oh yes, yes.

Related to that, you started working as a journalist in the 1970s and you've continued to do that. Did you start out as the books editor at *Essence* [magazine]?

JESSICA

Oh no, no, no. Before *Essence* I was, oh god, I did so many things.

CD

Theater critic?

JESSICA

I did that, certainly. I don't remember if that was before or concurrent with *Essence*. I did book reviews and interviews with the *Amsterdam News*.

CD

Which is the oldest black newspaper in the United States, right?

JESSICA

I believe so. And I did reviews and translated articles at some point from French to English for *Encore* [magazine], before I went to *Essence*.

CD

When did you start writing for non-black-specific publications, which I would jokingly call, "white publications" (because they tend to be pretty myopic)? I wondered if at any point you faced any discrimination when trying to write for other outlets or if it just kind of happened?

JESSICA

Not really, per se. I started out right where I lived, where I was in contact with people. And it was also a very exciting time because I was the second travel editor of *Essence*, the first black woman travel editor—prior to me it had been a black man. Those were things that were there, that were open, that were opening, that hadn't existed in that way before. It was just a world that was changing and I happened to be there at a time that it was changing. I wrote for *Black Enterprise*, I wrote for *Essence*, I wrote for *Encore* . . .

And that was it. I had written for the black publications—the majority ones—so in order to keep writing and in order to expand the world, then you want to write for other folks and do and say and write about other things.

CD

And did you find it easy to do that—to go from doing black publications to other stuff? Was it an easy transition?

JESSICA

Well yeah! I think it's limiting and balkanizing to assume that because one writes for one, one can't write for the other.

CD

Oh definitely! It's just that when you talk to women writers, especially food writers of color, today, they will say that they are so often not given opportunities that white writers are given, which is why I wondered if there was a difference; if, strangely, it was almost easier to do it before than it is now. It shouldn't be, there should be no difference.

JESSICA

I think there are several things that came with that. One is, there were a whole lot fewer black writers. So the pool was different; the possibilities were different; all sorts of things were just different. It's like comparing apples to oranges.

CD

Similarly, I've recently heard from women who write about travel, or want to write about travel, saying that these are jobs that always go to men—that people don't seem to think that woman can do travel writing.

JESSICA

Well, I certainly don't think that's true, and I think that may be a new paradigm. But we've got a whole lot of things: Men have gotten back into food writing and are dominating that in ways. There's this whole kind of masculine language that has taken over some of food criticism—just in terms of vocabulary. So there's all of that. But I mean, those pendulums swing back and forth, and in some cases, it's really about what you do and how well you do it.

CD

When did you start writing about food?

JESSICA

I probably started writing about food at *Essence*. As a travel editor, I was involved with the creation of the editorial calendar and one year it was like, *Okay how are we going to vary this?*, and then, *Let's do travel and the other months do travel and food*; so I started doing travel and food. That was relatively early on, in terms of the American perspective on things. I mean, there had been magazines like *Holiday* and magazines like *Gourmet*, but, at that point in time, many of the writers who worked for those publications were, in fact, white men. To write about travel and food was something that was different and certainly, as a black woman, very different. And I wrote about places that were of interest to the *Essence* readers—I went to Senegal, went to the Ivory Coast, I went to the Caribbean, I went places that were not just Paris and Venice.

CD

When did you segue into culinary studies and foodways. When did you really start to own that?

JESSICA

What I usually say is when my second book came out, which is *Iron Pots and Wooden Spoons* [1989], a woman named Nancy Harmon Jenkins was doing a series for the *New York Times* called Cooks on the Map. She got in touch with me and said she wanted to have me as one of the cooks on the map and was going to come out to my place and I could cook dinner for her, whatever.

So I did . . . and when the article came out [in 1990], it said that I was a food historian and it's almost like, you know, biblical: *In the beginning was the word*. People didn't even necessarily know what a food historian was, but once I was told I was one, then you go back, look at it, and rejig.

CD

My sense is that it wasn't really a thing when you started doing it, that there weren't a ton of food historians, even out there—

JESSICA

No, there were very, very few. I mean, Vertamae Grosvenor called herself the culinary anthropologist. I was the academic and working as an academic informed how I went about doing a lot of it.

CD

I also wonder, when you started, how many people were focused on the foodways of the African diaspora, specifically, too?

JESSICA

I think Vertamae, and me, and maybe a lady named Helen Mendez.

CD

Do you think it's expanded?

JESSICA

I mean, I think there is a lot more to be done. I think it is expanding. I think there are so many aspects to it: Are you talking about farmers? Are you talking about ingredients? Are you talking about ethnobotany? Are you talking about enslaved cooks? Are you talking about free cooks? What country are you talking about? Are you talking about food and religion?

CD

There is so much. You also have done radio and, with *My Welcome Table*, you were one of the first hosts on the Heritage Food Network, which has become this significant media outlet for people in the food world. Now, they're doing podcasts and everything, but when you started, it was pretty small. How did you end up doing that radio show?

JESSICA

By accident, once again: I was on Leonard Lopate's radio show for I don't even remember which book—went, saw it, saw the station, and thought, *Oh, this might be fun to do.* They talked to me, I talked with them, and there it was.

CD

I loved that show, by the way.

JESSICA

Thank you. I'm probably going to go back and do some more of them.

CD

That's very cool. When I think of everything that you've done, you have what almost seems like prescience for doing things early—and for doing them when other people aren't, especially when other black women aren't, but often it's just people in general aren't doing these things. And whenever I read a bio that's been written about you, it seems like no big deal, like you just did this stuff. But I wonder if that was true or if there were situations where you really felt like you were up against something or had to make a case for what you wanted to do.

JESSICA

I don't know, Charlotte. I really don't know. I think some of it is just because I have tended to be the avant-garde—often, simply, by myself—of many things. It's not always the fun place to be; in some cases, it wasn't like I really had a choice. I wrote a book about peppers and chilies before that became the massive thing it has become. I started talking about the African diaspora and the food of the African diaspora before it became, you know. A lot of it is just stuff that I saw that I wanted to do. It was very random; I wasn't particularly focused, which is probably one of the reasons I'm all over the map. What you probably know is only the tip of the iceberg, in terms of stuff that I have done.

CD

Do you ever feel like you don't get the recognition that you would like—or the work you deserve—for having done all that stuff and having done it early?

JESSICA

I don't think that's something you can take on. I think people do what they do, and I certainly didn't do it expecting recognition, so whether or not I get recognition is not immaterial, but not problematic. I mean, it's interesting, and occasionally I'm bemused just to see people get recognition, and know, okay, that's not the first, but that's not in terms of me, that's in terms of a lot of people.

CD

Looking specifically at the food world changing, in terms of making room for women or people of color—whether it's media or the restaurant industry—do you see more opportunity, and not just in employment, but I mean, in empowerment, in terms of ownership, and investment and awards? What change do you see?

JESSICA

First and foremost, it's something that I have heard from others and increasingly am looking at; the largest beneficiaries of the Civil Rights Act were white women, not African Americans and not African American women. That's a reality. When we talk about empowering women as people of color, that means that in many cases we are talking about all sorts of folks. My wheelhouse, if you will, is African American people. I am concerned in many ways with the rejigging of our national narrative, and we are rejigging it.

I remember this country before all of the immigration laws changed, and it is fascinating to me, not necessarily in a good way, that African Americans are still not very much further up on the scale than they were, as everyone else comes in and ascends. That is problematic.

CD

Yes, and I think too—and people could see it as a semantic argument, but it's not one—it's this idea that you really have to understand the difference between being an immigrant and being an African American, a black person in this country, where we're not talking about immigration, we're talking about enslavement. It's not the same thing.

JESSICA

It's not. It's very much not the same thing. It is what it is. I'm not saying there's no room for it in the national narrative, but it becomes the national narrative that I'm not a part of.

CD

I don't know if it's possible to be optimistic, but are you optimistic? What do you think would have to change, really, to make that happen?

JESSICA

I like to think I am maybe not optimistic, but hopeful. I think the current political climate makes that difficult and I'm not going into that. I'm not sure; I'm just trying to figure out where we are, and what these changes are making, and how that works, and what's going on, and all of the rest of it.

CD

What do you think of this idea or even the question of what constitutes American food? Has it changed? Has it gotten more limited? Do you think it's expanding? What is American food? How are we supposed to figure that out?

JESSICA

I think we try to think of it as monolithic; it's not. American food is like the food of just about every country I know of, regional. It is very specifically regional. It has to do with any number of things, ranging from patterns of migration to patterns of immigration and all of that goes into what is American food. I think

people sort of almost obfuscate the reality, which is, it's the food of a place that is very, very, very, different, that is unlike very many places in the world, and that has a history that is troubled, unresolved, and ongoing.

CD

Okay, cookbooks! I wanted to talk to you about cookbooks because you've done a lot of them. You've written about chilies and hot peppers before anybody was interested in them or thought they were cool, and you did *The Welcome Table*, which I personally love.

JESSICA

There was *Sky Juice and Flying Fish* [on traditional Caribbean cooking, 1991], and then *Tasting Brazil* [1992]; I think that's the way it went. And then, *The Welcome Table* [1995] and the Kwanzaa book [*A Kwanzaa Keepsake*, 1995]. And then a beauty book of Third World women's beauty things, many of which came out of the kitchen [*The World Beauty Book*, 1995]. I've done a lot of books. I coedited a French text on French as it is spoken outside of France per se.

CD

What do you think about cookbook publishing right now? And where it's going?

JESSICA

I really don't keep that much up on it. I know that there's a proliferation of them; they are all lovely, or many of them are beautifully illustrated. I didn't get color illustrations in any of my books until I guess, *Rum Drinks* [2013].

People now are getting book contracts because they blog. It's a very different world.

CD

Where would you tell younger food writers, or students of foodways, to look right now? And what advice would you give them, especially women of color or black women? What could they learn from you to move forward in their careers?

JESSICA

Learn from me? Not much.

CD

That's not true!

JESSICA

No, no, I'm not being disingenuous. I've had a career; I have had an interesting career; I have certainly done what I wanted to do. Whether or not I can consider that I've had a successful career is a whole 'nother question. I think that, in many ways, it is dependent on all sorts of things, not the least of which is what's going on in terms of, you know, who's getting book contracts? Who's doing what? Who's saying what? It's all about questions. And they are different.

CD

Yeah. I know it's corny, but for me, your work has definitely been eye-opening, but it also has taught me how to proceed in certain endeavors. I have found it immensely helpful.

JESSICA

Well, thank you! That's good to know! I know that there are people who feel that way and I am much pleased and very tickled. I just know that every time I think about writing a new book it's another struggle—to find a publisher, to find somebody who says, "Oh! People will be interested in that," or whatever. I don't blog. I don't have those numbers. I am not that person. I don't necessarily appear in those things the way other folks do. Some of those things are different and still difficult.

CD

I think it's hard because what you truly believe in is good work; what you value is not what other people think sells or what sells on Amazon.com. So there's that whole thing about playing the game, but if you don't really respect the rules of the game or you're not that interested in the rules of the game, you have this disconnect between the work you want to do and the work you understand would be deemed successful. And I think it's incredibly frustrating.

JESSICA

It is frustrating; I would be lying if I said it wasn't. No, it's frustrating, and it's sometimes disheartening, and it's sometimes disappointing. It's all sorts of things, but it is what it is.

CD

On a happier note, maybe, what informed your decision to move to New Orleans and what do you miss about New York? But also, what makes you so happy about being in New Orleans?

JESSICA

Well, I haven't moved to New Orleans yet; that is a question that I can't answer because I might get there and not like it as much as I think I will. I have had a house in New Orleans for twenty years now. So I'm not going to someplace with which I am unfamiliar. I like that it has an almost European feeling in the sense that people tend to have lives and not lifestyles, and it's possible to actually make a dinner date with a friend without weeks of backing and forthing and who's doing what. I like that, I very much like that. I like the fact that people take time for each other. Or at least the people I know—I don't know if that's the constant in New Orleans, but it is a constant among my friends. And I like that, I very much like that. I like that people entertain, people have friends over, people wonder about people they haven't heard from. I just like that human scale and it's something alive still in New Orleans . . . but I am someone who doesn't always fit in anywhere. I am at home in many ways in Paris, as I am in New York or as I am in London, or I might be anywhere.

CD

What are you excited about doing next? Even if someone says you can't do it, what would be a thing that you would like to do? What are you interested in?

JESSICA

Well, I want to write one more volume of the memoir.

CD

Yes! Please!

JESSICA

So does my publisher! I'm thinking about maybe doing a book sort of like *High on the Hog* [2011], about Afro-Latina stuff—something that people don't think about and are not that aware of.

CD

Yep!

JESSICA

I'd like to do travel. I mean, there's a whole lot of stuff. This is the first time in seventy years, or certainly in the fifty of those seventy years that I've been working, that, in some ways, I get to think about what I want to do.

CD

Wow!

JESSICA

And that's kind of crazy, interesting, and very unusual. It involves a lot of thought.

CD

That's incredible to me, this idea that we don't get to ask ourselves that question until so much later.

JESSICA

Well, I think that's my generation. I think your generation definitely asks that question and chooses or makes many life decisions based on their answer to it. I think my generation was a lot more, I don't know, I just had my fiftieth college reunion, and we talked about all manner of things, among them, the whole notion of how planned was your life. This entire career was absolutely random; it wasn't something in any way, shape, form, or size planned. It did what it did. And now looking at it, are there things I would change? Possibly. I usually say that I lived somewhere between Frank Sinatra and Édith Piaf. Regrets, I have a few, but then again too few to mention, and no, I don't regret anything. That's pretty much it!

Charlotte Druckman

We are our stories, stories that can be both prison and
the crowbar to break open the door of that prison.

REBECCA SOLNIT, *The Mother of All Questions*

I'm a woman of my word, now you have heard
My word's the only thing I truly need.

CHAN MARSHALL, "Woman"

The C-Word

C

omplicity.

It speaks of itself in hushed tones, with that soft, conspiratorial hiss in its second syllable. Defined as an involvement in wrongdoing, not the wrongdoing itself, it's a fuzzy criminality. You could say it's a peripheral transgression, relative to the main malfeasance. As a culture, we have treated it accordingly. Pushed aside, building up in the corners of our minds like black mold, it remains the one subject in the wake of #MeToo we—women—seem not to want to touch, and that, one could argue, has always been treated as taboo in the greater public discourse.

To rally women to confront their complicity together probably sounds like planning a witch-hunt orchestrated by witches. It can all go wrong so fast in a situation where innocence and guilt are knotted up; what was intended as a productive, ultimately empowering parsing of accountability can register as victim-blaming or shaming and as the passing of judgment. But I'm convinced we have to discuss it.

What I am not at all sure of is *how*. I can only hope that this is a start.

Complicity. Power can't function without it, but that goes both ways. Complicity is harnessed to fortify, exercise, and abuse power, institutionally or personally. The more imbalanced the system, the more severe and oppressive the complicity it demands.

Within the context of this anthology, I'm concerned by our own complicity in the systemic disempowerment of women; with how we have, whether against our wills, inadvertently or deliberately, been accomplices in suppressing—or oppressing—one another, which, simultaneously, keeps us all down.

Most of our countless infractions don't fit so neatly into a category—extenuating circumstances render each individual act unique. They comprise a range, and there is also the complicity involved in being aware of these acts, singular or collective, and not saying anything. Silence is a less obvious, less aggressive species of complicity, but damaging in its own right and just as relevant to this conversation.

If silencing others is an abuse and confirmation of power, then staying silent in the face of that abuse when you are cognizant of it becomes an act of validation and maintenance of that power. When you allow another woman to either suffer under it, or leave her to speak her experience on her own, you, too, have committed an act of silencing—of yourself—at the expense of someone else and, ultimately, of your own freedom. Still, up until very recently, we left those who came forward to fend for themselves. We watched as, one by one, they were put on trial in the court of public opinion—She v. The Patriarchy. We liked to fool ourselves into thinking that it would be enough for a single brave woman to tell the truth, and that she could stand in—and up—for us all. We were too frightened.

Silence can be kept for fear of being punished for speaking out—by being physically attacked, slandered, socially ostracized, stripped financially, fired, or disempowered (a somewhat paradoxical concern: If you really had power, you wouldn't have to fear being punished). Shame can hold tongues and squash stories just as well, quietly eating away at victims as they turn on themselves. This, of course, is what the men in charge (a redundant phrase) continue to count on. They assume we will not accuse or bear witness because we are afraid or because we have internalized their hate.

Fear, shame, and the silence they instill cripple the individual and divide communities, which grants those who wield power more of it. "Terror can rule absolutely only over men who are isolated against each other," Hannah Arendt wrote in *On Totalitarianism*, "Therefore, one of the primary concerns of all tyrannical governments is to bring this isolation about . . . its hallmark is impotence insofar as power always comes from men acting together." This doesn't apply strictly to tyrannical governments; it extends to any patriarchy. Arendt's is a universal truth: "Isolated men are powerless by definition."

If, by keeping us silent, our complicity isolates us, then talking about it should unite us. It is also in speaking that we free ourselves. I've always thought of it as both a kind of spell-breaking and a denial, or even rejection, of what seems like an impenetrable system that operates on socialized blind faith. If everyone assumes a group of people has power, it perpetuates whatever stronghold they have and might even endow them with more. Do you remember, in *Alice's Adventures in Wonderland*, when the Knave of Tarts, accused of stealing the Queen's tarts, is put on trial—a trial ruled by a breakdown of logic and language? Alice, as the voice of reason (and of Reason), is shushed, and then sentenced to death for protesting the absurd—and, therefore, unjust—order of things:

> "Stuff and nonsense!" said Alice loudly. "The idea of having the sentence first!"
>
> "Hold your tongue!" said the Queen, turning purple.
>
> "I won't!" said Alice.
>
> "Off with her head!" the Queen shouted at the top of her voice. Nobody moved.
>
> "Who cares for you?" said Alice (she had grown to her full size by this time). "You're nothing but a pack of cards!"
>
> At this the whole pack rose up into the air, and came flying down upon her: she gave a little scream, half of fright and half of anger, and tried to beat them off, and found herself lying on the bank, with her

head in the lap of her sister, who was gently brushing away some dead
leaves that had fluttered down from the trees upon her face.

I think about this all the time, in all sorts of contexts, this idea that so many of the rules and hierarchies we've had in place—and accepted—for so long, have a "because I said so" ring to them. And I wonder what would happen if we were to treat them that way, as arbitrary and meaningless, and question the authority of those who are empowered by and enforce them. The trick, in Wonderland at least, isn't just to recognize the pack of cards for what it is: it's to *say* it. That's what wakes—and saves—Alice from her dream.

I know it's only Wonderland, that in actuality, a child has no power,* and a woman less than a man. But even here in the real world, Rebecca Solnit writes in *The Mother of All Questions*, "Now, when women begin to speak of their experience, others step forward to bolster the earlier speaker and to share their own experience. A brick is knocked loose, another one; a dam breaks, the waters rush forth." When we speak together, our individual risk of recrimination is diminished and we become the threat. But that requires us to unite, and we can't do that unless we've freed ourselves, each of us, from our self-isolation. And that is only possible if we confront our complicity. It's the mortar that holds those bricks. Blast it, and we can knock them all loose; we can scatter the playing cards and break the spell.

What would sharing this particular form of experience entail? It's not a spectacle meant to entertain, shock, or provoke some intended audience. When I see women criticizing each other for complicit behavior on Twitter—whether it's one calling another out or a pile-on—I shudder. It tends toward bullying and only serves to feed a vicious cycle of complicity; not only is it divisive, but it also provides ammunition to those who would like to believe that women are a bunch of squabbling shrews or mean girls, or that we have acted just as badly as the men involved and should be punished to the same degree. It does not send a message of unity or strength. At best, it reads as virtue signaling on the part of the accusers; at worst, as a takedown of the accused for sport.

Complicity isolates us because it breeds self-hatred and mistrust of others. Getting past it requires restorative self-disclosure and, when relevant, respectful feedback, not forced confession or condemnation. It requires a safe space; no men allowed, no official press release to follow. Addressing it is something we do for ourselves and, collectively, for one another, and never as a performance, which would imply both manipulation and selective censoring and might suggest it was being

---

*The gruesome irony that Alice Liddell, the girl who inspired this book, was at the mercy of and possibly molested by its author, Lewis Carroll, who has, in recent years, been accused of pedophilia, does not escape me.

done primarily for the benefit of someone other than the complicit party or her community. Naturally, this rules out social media altogether.

And, on that subject, a December 2018 Amnesty International study of online abuse limited to Twitter of female politicians and journalists in Great Britain and the United States found that, as reported in *Wired*, "Women of color in the study were 34 percent more likely to be the targets of harassment than white women. Black women were targeted most of all: One in every 10 tweets sent to them was abusive or problematic, whereas for white women it was one in 15."

A few months earlier, the National Women's Law Center (NWLC) published a report on sexual harassment in the private sector, examining charges filed by women between 2012 and 2016. "In every industry," it stated, "black women are disproportionately represented among women who filed sexual harassment charges." The report went on to quote Emily Martin, vice president for Education and Workplace Justice at the NWLC, who said, "The statistics confirm that sexual harassment is alive and well across all industries—and women of color working low-wage jobs are facing the brunt of the abuse." Institutional feminism's track record on the inclusion and support of women of color has been undeniably lousy. We (white women) seem, finally, to be paying attention to and understanding the privilege and exclusivity that shaped the movement in its previous waves. But we have a long way to go.

In "Your Reckoning. And Mine," for *New York* magazine's The Cut, Rebecca Traister wrote about how women were reacting to the Harvey Weinstein allegations and their ripple effect—an empowering of women to come forward about other abuses in other industries, and a communal unleashing of anger:

> There is another realm of anger here, arising from our knowledge that even the long-delayed chance to tell these repugnant truths is built on several kinds of privilege. As others have observed, it matters that the most public complaints so far have come from relatively affluent white women in elite professions, women who've worked closely enough with powerful white men to be available for harassment. Racism and class discrimination determine whose stories get picked up and which women are readily believed.

While women of color have been the victims of more abuse, they are also more actively deterred from speaking up—they are afforded neither the platform nor the trust, which translate, respectively, to interest or respect. I realize this isn't just true of harassment and abuse. Women of color are rarely given the spotlight even in positive instances. In the food world, we can complain that women have gotten short shrift press-wise, compared to the attention men have received. Look at profiles of chefs and at media coverage in general. But then look at the number of women written about, or featured on screen, and ask yourself how many of them are women of color. Similarly, consider who is being assigned, or assigning, those stories. This isn't about the food industry or media, explicitly; I just use it as an example because it's the one I know best. If I, white-woman me, work in a company or a field and I see that kind of disparity in opportunity, and I don't speak up, what does that say about me? (Complicit.) Or, what if I don't bother paying attention in the first place and so remain oblivious to it? (Also complicit.)

There is complicity even in our complacency or ignorance, to everyone's detriment. The discrimination or abuse of women of color (or LGBTQ women, or of anyone who identifies as a woman) is discrimination or abuse of women, period. It sounds so obvious. But I think, sometimes, when something isn't happening to you or anyone like you, you think it isn't happening to anyone; or worse, maybe you think it doesn't matter. It matters. Let's go back to the Arendt principle of isolation. Fragmentation will never result in our dismantling the patriarchy and achieving parity. I'm not the first to say it, but it bears repeating: We rise together.

We can only lift our worth and the worth and quality of our work—and our lives—if we lift each other up together, if we push back together. If, as a woman with privilege—white or otherwise—you truly believe you aren't talented enough to get ahead in the workplace, or anywhere else for that matter, without handicapping the system (in a way that ultimately shoots yourself in the foot), by allowing "some" women to continue to be degraded and held back while you "advance" in what will surely remain a man's world, then sure, stay silent. Maintain the status quo; continue to live in a society where men believe they're entitled to mistreat and are superior to or guaranteed more success than women. Go right ahead and keep yourself down for the sake of a few more perks.

If you believe in equality, an equal distribution of power, and in any kind of real merit-based system, you have to believe not just in feminism, but in an inclusive feminism (which is the only legitimate feminism). You have to be the first to say no when you see another woman with less agency—or privilege—being overlooked (or worse), until we are all seen as equal, by each other (as women) and by men. So long as we know another woman's voice will be silenced, disregarded, or challenged, those of us whose voices may carry farther or hold more sway must use them to amplify hers. And we must do that for each other, together. Anything short of that? Complicity.

You know it when you see it. But sometimes, you don't see it, or you don't want to (same thing). Sometimes, you see it and you know it, and then you try to pretend you don't. You do see it, though. And it makes you feel shitty about yourself—makes you withdraw and go quiet or act out defensively. When other women are able to name and acknowledge their own complicity—in its many incarnations—it should alleviate some of their remorse by making them realize they're not alone in it. It can also serve as an informative—nonjudgmental, one hopes—way to help those women who haven't recognized their involvement in upholding the established power structure, do so. Because you have to know how you've been complicit in order to stop.

* * *

I decided to try an experiment, using what I think—and hope—is the safe space of this book to encourage that acknowledgment and, perhaps, generate a dialogue around it. It starts with this essay, but it's driven by what follows. I asked the women whose opinions and ideas you've read scattered throughout this book to share their thoughts on complicity. Participation was optional, so was anonymity. Naming names was never the goal. I wasn't sure if there would be any takers, but there were. There were a lot, and, for me, the effect was incredible, if a little overwhelming; the amount of embarrassment, regret, fear, and anger so many of us have been carrying is immeasurable. I have so much admiration and respect for everyone who spoke up. Maybe more important, I have been made aware of forms of complicity I had never considered and was perpetuating myself. It gives you a lot to think about—and, yes, to agonize over. But it also shows you how pervasive and inescapable complicity is, how it works, and, to some degree, how the system it's part of functions.

Although this is a reflection of the experiences of women who work in or adjacently to the food world in some capacity, most of it is applicable to other fields and to society at large. It has strengthened my belief that being silent about our complicity is the first silence—and the first form of complicity—we need to break. "Silence and shame are contagious," Solnit writes. "So are courage and speech."

What are some ways in which we, or you, have been complicit? When did you play a part in upholding white patriarchy by staying silent, not supporting or defending, or actively sabotaging other women?

RUBY TANDOH

Because the food world is such a small one, I think most of us will have worked at some point in close proximity to someone we knew to be bad, problematic, or just unkind. I certainly have, and I've bit my tongue for fear of falling out of favor with editors. It's tough. I think it's really important to interrogate that complicity at every opportunity though. There have been times when I've not done enough, but there have also been times when I've gone out in a blaze of glory, burning every single bridge on my way out. We each need to carry our share of responsibility for upholding these rotten structures; we owe it to ourselves and to the people around us to break down the barriers, even if it means we might miss out on some commission or other. We have to show solidarity, and solidarity means taking a share of the hurt so that others don't have to. There's no easy or painless way forward.

JASMINE MOY

I took for granted that the industry would always and forever be a hostile place for women. My first job was as a hostess at a restaurant when I was fifteen, and I waited tables straight through to my graduation from law school. It never once occurred to me that there might be a different way or that I shouldn't have to put up with having my ass grabbed by a customer or have to turn down advances from line cooks. Anyone who won't admit that they were complicit in that culture isn't looking hard enough at their own history.

CHANDRA RAM

I grew up the only girl in the family, with three brothers. And in high school and college, I had a lot of male friends, especially when I started working in restaurants. So, when I went into the kitchen and later, in culinary school, I was more than ready to be "one of the guys." I contributed to all the sex jokes on the line to prove that I was too cool to be bothered by them. And once I moved into the business world and journalism, I continued to laugh and joke awkward or uncomfortable moments away, instead of call people out on them. I regret that, because in the times I've spoken out, younger women have thanked me for doing so, because the world still hasn't changed enough for them.

MARISA DOBSON

Throughout my entire adolescence and my early twenties, I loudly identified as one of those girls who preferred the company of men, because "I wasn't down with the drama and the bitchiness" inherent in the company of women. When

I recently read Naomi Pomeroy's "confession" ["As a Chef and a Woman, I Regret Joining the Boys' Club" via *Eater*] and listened to the "Five Women" episode of *This American Life*, I heard very clear echoes of my own behavior—even similar phrasing. I wanted to be the "cool girl." I wanted to beat the system at its own game (without questioning whether it was a game I should be playing or even had a chance of "winning"!). I've always been afraid of weakness, and since weakness = women, I laid a foundation for a deep-set misogyny. Even my queerness was filtered through this lens, since my first same-sex relationships were coercive, and I built a sort of harem, with myself as a kind of madam. Looking back at it now, in my thirties, I can see that I was serving up threesome after threesome for the pleasure of white men. And I know I often clothed this in the language of sexual freedom, when I was really operating out of a sense of fear and detachment from my own desires. I wish I could go back now and protect those girls, rather than exploit them.

JEN AGG

I've always been fascinated by boys clubs. They had all the power, and I wanted it. So instead of cultivating relationships with women early in my career, I was more drawn to male friendships. And sometimes this is still the case, even though I'm aware of it. Lately (in the last few years), I have sought out friendships with brilliant women. But I'm embarrassed it's something I have to check myself on.

ANN CASHION

Early in my career, I was advised not to identify as a woman chef, but rather as just a chef. I think that was actually good advice. But it did mean that I was less attuned to the indignities and barriers that women in our industry (me included) often face, and that I was only a half-hearted member of organizations that support women, like WCR [Women Chefs and Restaurateurs]. I did my bit, but I bet I could have provided more leadership if I'd tried.

ANONYMOUS

Women need to be kinder to each other in this business. Period. Across the board.

MAISIE WILHELM

I read *Heat* when it came out, and I didn't think, *Oh my god, Mario* [Batali], *what a chauvinist pig. That behavior is immoral and I should take a stand against it.* I guffawed at him, and laughed. I am complicit. I should have known better. But society has changed since then and made it easier for me, in that same situation, to stand up and say, "You can't behave that way," which I am doing more now. But I wish I had been braver and more aware back then.

JULEE ROSSO

I was complicit by remaining silent. I didn't speak up and try to convince the men I worked with in the Fashion/Advertising business in the 1960s and '70s that they were out of line. Instead, I just worked harder than anyone else and tried to earn everyone's respect, one day at a time. That often earned me respect; but with insecure men (and women), it created animosity. And when they thought I was earning more than they were, well, things could get ugly. The green-eyed monster knows no gender.

When men used really shocking vulgar language (when there was still such a thing), I'd ignore them rather than call them out on it. I'm afraid giving people the silent treatment has always been my MO (it was my dad's way), and often it's not effective; when people don't really know your normal demeanor, it goes right over their heads.

For the past forty-one years, I've owned my own businesses, which have been mostly comprised of women. Now, I need to earn respect from lawyers, accountants, and industry colleagues, who sometimes don't listen. The gentlemen I've served with on food industry boards over the years were always respectful of my opinions. Kudos to them.

WENDY MACNAUGHTON

I try to keep things comfortable by avoiding confrontation in the moment. I think it's taking the high road, when in fact I'm keeping the status quo in place.

JOANNE CHANG

I know I have been in situations in the kitchen in which guys are "just being guys"—talking about women, making dirty jokes, etc.—and I've just smiled and either laughed along or ignored it. I was a young cook surrounded by mostly men and I didn't know how to react. Of course, now, my older self wishes I had had the wherewithal and guts to say, "Hey, that's not cool. Can we stop talking about this?"

RACHEL BOSSETT

I have witnessed a young female cook be intimidated out of the kitchen by our fellow male cooks. It was my first kitchen job, and I hadn't realized what was happening until much later, but I said and did nothing to stop what happened to her.

KIM ALTER

As a young cook I witnessed (and experienced) sexual harassment and didn't speak up about it. I was told that if I ever opened my mouth, I would never get a job, which I believed at the time. I was too scared and worried about losing my career to stand up.

CHARMAINE MCFARLANE

My choice of words and sense of humor hasn't always been respectful toward women. In my early years in the kitchen, my favorite prank was to butcher a skinless chicken breast, garnish it with my own hair to resemble a hairy vagina, and leave it on a coworker's cutting board. I've often had a good laugh about naming a dish of two over-easy eggs on a biscuit "Grandma's floppy tits," while failing to find humor in any dish that resembles "Grandpa's saggy balls." One way in which we are complicit in upholding the patriarchy is fucking the chef with the hope or expectation of advancing through the kitchen ranks. Or thinking that hooking up is fun, harmless, and will build camaraderie between male and female cooks. It does not. Instead, it devalues and discredits female cooks and creates the expectation that female cooks are available, and only in a superior position because they're fucking the chef.

In a broader sense, we justify our own non-action by recalling how tough kitchens were when we, as chefs, were rising through the ranks, and our accomplishments since. When outed for tolerating a sexually abusive culture, we then acknowledge that, in retrospect, we should have done more, and deeply regret our inaction. This reminds me of the time I was placed in a chokehold by a grill cook, who was trying to kiss me, after I repeatedly refused. When I spoke to the chef the next day, he was very apologetic, adding that the grill cook had "a thing for the pastry girls." The pastry chef and one of the pastry cooks knew about these proclivities and I felt betrayed that, as women, they never mentioned it. I swore to be more protective of my cooks

(which has caused friction between my bosses and myself), thus earning me the moniker, "Mama Bear." In light of the #MeToo movement, I've actively referred female colleagues to other kitchens for employment, especially if they are currently working for perpetrators of sexual harassment and inequality.

***

BONNIE MORALES

I am guilty of perpetuating the presumed "tough it out" mentality of kitchens. As an owner of my own restaurant, I have the opportunity to rewrite the rules. At first, I just fell right into the role I've seen a bunch of middle-aged white dudes with anger-management issues play. But at one point, I just woke up and realized that I felt like crap, I was making other people feel like crap, and I was just acting the way that was modeled to me, without any intention behind my actions. I work hard every day at creating a work environment that is professional. I don't mince words and I am very direct, but I don't belittle or embarrass. Well, sometimes I do— but only in good fun.

***

ANONYMOUS

My kitchen experience has been varied in that I have held jobs on the savory line, in the pastry corner, and with both men and women at the helm. I have had an incredible experience in the trenches with people of all races, colors, and genders. The kitchen, for me, is an incredible, intense, hyperfocused, structured playing field of talent. I am a competitive person by nature and *love* camaraderie and getting through chaos with a team. I have excelled in all my kitchen jobs by working my ass off, keeping my station spotless, and keeping my mouth shut. I am fast, efficient, and I love to help others get to the end goal of happy customers. I hate complainers—people who need more breaks than necessary and who complain about paper cuts; I see them as a weak link and would like them removed from the team. I have worked for chefs who were kind, pompous, assholes, and idiots, but all of them played a part in the type of owner I strive to be. I struggle with what I expect from my employees versus what is appropriate.

I feel so awkward saying this, and have erased this sentence a hundred times, but the people who have disrespected me the most in kitchens are women and women owners. That is awful, but that is my experience.

CAROLINE FIDANZA

I can be envious of other people in the industry, especially the ones who most resemble me. I undervalue certain kinds of businesses (cookie makers) over others (sandwich makers). I tend to view restaurant work as harder and better than other kinds of industry work, and I realize that I'm wrong—everyone works hard and cares.

EMILY FARRIS

You'll probably get seventy-five versions of this answer, but: I was raised to see other women as my competition. And for years, I bought into it. But someone else's success is not my failure—and I think that's especially true for women. The more we can support each other and help each other succeed, the better it will be for all of us.

TIFFANI FAISON

I was competitive with other women more than with men. Now, I understand why and have worked on forgiving myself, but it still burns me. I've thought a ton about this and, totally unscientifically, here's my take: Women are more competitive with other women because, historically, when we were included professionally, there were only a certain number of "slots" for us. Instead of fighting against the low number of slots, we fought each other for the slots themselves. The number of "slots" is where my energy is focused now.

ANONYMOUS

I have felt so many times in the past that my female colleagues, instead of being supportive and being truly happy about my success, sometimes approach it with a jealousy and grudging behavior because there are so few top female chefs in my city—meaning there is a sense that there aren't enough accolades to go around for the men *and* the women. It is really indicative that in the pre-Me Too era, women chefs were having a very difficult time getting recognition. I asked some women chefs for advice on how to open my first restaurant and they ignored me completely, only to befriend me after the restaurant was a success. That is a problem.

There has also been a lot of silence about the disgusting behavior of some male chefs. Generally, the industry has overlooked men making begrudging, snide comments or inappropriate behavior and, in this way, has supported the boys club and the rat-pack culture. The most common offense is looking the other way when someone is behaving offensively and basically being an egotistical pig. I don't want to attribute this responsibility to female chefs because, essentially, we have all been sort of powerless in the power paradigm. The fear of retaliation or ostracism for speaking out and standing your ground is real. The true responsibility lies squarely with the writers, journalists, event organizers, and industry colleagues, male and female, who have celebrated these people relentlessly, only to assist in tearing them down twenty years later when revelations come out. How much progress for women was sacrificed in those twenty years when everyone was looking the other way? How many women didn't make it, or were pushed out of the industry?

Honestly, in dozens of ways, speaking personally. But, I think, more when I was a magazine editor than when I was a cook. I remember working at not be seen as "feminine" when I was an editor in the early aughts. I cultivated a kind of hardened cynicism that isn't natural to me. I'm not saying that kind of hardness is necessarily male. But I think I used it to get a leg up on other, less obviously wry and sarcastic women. Similarly, there were no people of color on staff at the magazine where I worked and, though I noticed it, I never mentioned it. That certainly counts as complicity. The other instances I can think of are softer complicity, but merit mention: At both the restaurant kitchen I ran as head chef and at Chez Panisse, there was a conspicuous absence of people of color. My kitchen was in Georgia, making it all the more glaring that we didn't have any African American cooks. I was also the only woman in the kitchen, other than one of my restaurant partners, who cooked for a little while before moving to FOH [front of house]. That seems bizarre to me. Did only men apply? When I got only male applications, did I really do nothing to solicit female applications? Both seem impossible now. But I know I didn't have a single female cook. I think, for a lot of my pre-writing career, I prided myself on being able to function well and rise and achieve in the male-dominated universe. It was one of the things I had going for me. I don't think challenging it really ever occurred to me. I think I must have thought: I'm well adapted to this, which works to my advantage. Which is so bizarre to me now.

ANONYMOUS

When you're afraid to speak up because you fear retribution or you're scared of the repercussions in your industry, this is in some way being complicit, even if it is essentially against your will—you're a victim. I know a lot of women of color in the food media industry who are sitting on awful stories of discrimination or really suspicious unprofessional business practices but don't speak out because the industry is so small, they fear never working again, and they're probably right. If the stories came out, I don't think anyone would feel bad or start to look into how those women were mistreated. Those who control the industry have no incentive to care, so they're all complicit. They participate in the behavior, they know it goes on—they reward it. I've really seen that in publishing and in print and online media, and am glad people like Julia Turshen are trying to effect change by building a longer table.

SOFIA PEREZ

When you are already in a less-powerful position (by virtue of being a woman in a male-dominated world), it is simpler to smile and go along with whatever BS is being directed your way than to speak up in your own defense (or in that of other women). As a white woman, it is even easier to go this route, because—while you are still seen as the other—you are decidedly less other to the white male establishment than women of color. As a blunt New Yorker, I tend to be pretty direct in the face of bad behavior, but when I was younger (in my pre-culinary journalism phase), there were definitely times that I opted for blending into the curtains behind me instead of being the "shrill" woman who stands up for herself. I wish now that I (and others) had spoken up at every opportunity and joined together sooner to dismantle the bricks of those silos into which we were placed.

ALISON CAYNE

I know there have been times in the past where I played more naïve or helpless than I was in order to get what I needed or wanted from men. It was how I was taught, in the sense that I've grown up believing that manipulation was my power. I think, at the end of day, it just perpetuates the cycle. I'm hoping that's changing.

AUBRIE PICK

My mom was a single working mother in the early eighties and she was a badass. Our family motto was "girls can do anything," which we repeated to each other all the time. I believed it so thoroughly that it never occurred to me that other people might not know it, too. She raised me to be strong and independent and to work hard. She never told me about the odds that she faced in her professional life, and my understanding of what it took to be successful as a woman wasn't complete. As I made my way as an adult in the world, I think I used my ignorance to ignore the facts I saw around me. I thought that hard work could overcome any obstacle—it had worked for my mom, right?—so women who couldn't overcome obstacles weren't working hard enough. I'm embarrassed to admit just how long it took for me to really shake that notion.

MELANIE DUNEA

Complicit? Disagree. Forced to comply? That's more like it. The system has been unchallengeable until now, especially for the lone-soldier freelancer. Speak up = no work and alienation. There is no human resources department in the real world.

NAOMI TOMKY

Oh man . . . so I'm still really frightened to talk about how much I'm paid for each piece. I try to do it as much as possible, because we need to share amounts, but I'm also afraid it would show I didn't negotiate enough or would sour an editor on working with me. Ditto on sharing editor contacts. Both of which I think need to be public information for more equal footing.

HANNA RASKIN

I previously worked for Village Voice Media, which means profits from Backpage.com [known for its sex- and prostitution-related advertisements and shut down by the FBI in 2018] helped pay my salary. While I wasn't aware at the time of the extent to which our journalism was underwritten by the physical and sexual abuse of girls, I didn't look into it, either.

REBEKAH DENN

For most of my career, I worked for large corporations with very hierarchical newsrooms. For what it's worth, I had some female bosses and they were, for the most part, fantastic—but we were all stuck in the same system. I feel like I adapted to the system instead of recognizing and actively trying to change it.

KATHLEEN SQUIRES

In retrospect, I feel awful about being a part of chef-hero worship as a part of some assignments I was given over the years. Today, I would completely turn down that kind of garbage job, but back in the day, I needed to take on every job I could get.

JORDANA ROTHMAN

I have this memory of my pinboard at *Time Out New York* when I was the food and drink editor there years ago. I had cut out photos and stuck them up there, like the inside of a locker. There was one of Mario Batali, a pink and green coaster from the Spotted Pig, a photo of Anthony Bourdain, some others. I thought about this recently and realized that everyone up there is now dead, literally or figuratively. I think I was part of that worshipful culture at that time, a little dazzled. Ultimately, I know I contributed to a culture that made some of those men powerful, that allowed them to operate unchecked for so long. I'm ashamed of this, ashamed I didn't have the guile to ask questions or even, frankly, really tune into what was happening and why it was wrong. This would present itself later, and I would like to think I have done noble things for the culture in the years since. But I do live with it.

As for sabotage within the sisterhood . . . there have been times when I have had pangs of fear or a sense of threat that someone with a similar perspective or voice might ultimately be duplicative of my own—that absurd notion that "there can only be one." This vaporized for me when I dug a little deeper into the legendary Mimi Sheraton–Gael Greene rift. I still don't know what truly caused it, but seen through the lens of a modern perspective, I can't help but think it was rooted, to some extent, in that same sense of toxic competition and survival. I don't want to carry something like that with me for a lifetime, so now I ascribe more to the JFK idiom about the rising tide and all the boats.

ANONYMOUS

I worked with well-known people whose behavior made my self-respect suffer, and I continued working with them for too long.

KRISTY MUCCI

I've never told anyone what's what after I've gotten absurd comments about working in food or my body. It makes me cringe that I've only ever been polite about it. I just try to delicately squirm out of the conversation, instead of saying "this is not okay." I think my silence means that they'll go on making those comments or asking those questions, I'm sure only to women, without thinking about it, and I'm so sorry for it.

ANONYMOUS

In the face of so many conversations about #MeToo and egregious, salacious sexual harassment in the workplace, I have been thinking about the much more insidious, slippery examples of sexual harassment I witness on a regular basis in my job. When there is a common understanding that the men at the top are "feminists," it becomes even more challenging to make a case for why "locker-room talk" is damaging and harmful.

I enjoy a privileged position as "one of the guys" among the owners of the company. They consider me a close friend, fun, someone around whom they can talk freely. I enjoy certain privileges as a result—special treatment that makes my life much easier than most of my coworkers'. So when one of my bosses makes an off-color comment about one of my colleagues' bodies, or he pontificates on how they are in bed, I often laugh it off, just praying the moment will pass. When I receive "compliments" on my own physical appearance, I don't draw the line. In the instances when I have pushed back, I have been temporarily iced-out, and made to feel like my insider status has been revoked. I feel guilty for being complicit in this behavior, which has serious ramifications, even if no physical lines have been crossed. It's a reminder that the choice is to participate or suffer the consequences. It's a reminder that we are always evaluated by our sexuality, our looks, and our ability to assimilate to a man's world.

ANONYMOUS

I didn't fight hard enough to cover female chefs who didn't fit under the "sample size" criteria earlier in my career. At one point, I perpetuated the "mean-girling" that had once been directed at me. Just as certain women who were intimidated by my ambition tried to stomp it out of me, I did the same to a junior colleague, which I regret.

ALI ROSEN

While I do showcase a lot of different talent, I am not unaware of the value of food celebrities appearing on my TV show. I have definitely allowed myself to be spoken down to in order to continue with an interview. I have been shocked how an entire team of people can stand around and hear someone saying something vulgar to me (or others) and just chalk it up to "chefs being chefs." I assumed it was just the cost of being a journalist in food, and I now wish I had been a leader in saying no.

ANONYMOUS

By not paying attention soon enough. By not actively seeking out best practices in diversity and inclusion in hiring and representation. By not acknowledging that unpaid internships (when they were still commonplace, up until a few years ago) meant that scarce entry-level positions would only go to the most privileged candidates. By not fighting for the budgets to do it any other way.

REGINA SCHRAMBLING

I used to tell an aggrieved story about an editor at a magazine for black women rejecting (very nicely) my food/travel pitch because "it's a great topic, but you aren't the right writer." In retrospect, and thanks largely to Twitter consciousness-raising, I completely agree.

ANONYMOUS

I know that I support everything I come across that I like, and that I never act like propping someone up will harm me, because I don't think this way. But so much of the recipe-writing and cookbook-publishing world is simply made up of white, privileged women who have had more opportunities than anyone else gets (and who get to write recipes like "Mexican Chicken Salad"—"Mexican" because it has, like, beans or cilantro or cumin in it—ad infinitum, unquestioned, and uncriticized, including one I'm looking at right now from one of the biggest names in cooking, and I just can't believe this is still a thing). It's so much harder for people of color and others outside of this universe to get published, to get heard, to get to write about their own food. I'm not sure I'm doing enough to ensure I'm looking for voices I don't usually get to hear.

ESTHER TSENG

In a broader sense, I just want to do a better job reversing the negative effects of anti-blackness in the Asian American community. I want to help create an abundance model rather than a scarcity model when it comes to representation.

JASMINE LUKUKU

I don't have a specific example, but I have been reflecting on my own proximity to whiteness. I grew up in Western Canada with a white mother, white friends, white food, white teachers . . . a whole lot of whiteness. This proximity to whiteness has definitely given me privileges and biases. I am working on undoing the programming.

NICOLE A. TAYLOR

I've been wronged a lot by white women in food. I'm working on forgiveness. For people who wronged me, who didn't understand equity, inclusion, etc. I would just get angry and never give them a second chance. I'm trying to figure out better ways to bridge the gap if I feel they're worthy. But I don't feel like I've ever been complicit or participated in the patriarchy by being silent. I've been a part of the resistance since even before the resistance kicked off. I look at a lot of white women in the resistance now and think, five years ago you were clueless. Should I forgive you now?

THERESE NELSON

I think I've been complicit in not really understanding and showing up for non-cis women. I battle on my own ethnic- and gender-related battlegrounds and, in the midst of my own privilege, I often forget that, because I subscribe to a traditional identity, I don't have to confront the exhausting task of qualifying my humanity in that way. It's something I constantly check myself on, but it's only been over the last few years that it's begun to occur to me.

LIGAYA MISHAN

I've had a very fortunate career, in that at each media organization I've worked for—and note that there have been only two, the *New Yorker* and the *New York Times*—I've had multiple role models, women in positions of power looking out for and giving a helping hand to women just getting their start. I hope that I haven't been complicit in white patriarchy, but I may have been, by simply not being adversely affected by it. I suppose I've been able to ignore it as a problem.

JENI BRITTON BAUER

I have totally been complicit. But also, not to make an excuse, you can't model behavior that you have not seen. You can't. Once I saw someone someone behave in a way that rejected the status quo, I began to do it, too.

CHARLOTTE DRUCKMAN

I've had the advantage of being able to see everyone else's responses before answering this—my own—question. Before, I found I was harping more on my inexcusable tolerance for what I dismissed as "drunken chef" behavior, which was how I categorized any (male) chef who I'd heard would get "handsy" or say inappropriate, repugnant, sexist things when drinking and "letting loose" (as I thought of it). I don't know why I didn't see that it's all part of the same—the same misogyny and entitlement that drives other men to force themselves on, or emotionally and psychologically abuse women. Some men don't go that far, but they shouldn't get a pass or a pat on the back. It's all rooted in the belief that women are less than they are, and in hate.

Before I saw these responses, I also spent a lot of time thinking about how there isn't enough editorial coverage of women of color, and how whatever coverage there is seemed really pat and, in its own way, patronizing. This is true of coverage of women in general, but it is more glaring when it comes to women of color. I worried that I haven't done enough to correct that, as a freelancer, in terms of stories I pitched or wrote. And I felt hypocritical and ignorant, because I've spent so much time talking and writing about the representation (or lack thereof) of women in the food world, and trying to cover as many (white, it would seem, in hindsight) as I could.

More recently, I've become aware of the fact that this isn't only about who is covered, but who does the covering. Women of color in my own field—publishing—have been disregarded time and time again, so they've been denied bylines, editor positions, and book deals. The skills and talent are there, and so is a diversity of perspective and knowledge we're all missing out on. I don't want to keep reading the same stories by the same people. Do you? I will continue to try to correct that imbalance in whatever way I can.

As I took in everyone's statements, I found myself starting to feel like I'd missed a ton and, more disarming, that I might never really be able to account for all of my complicit behavior or even to catch it all going forward. I can only hope that pages like these, and being lucky enough to be surrounded by women like the ones in this book, will keep me constantly mindful and vigilant—and that we can do that for each other.

IF WE WERE IN CHARGE OF THE WORLD

What RULES would you *put into effect* if you were in charge of the world—or, if you're *willing to share* the POWER, we (women) were in charge of the world?

In 1981, Judith Viorst's *If I Were in Charge of the World and Other Worries* made its debut. My mother gave me a copy. I still have it and regularly reread the titular poem and think about what I'd do if I controlled the universe. In the world of Viorst's ruling narrator, "a chocolate sundae with whipped cream and nuts would be a vegetable," and Monday mornings would be scrapped, along with allergy shots, oatmeal, and someone named Sara Steinberg, who I always pictured as a pale, stringy blonde-haired menace. No one would tell you not to punch your sister, because you wouldn't have sisters at all. Given the opportunity back then, I probably would have axed Monday mornings, too. (Now, I'd just extend every weekend through Monday, effectively getting rid of the whole day altogether.) But I would never have gotten rid of sisters. I've always wished I had some.

JULEE ROSSO

Judith Viorst was one of a kind . . .

* * *

If I were in charge of the world:

Google wouldn't be.

Trump would be history.

Everyone would respect one another. People would not compete for importance. Pretension would be shunned.

Schools would be safe. Neighborhoods would be safe. Parents wouldn't spend half their time driving kids places. Kids wouldn't be pampered. Parenthood would not be idolized. Enjoy it all but grow up.

Money and power would not be singular goals.

Curiosity and intellect would be rewarded.

The arts would be supported by all.

We'd all get to drive great vintage cars.

We'd all be speed-readers and innately speak as many different languages as we liked, making global friendships easier.

Everyone could live on a Great Lake such as I do with sunsets on the horizon every single night and stars that drop into the water.

RACHEL BOSSETT

Humans are social animals and should be more concerned about our fellow humans, as opposed to greed and powerlust. We'd focus on helping others and creating safe environments for everyone to flourish. The matriarchal colonies of the world (bees, elephants, orca whales, meerkats, etc.) do it right. They are concerned about the welfare of their colony, their family, their friends, instead of just being concerned about themselves. The world needs more community and less division. How I'd write rules to accomplish that? I don't know yet.

KRISTINA GILL

Wow . . . rules . . . First would be that you have to know what a double negative is in order to be president! Seriously though, I'd rather think in terms of equal application of the rules for everyone, regardless of who you are.

ESTHER TSENG

Do not refer to a woman's appearance when addressing her.

Address a woman's work, and stay on topic, when you are addressing her from a position of power. Do it humanely when you have criticism to offer. Ask yourself whether you would say this to a man if you had the same things to say.

NICOLE RICE

Be kind.

JULIA TURSHEN

1. Try hard not to be an asshole.

2. Lift up as you rise.

CHRISTINA TOSI

Trust yourself when all doubt you.

Ask yourself every night before bed, what did I do today to make this place a little better? (Did I do something big, or more importantly, little, with intention, to help someone or something, to remind that person or thing that this place is pretty magical, even amidst the hubbub?)

Treat success and failure the same. They're both huge accomplishments if you let them in far enough.

SOFIA PEREZ

If I were in charge of the world, I would force everyone to travel overseas and spend a week cooking in a home kitchen under the tutelage of a local resident (preferably, a woman); there's no better way to learn adaptability (both in life and cooking), obtain a visceral understanding of the local culture, and provide a new framework for seeing your own world. Cooking without the crutch of your usual tools and ingredients is an illuminating, humbling, and expansive process. It connects us to the eternal story of humanity in a world where it is all too easy to be disconnected.

SARA LEVEEN

If I were in charge of the world, everyone could afford to visit the destination of his/her dreams at least once and it would always be safe. If I were in charge of the world, everyone could eat a home-cooked meal in the country whose cuisine he/she loves the most.

KRISTY MUCCI

No one is allowed to be a creep and get away with it.

Less chef-worship. It's boring.

If you're mean, or gossipy, or rude, or inappropriate, you don't get work.

This community is really here for its people. All of them.

No cookbooks written by people who don't actually cook, because that's hard work and it should be respected and taken seriously. No more ghostwriters; give people proper credit.

HANNA RASKIN

I just want restaurants to list their hours and phone number on their websites.

CHARMAINE MCFARLANE

If I was in charge of the world, health education—physical, mental, and nutritional—and culinary awareness would be an integral part of our society. As a former nutrition major and one who cooks for a living, I'm dismayed by how many people are ignorant of where their food comes from. Do you know how many guests tell me they can't have dairy and when I send them a dessert containing eggs, they send it back because "eggs are dairy"? In other words, they're getting their nutritional information and agricultural awareness from some corporate bureaucrat who noticed the eggs sell better when they're next to the milk.

And to encourage more awareness of where food comes from, I'd give tax rebates to property owners who devoted a percentage of their arable land to "victory" gardens instead of lawns and to renters who farmed a plot in a community garden or volunteered their time to working in an agricultural endeavor—a farm, a slaughterhouse, an apiary, a seed-saving organization, or a food pantry.

ANONYMOUS

Women who don't know about food and cooking, and who only hire their friends who are the same, will not be in charge of anything in the food world.

NICOLE TAYLOR

No cool kids table.

Once a month, reconnect with someone you haven't seen in six months to a year. Meet in person and talk.

Everyone needs to know how to roast a chicken and make a lemon pound cake.

TAMAR ADLER

Oh, man. If women were in charge of the world, schools would have kitchens and people would get paid living wages to cook our children real food in them. You know where else there would be real food? Prisons, hospitals, factories, post offices. I think enough mamas running things would turn around our garbage food system quicker than anything else could.

But, for that matter, if women ran things, I think the death penalty would disappear, work requirements for government assistance would disappear, our idiotic immigration system—which actually works to force people who would be doing cyclical migration to and from home countries to put down roots—would be changed to accommodate seasonal labor and natural human movement. Climate change would be accepted as fact and policies created to address it. We would start investing in education and recreation and health instead of the military.

How can I actually believe these things? Because I'm a mother now, and the mothers I know are great forces of good.

MARISSA LIPPERT

We communicate as humans, using both our hearts and minds first. We sit down to a meal to discuss important and non-important things. Breaking bread brings us together and equalizes things even if for a moment, or a meal. Always make your bed in the morning and say at least one kind thing to someone you do and don't know each day. Take time each day, five or ten minutes even, to go inward and connect with yourself.

ALISON CAYNE

If I were in charge of the world we'd communicate better: Listen, hoping to have our minds changed rather than our beliefs solidified, and speak from the kindest place to the kindest place of the other person. Corny, but how I feel. Also, we'd figure out how to balance consumerism and public policy.

ANN CASHION

Cellphones would be like cigarettes. They would not be allowed to advertise, they would carry mandatory health advisories, and their use would be banned from all public places, including restaurants! Election Day would be a holiday and voting would be mandatory.

GILLIAN SARA SHAW

Social media would be abolished.

JULIA SHERMAN

I would outlaw conference calls (is anyone really paying attention?).

I would make fast food and Flaming Hot Cheetos illegal.

I would make it illegal to heckle women on the street, and flashers would face some sort of public humiliation.

Donald Trump would be excommunicated.

Federal funding would be put toward a male birth control pill, and women would actually learn about how their reproductive systems work in school.

I'd bring back Esperanto.

VIRGINIA WILLIS

More talking with people, less talking to people.

MARION B. SULLIVAN

If *we* were in charge of the world, we would never be mansplained to again. Oh boy!

TIFFANI FAISON

If I were in charge of the world, everyone would have a dog.

Everyone would have a friend or a loved one or a lover with a disability.

I would cancel David Chang and René Redzepi and all of that bro shit.

There would be no guilt.

Nachos would be salad.

Donald Trump would live in a jail in an orange jumpsuit that is way too small and there would be a panda cam on him at all times.

Women would lead everything for the next fifty years.

We would have real conversations about female fear and rage, and men would actually listen and work to understand.

We would raise children as communities.

There would be no drugs, no gangs.

All of the history books would be rewritten.

The entire Supreme Court would be women. All nine.

We would gut the prison system and start anew.

We would all take naps.

With our dogs.

KLANCY MILLER

We would all work toward the liberation of oppressed people all over the world. And everyone would get a thirty-day vacation. And excellent free therapy and healthcare for all. And everyone would have access to high quality housing and education and food— and you would not have to be rich to have these things. There would be no student loans.

MAISIE WILHELM

- Give everyone paid family leave for six months
- Mandate recycling and composting
- Abolish the electoral college
- Criminal justice reform
- Health care for all
- Never would have allowed the Republicans to block Merrick Garland's nomination
- Ban on orange streetlights (white better)
- Stabilize rent in NYC for all apartments

SIERRA TISHGART

I'd magically bestow men with the ability to get pregnant and give birth.

JOANNE CHANG

If I were in charge of the world I would make every kid learn the value of writing a thank-you note. I would teach everyone the importance of making eye contact and saying please with a smile. In the restaurant world I would have everyone BOH [back of house] work a day in the front and everyone FOH [front of house] work a day in the kitchen.

REGINA SCHRAMBLING

I would put whatever they're drinking in New Zealand in the whole world's water. It's the one place I've traveled where equality is on the menu— even a construction guy on the side of the road pulling us over because of a landslide on the highway ahead looked me and my consort in the eye directly to speak to us. It's also where they seem to understand a healthy environment is the future, not just for food. (Although the industrial aspect of sauv blanc was a little distressing.)

KATHLEEN SQUIRES

If I were in charge of the world writers would be better paid and not looked upon as "hobbyists" by people in other professions.

ANDREA NGUYEN

Bathroom grout would never get gross.

Kitchen cabinets would never get gummy.

Fridges would have endless capacity.

Greater empathy would lead people to better read one another's needs and wants.

JENI BRITTON BAUER

I don't want to be in charge of the world.

Dorie Greenspan

I believe award-winning cookbook author, *New York Times Magazine* columnist, and baking legend Dorie Greenspan is our greatest living recipe writer. She gives you all the information you could need—nothing extraneous—and is precise without being off-puttingly exacting in her descriptions of technical steps and their intended results. Other food writers are able to do that as well. What they don't do is magically anticipate the thing that will trip you up or make you doubt yourself seconds before your panic sets in, so you never have to worry. That's what Dorie does. It is emboldening and helps us become better home cooks. It's also what prompted me to ask the members of the Chorus: What is your favorite Dorie Greenspan recipe?

People picked everything from Apple Tarte Flambé to Pumpkin Stuffed with Everything Good, but the World Peace Cookie definitely got the most love. You can find the recipe for it in any number of places online, including Dorie's own website and in more than one cookbook. It seemed redundant to print it here. Instead, I hoped maybe its creator might be open to revisiting it and coming up with a version 2.0 for this anthology. It would be a tribute to her and gift to everyone else and would showcase how she develops and writes a recipe.

So I typed an email and put a wish out to the universe as I hit send.

Here is Dorie's response, in both email and recipe form.

A Good Cookie

Dear Charlotte,

I've been reluctant to change this recipe, since I've always thought it is perfect as is. Over the years, I've swapped peanut-butter chips for the dark chocolate bits. I've added toasted nuts to the dough—nice, but not more than that. I've added peppermint oil and liked the cookie, but felt it was more crush than true love. And, of course, living in the twenty-first century, I've sprinkled the tops of the cookies with flaky salt before baking them . . . and sometimes I still do. But in the end, while the little tweaks were good, none were better than the original and so I never made an official change.

When you asked me to rethink the cookie, I was game, but doubtful that I'd come up with something that would be good enough. I think this is more than good enough and I hope you agree.

I wanted this to be a good cookie, but also one that would be right for your work. I thought about the qualities that I admire in women and then tried to find flavor and texture equivalents that would work with chocolate. The cocoa nibs are there for strength, the pepper for that touch of unpredictability that I love in people and food, and the raspberries for sharpness and verve. I also added a little rye flour, for earthiness. The raspberries are fascinating because they take a little time to reveal themselves. While you taste them soon after the cookies cool, they really only come into their own a day later.

I'm sure you know the history of the cookie, but just in case, here's a quick résumé. Pierre Hermé, the French pastry chef, created this cookie [in 2000] to put on the dessert menu of a new restaurant off the Champs Élysées. He named it after the restaurant, Korova, and gave me the recipe to put in my 2002 book, *Paris Sweets*. Just before I was ready to turn in my manuscript for *Baking from My Home to Yours*, which was published in 2006, I ran into a New York City neighbor, Richard Gold, who told me that he loved those chocolate cookies, but he never called them by their name. Instead, Richard said, he called them World Peace Cookies, because if everyone in the world had them, he was sure peace would reign. With a name like that, I had to republish the recipe. In what might as well be a case study in marketing, the cookie's popularity took off once it had the perfect name.

Joshua [Greenspan, her son] and I made World Peace Cookies when we had our cookie shop, Beurre & Sel, and, of course, I included the recipe in my book, *Dorie's Cookies*. In fact, it's the cookie on the cover.

Now it's yours. Maybe you'll find a new name for it.

Oh, a bit more background. When Pierre Hermé gave me the recipe for this cookie, he said that it was inspired by the American chocolate-chip cookie. And maybe it was, but it seems a world away from what we know as the classic. I think he might have made the association because this cookie has some brown sugar in it, so it's slightly chewy; but to me, it seems more like shortbread. The salt, subtle, but present enough to have you returning for bite after bite, was revolutionary at the turn of the century. That we take it for granted now doesn't diminish its effect.

I've seen (and tasted) the cookie made with every kind of cocoa powder possible, but I rarely stray from Valrhona, which has a beautiful color and a full flavor. And while I know that some people use chocolate chips for the cookie, I wish I could convince everyone to use good quality bittersweet (or semisweet) chocolate and to chop it by hand into uneven pieces. One of the pleasures of using chunks, shards, and bits of chocolate is that every bite of the cookie is different—another win for unpredictability.

We Were in Charge of the World Cookies

Makes about 36 cookies

Notes on a couple of quirks in the dough and a plea for patience: This dough can be different from batch to batch—it always seems to turn out well no matter what, but the inconsistency can be frustrating. I've found that it's best to mix the dough for as long as it takes to get big, moist curds that hold together when pressed and then, when it comes out of the mixer, to knead it if necessary so that it comes together. When you're rolling it into logs, keep checking that the logs are solid—gently squeeze them to see if there are any hollow spots. Again, the dough can be capricious and it may not always roll into a compact log on the first (or second or third) try. Be patient. —DG

1 cup (136 grams) all-purpose flour	Pinch Piment d'Espelette (go small on your first batch)
½ cup (60 grams) (medium) rye flour	
⅓ cup (30 grams) Dutch-processed cocoa (I prefer Valrhona)	1 teaspoon pure vanilla extract
½ teaspoon baking soda	5 ounces (140 grams) chopped bittersweet chocolate
11 tablespoons (155 grams) unsalted butter at room temperature, cut into chunks	⅓ cup (45 grams) cocoa nibs
	½ cup (15 grams) freeze-dried raspberries, coarsely chopped or broken
⅔ cup (135 grams) light brown sugar	
¼ cup (50 grams) granulated sugar	Flaky salt, such as Maldon, for sprinkling (optional)
½ teaspoon fleur de sel (or ¼ teaspoon fine sea salt)	

1. Sift the flours, cocoa, and baking soda together in a bowl and set aside.

2. Working with a mixer (preferably a stand mixer fitted with the paddle attachment), beat the butter and both sugars together on medium speed until soft, creamy, and homogenous, about 3 minutes. Beat in the salt, Piment d'Espelette, and vanilla. Turn off the mixer, add the dry ingredients all at once, and pulse a few times to start the blending. When the risk of a flour storm has passed, turn the mixer to low and beat until the dough forms big, moist curds—this may take longer than you'd expect; don't be afraid to keep mixing. Toss in the chocolate pieces, nibs, and raspberries and mix to incorporate. This is an unpredictable dough (see above). Sometimes it's crumbly and sometimes it comes together and cleans the sides of the bowl. Happily, no matter what, the cookies are always great.

3. Turn the dough out onto a work surface and gather it together, kneading, if necessary, to bring it together. Divide the dough in half. Shape each half into a log that is 1½ inches (4 cm) in diameter. Don't worry about the length—get the diameter right, and the length will follow. (If you get a hollow in the logs, just start over.) Wrap the logs in plastic wrap and freeze them for at least 2 hours or refrigerate for at least 3 hours.

4. When you're ready to bake: Center a rack in the oven and preheat it to 325°F (165°C). Line a baking sheet with parchment paper or a silicone baking mat.

5. Working with one log at a time and using a long, sharp knife, slice the dough into ½-inch- (12 mm) thick rounds. (The rounds might crack as you're cutting them—don't be concerned, just squeeze the bits back onto each cookie.) Arrange the rounds on the baking sheet, leaving about 2 inches (5 cm) between them. If you'd like, sprinkle the tops of the rounds sparingly with flaky salt.

6. Bake the cookies for 12 minutes—don't open the oven; just let them bake. When the timer rings, they won't look done, nor will they be firm, and that's just the way they should be. Transfer the baking sheet to a cooling rack and let the cookies rest until they are only just warm, at which point you can munch them, or let them reach room temperature (I think the texture's more interesting at room temperature).

7. Repeat with the remaining log of dough, always using a cool baking sheet.

A Conversation with Kim Severson

Honestly, I wish I could just type: "Kim Severson is my favorite journalist" and leave this introduction at that. Writing about your heroes is stressful enough, but when it's one who has set the bar for you in your own profession and whose byline both motivates you to do your job and to feel like you will never be worthy of saying you do, running for the hills (first choice) or letting it go with a presumably hyperbolic (it's not, though) six-word declaration and *then* running for the hills (second choice), seem like the only viable options.

But something about Kim—specifically, her being the ultimate team player and loyal to her clan—makes wimping out, despite its being the comfiest recourse, untenable. She believes in journalism, and she believes in the *New York Times*, the publication where she has worked for the last fifteen years.

Why is she my favorite journalist? You probably think it's because she writes about food. Wrong-o. I love how she reports the news; that this news just happens to be about food is the Luxardo cherry on top. She has a way of sneaking these sly, subtly cutting, deadpan observations or quotes into her features that never cross the line of bias, but leave a trail of crumbs for a secondary reading, should you be looking for one. And, at the same time, she's able to endow a story about something easily dismissed as trifling—cake contests or obsessive cookie decorators—with humanity and to turn it into a positive portrait of gay marriage or community building. She has traced the history and contributions of American slave cooking through a grain of rice, covered food stamp fraud, and recounted the misdeeds of a counterfeit artist.

She was my favorite long before she received the Pulitzer Prize in 2018, along with her "work wife," fellow reporter for the *New York Times*' Food section, Julia Moskin, for their contribution to the newspaper's watershed coverage of the #MeToo movement; they broke the story of restaurateur Ken Friedman's serial sexual harassment and assault of the women who worked for him at the Spotted Pig in New York City.

I encourage you all to pick up her memoir, *Spoon Fed*, where she candidly writes about her struggle with addiction and her path to self-discovery—and if you think that sounds too maudlin or "heavy" for you, I promise she'll crack you up along the way and you'll want to keep reading. Kim thinks meeting your heroes is the fastest route to seeing them knocked off their pedestals. She's proven herself wrong.

CD

The first thing I want to ask will seem a bit *duh* to you; I think people are not clear on the difference between food writing and food journalism. There's a lot of overlap, but journalism is a very specific profession with a set of standards and practices and I wonder if you could talk about what journalism means for you and what it is like to do the job of a journalist.

KIM

Okay, let's see. So I report news, right? And that news can look like, it can be about food, it can be about, you know, anything. I just see myself as a reporter first. I like to write about food and, I say this all the time, any story can be told through food. There are many people who I think are much better food writers than I am and much more lyrical about what happens when you slice an onion the right way or how certain dishes mingle with culture and become other dishes and all of that stuff, which is lovely.

But I am a very good reporter. At the [*New York*] *Times* we talk about reporting without fear or favor and the idea that you are not the story. In food writing, a lot, the author is the story, and journalists—we're really shifting right now a little, but you never want to really be the story; you want to just tell the story. I'm a stand-in for my readers, so I go out and say what's happening and, for a levelheaded, sensible person, what is the truth here, what happened? And the truth, as we know, is often very gray and has lots of sides, so we have to ask a lot of people questions.

You also have to be smart enough to know when somebody is lying to you, and you have to know where to find the receipts. In journalism, especially—we're seeing it really refined now in the age of Trump, you really have to have your shit sealed up pretty tight and know what your mission is, and the mission is to tell people what happened and give them some context. It's pretty simple, but in order to do that, it's just a lot of what seems like grunt work. You have to have a 360-degree view of whatever it is you're writing about and make sure you know everything—if you can, which is hard to do—so that you're not telling a story that's spun or that's not right.

You also have to figure out: Is this the right story to tell now and why. So, does this have news value? Does this meet what your audience needs to know? Is it a big enough story to put in the paper? Is it worth you spending your time on? Does this matter? Why does this matter? And you make all these choices when you decide what story to report. I think all of that is really different than food writing, you know?

It's journalism, it's making daily choices about what readers need to know. The other journalistic line I love is, "you want to comfort the afflicted and afflict the comfortable," and that's the big motto. And I think there's something to that. We're supposed to speak truth to power; we're supposed to help the underdog; we're supposed to be fair and not be afraid to stand up in front of people and ask questions.

We're not here to tear down the present; we're not here to build up the present. We're just here to report on what the reaction to the present is and I think people feel like we are supposed to be crusaders. Sometimes I think journalists are crusaders—maybe you want to say this housing project has lead in its pipes; it shouldn't have that. That's a crusade. But we're not supposed to be putting forth a political viewpoint, you know?

CD

I think people want everything now to be an op-ed; they just don't know that's what they want so they get frustrated.

KIM

It's not our job to be the judge and jury.

CD

But what I do think happens is that, in situations where you have less access to the truth, that idea of the crusade changes. Right now, because of Trump, I think we have this feeling that everything is being obscured, and then the pressure on newspapers to get there—that feeling of crusade-ship is intensified. So I kind of get it, you know. But I feel like if you're living in an age where there's more transparency then you don't think about it as much.

KIM

Right, I think that's true.

CD

I love your memoir *Spoon Fed* and feel like I totally got how you had been in the kitchen from day one, and at the same time, that you were interested in journalism early on, but I want to know how or when you figured out you wanted to put them together. How did you decide you wanted to cover food? Could have been crime, could have been politics . . . When did that happen and what do you think it was?

KIM

That's so interesting. I have no idea, but I do know, in college, I did a little bit of restaurant criticism and I waited tables, and I was a short order cook too, because I had to work my way through college partially, and I was the assistant manager at a Little Caesars pizza; I was very proud of that.

And I can remember reading *Gourmet* magazine and thinking, *I will never be able to get a story in this magazine*, and it seemed so far away; but I wanted to for some reason—I think because, when I was in high school, I kind of found my home with the nerd journalists, and then I also had this big family food thing going on; the table was where I could get noticed and where everything happened in my family.

I think those two driving things in my life, it just seemed like a marriage, you know? I remember dabbling a little in college, but of course we were post-Watergate babies and it was all about doing cops and courts—this is back in the day when you could jump from small newspaper to the next size up.

But then when I got to Alaska, which is a great place because there's so much heavy-lifting; if you just pick up a bucket and start bailing, you can become things . . . because there's just not that many people and there's all this money, and you're like, *Okay, I'll do that*, and they're like, *Fine you can be a federal judge*. And so I just started. They had kind of a bad restaurant critic, and I was doing feature editing then, and I just said, "Well, why don't you let me do that?" Because I like to eat a lot and cook and I was a big wine drinker, then.

And then there was so much power that came out of that. I just felt like I had this audience in the palm of my hand . . . and everybody wanted to follow it and it was a really interesting piece of built-in community. When you were writing for the food people, people who are interested in food, that was a specific community and I could plug right into them. News and all that other stuff is a little more vague, but food people are food people, right?

So there are newspaper people and food people; it's like a perfect marriage.

CD

I think the reason I asked you that is you're one of the people that made me want to do my job, but I think I took it for granted. I realized this when I was reading *Spoon Fed*. I don't want to say you invented food journalism, but there was definitely a moment in that book where you were like, *I saw that I could apply these—*

KIM

News standards to food, yeah.

Exactly. And saw that you could talk about things like politics or business or agriculture and do it through food.

They were not doing it back in the day. Marian Burros was, sort of, a little bit, but she wasn't quite. I mean, she came in as a food person, and then I came in as a newsperson and started writing about food. I remember when I got hired at the [*San Francisco*] *Chronicle* in like '99, that was right when it was pre–Michael Pollan and food as news; childhood obesity had just been declared an epidemic by the Surgeon General. There was this growing awareness that what we were eating, and food, and news issues were merging in a way.

It was just the beginning of this wave. Michael Bauer—god bless him, to his credit, he kind of saw that, and Alice Waters and the whole where-your-food-comes-from farmer stuff was just starting. The *Chronicle* saw that we could get food news on the front page that wasn't *Oh the taco place!* or whatever; you could tell your news stories from the plate. I don't think anyone else was really doing that at all at that time, so I felt like we really created a pretty good model for it there.

I feel like the tendency is always to ask people about their food inspiration but I'm actually wondering which journalists you had been reading when you were younger and who you were admiring from that perspective?

Well it's interesting, I was such a post-Watergate baby in that Woodward and Bernstein were like that idea that you could be that swashbuckler, and also [Christopher J. Koch's] *The Year of Living Dangerously* which sounds weird—

No, I get it.

But that idea of an emotionally invested reporter was just perfect for me . . . that kind of stuff. It's so funny when I think back, but there was a woman named Edna Buchanan [Pulitzer Prize–winning crime reporter for the *Miami Herald*]. She was huge and Molly Ivins [syndicated newspaper columnist, political commentator, and humorist from Texas]—I remember Molly Ivins came up to Anchorage to talk to us and we were all like young reporters and at that time nobody smoked in the newsroom anymore, but she was a huge smoker, so we took her to the cafeteria (it was in the late eighties, early nineties, or whatever). And she just lit up a cigarette and she was smoking, and we didn't have any ashtrays, and she had a covered coffee cup that she put her cigarette out in. And I remember it burned through, and some of the coffee and the ashes leaked through, and she didn't give a fuck and I was just like—

She's so cool.

Molly Ivins, you are the coolest. Some women like that were cool role models to me. And I remember the first women who were covering Congress—and some of them, like Elisabeth Bumiller, are still working here [at the *New York Times*]—and the idea that women had to fight to cover that. That whole generation of women was, at least professionally, who were interesting to me. And even meeting Jimmy Breslin at one point was a big thing for me, when I finally met him. Although all he wanted to talk about was the George Foreman grill and I was sort of ultimately disappointed.

George Foreman grill.

Yeah, he was all excited he had one and he was like, *Yeah, I can cook everything.* And I said,

"Okay, yes, sir." (You know, you never want to meet your heroes.) I always thought about the story he wrote about John F. Kennedy's—the guy who dug his grave, right? That famous story and he talks about him, the guy [Clifton Pollard], putting on his khakis in the morning and eating his eggs. And he gets a call; he knew what he was gonna do. So I always think about that: How do I look left when everybody's looking right? How do I get to that story?

CD

I think, for people who do food journalism, there tends to be a chip on the shoulder or tendency to feel somehow like you're not being taken as seriously because it's food, and I wonder if this is something that you felt at any point?

KIM

Oh, all the time and still—and I think even here [at the *Times*], people don't get what we do. Everybody thinks that food writing is easy to do, in a way, because everybody eats. It's like, *Oh, everybody goes to the movies!* But you don't expect everybody to be a movie critic . . . Food is different like that. But I've sort of been able to turn that so I can show up places and just be like, *I'm just the food writer. I'm just the recipe girl,* and then it lowers defenses. In some ways, it's kind of like I've kind of jui-jitsued it into an advantage for me.

Although now it's not the case here, it was, for a long time, hard to argue that a food news piece had enough value to get on the front page. Because it used to be there was, like, the women writing in the food section—you know, the Marian Burros era—and then all the gay male food critics—the Craig Claiborne model—and then you might have like a weird old grumpy guy covering the farm bill off the ag beat in Congress. It's taken a long time for newspapers to change that way, but now that food is the cultural currency of our time, it's easy, if you have a good reporter, to get all that.

CD

It's actually, in some ways, screwed women over because it's become a viable source of income.

KIM

And men love it.

CD

So what are some of the stories that you've written that you've been the proudest of? And I don't mean your favorite or even if it was something like you know was good because it got recognized; I just mean for you, at the time?

KIM

I mean, I've written thousands of news stories so it's hard to just . . . it's weird but the very first profile I did of Rachael Ray was kind of a big deal, because the editors here were way not into that; they were like, *We don't do those kinds of stories*, and I caught the timing just right on her. It was right before the wave broke; she hadn't had her magazine or her TV [talk] show yet. So I felt like the timing of that one was great, and that was stuff that people were into.

There were a lot of stories that were really hard to get when I was doing the national desk. There was one about a man in Jackson [Mississippi], who got beat up and killed—an African American man [James C. Anderson]—by a bunch of white teenagers. He had been at a hotel room, and he was gay. He had a partner; they had a kid, but he was out like at four in the morning, leaving this hotel room. And these kids were just out— they were driving from the white suburbs to beat people up in Jackson and they killed this guy. It was pretty brutal. Drove over him in a parking lot, and there was a camera from the hotel [recording] that happening.

It was a news story, but I had to deal with a very on-the-DL African American man whose family—the dead guy's family—didn't want to talk about him being gay at all, but then we had a grieving partner who also . . . It was hard to get his trust. Then I was dealing with race relations; I had to go deal with these yahoo idiot kids in this white community. And I had twenty-four hours to do it in, or thirty-six—but those kinds of stories where you have to jump into many different cultures and try to come up with a story in a very short period of time. This was in Jackson with its whole history of homophobia and racism and then this murder happened.

CD

And that's a crusade story too, right? I mean, obviously, you want to do every story right, but I think about what *right* means in those kinds of stories because they're so much more loaded.

KIM

Right, and you're not just: "Black Man Killed in Jackson." You have to nuance what it was like for that family; you have to nuance what it's like to be gay but in the closet in Jackson, and then you have to nuance the tension between these white and black neighborhoods.

Another story that comes to my mind that I was really proud of that I don't think people understood how fricking hard it was to get, but I did a story—all the Paula Deen stuff was happening and I went and found her black cook, Dora Charles.

CD

I loved that story, yeah.

KIM

I drove to Savannah three or four times just to get enough where she would meet with me at the Panera Bread to say, "maybe I'll talk to you." She was so scared and so scared of Paula—like, Paula's a thug; Paula had her

thumb on all these people . . . and then finally we started cooking and talking, and then she relaxed and talked, and it was just by a thread, and there was the timeline. But to get to the point where Dora Charles's story could be told, it was fucking hard.

It was just this continual, steady having to pull and then meeting her and being able to be like, *You have a story to tell. I understand you're afraid of Paula but we can tell this story.* And then meanwhile, I'm also working with Paula's people who are full-court press trying not to have me talk to her, and people who worked at the restaurant, still . . .

Anyway, so those kinds of stories where there's a huge amount of stuff that goes into it, so then you have your nice little two-thousand-word story.

CD

I think it's really interesting because, honestly, I don't think people realize—

KIM

What it takes to get a good story.

CD

Yes, I don't think that they realize what the actual work is.

KIM

Getting in the fucking car and driving and then another phone call and not stopping and calling them back and—

CD

Managing people's psyches.

KIM

That's really what it is. And then giving them respect, and being like, *Okay, I'm going to write this story; it's going to look like this.* You don't want to surprise anybody. You want to be able to stand on this story. I mean, they might not like this story the next day, but you have to be able to stand strong on it. I always think about this like, *If I had to go on trial for any of my stories, could I back everything up, you know?* I always think about that.

CD

One of the things I think about a lot is the compartmentalization when you are having these experiences, because people are sharing a lot. This is true too of the [Pulitzer-winning, #MeToo] Ken Friedman/Spotted Pig story; I mean, you have people who—it's not just that they're trusting you, it's that they're sharing really disturbing things with you.

And obviously what they've gone through is much worse than your listening to what they've gone through, but it's still something that you then—

KIM

Oh, it's fucked me up. The fucking sexual harassment stories were hard—triggering my own background and then you are holding their stories.

A lot of the times, you're the first person, maybe, besides the cop, or maybe besides a boyfriend or girlfriend, who they tell their story to so you just have to—you just hold it, and just listen. I always think about what I would want, you know? How would I want somebody to talk to me? It's a huge honor to hold somebody's truth for them and I feel like that's the higher bit about journalism, is you get to hold people's stories for them and help them a little bit, you know?

CD

Yeah, it's hard though. I don't think people realize sometimes.

KIM

And we're not trained counselors. Thank god for Kat Kinsman [founder of Chefs with Issues] and the whole reminder of #selfcare. I don't think journalists do enough to take care of themselves, you know, that's why everybody drinks and smokes. It's like cops.

CD

I don't think people recognize that journalists are going through it, either, so I think that there's that.

KIM

You know, we just need to take care of ourselves.

CD

Yeah. I love that in *Spoon Fed*, and it's been nearly ten years since you wrote it, you describe, I think, your first day at the *New York Times*, on your way to the cafeteria, how you take a detour and you walk through the hall of Pulitzers, right?

KIM

Was just right up there, yeah. I remember that.

CD

And your response is, *Oh god, I'm fucked, I'm in way over my head.* Did you ever think, *I would like to get this one day?* Or, *I think I can do this?*

KIM

In all sincerity, I never thought that I was good enough or that I would get a Pulitzer. It just wasn't going to be my thing. I just never thought that I was good enough or the field was, because you know when [restaurant critic, RIP] Jonathan Gold won for food criticism that was a big day for all of us, because he was the first food writer to get one. I just thought, *How can I be good enough to be in a room with people who won Pulitzers?* So the fact that I got in the room . . . That was the goal. But I honestly never, and I don't mean this with any sense of false humility or anything, I just . . . am not good enough to win a Pulitzer.

CD

I disagree. But I would say that when you write about food, it's not the first thought on your mind: *You know what? Goddamnit, one day I'm gonna get this award!* How much has changed, in the food world or in food media, since you first walked through that hall of Pulitzers [in 2004]?

KIM

It's a whole different world now, right? There's all these smart young people writing about food . . . We didn't do much digital storytelling then, and visual storytelling is so big and, you know, I think the world exploded. There's a lot more people who are just hot-taking and I can hardly keep up with what everybody's opinion is about everything. That's changed. I think the James Beard Foundation is a different organization. And I feel like newspapering has changed a lot, but in many ways it's still the same and it's become even more important in all of this noise. I think the tent poles of good journalism, they just become stronger. But then at the same time, [*New York Times* reporter] Julia [Moskin] and I, we were joking last night; I'm like, *Okay, we should make a bet, what's going to fall off first, Instant Pot or keto?* I just feel like that old, *I've seen 'em all.* Like, *I'll tell you what, I think that Instant Pot's going before keto.* And so in some ways you see the way people eat has changed a lot but—

CD

But the fact that of there being trends is the same.

KIM

Yeah, that's all the same. And every January people are gonna write weight-loss stories and every Thanksgiving . . . you know. There's something lovely about that though.

CD

One of the things that I think is really hard and tricky is that, let's say most of us of a certain age or generation, the things that made us want to be journalists or writers feel really antithetical to a lot of what we need to do now as writers, which is self-promote. You're supposed to have a brand or, I still don't know what it means, a "platform." How much

pressure do you feel to use social media? What do you think that dynamic is now between how much of it is about the story and how much of it is about you having written the story?

KIM

Well I don't think that I could ever win at the social media game because I'm just not that person in a way. But I do know that I think back to, like, Calvin Trillin: I remember I'd read one of his stories in the *New Yorker* and it was really like, *How can I ever do this?* Those great writers. I'm like, *Does he have to worry about his platform? What would he be doing now if he had to tweet?* I love Twitter as a reporting tool, and Instagram is a good reporting tool. I don't have a big Instagram game because I just don't have time, but I do it because I take so much from Instagram and Twitter. I have to contribute.

CD

You have to give back.

KIM

I'll put a picture up but I am very conscious of the fact that my last name is *New York Times*, because I don't wanna hurt the brand, you know, which sounds weird. I've been lucky that I'm attached to an organization. And I think about it like this—and I think we get memos about this all the time—but some of the journalists like Maggie Haberman and the people who are reporting right now and getting just attacked, and they're on the frontlines of good journalism and democracy, we're here rolling bandages and growing the victory garden, right? Our little features and whatever we're doing—and giving people their Thanksgiving stories; all that matters is to keep the *Times* making money and looking good, and it's my job to not make it harder for those guys. I have a real belief in that. Social media, you know, it's just part of a greater whole.

CD

Knowing what people expect from the Food section, and also being aware of the idea that for the *New York Times*, it's a moneymaking juggernaut (while Maggie Haberman's getting yelled at by Donald Trump), how does that change the kinds of stories that you do? Or, do you feel more like, *I've got to put a recipe on it?*

KIM

I think the reason I get to do the really big things is because I show up and do the little things. So I'm not above doing a fucking recipe for my section because we need to do a recipe, and that's fine if that's how they want to use my time. I'm just such a worker-among-workers kind of person, so I'm like, *Okay, well I gotta do this because you need a recipe.* But then I get to go fly to fucking Puerto Rico with [chef] José Andrés, so, you know.

CD

It's worth it. I think I get annoyed more by the principle of the thing, because I think about how much it's curtailing the kinds of stories that we would like to write. It's like, *Ugh, if it doesn't have a recipe on it . . .*

KIM

I know, *Imagine if I was just doing this . . .* Yeah, so all my stories don't have to have recipes, but also, it's that dance-with-the-one-that-brung-you thing; I just never want to give them a reason to not let me do what I want to do, you know what I mean? And I think that's important, especially for younger women: Show up and be so useful to your job. And then push, and then the trick is learning when to push back and say no, and how to manage up all that stuff.

The other thing that somebody told me early on, and it was just such great advice, is when all that criticism is coming in, just stay as close to the story as you can. If you can just get really narrow on the work then all that noise goes away; stay close to the work

and it's kind of simple. Be a craftsman, be a good worker.

CD

I always say trust the story.

KIM

I think, also, writers need to be the Easy-Bake Oven of rewriting, so when your editor doesn't like something, you just be like, *Let me know; I'll fix it for you.*

CD

Do you think that you'll leave Atlanta? Are you really happy there? You've lived in all these cities, so I have to ask.

KIM

I know. I've lived in every corner. My family is in there now; I'm divorced and I share custody of my daughter with a CNN writer. I'd have to move all my sister wives back to New York, and then my partner, who I've been with for, like, eight years, her eighty-three-year-old mom lives there. Also, it's super convenient for my job because I travel two or three times a month, so I can just jump; the airport is good. And right now, the paper really likes me being not in New York, and I think that's good because I cover the country.

CD

It's also refreshing not to be in New York.

KIM

Yeah, my big joke is when I moved to Atlanta from New York, I immediately felt skinny and rich. It was fantastic. But I don't know, when [my daughter] Tammy goes to school, maybe. I ultimately would like to live on the West Coast. I realize that I want to live near the Pacific Ocean, and it could be Seattle or Vancouver or California, but I am such a Pacific Ocean person, and so it is my great irony that I've sort of endured in the American South, although it's been great and informative and I've learned a ton. I think my soul needs to look at the Pacific Ocean, that is absolutely true.

Do you have anything in terms of career stuff
that you haven't done that you would like to do?

I mean, I would love to write a novel one day. I
don't think that I'm good enough, but I would
like to . . . I moderate a lot of panels and I'm
always doing that sort of thing and I love it.
It's really easy for me to be onstage. I just had
to do this onstage interview with Ina Garten
that actually ended up being in front of two
thousand people, for an hour, but it was so
fun; it was just easy to get the whole audience
together with a joke and I loved that. So maybe
one day I would love to be more of an onstage
storyteller? I don't know how to do that, really,
but I would love to do more of that.

Kristina Gill

I have mixed feelings about the genre of cookbook that presents readers with the cuisine of a city; I find the results work better as travel guides than something I might turn to in my kitchen when figuring out what to make for dinner. *Tasting Rome* was the first of this ilk to convince me otherwise—to prove that this concept can be executed in a way that speaks to home cooks while still capturing the gestalt of a place. The recipes and prose are evocative of the book's titular city, but the photos are the most transporting part of the equation. Kristina Gill, a Nashville native, who has lived in Rome for the last fifteen years and is the food and drinks editor at Design*Sponge, took them. Her images have appeared in publications like *National Geographic Traveler, Atlas, Bon Appétit*, and *Kinfolk*.

She coauthored *Tasting Rome* with another American expat based in the Eternal City, food writer Katie Parla. When Kristina told me the vision for the cookbook was hers, I wondered what other projects she might cook up and thought I'd give her a few pages to combine her words and images in a different context.

A Fig by Any Other Name

never really thought about the symbolism of what I ate until I moved to Italy. I was struck by how often women were compared to food. The vagina was referred to as a potato—or *patata*; an ugly woman as a scorpion fish—or *scorfano*. Anything large and round, like a caciocavallo cheese, was used in metaphors to describe men's testicles. I remember a vendor at the market explaining that the more flavorful fennel bulb was male; it, too, was round while its female counterpart was more oval. He grabbed a sphere-shaped one to show me and exclaimed, "This one is so masculine he still has his pants on!" This sometimes vivid, sometimes jarring language, which went unquestioned, highlighted an annoying intersection of sex and food. Were my market purchases—or a dinner I prepared them with—the culinary equivalent of double-entendres? What if I were eating something in public that had a meaning I didn't know about? And if so, was I inadvertently communicating a message to others?

Probably what bothered me the most was that the male symbolism usually had a comic overtone—penis-shaped pasta or the Umbrian specialty, a round nobbly salame called "Grandpa's Balls"—but the female did not. Discussing this disparity in metaphors with my Italian husband, he proved my point. His immediate response was that "grandpa's balls" are objectively funny. (See Charmaine's story on page 344.) However, he followed this by saying that Italians use so many food metaphors, good or bad, because they just can't help talking about food and simply find a way to insert it into most any context.

In putting together this collection of images, I explored many ideas about how produce and culinary utensils could be used to make a feminist statement. I wanted this to be a (mostly) lighthearted conversation piece about food and women. I opted to shoot the objects with a macro lens in order to highlight the details in the products that we could identify with women, if we wished to do so.

Walnuts

Here we have the sole image in the collection that focuses on male imagery, depending on how you see it. The shells with their wrinkles look like a sea of testicles, or "nut sacks," as some people prefer to say. At the center is a nutcracker, or, as I think of her, ballbreaker—a strong woman who has already made her mark in the field of nuts that surround her. With a bit more time, she will be the last one standing.

Mussels

During her campaign for the European Parliament, Italian politician Giorgia Meloni was accused on Twitter of using a photoshopped picture of herself for her campaign posters. The trolling was so extensive it began to distract from her campaign. Forced to respond, she said that every time she managed to take a decent photo, she was accused of photoshopping the image and she'd gotten the message: the world thought she was ugly (IL MONDO MI CONSIDERA UNA COZZA). To take the bull by the horns, she posted her campaign poster again with a COZZA (mussel) on it, the joke being that Italians refer to an ugly woman as a COZZA. Meloni didn't win her election, but she shut her critics down. Meloni 1, Haters 0. (I bet you were thinking this story would be about vaginas.)

Zucchini

The wonderful zucchini, though we most often treat her as a vegetable (one of my favorites), is really a fruit and it begins as a gorgeous flower—a female flower that brings forth sustenance. The male flower remains unchanged, offering us nothing but its fast-fading beauty. You can't have one without the other, but she always has more to offer when left to flourish.

Pomegranates

In the days surrounding Dr. Christine Blasey Ford's testimony to the Senate Judiciary Committee in 2018, countless people, especially women, spoke emotionally about their own experiences of sexual assault. For many, it was their first time ever sharing. These survivors' friends, families, and even strangers supported them and let them know they were not alone. The composition of the pomegranates—the vulnerable, sliced-open ones tightly surrounded by whole ones, sometimes bruised but still up to the task—represents that indelible snapshot in time.

Figs

A quick Italian lesson. In vulgar dialect, fig, or FIGA *(also* FICA*) means vagina (or whatever your favorite vulgar term for the same is in American English).* FIGO, *however, means cool (this book, for example, is* MOLTO FIGO*). Don't mix up the two . . .*

Spoons

Husband-and-wife woodworking team, Andrea Brugi and Samina Langholz, both produce pieces for their demi-eponymous brand (his, not hers). Samina has asserted her own dominion over their products; because of the time she spends handcrafting each spoon, she feels as though they have become a part of her family upon completion. So she names them after family members—mother and father, for example. Ever since she told me that, I've found, when I use flatware, I sometimes think of the spoon as round and safe, almost protective of the food I'm eating. The spoons (or stirrers) here represent equality among women, whether they're single, or coupled, with or without children.

Minne di Sant'Agata

Saint Agatha's breasts (**MINNE** is southern Italian dialect for breasts). Giuseppe Tomasi di Lampedusa wrote about the deliciousness of this Sicilian sweet in his historical novel, **IL GATTOPARDO** (**THE LEOPARD**). At the shop where I purchased the pastries, I discussed Italian food references with a young saleswoman who said she felt that women in Italy have just accepted how their bodies are referred to so casually, so frequently, and often quite vulgarly by food metaphors. The running commentary, she said, was annoying and at times made women feel ashamed of their bodies.

The variation pictured here is filled with ricotta cheese and chocolate chips, covered with marzipan, coated in a sugar glaze, and topped with a candied cherry. The scalloped paper they're served in is evocative of lacy lingerie, and the gold dessert platter gives these **MINNE** a touch of class.

BRIGHT IDEAS

Is there a
FOOD PRODUCT
or GADGET—
practical or otherwise—
that *doesn't exist
but should*?

TAMAR ADLER

What about eliminating food products and gadgets?

MAISIE WILHELM

I wish there were a way to keep my herbs fresher longer in the fridge.

HANNA RASKIN

Spicy salad dressing.

AMY BRANDWEIN

Perfect disposable plate wipers.

TIFFANI FAISON

A robot that lifts, cleans, and puts away all heavy appliances.

Effective kitchen cleaners that won't burn a hole in your skin.

NICOLE ADRIENNE PONSECA

An electronic coconut opener that opens it like a can.

CHRISTINE MUHLKE

A self-cleaning juicer.

ALI ROSEN

An avocado slicer so that I don't have to read another story about "avocado hand."

CATHY BARROW

I want a magical tool that will blanch/skin hazelnuts and another that will pick the leaves off thyme branches, two of the most annoying kitchen tasks around. Maybe something that would peel tomatoes and peaches, too.

SOFIA PEREZ

I would pay good money for an easy way to peel roasted peppers without scalding my fingers and scattering little bits of pepper skin all over my kitchen counter and floor. Sure, I could buy the jarred variety, but their flavor and texture never come close to the peppers I've roasted at home.

ANN CASHION

Pit-less Concord grapes. A hydraulic oyster shucker that pops off the top shell, leaving the oyster and its liquor intact.

EMILY FARRIS

I want something to dice onions for me. I want a perfect fucking dice. And no tears.

REBEKAH DENN

An idiot-proof mandoline. Everyone I know seems to have a story of getting their hands slashed, just like all my bike-riding friends in Seattle have had broken collarbones.

ERIN MCKENNA

Gloves made just for peeling apples, potatoes, etc. I always cut my finger every Thanksgiving while peeling apples for pie!

REBECCA FLINT MARX

A tool that would have one setting to peel and chop garlic for you, and another setting to taser sexual predators.

An air freshener that would rid the kitchen of unwanted smells and sexism/racism/homophobia, both casual and deeply ingrained.

NAOMI TOMKY

Can we get one that announces to GOP officials what percent of what they're eating was grown/made by immigrants?

JOANNE CHANG

A stand mixer that has a heat element underneath so you can whip over heat.

JORDANA ROTHMAN

A weighted whisk that can stay in the bowl when you let go of it.

CAROLINE FIDANZA

Slotted ladle. It exists but it's never big enough. A stainless-steel mixing bowl that is somewhat elliptical for easy pouring.

RACHEL BOSSETT

We need a spatula that can dig out the stuff that stays under the blade of a blender. It always seems like so much usable waste gets stuck under there, and it bothers my attention to detail.

JASMINE LUKUKU

I wish natural peanut butter manufacturers would build a paddle into the lid so that we could stir the peanut butter without having to open it.

KRISTINA GILL

The Jetsons had a sort of vending machine that produced all their meals. That would be nice.

JULEE ROSSO

Dinner in a Bag Delivered by Magic (But Not by Drone): A complete mélange of meals (with a broad assortment of dishes from every world cuisine), with the very, very, very best ingredients (heirloom/organic produce and heritage/freely walking around/wild protein), seasoned to absolute perfection (appropriately sauced or not), frozen in a bag (but with no residual effects of freezing)—with no preservatives/gums/stabilizers, ZERO unnatural ingredients—to be tossed into a skillet or roasted . . . and ready in fifteen to twenty minutes. I'd rather cook what I want to, when I want to, not every night at six.

MARION B. SULLIVAN

Potato chips that don't make you fat.

GINA HAMADEY

Can fancy, homemade, naturally dyed and flavored Jell-O be a thing?

KATHLEEN SQUIRES

An Instant Pot that grills and deep-fries and listens to your pitches and offers sound critical feedback.

What about restaurant concepts—legit or ludicrous—that haven't been tried?

JULIA SHERMAN

I wish America was better with the single-item restaurant. In other parts of the world, there is more focus in the restaurant scene, and I think the execution tends to be better for that reason. In Japan, there's the okonomiyaki place, or the spots that only serve chicken yakitori. In Vietnam, there's the giant cafeteria set-ups that don't even have menus, they just shuttle out banh xeo [sizzling crepes], or Hainan chicken and rice that is as damn near perfect as it can get. I see how it could get old for the chef, making the same food every day, but I love the commitment to mastery, simplicity, and the unfussiness of it all. I would be a regular if New York had a restaurant that only served turkey sandwiches or Greek salads. What a reprieve from tasting menus and seasonal specials!

AISHWARYA IYER

An idli shop (it's a south Indian steamed rice cake).

HANNA RASKIN

A sweet potato bar.

ALISON CAYNE

I'd like a fried rice bar.

JORDANA ROTHMAN

An all-nacho restaurant, with tabletop broilers of course.

LIGAYA MISHAN

A restaurant that specializes in the crispy, near-burnt rice scraped from the bottom the pot, called by various cultures tahdig (Iran), xoon (Senegal), nurungji (Korea), concón (Dominican Republic), guo ba (China), and socarrat (Spain).

GINA HAMADEY

Modernized moo shu pork/chicken/everything.

RACHEL BOSSETT

All-cheese everything.

JOANNE CHANG

Congee bar—it would be a very small restaurant but I would eat there every day.

SOFIA PEREZ

Tapas are everywhere, in every form, but what we need in the United States is the true tapas concept—seven or eight (separately owned and operated) establishments in a small two-to-three block area, with each place producing its specialty(ies), so that customers can go on a true tapas crawl, the way they do in Spain. NO ONE in the States (that I've seen, anyway) has yet to get the tapas concept right—not its authentic spirit, how they are consumed, and how they fit into the larger food culture of a town or city.

EVA KARAGIORGAS

This is not fun but why can't anyone make a very good Greek restaurant! There are zero. Name one.

JULIE ROSSO

In the United States, the Japanese sushi bar concept applied to other foods—where all sorts of specialties from world cuisines are placed on little plates, traveling on little trains on tracks passing in front of you, at a counter, for you to select, enjoy, and pay for on the way out after the plates have been counted.

KIM ALTER

When I was just starting to cook, I wanted a restaurant called Host. It would host a chef from a faraway place for a few nights and then the local staff would run the menu for a few weeks. I always thought about this because of the expense to travel . . . The price tag on what it would cost to run a place like this would be $$$.

WENDY MACNAUGHTON

A twenty-four-hour savory bakery.

ANN CASHION

The Bid. The expediter could perform the duties of auctioneer, auctioning off single dishes and menu packages of various courses to the diners. The restaurant would be able to charge the limit of what the market bears; customers could stop complaining about pricing.

REBEKAH DENN

You Can't Make This at Home (not just spherified-hay-smoked-pear-essence, but any food that's just better made with restaurant-quality/restaurant-size gear).

KRISTINA GILL

I loved the restaurant in the movie *Fast Food, Fast Women* by Amos Kollek. It charged diners based on the amount of time they occupied the table rather than the food they ordered.

ALI ROSEN

Whoever invents an adult restaurant (with good food) that has babysitters and a play area in the back would win my eternal gratitude and patronage.

ANITA LO

Front and back of the house get the same hourly salary.

ERIN MCKENNA

An Ugly Fruit and Vegetable restaurant that specializes only in food that is going to get wasted.

REBECCA FLINT MARX

I've long dreamed of Detritus, a restaurant that only serves things like brownie edges, the burnt, crispy scraps stuck to the bottom of the pan, and the curdled bits of egg that get left in the strainer when you make custard or curd.

A restaurant with tables designed for odd numbers of people (one, three, five . . .), shaking up the complacency of pairs.

KAREN HUDES

Updated cafeteria-style places for breakfast and lunch, offering memberships.

JASMINE LUKUKU

All I want in this life is for someone to open a tiny little natural wine bar within a two-block radius of my apartment. I'd like this wine bar to serve Japanese convenience store snacks (katsu sandwiches, rice crackers, onigiri) and some good ol' fashion potato chips.

The room would be colorful and decorated with eighties modernist furniture.

The soundtrack would lean heavily on Steely Dan's catalog.

CHANDRA RAM

Jen Pelka suggested this (so I'm stealing it): an all-Burgundy wine bar—pinot noir, white Burgundy, and snacks. I'd live there.

And because there aren't already enough cookbooks in the world . . . what's one that hasn't been written and should be, serious or silly?

REBEKAH DENN

The *Your Parents Are Already Proud of You Cookbook*.

ANDREA NGUYEN

The White Evangelical Cookbook. I think this could become an American cult classic like *White Trash Cooking*. It would need to be written by someone who identifies as evangelical but who has developed enough distance and perspective on the group to have some fun (fueled by fondness). Also *The Bountiful Bunker: Surviving the Nuclear Winter in Culinary Style*.

ANN CASHION

The Instant Pot, Air-Fryer, Sous Vide, Better Sex and Diet Cookbook—instant bestseller!

REBECCA FLINT MARX

I was sitting in a hot tub the other night and thinking that someone should write a cookbook that's all about how to sous vide food in a hot tub, because really, that's all sous vide is, right? It would be the ultimate lazy hedonist's cookbook: All you'd have to do is get into a hot tub with some vacuum-sealed salmon or eggs or whatever, and then set a timer and sit back with a glass of wine and wait. Seventies-era sleaze meets twenty-first-century gimmickry. What could go wrong?

HANNA RASKIN

I'm seriously contemplating a Chinese takeout cookbook.

WENDY MACNAUGHTON

Dinner Parties for Procrastinators (cooking for twelve people in under thirty minutes).

KIM ALTER

I don't know if this has happened, I am sure it has, but I want to write a book with all of my different menus. And each menu will include another part that talks about inspiration, farmers, mentors, etc. I wouldn't want the book to focus solely on me. So I would want to highlight people who made me who I am in the business or maybe have a page with their thoughts, recipes, inspirations, how they became who they are, etc.

MARION B. SULLIVAN

Combine the knowledge of Harold McGee, Alton Brown, Michael Ruhlman, James Peterson, and Shirley Corriher in a magic food processor and pulse them into a book of simple culinary principles for the home cook.

HOMA DASHTAKI

I think there should be a cookbook written on foods that are impossible to get right! Like, *Here is a recipe for a soufflé or the Iranian rock candy called* nabat, *but chances are even if you follow the recipe you will lack*

the finesse to get it right about 50 percent of the time. Good luck.

I think a lot of difficult to explain, intuitive dishes are not written about because they just fail more often than not.

ERIN MCKENNA

How to Un-Fuck Your Fucked Cake.

CHARMAINE MCFARLANE

A stale bread cookbook titled *Beyond Bread Pudding . . .* that would give practical recipes (besides the obvious and croutons) for using leftover bread and pastries—drinks, vinegars, ice creams, to name a few.

MICHELLE HERNANDEZ

I want to write a technical pastry book that explains the science of pastry and its ingredients. I am often asked by both home cooks and accomplished chefs how and why pastry works or doesn't work. A book like this would be an essential one for any cook's shelf. I've looked in both French and English and there is no similar book that exists yet.

JULIA SHERMAN

We are all so compelled by vintage cookbooks, but I don't know anyone who actually cooks from them. I would love for someone to comb through all the gross recipes to find (and translate) the recipes from past centuries that one would eat nowadays.

JORDANA ROTHMAN

I would love to see a new edition of Filippo Tommaso Marinetti's *La Cucina Futurista*. I mean, yes, sure, he was a fascist nationalist who hated pasta (it causes "lassitude, pessimism, nostalgic inactivity and neutralism"). But he has a recipe for hollowed-out oranges filled with salami and butter, so I'm in.

EVA KARAGIORGAS

A good Malaysian cookbook (hi, Mom!).

JASMINE LUKUKU

I'd love to see a cookbook that showcases variations on a dish based on regional preferences. Jollof rice is a good example of a dish with many regional variations. I think it would be fun to work your way through a couple of versions of well-known dishes.

JAMIE KANTROWITZ

Grandmother's Soups of the World or *The New Kosher*.

TIFFANI FAISON

I have actually thought about writing a *Cut the Shit* cookbook. Hacks to greatness; bullshit that shouldn't exist; make things simple, delicious, and free of extraneous ego.

THANK U
(REPRISE)

Dear **Bee**, **Carolita**, **Emily**, **Ev**, **Julia**, **Kristina**, **Korsha**, **Mari**, **Osayi**, **Priya**, **Rebecca**, **Sadie**, **Soleil**, **Tejal**, **Tienlon**, and **Von**:

I know I couldn't have pulled off any of this without EVERYONE involved. But I also know, without your essays, there would be no book at all. Thank you not just for your words and images, but also for believing in the project and taking the leap of faith required and, most of all, for trusting me. You amaze me. I loved every minute of working with and getting to know each of you better, even when I was "remindering." So thanks for that, too.

Much love and a lot of awe, CD

Dear **Betty**, **Carla**, **Cheryl**, **Devita**, **Diana**, **Jessica**, **Kim**, **Nigella**, **Pim**, **Rachael**, and **Preeti**:

"It was an honor." It's a hackneyed line these days, a throwaway. But what if you mean it? There really isn't a better way to say it. Thank you for your time, your patience, your uncensored thoughts and opinions, and your invaluable wisdom. Thank you for taking me—and this project—seriously. And, above all, thank you for giving me (and the rest of us) something to hold up, to try to live up to, and to carry forward.

Honored, CD

To the **Chorus**:

People should know how generous you all are—how you went into this without knowing exactly how it would turn out, and how you faced down that insane questionnaire with all of its twists and turns, and its questions that required real, typed-out answers (no checkboxes) and a lot of thought and truthfulness. And you did it only because I asked. I owe you, and so much more than money. You are the collective voice of this book, the Voice of Reason, Heart, Soul & Hope.

Eternal gratitude, CD

Dear **Holly**:

You got it from the very beginning. Then you let me do my thing—gave me the space I needed and your confidence in my vision. I've loved working on this collection with you. I knew I was in good hands and felt supported, which isn't always the case in the publishing industry. It's been a pleasure from start to finish, and I hope we get to do it again. Sorry for all the random last minute-style emails about obscure title ideas, inconsistent hyphenation, or whether it should be spelled "chili" or "chilli" or "chile."

xo, CD

Dear **Heesang**:

I'd admired your work from afar without knowing it was yours (special shoutout to *The World of Anna Sui*). You made this book visually embody everything I wanted it to be; it's incredible! Thank you so much. And thanks for being such an easy, open, and enthusiastic collaborator the whole way through. Can you design everything, please? Life would be so much better-looking, and just better in general.

CD

Thanks to **Annalea**, for managing it all and doing it so well, and to the entire team at Abrams who put so much love into this book. (Extra points go to **Hayley** for her patience with my analog ways.)

A thank-you to **Leyla Moushabeck** for being an objective set of eyes on my essays.

Thanks to **Felicia Gordon** for being the one reader I could trust at an uncertain and delicate moment.

Tamara Shopsin, thanks for making me like the title of this book after all.

Laura, Holly told me to keep these as short as possible. But we've been through this before, so I'll appease my editor and just say THANKS (again), because you'll KNOW.

Without **my family**, I wouldn't be me, and I wouldn't be typing these acknowledgments. Their love and support of and confidence in me, along with our sometimes differing opinions and the ensuing dustups are where this all began and are, in large part, responsible for what keeps it going.

Pawstein, kisses.

THE
CHORUS

I asked these extraordinary people, each of whom invested a lot of time and thought in this project, to provide their own job description, and I've tried my best to preserve their responses as writ.

TAMAR ADLER
Former chef, author, contributing editor at *Vogue*; Hudson, NY

JEN AGG
Restaurateur and author; Toronto, Canada

UMBER AHMAD
Founder, Mah-Ze-Dahr Bakery; New York, NY

KIM ALTER
Chef/owner, Nightbird and Linden Room; San Francisco, CA

TINA ANTOLINI
Journalist and audio producer; Oakland, CA

MASHAMA BAILEY
Executive chef, The Grey and The Grey Market; Savannah, GA

JULIA BAINBRIDGE
Writer, editor, podcast producer; Brooklyn, NY

CATHY BARROW
Cookbook author and freelance food writer; Washington, DC

RACHEL BOSSETT
Pastry chef; New York, NY

AMY BRANDWEIN
Chef/owner, Centrolina and Piccolina; Washington, DC

JENI BRITTON BAUER
Founder, Jeni's Splendid Ice Creams; Columbus, OH

ANN CASHION
Chef/co-owner, Johnny's Half Shell and Taqueria Nacional; Washington, DC

ALISON CAYNE
Founder, Haven's Kitchen; New York, NY

JOANNE CHANG
Co-owner, Flour Bakery + Café and Myers + Chang; Boston, MA

DIANNA DAOHEUNG
Executive chef, Black Seed Bagels; New York, NY

HOMA DASHTAKI
Yogurt maker; Brooklyn, NY

EMIKO DAVIES
Cookbook author and food writer; Florence, Italy

CLARE DE BOER:
Co–head chef, King; New York, NY

REBEKAH DENN
Journalist and critic; Seattle, WA

MARISA DOBSON
Consultant/owner, Scintillate; Baltimore, MD

HOLLY DOLCE
Associate publisher, Abrams; Brooklyn, NY

MELANIE DUNEA
Photographer and author; New York, NY

CATHY ERWAY
Cookbook author, food writer, podcast host; Brooklyn, NY

TIFFANI FAISON
Chef/owner, Sweet Cheeks Q, Tiger Mama, and Fool's Errand; Boston, MA

EMILY FARRIS
Food and lifestyle writer; Kansas City, MO

JAMIE FELDMAR
Journalist and cookbook writer; New York, NY

CAROLINE FIDANZA
Culinary director; Brooklyn, NY

REBECCA FLINT MARX
Journalist; Brooklyn, NY

KRISTINA GILL
Food editor, humanitarian adviser, photographer; Rome, Italy

GINA HAMADEY
Writer, editor, founder of Penknife Media, Inc.; Brooklyn, NY

MICHELLE HERNANDEZ
Pastry chef/owner, Le Dix Patisserie; San Francisco, CA

MAGGIE HOFFMAN
Food and drink editor, cookbook author; San Francisco, CA

KAREN HUDES:
Writer and editor; Brooklyn, NY

AISHWARYA IYER
Founder/CEO, Brightland;
Los Angeles, CA

NING (AMELIE) KANG
Restaurant owner, MáLà
Project; New York, NY

JAMIE KANTROWITZ
Founder, Countertop;
Venice, CA

EVA KARAGIORGAS
Partner, Mona Creative;
New York, NY

YASMIN KHAN
Food and travel writer;
London, United Kingdom

SARA LEVEEN
Restaurant owner,
Hanoi House and
Hanoi Soup Shop;
New York, NY

MARISSA LIPPERT
Founder, Nourish
Kitchen and Table and
Nourish Baby, chef,
registered dietician;
New York, NY

ANITA LO
Chef and cookbook author;
New York, NY

JASMINE LUKUKU
Founder, Black Food
Bloggers and actor;
Vancouver, Canada

WENDY MACNAUGHTON
Illustrator/
graphic journalist;
San Francisco, CA

CHARMAINE MCFARLANE
Pastry chef; Plainsboro, NJ

ERIN MCKENNA
Owner, EM Bakery
(aka BabyCakes NYC);
New York, NY

KRISTEN MIGLORE
Creative director, Genius,
Food52; New York, NY

KLANCY MILLER
Writer, cookbook author,
pastry chef; Brooklyn, NY

LIGAYA MISHAN
Hungry City columnist at
the *New York Times*;
New York, NY

BONNIE MORALES
Executive chef/owner,
Kachka and Kachinka;
Portland, OR

JASMINE MOY
Hospitality attorney;
New York, NY

KRISTY MUCCI
Writer and recipe
developer; New York, NY

CHRISTINE MUHLKE
Food consultant, writer,
founder of *Xtine* newsletter,
occasional cookbook
co-author; New York, NY

ANDREA NGUYEN
Writer, teacher, consultant;
Santa Cruz, CA

SAMIN NOSRAT
Writer, teacher, cook;
Berkeley, CA

DEB PERELMAN
Blogger and cookbook
author; New York, NY

SOFIA PEREZ
Journalist, writer, editor;
New York, NY

AUBRIE PICK
Photographer;
San Francisco, CA

NAOMI POMEROY
Chef/owner, Beast;
Portland, OR

**NICOLE ADRIENNE
PONSECA**
Restaurateur/founder,
Maharlika and Jeepney;
New York, NY

CHANDRA RAM
Editor, *Plate* magazine,
and cookbook author;
Chicago, IL

HANNA RASKIN
Food editor and chief critic
at the *Post and Courier*;
Charleston, SC

NICOLE RICE
Founder, Countertop;
Venice, CA

ALISON ROMAN
Food writer and cookbook
author; New York, NY

ALI ROSEN
Food journalist,
cookbook author, TV host;
New York, NY

HELEN ROSNER
Food correspondent
for the *New Yorker*;
Brooklyn, NY

JULEE ROSSO
Owner, Wickwood Inn
and cookbook author;
Saugatuck, MI

JORDANA ROTHMAN
Writer and editor;
Brooklyn, NY

REGINA SCHRAMBLING
Food writer; New York, NY

GILLIAN SARA SHAW
Baker/owner,
Black Jet Baking Co.;
San Francisco, CA

JULIA SHERMAN
Author, photographer,
cook, creative director;
Los Angeles, CA

ANA SORTUN
Chef/partner,
Oleana, Sofra, Sarma;
Cambridge, MA

KATHLEEN SQUIRES
Food and travel writer;
New York, NY

MARION B. SULLIVAN
Food writer and editor;
Charleston, NC

RUBY TANDOH
Food writer;
London, United Kingdom

NICOLE A. TAYLOR
Food writer and
cookbook author;
Brooklyn, NY

SIERRA TISHGART
Cofounder, Great Jones;
New York, NY

NAOMI TOMKY
Freelance food writer;
Seattle, WA

CHRISTINA TOSI
Pastry chef, CEO,
wife, sister, daughter;
New York, NY

MONIQUE TRUONG
Novelist, essayist,
lyricist/librettist;
Brooklyn, NY

ESTHER TSENG
Freelance writer;
Los Angeles, CA

JULIA TURSHEN
Cookbook author
and founder of Equity
at the Table;
Hudson Valley, NY

ALEX VAN BUREN
Food journalist;
Brooklyn, NY

MAISIE WILHELM
Founder of Palatine, a
culinary consultancy;
Brooklyn, NY

VIRGINIA WILLIS:
Cook and food writer;
Atlanta, GA

OLIVIA WILSON:
Pastry chef/restaurateur;
Richmond, VA

Special guest
appearances by:

DORIE GREENSPAN
On Dessert columnist
for the *New York Times
Magazine* and author of
thirteen cookbooks;
New York, NY/Westbrook,
CT/Paris, France

MEGAN KRIGBAUM
Wine and spirits writer,
and contributing editor at
Punch; Brooklyn, NY

HEESANG LEE
Graphic designer;
Brooklyn, NY

TAMARA SHOPSIN
Author, designer, illustrator;
Brooklyn, NY

Julia Kramer

At the very end of 2015, I picked up the issue of *Bon Appétit* in front of my door, expecting to find a whole bunch of unwanted advice on how to reset my diet for the new year and be a more responsible, healthier (or, to adopt the magazine's lingo, healthy-ish) eater. Instead, I found a story titled "Smoke Signals" about a baker named Tara Jensen, whose operation sits just off the French Broad River, around the bend from "a knoll called Walnut," beside an "algae-covered pond," outside a town in North Carolina you've probably never heard of, let alone been to. Jensen had, despite her remote location, developed something of a following, and Julia had gone to see what the fuss over the baker's pizza nights, and bread, and piecrusts was all about. It was one of the most gorgeous pieces of food writing I could remember reading in what felt like ages, and when I was done, I went back to the beginning to see who had written it. I was surprised it was Julia Kramer's only because as the deputy editor of *Bon Appétit*, she spends a lot of time editing other peoples' words and traipsing around the country to find "The Hot Ten," an annual list of America's best new restaurants.

As much as I look forward to that round-up every year, I can't help but wish she had a little more time to write features like the one about Jensen. I think Julia might wish the same; she told me as much when I asked her to contribute to this anthology. Then she surprised me by suggesting "a short piece of experimental fiction." She'd studied fiction writing as an undergrad at Pomona College in Claremont, California, and joked that she'd become the cliché her teachers had warned their students about: the kind of writer with a suitcase full of unfinished stories under her bed. Thank heavens for that suitcase, and for whatever kind of writer Julia is—and for Julia, for being that kind of writer.

Mother, 6:35 P.M.

Mother, *Access Hollywood* and

Mother, accidentally slicing finger and

Mother, baked potatoes and

    See also Mother, nonfat milk and

Mother, bowl of Raisin Bran for dinner
and

Mother, calendar and

Mother, "Can you please set the table?"
and

Mother, cash and

    See also Mother, hiding shit and

Mother, changing clothes and

    See also Mother, yellow sweat-
      pants and

Mother, chicken breast and

    See also Mother, Julia's Special
      Chicken and

Mother, chocolate chips and

    See also Mother, hiding shit and

Mother, cloth napkins and

Mother, colander and

Mother, conference calls and

Mother, conversation topics and

    See also Mother, calendar and;
      Mother, death and; Mother,
      shiva planning and

Mother, Cuisinart blade and

Mother, death and

Mother, defrosted chili and

    See also Mother, shiva planning
      and

Mother, Dijon mustard and

    See also Mother, Julia's Special
      Chicken and

Mother, Doing It All and

Mother, draining pasta and

    See also Mother, pasta with olive
      oil and

Mother, fears and

    See also Mother, mice and;
      Mother, taxis and

Mother, freezer and

    See also Mother, death and;
      Mother, shiva planning and

Mother, granite countertop and

Mother, hamburgers and

Mother, "Has anyone heard from your
father?" and

Mother, hiding shit and

    See also Mother, cash and;
      Mother, chocolate chips and;
      Mother, pearl necklaces and;
      Mother, spectre of
      anti-semitism and

Mother, immersion blender and

Mother, "It's 6:35, where is your father?"
and

Mother, Julia's Special Chicken and

Mother, leftovers

    See also Mother, defrosted chili
      and; Mother, roast chicken
      from Hole in the Wall and;
      Mother, shiva planning and

Mother, leggings and

Mother, Manischewitz matzo ball soup
mix and

Mother, mice and

Mother, Monterey Jack and

Mother, nonfat milk and

Mother, not eating dinner tonight and

Mother, pasta with olive oil and

Mother, pearl necklaces and

Mother, placemats and

Mother, quesadillas and

Mother, roast chicken from Hole in the
Wall and

> *See also* Mother, leftovers

Mother, roast salmon with leeks and

Mother, serrated knife and

Mother, shiva planning and

> *See also* Mother, conversation top-
> ics and

Mother, shredded mozzarella and

> *See also* Mother, baked potatoes
> and; Mother, nonfat milk and

Mother, Silpats and

Mother, speaker phone and

> *See also* Mother, "To listen to
> your messages, press one"
> and

Mother, spectre of anti-semitism and

Mother, sweet potato "fries" and

Mother, taxis and

Mother, television and

> *See also* Mother, *Access Hollywood*
> and

Mother, "To listen to your messages,
press one" and

Mother, "What train is your father on?"
and

Mother, wood-paneled refrigerator and

Mother, yellow sweatpants and